Baruch House Publishing
www.baruchhousepublishing.com
www.newmatthewbible.org

The Five Books of Moses

NMB
New Matthew Bible

Baruch House Publishing, British Columbia, Canada

We remember that which we first received,
and strengthen the things that are ready to die.
(Revelation 3:2,3)

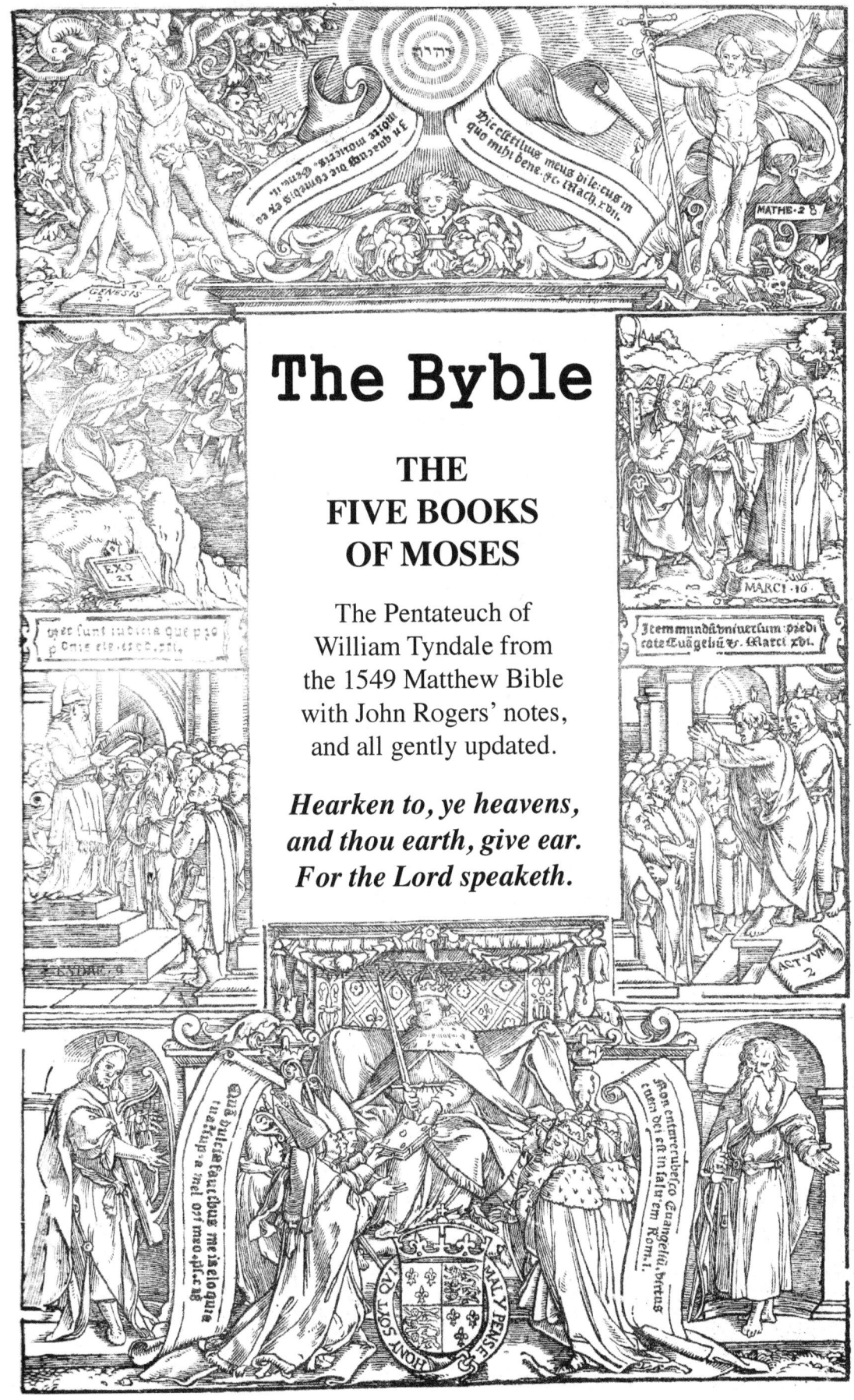

The Byble

THE FIVE BOOKS OF MOSES

The Pentateuch of William Tyndale from the 1549 Matthew Bible with John Rogers' notes, and all gently updated.

Hearken to, ye heavens, and thou earth, give ear. For the Lord speaketh.

The Five Books of Moses
The Pentateuch of the New Matthew Bible (NMB)
Copyright © 2024 Ruth Magnusson (Davis)
First published June 2024. Minor revisions to August 2025.

All rights reserved. This book may not be reproduced in whole or in part without written permission from the publisher (contact below), except scripture verses or notes may be freely quoted in the normal course, provided the New Matthew Bible is identified as the source, and except for such copying as is permitted by applicable law and reviewers for the public press.

Editing of Early Modern English text and interior layout
by Ruth Magnusson Davis.
Cover design by Iryna Spica.
Title page graphics (woodcuts) are from the editor's original,
ragpaper 1549 Matthew Bible.

Full Size edition ISBNs:
Paperback 978-1-7381208-0-2
Hardcover (case laminate) 978-1-7381208-1-9

Baruch House Publishing, British Columbia, Canada
www.baruchhousepublishing.com
www.newmatthewbible.org

**The Five Books of Moses in the Matthew Bible was William Tyndale's
original translation from the Hebrew almost 500 years ago.
Now gently updated by Ruth Magnusson Davis,
it may be fully appreciated by readers of the 21st century.**

**The Matthew Bible is a little-known Reformation Bible.
It formed the base of all major English Bibles,
including the KJV, though unacknowledged.**

**The Matthew Bible is the only English Bible attested
with martyrs' blood.**

William Tyndale, Bible translator and martyr, was strangled and burned at the stake in Vilvoord, Belgium, in the year 1536, when he was about forty-two years old. He had lived many years in exile from his native England, working under cover in order to avoid capture by enemies who wished to stop his pen. His first New Testament was published in 1526, and his final revision, which is here, in 1535.

John Rogers, martyr and friend of William Tyndale, collated and first published the Matthew Bible in 1537, using the scripture translations of William Tyndale and Myles Coverdale. His Bible was licensed by King Henry VIII, but was always unpopular with conservatives. In 1555, after Queen Mary ascended the throne, Rogers became her first burning victim, dying bravely in Smithfield and leaving a wife with ten children.

About the cover

The beautiful colour of the cover is *lapus lazuli*, or sapphire, one of the stones in the ephod that the Levitical priests wore when they ministered before the Lord in the tabernacle.

Table of Contents

Preface i
Abbreviations of the Names of the Books of the Bible iv

The Five Books of Moses:

Genesis 1
Tyndale's Prologue to Exodus (excerpts) 79
Exodus 80
Leviticus 142
Numbers 186
Deuteronomy 247

Preface to the Pentateuch of the New Matthew Bible

THE MATTHEW BIBLE was first published in 1537, in a time when God's word had for centuries been locked up in Latin, a language that the people could not understand. But God worked through his chosen vessels during the Reformation to open his word to England again in her own language. These vessels, the men who laboured for God's word in English, were three: William Tyndale and Myles Coverdale, the translators of the Matthew Bible, and their friend John Rogers, who compiled the Bible and oversaw publication.

The book that you hold in your hands is the Pentateuch of the Matthew Bible – that is, the first part of the Old Testament, being the five books of Moses – now gently updated for the 21st century. The Pentateuch was William Tyndale's original translation from the Hebrew, and Coverdale assisted him. John Rogers added the introductory chapter summaries and expository notes that you will find here, some of which were his own and others that he gleaned from various sources. The full story of the making of the Matthew Bible (MB), with also a review of some revisions to the original translations that have occurred since the Reformation, is in my two-part history, *The Story of the Matthew Bible*.

This updated Pentateuch is a publication of the New Matthew Bible Project. Our goal is to minimally update the original English translations while retaining their style. We must also, of course, render faithfully their meaning and message, which sometimes differs from later Bibles in ways both great and small. An example of a difference is in the historical books, where the MB says that the Canaanites conquered by Israel were required to pay tribute; some modern Bibles say they were made slaves and forced to do "hard labour." Another example is verse 4 of Genesis 19. Here the MB indicates that it was *all* the citizens of Sodom who surrounded Lot's house and demanded that he deliver up his guests to them, to do them evil; however, some modern versions say only men (or "males") were in the crowd.

The work of updating the nearly 500-year-old MB translation is vast in scope. The study of Early Modern English is ongoing, and always yields new insights with the help of the Oxford English Dictionary and good grammar studies. This editor's guidelines for updating are given in the preface to the October Testament, the New Testament of the New Matthew Bible.

A good resource for emending the Pentateuch was Myles Coverdale's own 1535 English Bible. His English was surprisingly more modern than Tyndale's. Martin Luther's lectures on Genesis were helpful. Pierre Olivetan's 1535 French Bible, which John Rogers knew and used, elucidated some verses or helped to confirm a consensus of opinion among his contemporaries. Occasionally, I emended a verse or passage from Rogers' own notes in the MB, where I judged it better to have the meaning in the text than in the margin. For example, several verses in Genesis 22 refer to Isaac as Abraham's "only son." However, Abraham in fact had other sons, and I recall stumbling over this as a new believer. But Rogers' note cleared it up: the Hebrew is an idiom, or figurative saying, and here "only" means "most beloved." Since this idiom is unknown in English, we cannot understand it. I therefore show the true intended meaning in the text.

Where I drew from Rogers' notes or other sources for more than a routine emendation to a difficult text, I show it in the margin as follows:

e.f. JR = emended from John Rogers' notes in the Matthew Bible.

e.f. COV = emended from Myles Coverdale's 1535 Bible.

e.f. ML = emended from Martin Luther's commentaries or 1534 Bible.

e.f. OLIV = emended from Pierre Olivetan's 1535 Bible.

e.f. WYC = emended from the Wycliffe Bible (Praotes edition).

e.f. WT 1530 = emended from William Tyndale's 1530 Pentateuch (the original translation or his notes or prefaces).

e.f. VAR = emended from any number or variety of sources.

In addition, items relevant to understanding Rogers' (and my) notes are:

"LXX," "Greek," or "Grk" means the Greek Septuagint.

"Common translation (or, transl.)" means the Latin Vulgate Bible.

"Chald." or "Chaldee" refers to the Chaldee (i.e. Aramaic) translation.

"OED" means the Oxford English Dictionary. I use the online edition.

As in the October Testament, my notes (except where indicating emendations, as shown above) are within square brackets, to distinguish them from Rogers' notes.

Each scripture reference in the margins and notes needed to be individually updated. This was a laborious task due to many misprints and because the Matthew Bible did not use verse numbers. As well, it used different or inconsistent book names, usually following the Latin Bible; for example, "Thren" is Lamentations, iii.Reg. (3Kings) is 1Kings, and i.Par. is 1Chronicles. Furthermore, the marginal references to the Psalms followed the numbering system of the Septuagint, whereas the text followed the Hebrew numbering system; I have carefully re-keyed everything to the Hebrew. Yet again, in places the MB translation of the Apocryphal books differed greatly from others, and this made verse numbering very difficult for those books. Indeed, throughout the Bible differences in translation may mean that if readers check a scripture reference against another version, they might not see the reason for it. The reason will only become clear when the New Matthew Bible is finally complete.

Acknowledgements

I wish to acknowledge the valuable assistance of three people in this work: Ruth Soffos and Jesse Eldred versified the text and performed preliminary updating, while Janell Rutten proof-checked the versification and my first drafts. God, who works all in all things, marshalled together a team of precious people – a small group for a huge work – and I am grateful to them.

In closing, I pray that this Pentateuch, which is faithfully rooted in the original English translation, will bless those who read it as much it has blessed us to work on it. All glory be to God the Father, God the Son, and God the Holy Spirit.

Ruth Magnusson Davis, Autumn, 2023.

Abbreviations of the Names of the Books of the Bible

Old Testament

Ge	=Genesis
Ex	=Exodus
Lev	=Leviticus
Nu	=Numbers
De	=Deuteronomy
Jos	=Joshua
J'g	=Judges
Ru	=Ruth
1Sam	=1 Samuel
2Sam	=2 Samuel
1Ki	=1 Kings
2Ki	=2 Kings
1Ch	=1 Chronicles
2Ch	=2 Chronicles
Ezr	=Ezra
Ne	=Nehemiah
Es	=Esther
Job	=Job
Ps	=Psalms
Pr	=Proverbs
Ec	=Ecclesiastes
Song	=Song of Solomon
Isa	=Isaiah
Jer	=Jeremiah
La	=Lamentations
Eze	=Ezekiel
Dan	=Daniel
Ho	=Hosea
Joe	=Joel
Am	=Amos
Ob	=Obadiah
Jon	=Jonah
Mic	=Micah
Na	=Nahum
Hab	=Habakkuk
Zep	=Zephaniah
Hag	=Haggai
Zec	=Zechariah
Mal	=Malachi

Apocryphal Books

1Esd	=1 Esdras
2Esd	=2 Esdras
Tob	=Tobit
J'th	= Judith
Es(Gk)	= Rest of Esther
Wis	=Wisdom of Solomon
Ec'us	= Ecclesiasticus
Bar	= Baruch (& letter of Jeremiah)
So3	=The Song of the Three
Sus	= History of Susanna
Bel	= Bel and the Dragon
Man	= Prayer of Mannaseh
1Macc	=1 Maccabees
2Macc	=2 Maccabees

New Testament

M't	=Matthew
Mk	=Mark
Lu	=Luke
Joh	=John
Ac	=Acts
Ro	=Romans
1Co	=1Corinthians
2Co	=2 Corinthians
Ga	=Galatians
Eph	=Ephesians
Ph'p	=Philippians
Col	=Colossians
1Th	=1 Thessalonians
2Th	=2 Thessalonians
1Ti	=1 Timothy
2Ti	=2Timothy
Tit	=Titus
Ph'm	=Philemon
Heb	=Hebrews
Jas	=James
1Pe	=1 Peter
2Pe	=2 Peter
1Jo	=1 John
2Jo	=2 John
3Jo	=3 John
Jude	=Jude
Rev	=Revelation

The First Book of Moses
called
Genesis

Chapter 1

How heaven and earth, the light, the firmament, the sun, the moon, the stars, and all animals, birds, and fishes in the sea were made by the word of God. And how man also was created.

IN THE BEGINNING God created heaven and earth. ²The earth was without form and empty, and darkness was upon the deep water, and the Spirit of God moved* upon the water.

³Then God said, Let there be light; and there was light. ⁴And God saw the light, that it was good, and divided the light from the darkness, ⁵and called the light the day, and the darkness the night. And so of the evening and morning was made the first day.

⁶And God said, Let there be a firmamentᵃ between the waters, and let it divide the waters apart. ⁷Then God made the firmament, and parted the waters that were under the firmament from the waters that were above the firmament; and it was so. ⁸And God called the firmament heaven. And so of the evening and morning was made the second day.

⁹And God said, Let the waters that are under heaven gather themselves in one place so that the dry land may appear; and it came so to pass. ¹⁰And God called the dry land the earth, and the gathering together of waters he called the sea. And God saw that it was good. ¹¹And God said, Let the earth bring forth plants and grasses that sow seed, and fruitful trees that bear fruit, every one in its kind, having their seed in themselves upon the earth; and it came so to pass. ¹²And the earth brought forth plants and grasses bearing seed, every one in its kind, and trees bearing fruit and having their seed in themselves, every one in its kind. And God saw that it was good. ¹³And then of the evening and morning was made the third day.

¹⁴Then said God, Let there be lights in the firmament of heaven to divide the day from the night, so that they may be for signs, seasons, days, and years; ¹⁵and let them be lights in the firmament of heaven to shine upon the earth. And so it was. ¹⁶And God made two great lights: a greater light to rule the day, and a lesser light to rule the night. And he made stars also. ¹⁷And God put them in the firmament of heaven to shine upon the earth, ¹⁸and to rule the day and the night, and to divide the light from darkness. And God saw that it was good. ¹⁹And so of the evening and morning was made the fourth day.

²⁰And God said, Let the water bring forth creatures that move and have life, and birds to fly over the earth under the firmament of heaven. ²¹And God created great whales and all manner of creatures that

---

2Esd 6:38-40, Ec'us 18:1, Jer 10:12,13. Heb 1:10 Ps 102:25; 136:5-9. Isa 44:24
*Breathed or stirred.

2Esd 6:41 Ps 136:5,6 Pr 8:22-31

2Esd 6:42-44

2Esd 6:45,46 Ps 136:7-9 Jer 31:35

2Esd 6:47-52

live and move, which the waters brought forth in their kinds, and all manner of feathered birds in their kinds. And God saw that it was good. ²²And God blessed them,ᵇ saying, Grow and multiply; and fill the waters of the seas, and let the birds multiply upon the earth. ²³And so of the evening and morning was made the fifth day.

^{2Esd 6:53, 54.}

²⁴And God said, Let the earth bring forth living creatures in their kinds: beasts of pasture, and creatures that crawl, and animals of the earth in their kinds; and it came so to pass. ²⁵And God made the animals of the earth in their kinds, and beasts of pasture in their kinds, and all manner of crawling things of the earth in their kinds. And God saw that it was good.

^{De 4:32}
^{Ec'us 17:1-4}

²⁶And God said, Let us make man in our similitude and after our likeness, that he may have rule over the fish of the sea and over the birds of the air, and over the beasts of pasture, and over all the earth, and over all crawling things that go about on the earth. ²⁷And God created man after his likeness; in the likeness of God he created him;ᶜ male and female he created them. ²⁸And God blessed them, and God said to them, Grow and multiply and fill the earth; and subdue it, and have dominion over the fish of the sea and over the birds of the air, and over all the animals that move on the earth.

²⁹And God said, See, I have given you all the plants that sow seed which are on all the earth, and all manner of trees that have fruit in them and sow seed, to be food for you ³⁰and for all the animals of the earth, and for all the birds of the air, and for everything that goes about on the earth in which there is life, so that they may have every kind of plant and grass to eat. And even so it was. ³¹And God beheld all that he had made, and lo, it was exceedingly good. And so of the evening and morning was made the sixth day.

^{Ec'us 39:16}
^{1Ti 4:4}

The Notes

a) 6. Firmament: or heaven. Psalms 136:5 and 8:3. It is a Hebrew word and signifies thrusting forth or spreading abroad. [Luther: In the scriptures, *heaven* is the entire expanse of air, sky, and outer space which extends from the earth's surface upward: the horizon. In context, it may also refer to any part of this expanse: *birds of heaven* refers to the birds that live in the air we breathe, while *stars of heaven* refers to the upper spheres.]
b) 22. Here *blessing* is taken for increasing and multiplying.
c) 27. In or after the likeness of God: that is, in the form and appearance that was before appointed for the Son of God. Also, the chief part of man, which is the soul, is made to be like God in a certain correspondence of powers and functioning, so that in this we are made like God. Ecclesiasticus 17:5-11.

Chapter 2

The previous chapter is here repeated. The hallowing of the Sabbath day. The four rivers of Paradise. The setting of man in Paradise; the tree of knowledge is forbidden to him. How Adam named all the creatures. The creation of Eve. The institution of marriage.

Thus were heaven and earth finished, with all their apparel.ᵃ ²And in the seventh day God ended his work which he had done, and rested in the seventh day from all his works which he had made. ³And God blessedᵇ the seventh day and sanctified it;ᶜ for in it he rested from all his works which he had created and made.

⁴These are the origins of heaven and earth when they were created, in the time when the Lord God created heaven and earth, ⁵and all the shrubs of the field before they were in the earth, and all the plants of the field before they sprang up. For the Lord God had yet sent no rain upon the earth, neither was there yet anyone to till the earth; ⁶but there arose a mist out of the ground that watered all the face of the earth. ⁷Then the Lord God formed man, even from the dust of the earth, and breathed into his face the breath of life; and so man was made a living soul.

⁸The Lord God also planted a garden in Eden,ᵈ toward the east; and there he set man whom he had formed. ⁹And the Lord God made to spring out of the earth all manner of trees beautiful to the sight and pleasant to eat, and the tree of life in the midst of the garden, and also the tree of the knowledge of good and evil.

¹⁰And there sprang a river out of Eden to water the garden, and from there it divided itself and grew into four principal waters. ¹¹The name of the one is Pishon, which runs about all the land of Havilah. There is found gold ¹²(and the gold of that country is precious), and there is found bedellion, and a stone called onyx. ¹³The name of the second river is Gihon, which runs about all the land of India. ¹⁴And the name of the third river is the Tigris, which runs on the east side of the Assyrians. And the fourth river is the Euphrates.

¹⁵And the Lord God took Adam and put him in the garden of Eden, to cultivate it and to keep it. ¹⁶And the Lord God commanded Adam, saying, Of all the trees of the garden, see that you eat; ¹⁷but of the tree of the knowledge of good and bad, see that you eat not, for even the same day you eat of it, you will surely die.

¹⁸And the Lord God said, It is not good that man should be alone. I will make him a helper to keep him company. ¹⁹And after the Lord God had made from the earth all the animals of the field and all the birds of the air, he brought them to Adam to see what he would call them. And as Adam called all the living creatures, so are their names. ²⁰And Adam gave names to all the beasts of pasture, and to the birds of the air, and to all the animals of the field. But there was no help found for Adam, to keep him company.

²¹Then the Lord God cast a slumber on Adam, and he slept. And then he took out one of his ribs, and in its stead he filled up the place with flesh. ²²And the Lord God made of the rib that he took from Adam a woman, and brought her to Adam.

²³Then said Adam, This is now bone of my bones and flesh of my flesh; this shall be called woman, because she was taken of the man. ²⁴For this cause shall a man leave father and mother and cleave unto

his wife, and they shall be one flesh.

^{Mk 10:6-8}
^{Eph 5:31}
^{1Co 6:16}

²⁵And they were each of them naked, both Adam and his wife, and were not ashamed.

The Notes

a) 1. The apparel of heaven is the stars and planets, etc.
b) 3. *Bless* here is taken for magnifying and praising, as in Psalm 33:1-3.
c) 3. *Sanctifying* in this place is as much as to say, to dedicate and ordain a thing to his own use, as in Exodus 13:2 and 20:8.
d) 8. *Eden* signifies pleasures.

Chapter 3

The serpent deceives the woman. The serpent, the woman, and the man are cursed and driven out of Paradise. Christ our saviour is promised.

But the serpent was subtler than all the beasts of the field that the Lord God had made, and said to the woman, Yea, has God said indeed, You shall not eat from all the trees in the garden? ²And the woman said to the serpent, Of the fruit of the trees in the garden we may eat; ³but of the fruit of the tree that is in the midst of the garden, God said, See that you eat not; and see that you touch it not, lest you die.

⁴Then said the serpent to the woman, Tsk, you will not die. ⁵But God knows that whenever you eat of it, your eyes will be opened,^a and you will be as God, and know both good and evil.

2Co 11:3

⁶And the woman saw that it was a good tree to eat of, and fair to the eyes, and a tree desirable to give understanding. And she took of the fruit of it and ate, and gave to her husband also with her, and he ate. ⁷And the eyes of both of them were opened, and they understood that they were naked. Then they sewed fig leaves together and made themselves coverings.

Ec'us 25:24

⁸And they heard the voice of the Lord God as he walked in the garden in the cool of the day. And Adam hid himself, and his wife also, from the face of the Lord God,^b among the trees of the garden. ⁹And the Lord God called Adam and said to him, Where are you?

¹⁰And he answered, I heard your voice in the garden, but I was afraid because I was naked, and therefore hid myself.

¹¹And he said, Who has told you that you were naked? Have you eaten from the tree from which I bade you not to eat?

¹²And Adam answered, The woman that you gave to keep me company, she gave to me from the tree, and I ate.

¹³And the Lord God said to the woman, Why did you do this?

And the woman answered, The serpent deceived me, and I ate.

¹⁴And the Lord God said to the serpent, Because you have done this, most cursed are you of all beasts of pasture and of all beasts of the field: upon your belly shall you go, and earth shall you eat all the days of your life. ¹⁵Moreover, I will put hatred between you and the

woman, and between your seed and her seed. And that seed shall tread you on the head, and you shall tread it on the heel.^c

¹⁶And to the woman he said, I will surely increase your sorrow when you are with child, and with pain shall you be delivered. And you shall submit to your husband, and he shall rule you.

¹⁷And to Adam he said, Because you heeded the voice of your wife and have eaten from the tree of which I commanded you, saying, See you eat not from it – cursed is the earth on your account. In sorrow shall you eat of it all days of your life, ¹⁸and it will bear thorns and thistles for you. And you shall eat the plants of the field. ¹⁹In the sweat of your face shall you eat bread, until you return to the earth whence you were taken. For earth you are, and to earth you shall return.

²⁰And Adam called his wife Eve because she was the mother of all that lives.* ²¹And the Lord God made Adam and his wife garments of skins, and put them on them. ²²And the Lord God said, Lo,^d Adam is become as it were one of us, in the knowledge of good and evil. But now, lest he stretch forth his hand and take also of the tree of life, and eat and live forever –

²³And the Lord God cast him out of the garden of Eden to till the earth whence he was taken. ²⁴And he cast Adam out; and at the entrance to the garden of Eden he set cherubims, with a naked sword moving in and out to guard the way to the tree of life.

v16 e.f. ML, COV, OLIV.

Job 34:15

*[*Eve* means Life]

The Notes

a) 5. To have their eyes open is to know and understand.
b) 8. From the face of the Lord: that is, from his presence.
c) 15. The head of the serpent signifies the power and tyranny of the devil, whom Christ, the seed of the woman, overcame. The heel is Christ's manhood, which was tried with our sins.
d) 22. Here this word *lo* is taken for mockery.

Chapter 4

> Cain kills his righteous brother Abel. Cain despairs and is cursed. The birth of Enoch, Methushael, Jubal, Lamech, Seth, and Enosh.

And Adam lay with Eve his wife, who conceived and bore Cain and said, I have gotten a man from the Lord. ²And she went on to bear his brother Abel. And Abel became a shepherd, and Cain became a plowman.

³And it happened in the course of time that Cain brought from the fruit of the earth an offering to the Lord. ⁴And Abel, he brought also, from the firstlings of his sheep and from the fat of them. And the Lord looked to Abel and to his offering, ⁵but to Cain and to his offering he looked not.* And Cain was exceedingly angry, and glowered. ⁶And the Lord said to Cain, Why are you angry, and why do you glower? ⁷Do you not know, if you do well, you shall receive it? But if you do evil, straightaway your sin lies open in the door. Notwithstanding, let it be

Heb 11:4
*ie, the Lord was pleased with Abel and his offering, but not with Cain or his offering.

subdued to you, and see that you rule it.

⁸And Cain talked with Abel his brother. And as soon as they were in the fields, Cain fell upon Abel his brother and slew him.

Wis 10:3
1Jo 3:12
Heb 12:24
M't 23:35
Jude 1:11

⁹And the Lord said to Cain, Where is Abel your brother?

And Cain said, I do not know. Am I my brother's keeper?

¹⁰And the Lord said, What have you done? The voice of your brother's blood cried to me[a] out of the earth. ¹¹And now, cursed are you as pertaining to the earth, which opened her mouth to receive your brother's blood from your hand. ¹²For when you till the ground, she will henceforth not give her fruits to you. A vagabond and a wanderer you shall be upon the earth.

v12 e.f.
WYC.

Pr 28:17
Job 15:20-35

¹³And Cain said to the Lord, My sin is greater than that it may be forgiven. ¹⁴Behold, you have cast me out this day from the face of the earth, and from your sight I must hide myself; and I must be wandering and a vagabond upon the earth! Moreover, whoever finds me will kill me.

¹⁵And the Lord said to him, Not so, but whoever slays Cain will be punished sevenfold.

And the Lord put a mark upon Cain so that no one who found him would kill him. ¹⁶And Cain went out from the face of the Lord and dwelt in the land of Nod, on the east side of Eden.

¹⁷And Cain lay with his wife, who conceived and bore Enoch. And he was building a city, and called the name of it after the name of his son Enoch. ¹⁸And Enoch begat Irad, and Irad begat Mehujael, and Mehujael begat Methushael, and Methushael begat Lamech.

¹⁹And Lamech took to himself two wives; the one was called Adah and the other Zillah. ²⁰And Adah bore Jabal, from whom came those who dwell in tents and possess beasts of pasture. ²¹And his brother's name was Jubal; from him came all who exercise themselves on the harp and on wind instruments. ²²And Zillah, she also bore Tubal-Cain, a worker in metal and a father of all craftsmen in bronze and iron. And Tubal-Cain's sister was called Naamah.

²³Then said Lamech to his wives Adah and Zillah, Hear my voice, ye wives of Lamech, and hearken to my words! For I have slain a man and wounded myself, and have slain a young man and got myself bruised. ²⁴For Cain shall be avenged sevenfold, but Lamech seventy times sevenfold.

²⁵Adam also lay with his wife yet again, and she bore a son and called his name Seth. For God (said she) has given me another son, for Abel whom Cain slew. ²⁶And Seth begat a son, and called his name Enosh. And in that time people began to call on the name of the Lord.[b]

The Notes

a) 10. Cries: that is, calls for vengeance, as you have at Genesis 19:13.

b) 26. To call on the name of the Lord is to ask all things of him, and to trust in him, giving him the honour and worship that belong to him, as in Genesis 12:8.

Chapter 5

The genealogy of Adam to Noah.

This is the book of the genealogy of man, in the day when God created man and made him in the similitude of God. ²Male and female he made them, and called their names man, in the day when they were created.

³When Adam was 130 years old, he begat a son after his likeness and similitude, and called his name Seth. ⁴And the days of Adam after he begat Seth were 800 years, and he begat sons and daughters. ⁵And all the days that Adam lived were 930 years, and then he died.

⁶And Seth lived 105 years, and begat Enosh. ⁷And after he had begotten Enosh, he lived 807 years and begat sons and daughters. ⁸And all the days of Seth were 912 years, and he died.

⁹And Enosh lived 90 years, and begat Cainan. ¹⁰And Enosh, after he begat Cainan, lived 815 years and begat sons and daughters. ¹¹And all the days of Enosh were 905 years, and then he died.

¹²And Cainan lived 70 years, and begat Mahalaleel. ¹³And Cainan, after he had begotten Mahalaleel, lived 840 years and begat sons and daughters. ¹⁴And all the days of Cainan were 910 years, and then he died.

¹⁵And Mahalaleel lived 65 years, and begat Jared. ¹⁶And Mahalaleel, after he had begotten Jared, lived 830 years and begat sons and daughters. ¹⁷And all the days of Mahalaleel were 895 years, and then he died.

¹⁸And Jared lived 162 years, and begat Enoch. ¹⁹And after he begat Enoch, Jared lived 800 years and begat sons and daughters. ²⁰And all the days of Jared were 962 years, and then he died.

²¹And Enoch lived 65 years, and begat Methuselah. ²²And after he had begotten Methuselah, Enoch walked with God[a] for 300 years, and begat sons and daughters. ²³And all the days of Enoch were 365 years. ²⁴And Enoch lived a godly life, and then was seen no more because God took him away.

²⁵And Methuselah lived 187 years, and begat Lamech. ²⁶And Methuselah, after he begat Lamech, lived 782 years, and begat sons and daughters. ²⁷And all the days of Methuselah were 969 years, and then he died.

²⁸And Lamech lived 182 years, and begat a son; ²⁹and he called him Noah, saying, He will comfort us in our work, and in the sorrow of our hands upon the earth, which the Lord has cursed. ³⁰And Lamech lived after he had begotten Noah 595 years and begat sons and daughters. ³¹And all the days of Lamech were 777 years, and then he died.

³²And when Noah was 500 years old, he had begotten Shem, Ham, and Japheth.

The Notes

a) 22. To walk with God is to do his will, and to lead a life according to his word.

Chapter 6

The cause of the flood. God warns Noah of the coming of the flood. The preparation of the ark.

And it came to pass, when men began to multiply upon the earth and had begotten daughters, ²the sons of God^a saw the daughters of men, that they were fair, and took as their wives those whom they best liked among them all.

³And the Lord said, My Spirit shall not always strive with man, for they are flesh. Nevertheless, I will give them 120 years more.*

⁴There were tyrants in the world in those days; for after the sons of God had gone in to the daughters of men and had begotten children, the same children were the mightiest of the world, and men of renown. ⁵And when the Lord saw that the wickedness of man was increased upon the earth, and that all the imagination and thoughts of his heart was only evil continually, ⁶he repented‡ that he had made man upon the earth, and sorrowed in his heart. ⁷And he said, I will destroy mankind that I have made from off the face of the earth; both man and beast, and crawling things, and birds of the air. For I repent that I have made them.

⁸But yet Noah found grace in the sight of the Lord.

⁹These are the generations of Noah. Noah was a righteous man, and uncorrupt in his time, and walked with God. ¹⁰And Noah begat three sons: Shem, Ham, and Japheth. ¹¹And the earth was corrupt in the sight of God, and was full of wrongdoing. ¹²And God looked upon the earth, and lo, it was corrupt; for all flesh^b had corrupted their way upon the earth.

¹³Then God said to Noah, The end of all flesh is come before me,^c for the earth is full of their wickedness. And lo, I will destroy them with the earth. ¹⁴Make for yourself an ark of pine wood, and make chambers in the ark, and pitch it within and without with pitch. ¹⁵And this is how you shall make it: the length of the ark shall be 300 cubits, the breadth of it 50 cubits, and the height of it 30 cubits. ¹⁶You shall make a window above in the ark, and within a cubit measure shall you finish it. And the door of the ark you shall set in the side of it. And you shall make it with three lofts, one above another. ¹⁷For behold, I will bring in a flood of water upon the earth, to destroy from under heaven all flesh wherein is the breath of life, so that all that is on the earth shall perish.

¹⁸But I will make my covenant with you, and you will go into the ark with your sons, your wife, and your sons' wives with you. ¹⁹And of all that lives, whatsoever flesh it be, you shall bring into the ark of everything a pair, to keep them alive with you. And male and female see that they be, ²⁰of birds in their kind, and of beasts in their kind, and of all the crawling things of the earth in their kind. A pair of everything will come to you, in order to keep them alive. ²¹And take for you some of every kind of food that may be eaten, and lay it up in store by

Margin notes:
1Pe 3:18-20
*[ie, 120 more years before the flood, being opportunity to amend their ways]
Ge 8:21
‡[JR: The repentance of God is the changing of his action. 1Sam 15:11, Jer 18:10.]
Ec'us 44:17, 18.

you so that it may be food both for you and for them.
²²And Noah did according to all that God commanded him.

The Notes

a) 2. The sons of God are the sons of Seth, who had instructed and reared them in the fear of God. The sons of men are the sons of Cain, instructed by him to all wickedness. [Tyndale, 1530 Pentateuch: The descendants of Seth eventually fell from the right way. Then they subdued the world under them and became the tyrants and men of renown referred to in v4.]
b) 12. All flesh: that is, all people who live after the flesh [ie, who follow the lusts and affections of the flesh], as said in the 8th chapter of Romans.
c) 13. The end of all flesh is come before me: that is, the end of all people is come before me.

Chapter 7

> The entrance of Noah and those who were with him into the ark. The rising of the flood, by which all things did perish.

And the Lord said to Noah, Go into the ark, both you and all your household; for I have seen you righteous[a] before me in this generation. ²Of all clean beasts, take to you seven of every kind, the male and his female; and of unclean beasts a pair, the male and his female.[b] ³Likewise, of the birds of the air seven of every kind, male and female, to save seed upon all the earth. ⁴For seven days from now I will send rain upon the earth for forty days and forty nights, and will destroy all the things that I have made from off the face of the land.

⁵And Noah did according to all that the Lord commanded him. ⁶And Noah was 600 years old when the flood of water came upon the earth. ⁷And Noah went, and his sons, his wife, and his sons' wives with him, into the ark, away from the waters of the flood. ⁸And of clean beasts and of beasts that were unclean – of birds and of all that moves upon the ground – ⁹came pairs of every kind to Noah into the ark, a male and a female as God had appointed to Noah. ¹⁰And the seventh day, the waters of the flood came upon the earth.

M't 24:37-39
Lu 17:26,27
1Pe 3:18-20

¹¹In the 600th year of Noah's life, in the second month on the 17th day of the month, that same day all the fountains of the great deep were broken up,[c] and the windows of heaven were opened.[d] ¹²And there fell a rain upon the earth forty days and forty nights.

¹³And that same day, Noah, with Shem, Ham, and Japheth, Noah's sons, and Noah's wife and the three wives of his sons with them, went into the ark – ¹⁴both they and all manner of wild animals in their kind, and all manner of beasts of pasture in their kind, and all manner of creatures that crawl upon the earth in their kind, and all manner of birds in their kind – all manner of fowls, whatever had feathers. ¹⁵And they came to Noah into the ark by pairs, of all flesh that had the breath of life in it. ¹⁶And those that came, came male and female of every flesh, as God had appointed to him. And the Lord shut the door upon him.

¹⁷And the flood came forty days and forty nights upon the earth; and the water increased and bore up the ark, and it was lifted up from off the earth. ¹⁸And the water prevailed and increased exceedingly upon the earth, and the ark went upon the top of the waters. ¹⁹And the waters prevailed exceedingly above measure on the earth, so that all the high mountains that are under all the parts of heaven were covered; ²⁰even fifteen cubits above them did the waters prevail, so that the mountains were covered.

²¹And all flesh that moved in the earth – birds, beasts of pasture, and wild animals – perished, with all that crawled on the land and all mankind, ²²so that everything that had the breath of life in its nostrils throughout all the dry land died. ²³Thus was destroyed all that was upon the land, man, beast, and crawling things, with birds of the air, so that they were destroyed from the earth – save Noah only was preserved, and those that were with him in the ark.

²⁴And the waters prevailed upon the earth for 150 days.

Marginal references: Wis 10:4; Ec'us 40:8-10.

The Notes

a) 1. They are righteous before God who love their neighbours for God's sake unfeignedly, having the Spirit of God who makes them the children of God, and who are therefore accepted by God as just and righteous, as it is in Genesis 18:19.

b) 2,8. Clean beasts are such as they could lawfully eat, and the unclean are those that they could not eat, as it appears in Lev c11 and De c14.

c) 11. The fountains of the great deep, etc: that is, all the waters that were on the earth sprang up, increased, and multiplied.

d) 11. The windows of heaven opened, etc: that is, all the waters above the earth descended and increased the flood.

Chapter 8

After the sending forth of the raven and the dove, Noah went out of the ark. He offers sacrifice. The evil of man's heart.

And God remembered Noah, and all the living things and all the animals that were with him in the ark. Then God made a wind to blow upon the earth, and the waters ceased; ²and the fountains of the deep and the windows of heaven were stopped, and the rain of heaven was forbidden. ³And the waters receded from off the earth, and abated after the end of 150 days. ⁴And the ark rested upon the mountains of Ararat on the 17th day of the seventh month. ⁵And the waters kept decreasing until the tenth month, and the first day of the tenth month, the tops of the mountains appeared.

⁶And after the end of forty days, Noah opened the window of the ark that he had made ⁷and sent forth a raven, which went out, ever going and coming again, until the waters were dried up upon the earth.

⁸Then he sent forth a dove from him, to see whether the waters had gone away from off the earth. ⁹But when the dove could find no rest-

Marginal references: Ge 1:2; also Ge 7:11 above and note c.

ing place for her foot, she returned to him again to the ark, for the waters were yet upon the face of all the earth. And he put out his hand and took her, and pulled her to him into the ark.

¹⁰And he waited yet seven days more and sent out the dove again from the ark. ¹¹And the dove came back to him about eventide, and behold: there was in her mouth a leaf of an olive tree which she had plucked, by which Noah perceived that the waters were abated upon the earth. ¹²And he waited yet seven more days and sent forth the dove, which from that time came no more to him again.

¹³And it came to pass, the 601st year and the first day of the first month, that the waters were dried up upon the earth. And Noah took off the hatches of the ark and looked, and behold: the face of the earth was dry. ¹⁴So by the 27th day of the second month, the earth was dry.

¹⁵And God spoke to Noah, saying, ¹⁶Come out of the ark, both you and your wife, and your sons and your sons' wives with you. ¹⁷And all the living things that are with you, whatever flesh it be – both bird and beast, and all the creatures that crawl on the earth – bring out with you; and let them move, grow, and multiply upon the earth. Ge 1:22,28; 9:1,7.

¹⁸And Noah came out, and his sons, his wife, and his sons' wives with him. ¹⁹And all the beasts and all the crawling things, and all the birds, and everything that moved upon the earth, came also out of the ark – all of their kind together.

²⁰And Noah made an altar to the Lord, and took some of every clean beast and of every clean bird and offered sacrifice upon the altar. Lev c11
²¹And the Lord smelled a sweet savour^a and said in his heart, I will henceforth no more curse the earth on account of man; for the imagination of man's heart is evil even from his very youth. Moreover, from henceforth I will not destroy everything that lives, as I have done. ²²Neither shall sowing time and harvest, cold and heat, summer and winter, nor day and night cease, as long as the earth endures.

The Notes

a) 21. The Lord's smelling of savour is the approval and receiving of the works of the faithful, as in Exodus 29:18, Leviticus 1:9 & cc 2-4, etc.

Chapter 9

> God blesses Noah and his sons. He forbids to eat the blood of beasts and forbids the shedding of man's blood. The law of the sword. He makes a covenant that he will destroy the world no more by water, and gives the rainbow as a sign and confirmation of the covenant. Noah is drunken, and Ham uncovers him and gets his curse.

And God blessed Noah and his sons, and said to them, Increase and multiply, and fill the earth. ²The fear also and dread of you will be upon all beasts of the earth, and upon all birds of the air, and upon all that crawls on the earth, and upon all fishes of the sea, which are given Ge 1:22,28 into your hands. ³And all that moves upon the earth, having life, will be your food; even as the green plants, so I give you all things. ⁴But the flesh with its life, which is its blood, see that you eat not. ⁵For indeed, your blood, in which your lives are, I will avenge; even from the hand of all beasts will I require it, and from the hand of man.ᵃ From the hand of every man's brother will I require the life of man, ⁶so that he who sheds man's blood will have his blood shed by man; for God made man after his own likeness. ⁷See that you increase and grow; and occupy the earth, and multiply in it.

⁸Furthermore, God spoke to Noah and to his sons with him, saying, ⁹See, I make my covenant with you and your seed after you, ¹⁰and with all the living things that are with you, both bird and beast – all the creatures of the earth that are with you, of all that comes out of the ark, whatever creature of the earth it be. ¹¹I make my bond with you, that henceforth all flesh shall not be destroyed with the waters of any flood, and that henceforth there shall not be a flood to destroy the earth.

¹²And God said, This is the sign of my bond, which I make between me and you, and between all living things that are with you forever: ¹³I will set my rainbow in the clouds, and it will be a sign of the covenant made between me and the earth. ¹⁴So it will be that, when I bring in clouds upon the earth, the rainbow will appear in the clouds. ¹⁵And then I will think upon my covenant which I have made between me and you and everything that lives – whatsoever flesh it be – so that henceforth there shall be no more waters to make a flood to destroy all flesh. ¹⁶The rainbow shall be in the clouds, and I will look upon it to remember the everlasting covenant between God and everything that lives upon the earth, whatsoever flesh it be. ¹⁷And God said to Noah, This is the sign of the covenant that I have made between me and all flesh that is on the earth.

¹⁸The sons of Noah who came out of the ark were Shem, Ham, and Japheth. (And Ham, he was the father of Canaan.) ¹⁹These were the three sons of Noah, and from them was all the world overspread.

²⁰And Noah, being a husbandman, went forth and planted a vineyard. ²¹And he drank of the wine and was drunk, and lay uncovered in his tent. ²²And Ham, the father of Canaan, saw his father's nakedness and told his two brothers who were without. ²³And Shem and Japheth took a mantle, put it on both their shoulders, and walked backward and covered their father's private parts; but their faces were backward so that they saw not their father's nakedness.

²⁴As soon as Noah awoke from his wine and knew what his younger son had done to him, ²⁵he said, Cursed be Canaan, and a servant of all servants to his brethren! ²⁶And he said, Blessed be the Lord God of Shem, and may Canaan be his servant. ²⁷May God increase Japheth,ᵇ that he may dwell in the tents of Shem. And may Canaan be their servant.

²⁸And Noah lived after the flood 350 years, ²⁹so that all the days of

Noah were 950 years; and then he died.

The Notes

a) 5. Here is all cruelty forbidden to man, so that God will not let it be unavenged in beasts, much less in our neighbour.

b) 27. To increase: that is, to gladden, or give to be in peace and of good comfort, as in Genesis 26:22 and note a, and in Psalm 4:1.

Chapter 10

The genealogy of Japheth, Shem, and Ham.

These are the generations of the sons of Noah – of Shem, Ham, and Japheth, who begat children after the flood. ²The sons of Japheth were Gomer, Magog, Madai, Javan, Tubal, Meshech, and Tiras. ³And the sons of Gomer were Ashkenaz, Riphath, and Togarmah. ⁴And the sons of Javan were Elishah, Tarshish, Kittim, and Dodanim. ⁵From these came the isles of the Gentiles in their countries, every person in his speech, kindred, and nation.

⁶The sons of Ham were Cush, Mizraim, Put, and Canaan. ⁷The sons of Cush were Seba, Havilah, Sabtah, Raamah, and Sabtechah. And the sons of Raamah were Sheba and Dedan. ⁸Cush also begat Nimrod, who began to be mighty in the earth. ⁹He was a mighty hunter in the sight of the Lord, from whence came the proverb, He is as Nimrod, that mighty hunter in the sight of the Lord. ¹⁰And the beginning of his kingdom was Babel, Erech, Accad, and Calneh in the land of Shinar. ¹¹Out of that land came Ashur, who built Nineveh, Rehoboth Ir, Calah, ¹²and Resen between Nineveh and Calah, which is a great city.

¹³And Mizraim begat Ludim, Anamim, Lehabim, Naphtuhim, ¹⁴Pathrusim, and Casluhim, from whence came the Philistines and the Caphtorim.

¹⁵Canaan also begat Sidon, his eldest son, and Heth, ¹⁶Jebusi, Amori, Girgashi, ¹⁷Hivi, Arki, Sim, ¹⁸Arvadi, Zemari, and Harmati. And afterward the kindreds of the Canaanites spread abroad, ¹⁹and the borderlands of the Canaanites were from Sidon till you come to Gerar and to Gaza, and till you come to Sodom, Gomorrah, Admah, Zeboim – even to Lasha. ²⁰These were the children* of Ham in their kindreds, tongues, lands, and nations.

²¹And Shem, the father‡ of all the children of Eber and brother of Japheth the elder, begat children also. ²²And his sons were Elam, Ashur, Arphaxad, Lud, and Aram. ²³And the children of Aram were Uz, Hul, Gether, and Mash. ²⁴Arphaxad begat Shelah, and Shelah begat Eber.° ²⁵And Eber begat two sons; the name of the one was Peleg, for in his time the earth was divided, and the name of his brother was Joktan. ²⁶Joktan begat Almodad, Sheleph, Hazarmaveth, Jerah, ²⁷Hadoram, Uzal, Diklah, ²⁸Obal, Abimael, Sheba, ²⁹Ophir, Havilah, and Jobab; all these were the sons of Joktan. ³⁰And they dwelt from Mesha until

---

Margin references:
1Ch 1:1-23
1Ch 1:10
Ge 11:9
Jon 1:2
*[Children: descendants, tribe, people]
1Ch 1:17-25
‡[Father: patriarch, progenitor, or forefather]
°From Eber comes the designation *Hebrew*.

you come to Sephar, a mountain of the east land. ³¹These are the descendants of Shem in their kindreds, languages, countries, and nations.

³²These are the kindreds of the sons of Noah in their generations and nations. And from these came the people who were in the world after the flood.

Chapter 11

The building of the tower of Babel. The confusion of tongues. The genealogy of Shem, the son of Noah, until Abram, who goes with Lot to Haran.

And all the world was of one tongue and one language. ²And as people came from the east, they found a plain in the land of Shinar, and there they dwelt. ³And they said to one another, Come on, let us make brick and bake it with fire. So brick was their stone, and slime was their mortar. ⁴And they said, Come on, let us build ourselves a city and a tower, so that the top may reach to heaven! And let us make a name for ourselves, for perhaps we will be scattered abroad over all the earth.

⁵And the Lord came down^a to see^b the city and the tower that the children of Adam were building. ⁶And the Lord said, See, the people is one, and have one tongue among them all. And they have begun to do this, and will not leave off from all that they have purposed to do. ⁷Come, let us descend and mix up their speech right there, so that one will not understand what another says.

⁸Thus the Lord scattered them from there upon all the earth, and they left off building the city. ⁹Therefore the name of it is called Babel, because there the Lord confused the speech of all the world, and because from there the Lord scattered them abroad upon all the earth.

Ac 2:4-12

1Ch 1:17-27

¹⁰These are the generations of Shem: Shem was 100 years old, and begat Arphaxad two years after the flood. ¹¹And Shem lived after he had begotten Arphaxad 500 years, and begat sons and daughters. ¹²And Arphaxad lived 35 years, and begat Shelah;^c ¹³and he lived after he had begotten Shelah 403 years, and begat sons and daughters. ¹⁴And Shelah was 30 years old and begat Eber, ¹⁵and lived after he had begotten Eber 403 years, and begat sons and daughters. ¹⁶When Eber was 34 years old he begat Peleg, ¹⁷and lived after he had begotten Peleg 430 years, and begat sons and daughters.

¹⁸And Peleg, when he was 30 years old, begat Reu, ¹⁹and lived after he had begotten Reu 209 years, and begat sons and daughters. ²⁰And Reu, when he had lived 32 years, begat Serug, ²¹and lived after he had begotten Serug 207 years, and begat sons and daughters. ²²And when Serug was 30 years old he begat Nahor, ²³and lived after he had begotten Nahor 200 years, and begat sons and daughters.

Jos 24:2

²⁴And Nahor when he was 29 years old begat Terah, ²⁵and lived after he had begotten Terah 119 years, and begat sons and daughters.

²⁶And when Terah was 70 years old he begat Abram, Nahor, and Haran. ²⁷And these are the generations of Terah: Terah begat Abram,

Nahor, and Haran. And Haran begat Lot. ²⁸And Haran died before Terah his father in the land where he was born, at Ur in Chaldea.

²⁹And Abram and Nahor took wives for themselves. Abram's wife was called Sarai. And Nahor's wife was Milcah, the daughter of Haran, who was father of Milcah and of Iscah. ³⁰But Sarai was barren, and had no child.

Heb 11:11
2Esd 9:43-45

³¹Then Terah took Abram his son, Lot his grandson (Haran's son), and Sarai his daughter-in-law (his son Abram's wife), and they went with him from Ur in Chaldea to go into the land of Canaan. And they came to Haran and dwelt there. ³²And when Terah was 205 years old, he died in Haran.

Jos 24:3

The Notes

a) 5. God is counted to come down when he does anything among people on the earth that is not accustomed to be done, in some way showing himself present among people by his wonderful work, as it is in Psalms 18:6-19 and 144:5-7.

b) 5. To see the city: not that God does not see at all times, but only that he makes himself both to be seen and known in his wonderful works among people.

c) 12. Here The Seventy translators [i.e. of the Greek Pentateuch or Septuagint] leave out the generation of Cainan, who by the reckoning of the Hebrews begat Shelah when he was 30 years of age. Luke 3:35,36.

Chapter 12

Abram is blessed by God, and goes with Lot into a strange land that was shown to him in Canaan. God promises to give the same land to him and to his seed. Afterward, Abram goes into Egypt, and causes his wife Sarai to say that she is his sister. And she was ravished by Pharaoh, for which the Lord plagues him.

Then the Lord said to Abram, Go out of your country, away from your kindred and out of your father's house, into a land that I will show you. ²And I will make of you a mighty people, and will bless you and make your name great,ᵃ so that you may be a blessing. ³And I will bless those who bless you and curse those who curse you. And in you shall be blessed all the generations of the earth.

Jos 24:2,3
Ac 7:2-4
Heb 11:8-10

⁴And Abram went as the Lord bade him, and Lot went with him. Abram was 75 years old when he went out of Haran. ⁵And Abram took Sarai his wife and Lot his brother's son, with all their goods that they had gathered and soulsᵇ that they had gotten in Haran, and they departed to go into the land of Canaan. And when they were come to the land of Canaan, ⁶Abram went forth into the land till he came to a place called Shechem, and to the oak of Moreh. And the Canaanites dwelt then in the land.

Ge 14:13

⁷Then the Lord appeared to Abram and said, To your seed will I give this land.

And Abram built an altar there to the Lord who had appeared to

Ge 15:18-21
Ge 17:8
De 34:4
Ge 13:15

him. ⁸Then he went from there to a mountain that lies on the east side of Bethel and pitched his tent, Bethel being on the west side and Ai on the east. And he built there an altar to the Lord, and called on the name of the Lord. ⁹And then Abram departed and took his journey southward.

¹⁰After this there came a dearth in the land, and Abram went down into Egypt to sojourn there; for the dearth was sore in the land. ¹¹And when he was near to entering into Egypt, he said to Sarai his wife, Behold, I know that you are a fair woman to look upon. ¹²It will come to pass therefore, when the Egyptians see you, that they will say, She is his wife – and so they will slay me and keep you alive. ¹³Say, I pray you therefore, that you are my sister, so that I may fare the better by reason of you, and so that my soul may live for your sake.

<small>Ge 20:1-7</small>

¹⁴As soon as he came into Egypt, the Egyptians saw the woman, that she was very fair. ¹⁵And Pharaoh's lords saw her also, and praised her to Pharaoh. So it came about that she was taken into Pharaoh's house, ¹⁶who treated Abram well for her sake, so that he had sheep, oxen, and he-donkeys, and menservants and maidservants, and she-donkeys and camels.

¹⁷But God plagued Pharaoh and his house with great plagues because of Sarai, Abram's wife. ¹⁸Then Pharaoh called Abram and said, Why have you dealt thus with me? Why did you not tell me that she was your wife? ¹⁹Why did you say that she was your sister, and cause me to take her as my wife? But now, lo, here is your wife. Take her, and be walking.

²⁰Pharaoh also gave a charge to his men over Abram, to lead him out with his wife and everything that he had.

The Notes

a) 2. To bless means here to be made happy and fortunate. And to make great his name is to advance and extol him above other people.
b) 5. Here *souls* are taken for his servants and maids, who were very many, as you may see in Genesis 14:14.

Chapter 13

> Abram and Lot depart out of Egypt. And Abram divided his land and herds with his brother Lot. Here again is promised to Abram the land of Canaan.

Then Abram departed out of Egypt, both he and his wife with everything that he had, and Lot with him, toward the south. ²Abram was very rich in livestock, silver, and gold. ³Then he turned in his journey from the south toward Bethel, to the place where his tent was at the first between Bethel and Ai, ⁴the place of the altar that he had made before. And there Abram called upon the name of the Lord.

<small>Ge 12:8</small>

⁵Lot also who went with him had flocks, herds, and tents, ⁶so it was that the land was not able to receive them, that they could dwell together. For their possessions were so great that they could not dwell

<small>Ge 36:7</small>

together. ⁷And there fell a strife between the herdsmen of Abram's livestock and the herdsmen of Lot's livestock. Moreover, the Canaanites and the Perizzites also dwelt at that time in the land.

⁸Then Abram said to Lot, Let there be no strife, I pray you, between you and me, and between my herdsmen and yours; for we are brethren.ᵃ ⁹Is not all the whole land before you? Depart, I pray you, from me. If you will take the left hand, I will take the right; or if you take the right hand, I will take the left.

¹⁰And Lot lifted up his eyes and beheld all the country round about the Jordan, which was a land abundant in water everywhere (before the Lord destroyed Sodom and Gomorrah) – even like the garden of the Lord, and like the land of Egypt till you come to Zoar. ¹¹Then Lot chose all the plain of the Jordan, and took his journey toward the east; and so departed the one brotherᵃ from the other. ¹²Abram dwelt in the land of Canaan, but Lot in the cities of the plain, and he tented till he came to Sodom. ¹³But the people of Sodom were wicked, and sinned exceedingly against the Lord.

¹⁴And the Lord said to Abram after Lot departed from him, Lift up your eyes, and look from the place where you are northward, southward, eastward, and westward. ¹⁵For all the land that you see, I will give to you and to your seed forever.ᵇ ¹⁶And I will make your seed as the dust of the earth, so that if a man could number the dust of the earth, then could your seed also be numbered. ¹⁷Arise, and walk about the land in the length of it and in the breadth, for I will give it to you.

¹⁸Then Abram took down his tent and went and dwelt in the oak grove of Mamre, which is in Hebron;ᶜ and he built there an altar to the Lord.

The Notes

a) 8,11. The Hebrews often understand by this word *brother* [plural, *brethren*] all descendants, relations, and neighbours, and all who are of one stock. Romans 9:3, John 7:3.

b) 15. *Forever* [Heb. *o-lawm*] is not here taken for a time without end, but for a long season that does not have its end appointed. Exodus 12:14, 17, etc. [Ed: John Rogers often emphasized this idiomatic use of *forever* in the Hebrew scriptures. See especially note b on Exodus 15:18.]

c) 18. Hebron is the name of a city where Adam, Abraham and his wife with Isaac, etc., were buried, as in Genesis 23:17-20.

Chapter 14

Lot is taken prisoner. The victory of Abram over the Sodomites. Abram rescues Lot. Melchisedek offers gifts to Abram. Abram pays tithes to Melchisedek. Abram keeps nothing of the king of Sodom's goods.

And it happened within a while that Amraphel king of Shinar, Arioch king of Ellasar, Chedorlaomer king of Elam, and Tidal king of the nations, ²made war with Bera king of Sodom, with Birsha king of Gomorrah, with Shinab king of Admah, with Shemeber king of Zeboim, and with the king of Bela^a (which Bela is called Zoar). ³The latter kings all came together to the vale of Siddim, which is now the Salt Sea. ⁴For twelve years they had been subject to king Chedorlaomer, and in the thirteenth year they rebelled.

⁵Therefore, in the fourteenth year Chedorlaomer and the kings that were with him came and smote the Rephaims^b in Ashteroth Karnaim, the Zuzim in Ham, the Emim in Shaveh Kiriathaim, ⁶and the Horites from their own Mount Seir as far as the plain of El Paran, which borders upon the wilderness. ⁷And then they turned and went to the Well of Judgment (that is, Kadesh), and smote all the country of the Amalekites, and also the Amorites who dwelt in Hazezon Tamar.

⁸Then went out the king of Sodom, the king of Gomorrah, the king of Admah, the king of Zeboim, and the king of Bela (now called Zoar). And they arrayed their men in order to fight with them in the vale of Siddim; ⁹that is to say, with Chedorlaomer the king of Elam, with Tidal king of the nations, with Amraphel king of Shinar, and with Arioch king of Ellasar: four kings against five. ¹⁰And that vale of Siddim was full of slime pits. And the kings of Sodom and Gomorrah fled, and fell there. And the men who remained escaped to the mountains. ¹¹And the four kings took all the goods of Sodom and Gomorrah and all their victuals, and went their way. ¹²And they also took Lot, Abram's brother's son, with his goods – for he dwelt at Sodom – and departed.

¹³Then one who had escaped went and told Abram the Hebrew, who was dwelling in the oak grove of Mamre, the Amorite brother of Eshcol and Aner, who were allied with Abram. ¹⁴When Abram heard that his nephew was taken, he armed his servants born in his own house – three hundred and eighteen men – and went in pursuit till they came to Dan. ¹⁵And he set himself and his servants in array and fell upon them by night, and smote them, and chased them away to Hobah, which lies on the left hand of Damascus. ¹⁶And he brought back all the goods, and also his nephew Lot and his goods, with the women also and the people.

¹⁷And as he returned from the slaughter of Chedorlaomer and the kings who were with him, the king of Sodom went to meet him in the vale of Shaveh, which now is called King's Dale. ¹⁸Then Melchisedec king of Salem^c brought out bread and wine. And he, being the priest of the most high God, ¹⁹blessed him, saying, Blessed be Abram^d unto the most high God, possessor of heaven and earth. ²⁰And blessed be God the Most High, who has delivered your enemies into your hands.

And Abram gave him tithes of everything.

²¹Then the king of Sodom said to Abram, Give me the souls,^e and keep the goods for yourself. ²²And Abram answered the king of Sodom, I lifted up my hand to the Lord God, most high possessor of heaven and earth, ²³that I will not take of anything that is yours so much as a thread or a shoe latchet, lest you should say, I have made Abram rich! – ²⁴save only that which the young men have eaten, and the

Ge 13:18

Heb c7

shares of the men who went with me, Aner, Eshcol, and Mamre; let them take their shares.

The Notes

a) 2. Bela (or Zoar) is that town which Lot desired for his refuge when he came out of Sodom. Genesis 19:19-22.

b) 5. Rephaims are accounted in the scripture for giants (as in 2 Samuel 5:18 and Isaiah 17:5), who lived by theft and robbery.

c) 18. The Jews supposed Melchisedec to be Shem the son of Noah, because after the flood he lived 500 years, and after the death of Abraham he was (by God's providence) the king of Salem.

d) 19. Blessed be Abram: that is, praised be Abram. And (v20) praised be the most high God, as it is in Genesis 47:10.

e) 21. Souls are men and women, as in Genesis 46:15 and Deuteronomy 10:22.

Chapter 15

> The land of Canaan is yet again promised to Abram. God promises him seed. He believes and is justified. The prophecy of the bondage in which the children of Israel would be under Pharaoh, and of their deliverance.

After these events, the word of God came to Abram in a vision,^a saying, Fear not, Abram; I am your shield, and your reward will be exceedingly great.

²And Abram answered, Lord Jehovah, what will you give me? I go childless, but the steward of my house, this Eliezer of Damascus, has a son. ³And Abram said, See, to me you have given no seed; lo, a servant born in my house will be my heir.

⁴And behold, the word of the Lord spoke to Abram, saying, He shall not be your heir, but one that will come out of your own body shall be your heir. ⁵And he brought him outside and said, Look up to heaven and count the stars, if you are able to number them. And he said to him, Even so shall your seed be.

De 10:15
Ro 4:18

⁶And Abram believed the Lord,^b and it was counted to him for righteousness. ⁷And he said to him, I am the Lord that brought you out of Ur in Chaldea to give you this land, to possess it.

Ro 4:3,22
Ga 3:6

⁸And Abram said, Lord God, how can I know that I will possess it? ⁹And he said to him, Take a heifer of three years old, a she-goat of three years old, a three-year-old ram, a turtle dove, and a young pigeon.

¹⁰And Abram took all these, and divided them in the middle and laid each half opposite the other; but the birds he did not divide. ¹¹And birds of prey fell on the carcasses, but Abram drove them away. ¹²And when the sun was down, there fell a slumber upon Abram; and lo, fear and great darkness came upon him. ¹³And the Lord said to Abram, Know this for certain: that your seed will be strangers in a land that does not belong to them. And they will make bondmen of them, and ill-treat them for 400 years. ¹⁴But the nation whom they serve, I will

Ac 7:6,7
J'th 5:11
Ex 12:40-44

Ex 12:31-36 judge,^c and afterward they shall come out with great substance. ¹⁵Nevertheless, you will go to your fathers in peace, and will be buried when you are of a good age. ¹⁶And in the fourth generation,^d they will return here again; for the wickedness of the Amorites is not yet full.

¹⁷When the sun was down and it was dark, behold, there was a smoking furnace, and a firebrand that went between^e the said pieces. ¹⁸And that same day the Lord made a covenant with Abram, saying, Gal 3:16 To your seed I will give this land, from the River of Egypt even to the Ge 24:7 great river Euphrates: ¹⁹the Kenites, the Kenezzites, the Kadmonites, ²⁰the Hittites, the Perizzites, the Rephaims, ²¹the Amorites, the Canaanites, the Girgashites, and the Jebusites.

The Notes

a) 1. The word of the Lord comes when he shows anything to us by revelation, as it is used in various places of the scripture, and especially in the Prophets. It is a manner of speech of the Hebrews.

b) 6. To believe is to have a sure trust and confidence to obtain the thing promised, and not to have any doubt in him who promises. Romans 4:3, Galatians 2:16; 3:6-9.

c) 14. To judge is here to take vengeance. Psalm 35:1-8.

d) 16. A generation or an age is here taken for 100 years, as in Ge 6:9.

e) 17. This word *went between* is taken for burning or consuming.

Chapter 16

Sarai gives Abram leave to take her maid Hagar as a wife. Hagar despises her mistress, for which she was ill-treated by Sarai and therefore runs away. The angel meets her, commands her to turn back, and promises her seed. And he names her first child Ishmael.

Sarai, Abram's wife, bore him no children. But she had a handmaid, an Egyptian whose name was Hagar. ²And so she said to Abram, Behold, the Lord has closed me so that I cannot bear. I pray you, go in to my maid.^a Perhaps I can be multiplied by means of her.

And Abram heeded the voice of Sarai. ³Then Sarai Abram's wife took Hagar her maid, the Egyptian, and gave her to her husband Abram to be his wife, after Abram had dwelt ten years in the land of Canaan. ⁴And he went in to Hagar, and she conceived.

But when Hagar saw that she had conceived, her mistress was contemptible in her sight. ⁵Then said Sarai to Abram, You do me injustice, for I have given my maid into your bosom,^b and now, because she sees that she has conceived, I am contemptible in her sight! May the Lord judge between you and me.

⁶Then Abram said to Sarai, Behold, your maid is in your hand. Do with her as it pleases you.

And because Sarai dealt severely with her, Hagar fled from her. ⁷And the angel of the Lord found her beside a fountain of water in the wilderness, by a well in the way to Shur. ⁸And he said, Hagar, Sarai's maid, from whence do you come, and where will you go?

And she answered, I flee from my mistress Sarai.

⁹And the angel of the Lord said to her, Return to your mistress again, and submit yourself under her hands. ¹⁰And the angel of the Lord said to her, I will so increase your seed, that it may not be numbered for multitude. ¹¹And the Lord's angel said further to her, See, you are with child and shall bear a son. And you shall call his name Ishmael, because the Lord has heard your tribulation. ¹²He will be a wild man, and his hand will be against every man, and every man's hand against him. And yet, he will dwell close by all his brethren.

¹³And Hagar called the name of the Lord who spoke to her, You-are-the-God-that-looks-on-me. For (she said), I have assuredly seen here the back parts of him who sees me.ᶜ ¹⁴Therefore, she called the well The-well-of-the-Living-who-sees-me, which well is between Kadesh and Bered.

¹⁵And Hagar bore Abram a son. And Abram called the name of his son whom Hagar bore, Ishmael. ¹⁶And Abram was 86 years old when Hagar bore him Ishmael.

Ge 17:16
J'g 13:3
M't 1:20,21
Lu 1:13

Ge 24:62

The Notes

a) 2. To go in to her maid is to have carnal copulation with her, as the words *know* and *sleep* do also signify.

b) 5. *Bosom*, after the manner of the Hebrews, is taken for consorting with a woman. And it is also taken for faith, as in Luke 16:22 of Lazarus.

c) 13. They who see the back parts of God are those who, by revelation or otherwise, have perception or knowledge of God.

Chapter 17

> Abram is called Abraham, and Sarai is named Sarah. The land of Canaan is here the fourth time promised. Circumcision is here instituted. Isaac is promised. Abraham prays for Ishmael.

When Abram was 99 years old the Lord appeared to him, saying, I am the almighty God; walk before me, and be uncorrupt. ²And I will make my bond between you and me, and will multiply you exceedingly.

³And Abram fell on his face. And God talked further with him, saying, ⁴I am; behold, my covenant is with you, that you shall be a father of many nations. ⁵Therefore, you shall no more be called Abram, but your name shall be Abraham. For I have made you a father of many nations, ⁶and I will multiply you exceedingly, and will make nations of you; yea, and kings shall come out of you. ⁷Moreover, I will make my bond between me and you, and your seed after you in their times, to be an everlasting covenant, so that I will be God to you and to your seed after you. ⁸And I will give to you and to your seed after you the land wherein you are a stranger, even all the land of Canaan, for an everlasting possession, and will be their God.

⁹And God said to Abraham, See that you keep my covenant, both

Ge 5:24;
6:18.

Ec'us 44:19

Ac 7:5

you and your seed after you in their times. ¹⁰This is my covenant, which you shall keep between me and you and your seed after you: that you circumcise all your menchildren. ¹¹You shall circumcise the foreskin of your flesh, and it will be a sign of the bond between me and you. ¹²Every manchild, when it is eight days old, shall be circumcised among you in your generations; and all servants also, born at home or bought with money, even though they be strangers and not of your seed. ¹³The servant born in your house and he also who is bought with money must be circumcised, so that my covenant may be in your flesh for an everlasting bond. ¹⁴If there is any uncircumcised manchild, who has not the foreskin of his flesh cut off, his soul shall perish from his people because he has broken my covenant.

¹⁵And God said to Abraham, Sarai your wife shall no more be called Sarai, but her name will be Sarah. ¹⁶For I will bless her and give you a son by her, and will bless her so that people – yea, and kings of people – shall come of her.

¹⁷And Abraham fell upon his face and laughed, and said in his heart, Can a child be born to him who is 100 years old? And can Sarah, who is 90 years old, bear? ¹⁸And Abraham said to God, O that Ishmael might live in your sight!

¹⁹Then said God, Sarah your wife will bear you a son indeed, and you shall call his name Isaac. And I will make my bond with him, so that it will be an everlasting bond unto his seed after him. ²⁰And as concerning Ishmael also, I have heard your request; lo, I will bless him and increase him, and multiply him exceedingly. Twelve princes shall he beget, and I will make a great nation of him. ²¹But my bond I will make with Isaac, whom Sarah will bear to you at this time in twelve months.

²²And God left off talking with him and departed up from Abraham. ²³And Abraham took Ishmael his son, all the servants born in his house, and all who were bought with money – as many as were menchildren among the people of Abraham's house – and circumcised the foreskin of their flesh that very same day, as God had said to him. ²⁴Abraham was 99 years old when he cut off the foreskin of his flesh. ²⁵And Ishmael his son was 13 years old when the foreskin of his flesh was circumcised. ²⁶That same day Abraham was circumcised, and Ishmael his son. ²⁷And all the males in his house, whether they were born in his house or bought with money, though they were strangers, were circumcised with him.

Chapter 18

There appeared three men to Abraham. Isaac is promised to him again, at which Sarah laughed. The destruction of the Sodomites is declared to Abraham. Abraham prays for them.

And the Lord appeared to Abraham in the oak grove of Mamre as he sat in his tent door in the heat of the day.ᵃ ²And he lifted up his eyes and looked, and lo, three men stood not far from him. And when he saw them, he ran to meet them from the tent door, and fell to the ground ³and said, Lord, if I have found favour in your sight, go not by your servant! ⁴Let a little water be fetched, and wash your feet, and rest yourselves under the tree; ⁵and I will fetch a morsel of bread^b to refresh your hearts. And then go your ways, for even for this have you come to your servant.

And they answered, Do even so, as you have said.

⁶And Abraham hastened into his tent to Sarah and said, Make ready at once three pecks of fine meal, knead it, and make cakes.

⁷And Abraham ran to his cattle and fetched a calf that was tender and good, and gave it to a young man who made it ready at once. ⁸And he took butter and milk with the calf that he had prepared and set it before them, and stood himself by them under the tree. And they ate.

⁹And they said to him, Where is Sarah your wife?

And he said, In the tent.

¹⁰And the Lord said, I will come again to you as soon as the fruit can live; and lo, Sarah your wife shall have a son.

Now Sarah heard this from the tent door that was behind his back. ¹¹But Abraham and Sarah were both old and well stricken in age, and it had ceased to be with Sarah after the manner of wives. ¹²And Sarah laughed in herself, saying, Now I am grown old; shall I give myself to pleasure, and my old lord also?

¹³Then said the Lord to Abraham, Why does Sarah laugh, saying, Will I really bear a child now, when I am old? ¹⁴Is the thing too hard for the Lord to do? In the time appointed I will return to you, as soon as the fruit can have life, and Sarah shall have a son.

¹⁵Then Sarah denied it, saying, I did not laugh! For she was afraid.

But he said, Yes, you laughed.

¹⁶Then the men stood up from there and looked toward Sodom. And Abraham went with them, to bring them on the way. ¹⁷And the Lord said, Can I hide from Abraham that thing which I am about to do, ¹⁸seeing that Abraham shall be a great and a mighty people, and all the nations of the earth shall be blessed in him? ¹⁹For I know him, that he will command his children and his household after him to keep the way of the Lord, to do according to right and conscience, so that the Lord may bring upon Abraham that which he has promised him.

²⁰And the Lord said, The outcry against Sodom and Gomorrah is great, and their sin is exceedingly grievous. ²¹I will go down and see whether the people have done all together according to the cry that has come to me or not, so that I may know.

²²And the men departed from there and went toward Sodom. But Abraham stood yet before the Lord, ²³and he drew near and said, Will you destroy the righteous with the wicked? ²⁴If there are fifty righteous within the city, will you destroy it, and not spare the place for the sake of fifty righteous who are in it? ²⁵Far be it from you to do after this manner and slay the righteous with the wicked, so that the

righteous are as the wicked! Far be that from you. Should not the judge of all the world do according to right?

²⁶And the Lord said, If I find in Sodom fifty righteous within the city, I will spare all the place for their sakes.

²⁷And Abraham answered and said, Behold, I have taken upon me to speak to the Lord, and yet am but dust and ashes. ²⁸What if there lack five of fifty righteous: will you destroy all the city for the lack of five?

And he said, If I find there forty-five, I will not destroy them.

²⁹And Abraham spoke to him yet again and said, What if there be forty found there?

And he said, I will not do it for the forty's sake.

³⁰And he said, O, let not my Lord be angry that I speak: what if there be found thirty there?

And he said, I will not do it if I find thirty there.

³¹And Abraham said, O see, I have begun to speak to my Lord: what if there be twenty found there?

And he said, I will not destroy them for twenty's sake.

³²And Abraham said, O let not my Lord be angry that I speak yet, but even once more only: what if ten be found there?

And he said, I will not destroy them for ten's sake.

³³And the Lord went his way as soon as he had left communing with Abraham, and Abraham returned to his place.

Ge 2:7

The Notes

a) 1. The heat of the day is taken for noon.
b) 5. By *bread* in the scripture is understood every kind of food that is fit for man's eating, as in 1Samuel 28:22.

Chapter 19

> Lot received two angels into his house. The unclean lusts of the Sodomites. Lot is delivered and asks to dwell in the town of Zoar.

And there came two angels to Sodom in the evening, and Lot was sitting at the gate of the city. And Lot saw them and rose up to meet them, and he bowed himself to the ground with his face. ²And he said, See, lords, turn in I pray you, into your servant's house. And stay all night, and wash your feet, and rise up early and go on your ways.

And they said, Nay, but we will stay in the streets all night.

³Then he compelled them exceedingly. And they turned in to him and entered into his house, and he made them a feast and baked sweet cakes, and they ate. ⁴But before they went to rest, the people of the city of Sodom compassed the house round about, both old and young – all the people from all quarters. ⁵And they called to Lot and said to him, Where are the men who went into your house tonight?ª Bring them out to us so that we can do our lust with them.

⁶And Lot went out at the door to them and shut the door after him,

Ge 33:3,6,7
Heb 13:2

Lu 24:29
Tob 12:19

⁷and said, No, for God's sake brethren, do not so wickedly! ⁸Look, I have two daughters who have known no man; them I will bring out to you. Do with them as it seems good to you. Only to these men, do nothing; for that is why they came under the shelter of my roof.

⁹And they said, Come here! And they said, Did you not come in to sojourn here, and will you now be a judge? We will surely deal worse with you than with them!

And as they pressed in hard upon Lot and would have broken down the door, ¹⁰the men put forth their hands, pulled Lot into the house to them, and shut the door. ¹¹And the people who were at the door of the house they struck with blindness, both small and great, so that they could not find the door. ¹²And the men said moreover to Lot, If you have yet here any son-in-law, or sons or daughters, or whomever you have in the city, bring them out of this place. ¹³For we must destroy this place, because the outcry against the people is great before the Lord. Therefore, he has sent us to destroy it.

¹⁴And Lot went out and spoke to his sons-in-law (who were to have married his daughters) and said, Stand up and get out of this place, for the Lord will destroy the city! But he seemed as one joking to his sons-in-law. ¹⁵And as the morning arose, the angels hurried Lot, saying, Stand up! Take your wife, your two daughters, and that which is at hand, lest you perish in the sin of the city. ¹⁶And as he delayed, the men caught him, his wife, and his two daughters by the hands, because the Lord was merciful to him. And they brought him forth and set him outside the city. ¹⁷When they had brought them out, they said, Save your life! And look not behind you, neither stop in any place of the plain, but save yourself in the mountains, lest you perish.

¹⁸Then said Lot to them, O nay, my lord; ¹⁹behold, inasmuch as your servant has found grace in your sight, now make your mercy great, which you show to me in saving my life. For I cannot save myself in the mountains, lest some misfortune fall upon me and I die. ²⁰See, here is a town nearby to flee to, and it is a little one. Let me save myself there. Is it not a little one? Then my soul may live.

²¹And the angel said to him, See, I have received your request concerning this thing, and I will not overthrow this town for which you have spoken. ²²Hasten and save yourself there, for I can do nothing till you are gone in there.

And therefore the name of that town is called Zoar.* ²³And the sun was upon the earth when Lot entered into Zoar. ²⁴Then the Lord rained upon Sodom and Gomorrah brimstone and fire, from the Lord out of heaven, ²⁵and overthrew those cities and all the region, and all who dwelt in the cities, and that which grew upon the ground. ²⁶And Lot's wife looked behind her, and was turned into a pillar of salt.

²⁷Abraham rose up early and went to the place where he had stood before the Lord, ²⁸and he looked toward Sodom and Gomorrah, and toward all the land of the plain. And as he looked, behold, the smoke of the land rose as if it were the smoke of a furnace. ²⁹But

2Pe 2:6-9
Wis 10:6
Am 4:11
Lu 17:28-30
Jude 1:6,7

yet, when God destroyed the cities of the region, he thought upon Abraham and sent Lot out from the danger of the overthrowing, when he overthrew the cities where Lot dwelt.

³⁰Then Lot departed out of Zoar and dwelt in the mountains, and his two daughters with him, because he feared to remain in Zoar. He dwelt therefore in a cave, both he and his two daughters also. ³¹Then said the elder to the younger, Our father is old, and there are no more men in the earth to come in to us after the manner of all the world. ³²Come, therefore; let us give our father wine to drink, and let us lie with him so that we may preserve seed by our father.

³³And they gave their father wine to drink that same night. And the elder daughter went and lay with her father. And he perceived it not, neither when she lay down nor when she rose up.

³⁴And on the morrow the elder said to the younger, See, last night I lay with my father. Let us give him wine to drink this night also, and you go and lie with him, and let us preserve seed by our father. ³⁵And they gave their father wine to drink that night also, and the younger arose and lay with him. And he perceived it not, neither when she lay down nor when she rose up.

³⁶Thus were both the daughters of Lot with child by their father. ³⁷And the elder bore a son and called him Moab, who is the father of the Moabites to this day. ³⁸And the younger bore a son and called him Ben-Ammi, who is the father of the children of Ammon to this day.

The Notes

a) 5. The night is here taken for the evening, which is the beginning of the night, as in Proverbs 7:9.

Chapter 20

> Abraham went as a stranger into the land of Gerar.
> The king of Gerar takes away his wife.

And Abraham departed from there toward the south country. And he dwelt between Kadesh and Shur, and sojourned in Gerar. ²And Abraham said of Sarah his wife that she was his sister. Then Abimelech, the king of Gerar, sent and fetched Sarah away.

Ge 12:13; 26:7.

³And God came to Abimelech by night in a dream and said to him, See, you are but a dead man because of the woman that you have taken away, for she is a man's wife.

⁴But Abimelech had not yet come near her, and therefore said, Lord, would you slay righteous people? ⁵Did he not say to me that she was his sister? Yea, and did she not say herself that he was her brother? With a pure heart and innocent hands I have done this.

⁶And God said to him in a dream, I knew well that you did it in the pureness of your heart, and therefore I kept you so that you would not sin against me; neither did I suffer you to come near her. ⁷Now therefore, deliver to the man his wife again, for he is a prophet. And let him

pray for you so that you may live. But if you do not deliver her back, be sure that you shall die, with all that you have.

⁸Then Abimelech rose up early in the morning, and he called all his servants and told all these things in their ears. And the men were sore afraid. ⁹And Abimelech called Abraham and said to him, What have you done to us? And how have I offended against you, that you should bring on me and on my kingdom so great a sin? You have done things to me that ought not to be done. ¹⁰And Abimelech said moreover to Abraham, What did you see, that moved you to do this thing?

¹¹And Abraham answered, I thought that perhaps the fear of God^a was not in this place, and that men would kill me for my wife. ¹²Yet indeed she is my sister – the daughter of my father, but not of my mother – and became my wife. ¹³And after God caused me to wander out of my father's house, I said to her, This kindness shall you show to me in all the places where we go: to say of me that I am your brother.

¹⁴Then Abimelech took sheep and oxen, menservants and womenservants, and gave them to Abraham, and delivered Sarah his wife to him again. ¹⁵And Abimelech said, Behold, the land lies before you; dwell where it pleases you best. ¹⁶And to Sarah he said, See, I have given your brother a thousand pieces of silver; behold, this will be to you a recompense, and to all who are with you and to all people, a vindication of your honour.

v16 e.f. JR.

¹⁷And so Abraham prayed to God, and God healed Abimelech and his wife and his maidservants, so that they bore children. ¹⁸For the Lord had closed all the wombs of the house of Abimelech because of Sarah, Abraham's wife.

The Notes

a) 11. Among the Hebrews, the fear of God is principally taken for the honour and faith that we owe to God, and that with such a love as the child has for the father.

Chapter 21

Isaac is born. Hagar is cast out with her young son Ishmael. The angel helps and comforts Hagar. The covenant between Abimelech and Abraham.

The Lord visited Sarah as he had said, and did unto her as he had promised. ²And Sarah was with child and bore Abraham a son in his old age, at the same time that the Lord had appointed. ³And Abraham called his son who was born to him, whom Sarah bore him, Isaac. ⁴And Abraham circumcised Isaac his son when he was eight days old, as God had commanded him.

Ge 17:6; 18:10,14.
Ga 4:21-31
Heb 11:11
M't 1:2
Jos 24:3
Ge 17:10

⁵And Abraham was 100 years old when his son Isaac was born to him. ⁶And Sarah said, God has prepared joy for me, and whoever hears will rejoice with me. ⁷She said also, Who would have said to Abraham that Sarah should have given children suck, or that I should have borne him a son in his old age?

v6 e.f. COV.

⁸And the child grew and was weaned, and Abraham made a great

feast on the same day that Isaac was weaned.

⁹And Sarah saw the son of Hagar the Egyptian (whom Hagar had borne to Abraham), that he was a mocker. ¹⁰Then she said to Abraham, Put away this bondmaid and her son, for the son of this bondwoman will not be heir with my son Isaac!

¹¹But these words seemed very grievous in Abraham's sight, because of his son. ¹²Then the Lord said to Abraham, Let it not be grievous to you because of the lad and your bondmaid, but in all that Sarah has said to you, hear her voice. For in Isaac shall your seed be called. ¹³Moreover, of the son of the bondwoman I will make a nation, because he is your seed.

¹⁴And Abraham rose up early in the morning, and took bread and a bottle with water and, putting it on her shoulders, gave it to Hagar with the lad also, and sent her away. And she departed, and wandered up and down in the wilderness of Beersheba. ¹⁵When the water that was in the bottle was gone, she cast the lad under a bush, ¹⁶and went and sat out of sight a great way, as it were a bowshot off; for she said, I cannot see the lad die! And she sat down out of sight and lifted up her voice and wept.

¹⁷And God heard the voice of the child. And the angel of God called Hagar out of heaven and said to her, What ails you, Hagar? Fear not, for God has heard the voice of the child where he lies. ¹⁸Arise, lift up the lad, and take him in your hand; for I will make of him a great people.

¹⁹And God opened her eyes, and she saw a well of water. And she went and filled the bottle with water and gave the boy a drink. ²⁰And God was with the lad, and he grew and dwelt in the wilderness, and became an archer. ²¹And he dwelt in the wilderness of Pharan. And his mother got him a wife out of the land of Egypt.

²²And it chanced the same season that Abimelech, with Phichol his chief captain, spoke to Abraham, saying, God is with you in everything that you do. ²³Now therefore swear to me, right here by God, that you will not hurt me or my children, nor my children's children, but that you will deal with me and the country where you are a stranger according to the kindness that I have shown you.

²⁴Then Abraham said, I will swear. ²⁵But Abraham rebuked Abimelech for a well of water that Abimelech's servants had taken away. ²⁶And Abimelech answered, I do not know who did it. Also, you did not tell me, nor did I hear about it until this day.

²⁷And Abraham took sheep and oxen and gave them to Abimelech, and they made both of them a bond together. ²⁸Then Abraham set seven lambs by themselves, ²⁹and Abimelech said to Abraham, What is the meaning of these seven lambs that you have set by themselves? ³⁰And he answered, Seven lambs must you take from my hand so that it may be a witness for me, that I dug this well.

³¹And so the place is called Beersheba,* because they swore, both of them. ³²Thus they made a bond together at Beersheba.

*[ie, Well of the Seven, or Well of the Oath]

Then Abimelech with Phichol, his chief captain, rose up and turned again to the land of the Philistines. ³³And Abraham planted a wood in Beersheba and called there on the name of the Lord, the Everlasting God. ³⁴And he dwelt in the Philistine land a long season.

Chapter 22

The faith of Abraham is proved in offering his son Isaac. Christ our saviour is promised. The children of Abraham's brother Nahor.

After these things God did prove Abraham, and said to him, Abraham! And he answered, Here am I. ²And he said, Take your most beloved son Isaac,ᵃ whom you love, and go to the land of Moriah, and sacrifice him there for a sacrifice upon one of the mountains that I will show you.

³Then Abraham rose up early in the morning and saddled his donkey, and took two of his young men with him and Isaac his son; and he split wood for the sacrifice, rose up, and set off for the place that God had appointed to him.

⁴On the third day, Abraham lifted up his eyes and saw the place afar off, ⁵and said to his young men, Wait here with the donkey. I and the lad will go yonder and worship,* and will come again to you.

⁶And Abraham took the wood for the sacrifice and laid it upon Isaac his son, and took fire in his hand, and a knife. And they went both of them together.

⁷Then Isaac spoke to Abraham his father and said, My father? And he answered, Here am I, my son. And he said, See, here is fire and wood, but where is the sheep for sacrifice? ⁸And Abraham said, My son, God will provide himself a sheep for sacrifice.

So they went both together. ⁹And when they came to the place that God showed him, Abraham made an altar there and set the wood in order; and he bound Isaac his son and laid him on the altar, above upon the wood. ¹⁰And Abraham stretched forth his hand and took the knife, to have killed his son.

¹¹Then the angel of the Lord called to him from heaven, saying, Abraham, Abraham!

And he answered, Here am I.

¹²And he said, Lay not your hands upon the child, neither do anything at all to him. For now I knowᵇ that you fear God, in that you have not kept your most beloved son from me.

¹³And Abraham lifted up his eyes and looked about, and behold, there was a ram caught by the horns in a thicket. And he went and took the ram, and offered him up for a sacrifice in the stead of his son. ¹⁴And Abraham called the name of the place The-Lord-will-see. Therefore it is a common saying this day: In the mount will the Lord be seen.

¹⁵And the angel of the Lord called to Abraham from heaven the second time, ¹⁶saying, I swear by myself (says the Lord), because you

Side notes:
J'th 8:24-26
Ec'us 44:19,20.
Heb 11:17
v2 e.f. JR. See note a.

*To worship is here to do sacrifice.

Jas 2:21
1Macc 2:52

Heb 6:13-15
Ps 105:6-9
Lu 1:73
Ec'us 44:
20,21.
Ge 24:60;
12:2,3.
Ac 3:25
Ga 3:8

have done this thing, and have not spared your most beloved son, [17]I will bless you and multiply your seed as the stars of heaven and as the sand upon the sea side. And your seed shall possess the gates of his enemies. [18]And in your seed shall all the nations of the earth be blessed, because you have obeyed my voice.

[19]So Abraham turned back to the young men, and they rose up and went together to Beersheba. And Abraham dwelt at Beersheba.

[20]And it chanced after these things that someone told Abraham, saying, Behold Milcah! She has also borne children to your brother Nahor: [21]Huz his eldest son, and Buz his brother, and Kemuel the father of the Syrians; [22]and Chesed, Hazo, Pildash, Jidlaph, and Bethuel. [23]And Bethuel begat Rebecca. These eight did Milcah bear to Nahor, Abraham's brother. [24]And his concubine called Reumah, she bore also Tebah, Gaham, Thahash, and Maachah.

The Notes

a) 2. *Only son* [original translation] means only beloved or most chiefly beloved above others, after the Hebrew idiom, as in Pr 4:3. [For clarity, the idiom was emended to *most beloved son* in verses 2, 12, and 16. Ed.]
b) 12. I know: that is, I have experience that you fear God, as in Philippians 4:10.

Chapter 23

Sarah dies, and she is buried in the field that Abraham bought from Ephron the Hittite.

Sarah was 127 years old (for so long did she live), [2]and then died in a head city called Hebron in the land of Canaan. Then Abraham came to mourn Sarah and to weep for her. [3]And Abraham stood up from the dead body and talked with the sons of Heth, saying, [4]I am a stranger and a foreigner among you; give me a burial ground with you, so that I may bury my dead out of my sight.

[5]And the children of Heth answered Abraham, saying to him, [6]Hear us, lord. You are a mighty man of God among us; in the finest of our sepulchres bury your dead. None of us will forbid you his sepulchre, that you should not bury your dead therein.

[7]Abraham stood up and bowed himself before the people of the land, the children of Heth. [8]And he talked with them, saying, If it be your will that I may bury my dead out of my sight, hear me, and speak for me to Ephron the son of Zoar. [9]And let him give me the double cave that he has in the end of his field, for as much money as it is worth. Let him sell it to me in the presence of you all, for a possession to bury in. [10](For Ephron dwelt among the children of Heth.)

Then Ephron the Hittite answered Abraham in the hearing of the children of Heth and of everyone who went in at the gates of his city, saying, [11]Not so, my lord, but hear me: I give you the field, and I give you the cave that is in it also. And in the presence of the sons of my people I give it to you, to bury your dead in.

¹²Then Abraham bowed himself before the people of the land, ¹³and spoke to Ephron in the hearing of the people of the country, saying, I pray you, hear me. I will give silver for the field; receive it from me, and so will I bury my dead there.

¹⁴Ephron answered Abraham, saying to him, ¹⁵My lord, hearken to me. The land is worth 400 sickles of silver. But what is that between you and me? Bury your dead.

¹⁶And Abraham hearkened to Ephron, and weighed out to him the silver as he had said in the hearing of the sons of Heth, namely 400 silver sickles of money, currency among the merchants. ¹⁷Thus was the field of Ephron before Mamre where the double cave is – including the field, the cave that is in it, and all the trees of the field that grow in all the borders round about – made sure ¹⁸to Abraham for a possession, in the sight of the children of Heth and of everyone who went in at the gates of the city. ¹⁹And then Abraham buried Sarah his wife in the double cave of the field that lies before Mamre, otherwise called Hebron, in the land of Canaan. ²⁰And so both the field and the cave that is in it were made to Abraham a sure possession to bury in by the sons of Heth.

Chapter 24

> Abraham makes his servant swear an oath, and sends him to seek a wife for his son Isaac. The servant was faithful and brought Rebecca, whom Isaac took as his wife.

Abraham was old and stricken in days, and the Lord had blessed him in all things. ²And he said to the senior servant of his house, who had the rule over all that he had, Put your hand under my thigh,ᵃ ³so that I may make you swear by the Lord who is God of heaven and God of the earth, that you will not take a wife for my son from the daughters of the Canaanites among whom I dwell. ⁴But you must go to my country and to my kindred, and there take a wife for my son Isaac.

⁵Then said the servant to him, What if the woman will not agree to come with me to this land? Shall I bring your son back into the land that you came out of?

⁶And Abraham said to him, Beware of that, that you do not bring my son there. ⁷The Lord God of heaven who took me from my father's house and from the land where I was born, and who spoke to me and swore to me, saying, To your seed will I give this land – he will send his angel before you so that you may take a wife for my son from there. ⁸Nevertheless, if the woman will not agree to come with you, then you are discharged from this oath. But above all things, do not bring my son back there.

⁹And the servant put his hand under Abraham's thigh and swore to him concerning that matter.

¹⁰And the servant took ten camels from the camels of his master and departed, and had all manner of goods from his master with him;

Ge 12:7; 15:17-21.

and he stood up and went to Mesopotamia, to the town of Nahor. ¹¹And he made his camels lie down outside the town by the side of a well of water, in the evening about the time that the women come out to draw water. ¹²And he said, O Lord God of my master Abraham, send me good speed this day, and show mercy to my master Abraham. ¹³Lo, I stand here by the well of water, and the daughters of the men of this town will come out to draw water. ¹⁴Now, the young woman to whom I say, Lower your pitcher and let me drink – if she says, Drink, and I will give your camels to drink also, the same is she whom you have ordained for your servant Isaac. Yea, and by this I will know that you have shown mercy on my master.

¹⁵And it came to pass, before he had left speaking, that Rebecca the daughter of Bethuel, son of Milcah the wife of Nahor, Abraham's brother, came out with her pitcher upon her shoulder. ¹⁶The girl was very fair to look upon, and yet a maiden* and unknown by a man. And she went down to the well, filled her pitcher, and came up again. ¹⁷Then the servant ran to her and said, Let me sip a little water from your pitcher. ¹⁸And she said, Drink, my lord. And she quickly let down her pitcher upon her arm and gave him a drink. ¹⁹And when she had given him a drink, she said, I will draw water for your camels also, until they have drunk enough. ²⁰And she poured out her pitcher into the trough hastily, and ran again to the well to fetch water, and drew for all his camels.

*[ie, here, a virgin]

²¹And the fellow wondered at her. But held his peace, to be certain whether the Lord had made his journey successful or not. ²²And as the camels had left drinking, he took a golden earring of half a sickle weight, and two golden bracelets for her hands of ten sickles weight of gold,ᵇ ²³and said to her, Whose daughter are you? Tell me, is there room in your father's house for us to lodge in?

²⁴And she said to him, I am the daughter of Bethuel the son of Milcah, whom she bore to Nahor. ²⁵And she said moreover to him, We have straw and provender enough, and also room to lodge in.

²⁶And the man bowed himself and worshipped the Lord.ᶜ ²⁷And he said, Blessed be the Lord God of my master Abraham, who ceases not to deal mercifully and truly with my master, and has brought me by the way to my master's brother's house! ²⁸And the girl ran and told the people at her mother's house these things.

²⁹And Rebecca had a brother called Laban. And Laban ran out to the man, to the well. ³⁰For as soon as he had seen the earring and the bracelets upon his sister's hands, and heard the words of Rebecca his sister, saying, Thus said the man to me – then he went out to the man. And lo, he stood yet with the camels by the well side. ³¹And Laban said, Come in, O blessed of the Lord. Why do you stand without? I have prepared the house and made room for the camels.

³²And then the man went into the house. And Laban unbridled the camels, and brought straw and provender for the camels, and water to wash the man's feet and the feet of those who were with him. ³³And

there was food set before him to eat, but he said, I do not wish to eat until I have said my errand.

And Laban said, Say on.

³⁴And he said, I am Abraham's servant. ³⁵And the Lord has blessed^d my master out of measure, so that he has become great, and has given him sheep, oxen, silver and gold, menservants, maidservants, camels, and donkeys. ³⁶And Sarah, my master's wife, bore him a son when she was old, and to him he has given all that he has.

³⁷And my master made me swear, saying, You must not take a wife for my son from among the daughters of the Canaanites in whose land I dwell; ³⁸but you shall go to my father's house and to my kindred and there take a wife for my son. ³⁹And I said to my master, What if the wife will not follow me? ⁴⁰And he said to me, The Lord before whom I walk will send his angel with you and prosper your journey, so that you may take a wife for my son from my kindred and from my father's house. ⁴¹But if, when you come to my kindred, they will not give you one, then you will be discharged from this oath.

⁴²And I came this day to the well and said, O Lord, the God of my master Abraham, if it be so that you have made this my journey successful, ⁴³behold: I stand by this well of water. And when a virgin comes forth to draw water and I say to her, Give me a little water from your pitcher to drink, ⁴⁴and she answers me, Drink, and I will also draw water for your camels – that same is the wife whom the Lord has prepared for my master's son.

⁴⁵And before I had made an end of speaking in my heart, behold, Rebecca came forth with her pitcher on her shoulder, and she went down to the well and drew. And I said to her, Give me a drink. ⁴⁶And she made haste and took down her pitcher from off her, and said, Drink, and I will give your camels to drink also. And I drank, and she gave the camels drink also. ⁴⁷And I asked her, saying, Whose daughter are you? And she answered, The daughter of Bethuel, Nahor's son, whom Milcah bore to him. And I put the earring upon her face and the bracelets upon her hands. ⁴⁸And I bowed myself and worshipped the Lord, and blessed the Lord God of my master Abraham, who had brought me the right way, to take my master's brother's daughter for his son. ⁴⁹Now, therefore, if you will deal mercifully and truly^e with my master, tell me; and if not, tell me also, so that I may turn to the right hand or to the left.^f

⁵⁰Then Laban and Bethuel answered, saying, This has come of the Lord; therefore, we cannot speak to you either good or bad. ⁵¹Behold, Rebecca is before your face. Take her and go, and let her be your master's son's wife, just as the Lord has said.

⁵²And when Abraham's servant heard their words, he bowed himself to the Lord flat upon the earth. ⁵³And the servant took out jewelry of silver, jewelry of gold, and clothing, and gave them to Rebecca. But to her brother and to her mother he gave spices. ⁵⁴And then they ate and drank, both he and the men who were with him, and stayed there

Ge 22:23; 24:24.

all night, and rose up.

And he said, Let me depart to my master. ⁵⁵But Rebecca's brother and mother said, Let the girl abide with us a while, even but ten days, and then go your ways. ⁵⁶And he said to them, Hinder me not, for the Lord has prospered my journey; send me away so that I may go to my master. ⁵⁷And they said, Let us call the girl and see what she says to the matter. ⁵⁸And they called Rebecca and asked her, Do you want to go with this man? And she said, Yes.

⁵⁹So they let Rebecca their sister go, with her nurse and Abraham's servant and the men who were with him. ⁶⁰And they blessed⁽ᵍ⁾ Rebecca and said to her, You are our sister; grow into a thousand thousands, and may your seed possess the gates of their enemies.

⁶¹And Rebecca arose with her maidservants, and they seated themselves up upon the camels and went their way after the man. And so the servant took Rebecca and went his way.

⁶²And Isaac was coming from the Well of the Living and Seeing. For he dwelt in the south country, ⁶³and had gone out to walk during his meditations⁽ʰ⁾ before eventide. And he lifted up his eyes and looked, and behold, the camels were coming. ⁶⁴And Rebecca lifted up her eyes; and when she saw Isaac she alighted from the camel ⁶⁵and said to the servant, What man is this, who comes toward us in the field?

And the servant said, It is my master.

And then she took her mantle and put it about her. ⁶⁶And the servant told Isaac all that he had done.

⁶⁷Then Isaac brought her into his mother Sarah's tent, and took Rebecca, and she became his wife, and he loved her. And so was Isaac comforted over his mother.

Ge 16:14

The Notes

a) 2. To put the hand under the thigh was an oath that the Hebrews used in such things as pertained to the testament and promise of God, as in Genesis 47:29.

b) 22. Earrings are decorative items for the face and forehead of the woman, or for the ears. And bracelets are to adorn the arms or hands.

c) 26,48. To bow and worship is here to give thanks, as in Genesis 23:7.

d) 35. God blesses us when he gives us his benefits. He curses us when he takes them away, as in 2Kings 20:17.

e) 49. Mercifully and truly is as much as to say, in this place, to show favour, gentleness, or kindness.

f) 49. The right hand or the left is no more but to say, tell me one thing or another so that I may know my next step, and is a Hebrew idiom.

g) 60. To bless one's neighbour is to pray for him and to wish him good, and not to wag two fingers at him.

h) 63. Meditations are the exercise of the spirit and lifting up of the mind to God.

Chapter 25

Abraham takes Keturah as his wife and begets many children. Abraham dies and gives all his goods to

GENESIS 25

Isaac. The family of Ishmael. The birth of Jacob and Esau. Esau sells his birthright for a dish of pottage.

Abraham took another wife, called Keturah, ²who bore him Zimran, Jokshan, Medan, Midian, Ishbak, and Shuah. ³And Jokshan begat Sheba and Dedan. And the sons of Dedan were Ashurim, Letushim, and Leummim. ⁴And the sons of Midian were Ephah, Epher, Hanoch, Abidah, and Eldaah. All these were the descendants of Keturah. ⁵But Abraham gave all that he had to Isaac. ⁶And to the sons of his concubines[a] he gave gifts, and, while he was still living, he sent them eastward, away from Isaac his son to the east country.

⁷These are the days of the life of Abraham that he lived, 175 years. ⁸And then he fell sick and died at a good age, when he had lived enough, and was put unto his people.[b] ⁹And his sons Isaac and Ishmael buried him in the double cave in the field of Ephron the son of Zohar the Hittite, before Mamre, ¹⁰which field Abraham had bought from the sons of Heth. There was Abraham buried, with Sarah his wife. ¹¹And after the death of Abraham, God blessed Isaac his son, who dwelt by the Well of the Living and Seeing.

¹²These are the children of Abraham's son Ishmael, whom Hagar the Egyptian, Sarah's handmaid, bore to Abraham. ¹³The names of the sons of Ishmael, with their names in their kindreds: the eldest son of Ishmael, Nebajoth; then Kedar, Adbeel, Mibsam, ¹⁴Mishma, Dumah, Massa, ¹⁵Hadar, Tema, Jetur, Naphish, and Kedemah. ¹⁶These are the sons of Ishmael, and these are their names in their towns and castles – twelve princes of nations.

¹⁷And these are the years of the life of Ishmael, 137 years. And then he fell sick and died, and was laid unto his people. ¹⁸And he dwelt from Havilah to Shur, which is before Egypt as you go toward the Assyrians. And he died in the presence of all his brethren.

¹⁹And these are the children of Isaac, Abraham's son. Abraham begat Isaac, ²⁰and Isaac was forty years old when he took to wife Rebecca, the daughter of Bethuel the Syrian of Mesopotamia and sister to Laban the Syrian. ²¹And Isaac made intercession to the Lord for his wife because she was barren, and the Lord was entreated, and Rebecca his wife conceived. ²²But the children strove together within her. Then she said, If it should come so to pass, what help is it that I am with child? And she went and asked the Lord.

²³And the Lord said to her, There are two manner of people in your womb, and two nations shall spring out of your bowels.[c] And the one nation will be mightier than the other, and the eldest will be servant to the younger.

²⁴And when her time came to be delivered, behold, there were twins in her womb. ²⁵And he who came out first was red and hairy all over, as it were a hide; and they called his name Esau.* ²⁶And afterward his brother came out; and his hand was holding Esau by the heel, for which his name was called Jacob.‡ And Isaac was sixty years old when Rebecca bore them.

Ge 15:15

1Ch 1:28-31

Ge 17:20

*[ie, Covered with Hair]
Ho 12:3
‡[ie, Who Supplants or Trips Up]

²⁷And the boys grew. And Esau became a skillful hunter and a tillman, but Jacob was a simple man,^d and dwelt in the tents. ²⁸Isaac loved Esau because he ate of his venison, but Rebecca loved Jacob.

²⁹Now Jacob prepared a pottage. Then Esau came in from the field and was weary, ³⁰and he said to Jacob, Let me eat some of the red pottage, for I am faint. And therefore his name was called Edom.*

³¹And Jacob said, Sell me this day your birthright.

³²And Esau answered, Lo, I am at the point of death, and what profit will this birthright be to me?

³³And Jacob said, Swear to me then this day.

And he swore to him, and sold his birthright to Jacob.

³⁴Then Jacob gave Esau bread and the pottage of red lentils. And he ate and drank, and rose up and went his way. And so Esau regarded not his birthright.

Marginal references: Ob 1:1-4; *[ie, Red]; Ge 47:31; Heb 12:16*

The Notes

a) 6. Concubines in the scripture are not harlots, but wives. However, they bore no rule in the house but were subject as servants, as Hagar was to Sarah, Ge 16:3. Also Bilhah, as in Ge 30:4. See also 2Sam 15, note b.

b) 8,17. To be put among his people is not only to be put in a goodly place of burial, but to be put with the company of the ancient fathers who died in the same faith that he did. [See also note b on Genesis 35.]

c) 23. By these two peoples is signified to us the law and the gospel, as you may read likewise in Galatians 4:24.

d) 27. Simple: he is simple who is without craftiness and deceit, and who continues in believing and in doing God's will.

Chapter 26

The journey of Isaac to Abimelech. The promises made to Isaac and his seed. Isaac is rebuked by Abimelech for calling his wife his sister. The quarreling of the shepherds for the wells. Isaac is comforted. The reconciliation between Abimelech and Isaac.

And there fell a dearth in the land, surpassing the first dearth that fell in the days of Abraham, and so Isaac went to Abimelech the king of the Philistines in Gerar. ²Then the Lord appeared to him and said, Do not go down into Egypt, but stay in the land where I say to you, ³Sojourn in this land. And I will be with you and will bless you, for to you and to your seed I will give all these countries. And I will perform the oath that I swore to Abraham your father, ⁴and will multiply your seed as the stars of heaven, and will give to your seed all these countries. And through your seed shall all the nations of the earth be blessed, ⁵because Abraham hearkened to my voice and kept my ordinances, commandments, statutes, and laws.

⁶And Isaac dwelt in Gerar. ⁷And the men of the place asked him about his wife. And he said that she was his sister, for he feared to call her his wife in case the men of the place killed him for her, because she was beautiful to the eye. ⁸And it happened, after he had been there

Marginal references: Ge 12:7; 13:14,15; 15:18-21; 22:17. Ec'us 44:22; Ge 12:11-13; 20:2.

a long time, that Abimelech king of the Philistines looked out at a window and saw Isaac having fun with Rebecca his wife. ⁹And Abimelech sent for Isaac and said, See, she is surely your wife; why did you say she was your sister? And Isaac said to him, I thought I might die because of her. ¹⁰Then said Abimelech, Why have you done this to us? One of the people might easily have lain with your wife, and so would you have brought sin upon us!

¹¹Then Abimelech charged all his people, saying, He who touches this man or his wife shall surely die for it.

¹²And Isaac sowed crops in the land, and reaped in the same year a hundred bushels, for the Lord blessed him. ¹³And the man became mighty, and went on growing till he was exceedingly great, ¹⁴and possessed flocks and herds and a mighty household. Therefore the Philistines envied him, ¹⁵so much so that they stopped up and filled with earth all the wells that his father's servants had dug in his father Abraham's time. ¹⁶Then Abimelech said to Isaac, Go away from me, for you are mightier than we a great deal!

¹⁷Then Isaac departed from there, and pitched his tent in the valley of Gerar and dwelt there. ¹⁸And Isaac dug open again the wells of water that were dug in the days of Abraham his father, which the Philistines had stopped up after Abraham's death. And he gave them the same names that his father had given them.

¹⁹As Isaac's servants dug in the valley, they found a well of springing water. ²⁰But the herdsmen of Gerar quarreled with Isaac's herdsmen, saying, The water is ours! Then he called the well Esek,* because they quarreled with him. ²¹Then Isaac's servants dug another well, and they contended for that also. Therefore he called it Sitnah.‡ ²²And then he left there and dug another well, for which they did not contend; therefore he called it Rehoboth,° saying, The Lord has now made room for us, and we are increased upon the earth.ᵃ

²³Afterward, Isaac departed from there and went to Beersheba. ²⁴And the Lord appeared to him the same night and said, I am the God of Abraham your father. Fear not, for I am with you, and will bless you, and will multiply your seed for my servant Abraham's sake. ²⁵And then Isaac built an altar there and called upon the name of the Lord, and there pitched his tent. And there Isaac's servants dug a well.

²⁶Then Abimelech came to him from Gerar, with Ahuzzath his friend and Phichol his chief captain. ²⁷And Isaac said to them, Why do you come to me, seeing you hate me and have put me away from you? ²⁸Then they said, We saw that the Lord was with you, and therefore we said that there should be an oath between us and you, and that we should make a bond with you,²⁹ that you will do us no harm, since we have not touched you and have done you nothing but good, and sent you away in peace. For you are now the blessed of the Lord.

³⁰And Isaac made them a feast, and they ate and drank. ³¹And they rose up early in the morning and swore with one another. And Isaac sent them away, and they departed from him in peace. ³²And that same

*[ie, Contention]

‡[ie, Opposition]

°[ie, Broad places]

Ge 21:22-24

*[ie, Seven, or, An Oath]
†[Well of the Oath]

day, Isaac's servants came and told him of a well that they had dug, and said to him that they had found water. ³³And he called it Sheba,* for which the name of the town is called Beersheba† until this day.

³⁴When Esau was forty years old, he took to wife Judith the daughter of Beeri, a Hittite, and Basemath the daughter of Elon, also a Hittite, ³⁵who were disobedient to Isaac and Rebecca.

The Notes

a) 22. Increased: as if to say, after such great pains and labours, God has given us peace and quietness. For quietness makes the heart blossom and expand, but sadness restrains it, as in Psalm 4:7,8.

Chapter 27

Jacob steals the blessing from Esau through his mother's counsel. Isaac is sad. Esau is comforted. The hatred of Esau toward Jacob.

And it came to pass that Isaac grew old, and his eyes were so dim that he could not see. Then he called Esau his eldest son and said to him, My son!

And Esau said to him, Here am I.

²And he said, Behold, I am old, and know not the day of my death. ³Now therefore take your weapons – your quiver and your bow – and go to the fields and catch some venison for me. ⁴And make me food such as I love, and bring it to me and let me eat, so that my soul may bless you[a] before I die.

⁵But Rebecca heard when Isaac spoke to Esau his son. And as soon as Esau was gone to the field to catch venison and bring it home, ⁶she spoke to Jacob her son, saying, Behold, I heard your father talking with Esau your brother and saying, ⁷Bring me venison and make me food, so that I may eat and bless you before the Lord before I die. ⁸Now therefore, my son, hear my voice and that which I tell you. ⁹Go to the flock and bring me from it two good kids, and I will make a dish from them for your father, such as he loves. ¹⁰And you will bring it to your father and he will eat, so that he may bless you before his death.

¹¹Then Jacob said to Rebecca his mother, Behold, Esau my brother is hairy and I am smooth. ¹²My father might feel me, and I will seem to him as though I went about to deceive him; and so shall he bring a curse upon me, and not a blessing.

¹³And his mother said to him, Upon me be your curse,[b] my son. Only hear my voice, and go and fetch me the kids.

¹⁴And Jacob went and fetched them, and brought them to his mother. And his mother made with them a dish his father loved. ¹⁵And she went and got good clothes that belonged to her eldest son Esau, which she had in the house with her, and put them on Jacob her youngest son; ¹⁶but the skins from the kids she put upon his hands and upon the smooth of his neck. ¹⁷And she put the meat and bread that she had made in the hand of her son Jacob, ¹⁸and he went in to his fa-

ther, saying, My father!

And he answered, Here am I. Who are you, my son?

¹⁹And Jacob said to his father, I am Esau, your eldest son. I have done as you bade me. Up and sit, and eat of my venison so that your soul may bless me. ²⁰But Isaac said to his son, How comes it that you found it so quickly, my son?

He answered, The Lord your God brought it to my hand.

²¹Then said Isaac to Jacob, Come near and let me feel you, my son, whether you are my son Esau or not.

²²Then Jacob went to Isaac his father, and he felt him and said, The voice is Jacob's voice, but the hands are the hands of Esau. ²³And he did not recognize him, because his hands were hairy like his brother Esau's hands; and so he blessed him. ²⁴But then he asked him, Are you my son Esau?

And he said, That I am.

²⁵Then he said, Bring to me, and let me eat of my son's venison so that my soul may bless you.

And he brought it to him, and he ate. And he brought him wine also, and he drank. ²⁶And his father Isaac said to him, Come near and kiss me, my son. ²⁷And he went to him and kissed him. And Isaac smelled the scent of his clothing and blessed him, and said, See, the smell of my son is as the smell of a field that the Lord has blessed. ²⁸May God give you of the dew of heaven and of the fatness of the earth,^c and plenty of wheat and wine. ²⁹May people be your servants and nations bow to you. Be lord over your brethren, and may your mother's children bow to you. Cursed be he that curses you, and blessed be he that blesses you.

³⁰As soon as Isaac had made an end of blessing Jacob, and Jacob was scarcely gone out from the presence of Isaac his father, then Esau his brother came in from his hunting. ³¹And he also had made a meat dish, and brought it in to his father and said to him, Arise, my father, and eat of your son's venison, so that your soul may bless me.

³²Then his father Isaac said to him, Who are you?

He answered, I am your eldest son Esau.

³³And Isaac was greatly astonished out of measure and said, Where then is he who hunted venison and brought it to me, and I ate it all before you came, and have blessed him, and he will be blessed still?

³⁴When Esau heard the words of his father, he cried out greatly and bitterly above measure and said to his father, Bless me also, my father!

³⁵But he said, Your brother came with subtlety, and has taken away your blessing.

³⁶Then said Esau, He may well be called Jacob, for he has undermined me now two times. First he took away my birthright, and see, now has he taken away my blessing also. And he said, Have you kept never a blessing for me?

³⁷Isaac answered and said to Esau, Behold, I have made him your lord, and all his mother's children I have made his servants. Moreover,

Ec'us 3:8
Heb 11:20

with wheat and wine I have established him.ᵈ What can I do for you now, my son?

³⁸And Esau said to his father, Have you but that one blessing, my father? Bless me also, my father! So Esau lifted up his voice and wept.

Heb 12:17

³⁹Then Isaac his father answered and said to him, Behold, your dwelling place shall have of the fatness of the earth and of the dew of heaven from above. ⁴⁰And by your sword shall you live, and shall be your brother's servant. But the time will come when you will get the mastery and loose his yoke from off your neck.

Ob 1:1-4

⁴¹And Esau hated Jacob because of the blessing that his father had blessed him with, and he said in his heart, The days of my father's sorrow are at hand, for I will slay my brother Jacob.

⁴²But these words of Esau her eldest son were told to Rebecca. And she sent and called Jacob her youngest son and said to him, Behold, your brother Esau is threatening to kill you. ⁴³Now therefore, my son, hear my voice. Get ready, and flee to Laban my brother at Haran. ⁴⁴And stay with him a while, until your brother's fierceness is assuaged, ⁴⁵and until your brother's wrath turns away from you and he forgets what you have done to him. Then I will send and fetch you away from there. Why should I lose you both in one day?

⁴⁶And Rebecca spoke to Isaac: I am weary of my life, for fear of the daughters of Heth. If Jacob takes a wife from the daughters of Heth, such a one as these are, or from the daughters of the land, what desire would I have to live?

The Notes

a) 4. Bless: that is, so that my soul may wish you good and pray to God for you.
b) 13. There are two kinds of curses used in the scripture. The one is in the soul and pertains to the soul, as sin and wickedness. And the other pertains to the body, as every temporal misery and wretchedness, as in Genesis 3:16-19 and Deuteronomy 28:15-68.
c) 28. By this word *dew* the Hebrews understand everything in the firmament that sustains the earth, such as the sun, moon, rain, and temperateness of weather. By the *fatness of the earth* they understand everything that is brought forth from beneath the earth, as Ge 45:18 and Nu 11:5.
d) 37. By wheat and wine is understood an abundance of all temporal things.

Chapter 28

Jacob is sent into Mesopotamia to Laban for a wife.
Esau marries an Ishmaelite. Jacob dreams a dream.
Christ is promised. Jacob makes a vow.

Then Isaac called Jacob his son and blessed him,ᵃ and charged him and said to him, See you do not take a wife from the daughters of Canaan; ²but arise and go to Mesopotamia, to the house of Bethuel your mother's father, and there take yourself a wife from the daughters of Laban, your mother's brother. ³And may God Almighty bless you, increase you, and multiply you so that you may be a multitude of people, ⁴and give you the blessing of Abraham – both to you and to your seed with you – so that you may possess the land wherein you are a stranger, which God gave to Abraham.

⁵Thus Isaac sent Jacob forth to go to Mesopotamia, to Laban the son of Bethuel the Syrian, and brother to Rebecca, Jacob's and Esau's mother.

⁶And Esau saw that Isaac had blessed Jacob and sent him to Mesopotamia to take a wife from there, and that as he blessed him he gave him a charge, saying, See you take not a wife from the daughters of Canaan. ⁷And he saw that Jacob had obeyed his father and mother and was gone to Mesopotamia, ⁸and also that the daughters of Canaan did not please Isaac his father. ⁹So then he went to Ishmael, and, besides the wives that he already had, took Mahala, the daughter of Ishmael Abraham's son and sister of Nabajoth, to be his wife.

¹⁰Jacob departed from Beersheba and went toward Haran, ¹¹and came to a place where he stayed all night because the sun was down. And he took a stone of the place and put it under his head, and laid down in the same place to sleep. ¹²And he dreamt, and behold: there stood a ladder upon the earth, and the top of it reached up to heaven. And see, the angels of God went up and down upon it; ¹³yea, and the Lord stood upon it and said, I am the Lord God of Abraham your father, and the God of Isaac. The land that you sleep upon I will give to you and your seed. ¹⁴And your seed shall be as the dust of the earth. And you shall spread abroad west, east, north, and south. And through you and your seed shall all the kindreds of the earth be blessed.ᵇ ¹⁵And see, I am with you, and will be your keeper in all places, wherever you go, and will bring you back again into this land. Neither will I leave you until I have made good all that I have promised you.

¹⁶When Jacob awakened out of his sleep, he said, Surely the Lord is in this place, and I was not aware! ¹⁷And he was afraid and said, How fearful is this place? It is none other but even the house of Godᶜ and the gate of heaven. ¹⁸And Jacob stood up early in the morning and took the stone that he had laid under his head, pitched it up on end, and poured oil on the top of it. ¹⁹And he called the name of the place Bethel;ᵈ for indeed, the name of the city was called Luz before.

²⁰And Jacob vowed a vow, saying, If God will be with me and will keep me in this my journey, and will give me bread to eat and clothes to put on, ²¹so that I come back again to my father's house in safety, then shall the Lord be my God. ²²And this stone that I have set up on end shall be God's house. And of all that you give me, I will give the tenth to you.ᵉ

The Notes

a) 1. Blessed means here to have prayed for good things for him, as in Genesis 27:4 and note a.

b) 14. Blessed means here to be increased and multiplied, as in Genesis 1:22 and note b.

c) 17. He calls it the house of God because of the household of angels that he saw there. We, in like manner, call the church of lime and stone the house of God because the people who come there are the church of God, as St. Paul teaches. 1Co 3:9 & 16, Col 2:19, Eph 2:19-22.

d) 19. *Bethel* signifies the house of God.

e) 22. Tithes [or tenths]: by tithes the ancient fathers mean all great rewards, as in Genesis 14:20.

Chapter 29

> Jacob goes to Laban and serves seven years for Rachel. Leah was brought to his bed instead of Rachel. He marries them both, and serves yet seven years more for Rachel. Leah conceives.

Then Jacob lifted up his feet and went toward the east country. ²And as he looked about, behold, there was a well in the field; and three flocks of sheep lay nearby, for at that well the flocks were watered. And there lay a great stone at the well mouth. ³And the custom was to bring the flocks there, and to roll the stone from the well's mouth and water the sheep, and then to put the stone back on the well's mouth in its place.

⁴And Jacob said to the people, Brethren, where are you from? And they said, We are from Haran. ⁵And he said to them, Do you know Laban, the son of Nahor? And they said, We know him. ⁶And he said to them, Is he in good health? And they said, He is in good health; and look, his daughter Rachel is coming with the sheep. ⁷And he said, Lo, it is still a long time till night, nor is it time to gather together the flocks: water the sheep, and go and feed them. ⁸But they said, We cannot until all the flocks are brought together and the stone is rolled from the well's mouth; and that is how we water our sheep.

⁹While Jacob was yet talking with them, Rachel came with her father's sheep, for she kept them. ¹⁰As soon as Jacob saw Rachel the daughter of Laban his mother's brother, with the sheep of Laban his mother's brother, he went and rolled the stone from the well's mouth and watered the sheep of Laban his mother's brother. ¹¹And Jacob kissed Rachel, and lifted up his voice and wept, ¹²and told her also that he was her father's nephew and Rebecca's son. Then Rachel ran and told her father.

¹³When Laban heard about Jacob his sister's son, he ran to meet him, and embraced him and kissed him, and brought him to his house. And then Jacob told Laban all the matter. ¹⁴Then Laban said, Well, you are my bone and my flesh. Stay with me for a month. ¹⁵And afterward Laban said to Jacob, Though you are my relation, should you therefore serve me for nothing? Tell me, what shall your wages be?

¹⁶And Laban had two daughters, the eldest called Leah and the youngest Rachel. ¹⁷Leah was weak-eyed;* but Rachel was beautiful and well favoured, ¹⁸and Jacob loved her well. And he said, I will serve you seven years for Rachel, your youngest daughter. ¹⁹And La-

*[WYC: bleary-eyed.]

ban answered, It is better that I give her to you than to another man. Stay therefore with me.

²⁰And Jacob served seven years for Rachel, and they seemed to him but a few days, for the love he had to her. ²¹Then Jacob said to Laban, Give me my wife, so that I may lie with her. For the time appointed to me has come.

²²Then Laban invited all the people of that place and made a feast. ²³But when the evening came, he took his daughter Leah and brought her to Jacob, and he went in to her. ²⁴And Laban gave Zilpah his maid to his daughter Leah, to be her servant.

²⁵And when the morning was come, behold: it was Leah. Then Jacob said to Laban, Why have you played thus with me? Did I not serve you for Rachel? Why then have you deceived me?

²⁶Laban answered, It is not the custom of this place to marry the youngest before the eldest. ²⁷Pass out this week, and then she will also be given you, for the service you will do for me yet seven years more.

²⁸And Jacob did so, and passed out that week, and then Laban gave him Rachel his daughter to wife also. ²⁹And Laban gave Bilhah his handmaid to Rachel his daughter, to be her servant. ³⁰So Jacob lay by Rachel also, and loved Rachel more than Leah, and served Laban yet seven years more.

³¹When the Lord saw that Leah was not regarded, he made her fruitful; but Rachel was barren. ³²And Leah conceived and bore a son. And she called his name Reuben,* for she said, The Lord has looked upon my tribulation, and now my husband will love me. ³³And she conceived again and bore a son, and said, The Lord has heard that I am unloved, and has therefore given me this son also. And she called him Simeon.‡ ³⁴And she conceived yet again and bore a son, and said, Now finally my husband will keep me company, because I have borne him three sons. And therefore she called his name Levi.° ³⁵And she conceived yet again and bore a son, saying, Now will I praise the Lord! Therefore she called his name Judah,* and left bearing.

Ho 12:12

1Ch 2:1
*[ie, Behold, a Son]

‡[ie, Heard]

°[ie, Joined]

*[ie, Praise]

Chapter 30

Rachel and Leah, both being barren, give their maids
to their husband, and they bear him children. Jacob
gets the better of Laban in the conceiving of the sheep
and goats. Jacob's wages for his service.

When Rachel saw that she bore Jacob no children, she envied her sister and said to Jacob, Give me children, or else I am but dead! ²Then Jacob was angry with Rachel, saying, Am I in God's stead, who keeps from you the fruit of your womb? ³Then she said, Here is my maid Bilhah. Go in to her, so that she may bear upon my lap and I may be increased by her.

⁴And she gave him Bilhah her handmaid as wife. And Jacob went in to her, ⁵and Bilhah conceived and bore Jacob a son. ⁶Then said Ra-

GENESIS 30

*[ie, Judge or Judging]

‡[ie, My Wrestling]

°[ie, Good Fortune or Luck]

*[ie, Happy]

chel, God has given judgment on my side, and has also heard my voice, and has given me a son. Therefore she called him Dan.* ⁷And Rachel's maid Bilhah conceived again and bore Jacob another son. ⁸And Rachel said, God has turned, and I have changed things with my sister, and have gotten the upper hand. And she called his name Naphtali.‡

⁹When Leah saw that she had left bearing, she took Zilpah her maid and gave her to Jacob to wife. ¹⁰And Leah's maid Zilpah bore Jacob a son. ¹¹Then said Leah, Good luck! and called his name Gad.° ¹²And Leah's maid Zilpah bore Jacob another son. ¹³Then said Leah, Happy am I, for the daughters will call me blessed. And she called his name Asher.*

¹⁴Now Reuben went out in the wheat harvest and found mandragorasᵃ in the fields, and brought them to his mother Leah. Then Rachel said to Leah, Give me some of your son's mandragoras! ¹⁵And Leah answered, Is it not enough that you have taken away my husband, but would you take away my son's mandragoras also? Then said Rachel, Well, let him sleep with you tonight, for your son's mandragoras. ¹⁶And when Jacob came from the fields in the evening, Leah went out to meet him and said, Come in to me, for I have bought you with my son's mandragoras.

*[ie, My Due Reward or Benefit]

‡[ie, Desired Dwelling]
°[ie, Judged] Of Dinah, see Ge 34

*[ie, He Will Add]

And he slept with her that night. ¹⁷And God heard Leah, and she conceived and bore to Jacob her fifth son. ¹⁸Then said Leah, God has given me my due because I gave my maid to my husband. And she called him Issachar.* ¹⁹And Leah conceived yet again and bore Jacob a sixth son. ²⁰Then she said, God has endowed me with a good dowry. Now my husband will dwell with me, because I have borne him six sons. And she called his name Zebulun.‡ ²¹After that she bore a daughter and called her Dinah.°

²²And God remembered Rachel, heard her, and made her fruitful, ²³so that she conceived and bore a son. And she said, God has taken away my rebuke. ²⁴And she called his name Joseph,* saying, May the Lord give me yet another son.

1Ki 11:21

Ge 39:2-4

²⁵As soon as Rachel had borne Joseph, Jacob said to Laban, Send me away so that I may go to my own place and country. ²⁶Give me my wives and my children, for whom I have served you, and let me go. For you know what service I have given you.

²⁷Then Laban said to him, If I have found favour in your sight – for I suppose that the Lord has blessed me for your sake – ²⁸name your wage and I will give it to you.

²⁹But he said to him, You know what service I have done for you, and in what condition your flocks have been under me. ³⁰For you had but little before I came, and now it is increased into a multitude, and the Lord has blessed you for my sake. But now, when can I provide for my own house also?

³¹And he said, What shall I give you?

And Jacob answered, You shall give me nothing at all, if you will do this one thing for me, and then I will go back and feed your flocks

44

and take care of them: ³²I will go through all your flocks this day and separate from them all the sheep that are speckled and of different colours, and all the black sheep among the lambs, and the calico and speckled among the goats. And the same will be my wages. ³³In this way, my righteousness[b] may answer for me when the time comes for me to receive my wages from you. So it will be that, whatever is not speckled and of different colours among the goats, or black among the lambs that are with me, let that be as stolen.

³⁴Then said Laban, Lo, I am content for it to be as you have said.

³⁵And that same day, Laban took out the he-goats that were striped and of different colours, and all the she-goats that were speckled and calico-coloured, and all that had white in them, and all the black among the lambs, and put them in the keeping of his sons. ³⁶Then he set a three-days' journey between himself and Jacob.

And so Jacob tended the rest of Laban's flocks. ³⁷And Jacob took green branches from poplar, hazel, and chestnut trees, and peeled white strips in them, and made the white in the wood appear. ³⁸And he put the branches that he had peeled before the flocks in the brooks and watering troughs when they came to drink; for they bred when they came to drink. ³⁹And the flocks conceived before the branches, and brought forth striped, speckled, and calico young. ⁴⁰And Jacob separated the lambs, and turned the faces of the animals toward striped things and toward all manner of black things throughout the flocks of Laban. And he made flocks of his own by themselves, which he did not put with the flocks of Laban.

⁴¹And always, in the first bucking time of the flocks, Jacob put the branches before the animals in the brooks so that they would conceive before the branches. ⁴² But in the latter bucking time he did not put them there, so the last brood was Laban's and the first was Jacob's. ⁴³And the man became exceedingly rich, and had many flocks, maidservants, menservants, camels, and donkeys.

The Notes

a) 14. *Mandragoras* [or mandrakes]: the Hebrews say this is a herb, or rather a root, which bears the shape of man's body. Others say it is an apple which, when eaten with meat, causes conception. Saint Augustine thinks that it pleases women because it has a pleasant savour, or rather for its choiceness, because there were not many of them to get.
b) 33. *Righteousness* signifies here true and faithful service.

Chapter 31

> At the commandment of God, Jacob departed from Laban and took his possessions with him. Rachel steals her father's images. Laban pursues Jacob. The covenant between Laban and Jacob.

And Jacob heard the words of Laban's sons, how they were saying, Jacob has taken away everything that was our father's, and from our father's goods has obtained all this honour! ²And Jacob saw the countenance of Laban, that it was not favourable toward him as it had been in times past. ³And the Lord said to Jacob, Turn back into the land of your fathers and to your kindred, and I will be with you.

⁴Then Jacob sent and called Rachel and Leah to the field, to his flocks, ⁵and said to them, I see your father's countenance, that it is not favourable toward me as in times past. Moreover, the God of my father has been with me. ⁶And you know how I have served your father with all my might, ⁷but your father has cheated me and changed my wages ten times. But God did not suffer him to hurt me. ⁸When he said, The speckled animals will be your wages, then all the flocks bore speckled young. If he said, The striped will be your wages, then all the flocks bore striped. ⁹Thus has God taken away your father's animals and given them to me. ¹⁰For in bucking time, I lifted up my eyes and saw in a dream, and behold: the rams that mounted the sheep were striped, spotted, and dappled. ¹¹And the angel of God spoke to me in a dream saying, Jacob! And I answered, Here am I. ¹²And he said, Lift up your eyes and see, how all the rams that leap upon the sheep are striped, spotted, and dappled. For I have seen everything that Laban does to you. ¹³I am the God of Bethel, where you anointed the stone and where you vowed a vow to me. Now arise and go out of this country, and return to the land where you were born.

Ge 28:16-22

Ge 32:9

¹⁴Then Rachel and Leah answered and said to him, We have no part nor inheritance in our father's house. ¹⁵He counts us as strangers, for he has sold us, and has consumed what he got for us. ¹⁶Moreover, all the riches that God has taken from our father, they are ours and our children's. Now, therefore, whatever God has said to you, that do.

¹⁷Then Jacob rose up, set his sons and wives up upon camels, ¹⁸and carried away all his livestock and all his substance which he had acquired in Mesopotamia, to go to Isaac his father in the land of Canaan. ¹⁹Laban was gone to shear his sheep, and Rachel had stolen her father's images. ²⁰And Jacob went away unbeknownst to Laban the Syrian, and did not tell him that he was leaving. ²¹So he fled with everything he had; he made himself ready, passed over the Euphrates River,* and set his face straight toward the mount Gilead.

Ge 38:13
1Sam 25:2

*[The Euphrates River divided Mesopotamia from the land of promise]

²²On the third day following, Laban was told that Jacob had fled. ²³Then he took his kinsmen with him and followed after Jacob a seven days' journey, and overtook him at the mount Gilead. ²⁴And God came to Laban the Syrian in a dream by night and said to him, Take heed to yourself, that you do not speak to Jacob anything but good.

²⁵And Laban overtook Jacob. And Jacob had pitched his tent in the mount, and Laban with his kinsmen pitched their tent also upon the mount Gilead.

²⁶Then said Laban to Jacob, Why have you done this, unknown to me, and carried away my daughters as though they had been taken captive with the sword? ²⁷Why did you go away secretly, unknown to me, and did not tell me, so that I could have brought you on the way

with mirth, singing, timbrels, and harps? ²⁸And have not suffered me to kiss my children and my daughters? You were a fool to do it, ²⁹for I am able to do you harm. But the God of your father spoke to me yesterday, saying, Take heed that you speak not to Jacob anything but good. ³⁰And now, though you went your way because you long after your father's house, yet why have you stolen my gods?

³¹Jacob answered and said to Laban, Because I was afraid, and thought that you would have taken away your daughters from me. ³²But with whomever you find your gods, let him die here before our kinsmen. Search for whatever is yours with me, and take it back. (For Jacob did not know that Rachel had stolen the images.)

³³Then Laban went into Jacob's tent, and into Leah's tent, and into the two maidservants' tents, but found them not. Then he went out of Leah's tent and entered into Rachel's tent. ³⁴And Rachel took the images and put them in the camels' straw, and sat down upon them. And Laban searched the whole tent, but found them not. ³⁵Then she said to her father, My lord, do not be angry that I cannot rise up before you, for the disease of women is come upon me.

So he searched, but found them not.

³⁶Jacob was angry and reproached Laban. Jacob also answered and said to him, How have I trespassed, or how have I offended, so that you pursued me? ³⁷You have searched all my things, and what did you find from all your household stuff? Put it here before your kinsmen and mine, and let them judge between us both. ³⁸These twenty years that I have been with you, your sheep and your goats were not barren, and I have not eaten the rams of your flock. ³⁹Whatever was torn by beasts I did not bring to you, but made it good myself; from my hand you required it, whether it was stolen by day or by night. ⁴⁰Moreover, by day the heat consumed me, and the cold by night, and my sleep departed from my eyes. ⁴¹This way I have passed twenty years in your house, and I served you fourteen years for your two daughters and six years for your flocks. And you have changed my wages ten times. ⁴²And if the God of my father – the God of Abraham, and the God whom Isaac fears[a] – had not been with me, surely you would have sent me away now empty-handed. But God saw my tribulation and the labour of my hands, and rebuked you yesterday.

⁴³Laban answered and said to Jacob, The daughters are my daughters, the children are my children, the flocks are my flocks, and all that you see is mine. And what can I do this day for these my daughters, or for their children whom they have borne? ⁴⁴Now therefore, come; let us make a bond, I and you together, and let it be a witness between you and me.

⁴⁵Then Jacob took a stone and set it up on end. ⁴⁶And he said to his kinsmen, Gather stones. And they took stones and made a heap, and they ate there upon the heap. ⁴⁷And Laban called it Jegar Sahadutha,* but Jacob called it Gilead.†

⁴⁸Then Laban said, This heap is a witness between you and me this

---

1Sam 13:13

1Ch 16:20, 21.

Ge c29

*[Syriac for Heap of Witness]
†[or Galeed, Hebrew for Heap of Witness]

Jos 22:26,27; 24:26,27. day. (Therefore, it is called Gilead.) ⁴⁹And this mound which the Lord sees (he said) is a witness between me and you, when we are departed one from another, ⁵⁰that you will not vex my daughters, nor take other wives in addition to them. There is no man here with us; behold, God is witness between you and me.

⁵¹And Laban said moreover to Jacob, See this heap, and this mark that I have set here between me and you.⁵²This heap is witness, and also this mark, that I will not pass over this heap to you, and you will not pass over this heap and this mark, to do any harm. ⁵³The God of Abraham, the God of Nahor, and the God of their fathers, be judge between us.

And Jacob swore by him whom his father Isaac feared. ⁵⁴Then Jacob did sacrifice upon the mount, and called his kinsmen to eat bread. And they ate bread and spent all night in the hill. ⁵⁵And early in the morning Laban rose up, kissed his children and his daughters, blessed them, and departed and went to his place again.

The Notes

a) 42. *Fear* is taken for honour, as above in Genesis 20:11 and note a.

Chapter 32

The vision of the angels. Jacob sends gifts to his brother Esau. How he wrestled with the angel, who changed his name and called him Israel.

So Jacob went forth on his journey. And the angels of God came and met him. ²And when Jacob saw them, he said, This is God's host! And he called the name of that same place Mahanaim.*

*[ie, Two Hosts or Camps]

Jos 24:4

³Jacob sent messengers before him to Esau his brother, to the land of Seir and the fields of Edom. ⁴And he instructed them, saying, See that you speak in this manner to my lord Esau: Your servant Jacob says, I have sojourned and been a stranger with Laban until this time, ⁵and have gotten oxen, donkeys, and sheep, and menservants and womenservants; and I have sent messengers to show it to my lord, so that I may find grace in your sight.

⁶And the messengers came back to Jacob saying, We went to your brother Esau and he is coming to meet you, and 400 men with him. ⁷Then Jacob was greatly afraid and knew not which way to turn himself. And he divided the people that were with him, and the flocks, herds, and camels, into two companies, ⁸and said, If Esau comes to the one part and attacks it, the other may save itself.

⁹And Jacob said, O God of my father Abraham and God of my father Isaac – Lord who said to me, Return to your country and to your kindred, and I will do all well with you – ¹⁰I am not worthy of the least of all the mercies and truth that you have shown to your servant. For with only my staff I came over the Jordan,ᵃ and now I have gotten two companies. ¹¹Deliver me from the hands of my brother Esau; for I fear him, that he will come and attack the mother with the children. ¹²You

said that you would surely do me good, and would make my seed as the sand of the sea, which cannot be numbered for multitude.

¹³And he tarried there that same night, and took out of the things that he had gifts for Esau his brother: ¹⁴200 she-goats and 20 he-goats, 200 sheep and 20 rams, ¹⁵30 milk camels with their colts, 40 cows and 10 bulls, and 20 she-donkeys with 10 foals. ¹⁶And he delivered them to his servants, each drove by itself, and said to them, Go ahead of me, and put a space between each drove. ¹⁷And he instructed the one in the lead, saying, When Esau my brother meets you and asks you, saying, Whose servant are you, and where are you going, and whose are these animals that go before you?– ¹⁸you must say, They are your servant Jacob's, and are a gift sent to my lord Esau; and behold, he himself is coming after us. ¹⁹And he so instructed the second, and so again the third, and likewise all who followed the droves, saying, See that you speak to Esau in this manner when you meet him. ²⁰And say moreover: Behold, your servant Jacob comes after us. For (he said) I will appease his wrath with the gifts that go before me, and afterward I will see him myself, so perhaps he will receive me to grace.

²¹So the gifts went before him, and he tarried that night in the tent. ²²And he rose up the same night and took his two wives, his two maids, and his eleven sons, and went over the ford Jabbok. ²³And he took them and sent them over the river, and sent over what he had, ²⁴and remained behind himself alone.

And there was a man who wrestled with him until the breaking of the day. ²⁵And when the man saw that he could not prevail against Jacob, he struck him under the thigh; and the sinew of Jacob's thigh shrank as he wrestled with him.

²⁶And the man said, Let me go, for the day is breaking.

But Jacob said, I will not let you go unless you bless me.

²⁷And he said to him, What is your name?

He answered, Jacob.

²⁸And he said, You shall be called Jacob no more, but Israel.* For you have wrestled with God and with men, and have prevailed.

²⁹And Jacob asked him, saying, Tell me your name!

And he said, Why do you ask my name? And he blessed him there.

³⁰And Jacob called the name of the place Pheniel.† For (he said) I have seen God face to face,ᵇ and yet my life is preserved.

³¹And as he went across Pheniel the sun rose upon him, and he limped upon his thigh. ³²Therefore the children of Israel do not eat of the sinew that shrank under the thigh to this day, because he struck Jacob under the thigh in the sinew that shrank.

The Notes

a) 10. To go with a staff is a manner of speaking of the Hebrews, which signifies nothing else than to go simply, barely, and without any riches or baggage, as in Mark 6:8.

b) 30. To see God face to face is to have a certain and sure knowledge of him, as in Exodus 33:11.

Margin notes:
- 1Ch 16:15-19
- v13 e.f. WYC.
- Ho 12:4
- *[ie, He Will Be Prince With God, or, Contender of God]; Ge 35:10.
- J'g 13:17,18
- †[ie, Face of God]

Chapter 33

Esau and Jacob reconcile. Jacob goes into Shechem.

Jacob lifted up his eyes and saw his brother Esau coming, and with him 400 men. And he divided the children among Leah, Rachel, and the two maids. ²And he put the maids and their children in front, Leah and her children after them, and Rachel and Joseph last of all. ³And he went before them, and fell on the ground seven times until he came to his brother.

⁴Esau ran to meet him, and embraced him, and fell on his neck and kissed him; and they wept. ⁵And Esau lifted up his eyes and saw the wives and their children, and said, Who are these that you have here?

And Jacob said, They are the children that God has given your servant.

⁶Then the maids came forward and bowed themselves. ⁷Leah also and her children came and bowed themselves. And last of all came Joseph and Rachel, and bowed down.

⁸And Esau said, What do you mean by all the droves that I met?

And he answered, To find grace in the sight of my lord.

⁹And he said, I have enough, my brother. Keep what you have for yourself.

¹⁰Jacob answered, Oh no, but if I have found grace in your sight, receive my gift from my hand. For I have seen your face as if I have seen the face of God. Therefore, receive me to grace, ¹¹and take the blessing that I have brought you. For God has given it to me freely, and I have enough of all things! And so he compelled him to take it.

¹²And Esau said, Let us take our journey and go, and I will go in your company.

¹³But he said to him, My lord knows that I have tender children, and ewes and cows with young under my hand which, if the men were to overdrive them but one day, the whole flock would die. ¹⁴Let my lord therefore go before his servant. I will drive slowly and gently, as the animals that go before me and the children are able to endure, until I come to my lord at Seir.

¹⁵And Esau said, Let me yet leave some of my folk with you.

But he said, What need is there? Let me find grace in the sight of my lord.

¹⁶So Esau went his way back the same day, to Seir. ¹⁷But Jacob took his journey toward Succoth, and built himself a house and made shelters for his animals. For this reason, the name of the place is called Succoth.*

¹⁸Then Jacob went peaceably to the town of Shechem in the land of Canaan, after he had come from Mesopotamia, and pitched before the city. ¹⁹And he bought a parcel of ground where he pitched his tent from the children of Hamor, Shechem's father, for a hundred lambs. ²⁰And he made there an altar, and there called upon the mighty God of Israel.

Es (Gk) 15:13. (at verse 10)

*[ie, Shelters]

Chapter 34

The ravishing of Dinah, Jacob's daughter, by Shechem. And of the great blood-shedding done by the sons of Jacob.

Dinah the daughter of Leah, whom she bore to Jacob, went out to see the daughters of the land. ²And Shechem the son of Hamor the Hivite, lord of the country, saw her, and took her and lay with her, and forced her. ³And his heart was bound fast to Dinah the daughter of Jacob. And he loved the girl, and spoke lovingly to her. ⁴And he spoke to his father Hamor, saying, Get me this maiden for my wife.

⁵And Jacob heard that he had defiled Dinah his daughter. But his sons were with the herds and flocks in the field, and therefore he held his peace until they returned. ⁶Then Hamor the father of Shechem went out to Jacob, to commune with him. ⁷And the sons of Jacob came out of the field as soon as they heard of it, for it grieved them. And they were not a little angry, because Shechem had wrought evil in Israel, in that he had lain with Jacob's daughter, which thing ought not to be done.

⁸And Hamor communed with them, saying, The soul of my son Shechem longs for your daughter; give her to him as wife. ⁹And make marriages with us: give your daughters to us and take our daughters to you. ¹⁰And dwell with us, and the land shall be at your pleasure. Dwell, and do your business, and have your properties in it.

¹¹And Shechem said to Dinah's father and her brothers, Let me find grace in your eyes, and whatever you say, that I will give. ¹²Ask freely of me both the dowry and gifts, and I will give as you may say to me; and give me the girl for my wife.

¹³Then the sons of Jacob answered Shechem and Hamor his father deceitfully, because he had defiled Dinah their sister. ¹⁴And they said to them, We cannot do this thing, to give our sister to one that is uncircumcised, for that would be a disgrace to us. ¹⁵We will we consent to you only if you will be as we are, so that all the menchildren among you are circumcised. ¹⁶Then we will give our daughters to you and take yours to us, and will dwell with you and be one people. ¹⁷But if you will not hearken to us to be circumcised, then we will take our daughter and go our ways.

¹⁸And their words pleased Hamor and Shechem his son. ¹⁹And the young man did not delay to do the thing, because he had delight in Jacob's daughter. He was also most esteemed by all who were in his father's house. ²⁰Then Hamor and Shechem went to the gate of their town and conferred with the men of their town, saying, ²¹These men are peaceable with us, and will dwell in the land and follow their occupations in it. And there is room enough for them in the land. Let us take their daughters as wives and give them ours. ²²But they will only consent to dwell with us and to be one people if all the menchildren that are among us are circumcised as they are. ²³Their goods, their substance, and all their flocks and herds are ours; only let us consent

v3 e.f. WYC.

2Sam 13:12

to them, so that they may dwell with us.

²⁴And everyone who went out at the gate of his town hearkened to Hamor and to Shechem his son. And all the menchildren were circumcised, all who went out at the gate of his town.

²⁵But on the third day, when it was painful to them, two of the sons of Jacob – Simeon and Levi, Dinah's brothers – took each of them his sword and went into the town boldly, and slew all the men. ²⁶And they slew also Hamor and Shechem his son with the edge of the sword, and took Dinah their sister out of Shechem's house, and went their way.

²⁷Then the sons of Jacob came upon the dead and plundered the town, because they had defiled their sister. ²⁸They took their flocks, herds, donkeys, and whatever was in the town and also in the fields – ²⁹all their goods, all their children, and their wives they took captive. And they carried off everything that was in the houses.

³⁰And Jacob said to Simeon and Levi, You have troubled me and made me stink to the inhabiters of the land, both to the Canaanites and also to the Perizzites. And I am few in number. Therefore, they will gather themselves together against me and slay me, and so I and my house will be destroyed.

³¹And they answered, Should they deal with our sister as with a whore?

_{Ge 49:5-7}
_{J'th 9:1-6}

Chapter 35

> Jacob goes up to Bethel and buries his images under an oak. Deborah dies. Jacob is called Israel. The land of Canaan is promised to him. Rachel dies in labour. Reuben lies with his father's concubine. The death of Isaac.

And God said to Jacob, Arise, and go up to Bethel and dwell there. And make there an altar to God, who appeared to you when you fled from Esau your brother.

²Then Jacob said to his household and to all who were with him, Put away the strange gods^a that are among you, and make yourselves clean and change your garments. ³And let us arise and go up to Bethel, so that I may make an altar there to God, who heard me in the day of my tribulation and was with me in the way that I went.

⁴And they gave to Jacob all the strange gods that were in their hands, and all the earrings that were in their ears, and Jacob hid them under an oak at Shechem. ⁵And they departed. And the fear of God fell upon the places that were round about them, so that they dared not pursue the sons of Jacob.

⁶So Jacob came to Luz in the land of Canaan, otherwise called Bethel, with all the people who were with him. ⁷And he built there an altar and called the place El Bethel,* because God had appeared to him there when he fled from his brother.

⁸Then Deborah, Rebecca's nurse, died, and was buried below

*[ie, God of Bethel]

Ge 24:59

Bethel under an oak. And the name of it was called the Oak of Lamentation.

⁹And God appeared to Jacob again after he came out of Mesopotamia, and blessed him, ¹⁰and said to him, Your name is Jacob. Notwithstanding, you shall be no more called Jacob, but Israel shall be your name. And so his name was called Israel.* ¹¹And God said to him, I am God Almighty. Grow and multiply, for a people and a multitude of people shall spring of you; yea, and kings shall come out of your loins. ¹²And the land which I gave Abraham and Isaac I will give to you; and to your seed after you I will give it also.

¹³And God departed from him in the place where he talked with him. ¹⁴And Jacob set up a mark in the place where he talked with him, even a pillar of stone, and poured a drink offering thereon, and poured also oil thereon. ¹⁵And he called the name of the place where God spoke with him, Bethel.*

¹⁶And they departed from Bethel, and when he was but a field breadth from Ephrath, Rachel began to travail in childbirth. And in travailing, she was in peril. ¹⁷And as she was in the pains of her labour, the midwife said to her, Fear not, for you shall have this son also. ¹⁸Then, as her soul was departing so that she would surely die, she called his name Ben-Oni.* But his father called him Benjamin.✝

¹⁹And thus Rachel died, and was buried along the way to Ephrath, which is now called Bethlehem. ²⁰And Jacob set up a pillar upon her grave, which is called Rachel's grave-pillar to this day.

²¹And Israel left there, and pitched his tent beyond the Tower of Eder.º ²²And it came to pass, as Israel dwelt in that land, that Reuben went and lay with Bilhah, his father's concubine. And it came to Israel's ear.

The sons of Jacob were twelve in number. ²³The sons of Leah: Reuben, Jacob's eldest son, and Simeon, Levi, Judah, Issachar, and Zebulun. ²⁴The sons of Rachel: Joseph and Benjamin. ²⁵The sons of Bilhah, Rachel's maid: Dan and Naphtali. ²⁶The sons of Zilpah, Leah's maid: Gad and Asher. These are the sons of Jacob that were born to him in Mesopotamia.

²⁷Then Jacob went to Isaac his father at Mamre, a principal city otherwise called Hebron, where Abraham and Isaac had sojourned as strangers. ²⁸And the days of Isaac were 180 years, ²⁹and then he fell sick and died, and was put unto his people,ᵇ being old and full of days. And his sons Esau and Jacob buried him.

The Notes

a) 2. The scripture calls all kinds of idols or images strange gods because the worshippers of them esteem them as gods.

b) 29. To be put unto his people: look in Genesis 25 and note b. [Luther: To say he was put unto or gathered unto his fathers bears witness to the future resurrection of the dead, in that we are gathered to a people and there preserved under the hands of God.]

Chapter 36

The wives of Esau. Jacob and Esau are rich. The genealogy of Esau. Esau dwells in the hill Seir.

These are the generations of Esau, who is called Edom. ²Esau took his wives from the daughters of Canaan: Ada the daughter of Elon, a Hittite; and Aholibama the daughter of Anah, which Anah was the son of Zibeon, a Hivite; ³and Basemath,ª Ishmael's daughter and the sister of Nebajoth. ⁴And Ada bore Eliphaz to Esau, and Basemath bore Reuel. And Aholibama bore Jeush, Jaa-lam, and Korah. These are the sons of Esau who were born to him in the land of Canaan.

⁶And Esau took his wives, his sons and daughters, and all the souls of his house, his goods, with all his livestock and all his substance which he had got in the land of Canaan, and went into a country away from his brother Jacob. ⁷For their riches were so great that they could not dwell together, and the land wherein they were strangers could not receive them because of their flocks and herds. ⁸Thus Esau dwelt in Mount Seir (which Esau is called Edom).

⁹These are the generations of Esau, father of the Edomites, in Mount Seir. ¹⁰The names of Esau's sons: Eliphaz the son of Ada, the wife of Esau, and Reuel the son of Basemath, the wife of Esau also. ¹¹And the sons of Eliphaz were Teman, Omar, Zepho, Gatam, and Kenaz. ¹²And Timna was concubine to Eliphaz, Esau's son, and bore Amalek to Eliphaz. These were the grandsons of Esau's wife Ada. ¹³And these are the sons of Reuel: Nahath, Zerah, Shammah, and Mizzah; these were the grandsons of Esau's wife Basemath. ¹⁴And these were the sons of Esau's wife Aholibama, the daughter of Anah son of Zibeon, whom she bore to Esau: Jeush, Jaalam, and Korah.

¹⁵The following were the chiefs of the descendants of Esau:

The children of Eliphaz, the first son of Esau, were these: chief Teman, chief Omar, chief Zepho, chief Kenaz, ¹⁶chief Korah, chief Gatam, and chief Amalek. These are the chiefs that came of Eliphaz in the land of Edom, and these were the grandsons of Ada.

¹⁷These were the children of Esau's son Reuel: chief Nahath, chief Zerah, chief Shammah, chief Mizzah. These are the chiefs that came of Reuel in the land of Edom, and these were the grandsons of Basemath, Esau's wife.

¹⁸These were the children of Aholibama, Esau's wife: chief Jeush, chief Jaalam, chief Korah. These chiefs came of Aholibama the daughter of Anah, Esau's wife.

¹⁹This was the family of Esau (which Esau is called Edom), and these were the chiefs descended from them.

²⁰These are the children of Seir the Horite, the inhabiter of the land: Lotan, Shobal, Zibeon, Anah, ²¹Dishon, Ezer, and Dishan. These are the chiefs of the Horites, the children of Seir in the land of Edom. ²²And the children of Lotan were Hori and Hemam. And Lotan's sis-

^23^The children of Shobal were these: Alvan, Manahath, Ebal, Shepho, and Onam. ^24^The children of Zibeon were Ajah and Anah; this was that Anah who found the mules* in the wilderness as he fed his father Zibeon's donkeys. ^25^The children of Anah were these: Dishon, and Aholibama the daughter of Anah. ^26^These are the children of Dishon: Hemdan, Eshban, Ithran, and Cheran. ^27^The children of Ezer were these: Bilhan, Zaavan, and Akan. ^28^The children of Dishan were Uz and Aran.

*[or, pools]

^29^These are the chiefs that came of Hori: chief Lotan, chief Shobal, chief Zibeon, chief Anah, ^30^chief Dishon, chief Ezer, chief Dishan. These were the chiefs that came of Hori in their chiefdoms in the land of Seir.

^31^The following are the kings who reigned in the land of Edom before any king reigned among the children of Israel:

^32^Bela the son of Beor reigned in Edom, and the name of his city was Dinhabah. ^33^And when Bela died, Jobab the son of Zerah out of Bozrah reigned in his stead. ^34^When Jobab was dead, Husham of the land of Temany reigned in his stead. ^35^And after the death of Husham, Hadad the son of Bedad, who slew the Midianites in the field of the Moabites, reigned in his stead; and the name of his city was Avith. ^36^When Hadad was dead, Samlah of Masrekah reigned in his stead. ^37^When Samlah was dead, Saul of the river Rehoboth reigned in his stead. ^38^When Saul was dead, Baal-Hanan the son of Achbor reigned in his stead. ^39^And after the death of Baal-Hanan the son of Achbor, Hadad reigned in his stead; and the name of his city was Pau. And his wife's name was Mehetabel, the daughter of Matred who was the daughter of Mezahab.

1Ch 1:43-50

Jer 49:13,22

^40^These are the names of the chiefs that came of Esau, in their kindreds, places, and names: chief Timnah, chief Alvah, chief Jetheth, ^41^chief Ahol-ibamah, chief Elah, chief Pinon, ^42^chief Kenaz, chief Teman, chief Mibzar, ^43^chief Magdiel, and chief Iram. These were the chiefs of Edom in their territories, in the lands that they held.

1Ch 1:51-54

This Esau is the father of the Edomites.

The Notes

a) 3. Basemath is otherwise called Mahala [Ge 28:9]. And also in other places in the scriptures there are different names given to one person. [As Ada was called Judith in Ge 26:34, and her father was there called Beeri the Hittite, etc.]

Chapter 37

> Joseph accuses his brothers. Joseph dreams, is hated by his brothers, and is sold to the Ishmaelites. Jacob bewails Joseph.

And Jacob dwelt in the land where his father was a stranger; that is to say, in the land of Canaan. ^2^And these are the generations of Jacob.

When Joseph was seventeen years old, he kept the flocks with his brothers; the lad was with the sons of Bilhah and Zilpah, his father's wives. And he told their father of the bad report that there was of them.

³And Israel loved Joseph more than all his children because he had begotten him in his old age, and he made him a coat of many colours. ⁴When his brothers saw that their father loved him more than all his brothers, they hated him and could not speak one kind word to him. ⁵Moreover, Joseph dreamed a dream and told it to his brothers, for which they hated him yet the more. ⁶He said to them, Hear, I pray you, this dream that I have dreamed. ⁷Behold, we were making sheaves in the field; and lo, my sheaf arose and stood upright, and yours stood round about and bowed down to my sheaf.

⁸Then his brothers said to him, What, will you be our king, or will you reign over us? And they hated him yet the more, because of his dream and of his words.

⁹And he dreamed yet another dream and told it to his brothers, saying, Behold, I have had one more dream; I thought the sun and the moon and eleven stars bowed down to me. ¹⁰And when he had told this to his father and his brothers, his father rebuked him and said to him, What does this dream mean, which you have dreamed? Will I and your mother and your brothers come and fall on the ground before you?

¹¹And his brothers hated him, but his father noted what he said.

¹²His brothers went to keep their father's flocks in Shechem, ¹³and Israel said to Joseph, Are your brothers not keeping the flocks in Shechem? Come, so that I may send you to them. And he answered, Here am I! ¹⁴And he said to him, Go, and see if it is well with your brothers and the flocks, and bring word back to me. And he sent him out of the vale of Hebron to go to Shechem.

¹⁵And a certain man found Joseph wandering out of his way in the field and asked him what he was looking for. ¹⁶And he answered, I seek my brothers; tell me, I pray, where they are keeping the flocks. ¹⁷And the man said, They are departed from here, for I heard them say, Let us go to Dothan.

Thus Joseph went after his brothers, and he found them in Dothan. ¹⁸But when they saw him afar off, before he came to them, they took counsel against him, to slay him. ¹⁹And they said to one another, Behold, this dreamer comes! ²⁰Come now, and let us slay him and cast him into some pit. And let us say that some wicked beast has devoured him, and let us see what his dreams will come to.

²¹When Reuben heard this, he went about to rescue him out of their hands and said, Let us not kill him. ²²And Reuben said moreover to them, Do not shed his blood, but cast him into this pit that is in the wilderness, and lay no hands upon him. (For he would have rescued Joseph out of their hands and delivered him to his father again.)

²³And as soon as Joseph came to his brothers, they stripped him

out of his gay coat that was upon him, ²⁴and they took him and cast him into the pit. But the pit was empty and had no water in it. ²⁵And they sat themselves down to eat bread. And as they lifted up their eyes and looked about, there came a company of Ishmaelites from Gilead, their camels laden with spices, balm, and myrrh; and they were going down into Egypt. ²⁶Then Judah said to his brothers, What does it avail, to slay our brother and keep his blood hidden? ²⁷Come on, let us sell him to the Ishmaelites. And let not our hands be defiled upon him, for he is our brother and our flesh.

Ac 7:9

And his brothers consented. ²⁸Then, as the Midianite merchants passed by, they drew Joseph out of the pit and sold him to the Ishmaelites for twenty pieces of silver. And the Ishmaelites brought him into Egypt.

²⁹And when Reuben came back to the pit and did not find Joseph there, he rent his clothes,ᵃ ³⁰and went back to his brothers, saying, The lad is not there, and where can I go? ³¹And they took Joseph's coat, and killed a goat and dipped the coat in the blood. ³²And they sent that gay coat, and caused it to be brought to their father, and said, We have found this; see if it is your son's coat or no. ³³And he identified it, saying, It is my son's coat! A wicked beast has devoured him, and Joseph is torn in pieces.

Ge 44:27,28

³⁴And Jacob rent his clothes and put sackcloth about his loins, and he sorrowed for his son a long season. ³⁵Then all his sons and all his daughters came to comfort him. But he would not be comforted, and said, I will go down into the grave to my son, mourning. And thus his father wept for him.

³⁶And in Egypt the Midianites sold Joseph to Potiphar, a lord of Pharaoh and his chief marshal.

Ps 105:17
Wis 10:13

The Notes

a) 29. Rent his clothes: It was a special custom among the Hebrews to rent or tear their clothes to signify grief, or at other grievous occasions, such as when the glory of God was contemned.

Chapter 38

> The marriage of Judah. The trespass of Onan and the vengeance of God that came thereupon. Judah lay with his daughter-in-law Tamar. The birth of Perez and Zerah.

And it came to pass at that time that Judah went out from his brothers, and turned in to a man called Hirah of Adullam. ²And there he saw the daughter of a man called Shua, a Canaanite, and he married her and went in to her. ³And she conceived and bore a son, and called his name Er. ⁴And she conceived again and bore a son, and called him Onan. ⁵And she conceived a third time and bore a son whom she called Shelah; and Judah was at Chezib when she bore him.

1Ch 2:3

⁶And Judah gave Er his eldest son a wife, whose name was Tamar.

GENESIS 38

1Ch 2:3

⁷But this Er, Judah's eldest son, was wicked in the sight of the Lord,ᵃ and so the Lord slew him. ⁸Then Judah said to Onan, Go in to your brother's wife and marry her, and stir up seed unto your brother. ⁹And when Onan perceived that the seed would not be his, when he went in to his brother's wife he spilled it on the ground, because he would not give seed unto his brother. ¹⁰And the thing he did displeased the Lord, for which he slew him also.

¹¹Then Judah said to Tamar his daughter-in-law, Remain a widow at your father's house till my son Shelah is grown. (For he feared that he might die also as his brothers had.) So Tamar went and dwelt in her father's house.

Ge 31:19
1Sam 25:2

¹²And in the process of time, the daughter of Shua, Judah's wife, died. Then Judah, when he had left mourning, went to his sheep shearers at Timnah with his friend Hirah of Adullam. ¹³And someone told Tamar, saying, Behold, your father-in-law is going up to Timnah to shear his sheep. ¹⁴And she put her widow's garments off from her, and then covered herself with a cloak and disguised herself. And she sat down at the way into Enaim, which is by the side of the highway to Timnah, because she saw that Shelah was grown and that she had not been given to him as a wife.

¹⁵When Judah saw her, he thought she was a whore because she had covered her face. ¹⁶And he turned to her by the way and said, Come, I pray you, let me lie with you. For he did not know that it was his daughter-in-law. And she said, What will you give me, to lie with me? ¹⁷Then he said, I will send you a kid from the flock. She answered, Then give me a pledge till you send it. ¹⁸Then he said, What pledge shall I give you? And she said, Your signet, your bracelet, and your staff that is in your hand.

And he gave them to her, and lay with her, and she was with child by him. ¹⁹And she got up and went and put her cloak from her, and put on her widow's garments again.

²⁰And Judah sent the kid by his neighbour from Adullam, to fetch his pledge back from the woman's hand. But he found her not. ²¹Then he asked the men of the same place, saying, Where is the whore who sat at Enaim along the road? And they said, There was no whore here. ²²And he went back to Judah, saying, I cannot find her, and also the men of the place said that there was no whore there. ²³And Judah said, Let her keep it for herself, lest we be shamed. For I sent the kid, but you could not find her.

²⁴And it came to pass that, after three months, someone told Judah, saying, Tamar your daughter-in-law has played the whore, and with playing the whore has become great with child. And Judah said, Bring her forth and let her be burned! ²⁵And when they brought her forth, she sent to her father-in-law, saying, By the man to whom these things belong, I am with child. And she said also, Look, whose are this seal, bracelet, and staff? ²⁶And Judah acknowledged them, saying, She is more righteous than I, because I did not give her to Shelah my son.

But he lay with her no more.

²⁷When the time came that she should be delivered, behold, there were twins in her womb. ²⁸And as she travailed, one put out his hand, and the mid-wife took and bound a red thread about it, saying, This one will come out first. ²⁹But he plucked his hand back again, and his brother came out. And she said, Why have you breached the womb first? – and called him Perez.* ³⁰And afterward his brother came out, who had the red thread about his hand, who was called Zerah.†

1Ch 2:4
v29 e.f. JR.

*[ie, Breach]
†[ie, Rising of Light]

The Notes

a) 7. To be wicked in the sight of the Lord is to walk in wickedness, knowing that the Lord sees us, and yet we will not repent.

Chapter 39

God prospers Joseph. Potiphar's wife tempts him. He is accused and cast into prison. God has mercy upon him.

Joseph was brought to Egypt, and Potiphar, a lord of Pharaoh's and his chief marshal, an Egyptian, bought him from the Ishmaelites who had brought him there. ²And the Lord was with Joseph, and he was a fortunate man, and he continued in the house of his master the Egyptian. ³And his master saw that the Lord was with him, and that the Lord made everything he did prosper in his hand. ⁴Therefore he found grace in his master's sight, and served him. And his master made him overseer of his house, and put all that he had in his hand. ⁵And as soon as he had made him overseer of his house and of all that he had, the Lord blessed this Egyptian's house for Joseph's sake; and the blessing of the Lord was upon all that he had, both in the house and also in the fields. ⁶And therefore he left all that he had in Joseph's hand, and looked to nothing that was with him save only the food that he ate.

Ge 37:28,36

And Joseph was a well-built man and handsome. ⁷And it happened after this that his master's wife cast her eyes upon Joseph and said, Come, lie with me! ⁸But he refused and said to her, Look, my master takes no concern for what he has in the house with me, but has committed all that he has to my hand. ⁹He himself is not greater in the house than I, and has kept nothing from me but you alone, because you are his wife. How then can I do this great wickedness, to sin against God?

1Sam 16:12

¹⁰But she spoke in this manner to Joseph day by day. Yet he would not hear her, to sleep with her or to be in her company.

¹¹And it came to pass about this time that Joseph entered into the house to conduct his business, and there was no one from the household nearby in the house. ¹²And she caught him by the garment, saying, Come, sleep with me! And he left his garment in her hand and fled and got out. ¹³When she saw that he had left his garment in her hand and fled, ¹⁴she called to the men of the house and told them, say-

ing, See, he has brought in a Hebrew to us, to do us shame. For he came in to me, to sleep with me. But I cried out with a loud voice, ¹⁵and when he heard that I lifted up my voice and cried, he left his garment with me and fled away, and got out.

¹⁶And she laid up his garment by her until her lord came home. ¹⁷And she told him the same thing, saying, This Hebrew servant that you have brought to us came in to me, to do me shame. ¹⁸But as soon as I lifted up my voice and cried aloud, he left his garment with me and fled out.

Ps 105:17,18

¹⁹When the master heard the words that his wife spoke (saying, This is what your servant did to me), he became angry. ²⁰And he took Joseph and put him in prison, in the place where the king's prisoners lay bound. And there he continued in prison.

²¹But the Lord was with Joseph and showed him mercy. And he gave him favour in the sight of the keeper of the prison, ²²who committed to Joseph's hand all the prisoners who were in the prison house. And whatever was done there, he oversaw it. ²³And the keeper of the prison looked to nothing that was under Jospeh's hand because the Lord was with him, and because whatever he did, the Lord made it to prosper.

Chapter 40

Joseph interprets the dreams of the two prisoners.

And it came about after this that the chief butler of the king of Egypt and his chief baker had offended their lord, the king of Egypt. ²And Pharaoh was angry with them, ³and imprisoned them in his chief marshal's house, in the prison where Joseph was bound. ⁴And the chief marshal put Joseph in charge of them, and he served them. And they continued a season in prison.

⁵And they each dreamed in one night, both the butler and the baker of the king of Egypt who were bound in the prison house – each of them his dream, and each man's dream of a different signification. ⁶When Joseph went in to them in the morning and looked upon them, behold, they were sad. ⁷And he asked them, saying, Why do you look so sad today? ⁸They answered him, We have dreamed a dream, but have no one to interpret it. And Joseph said to them, Interpreting belongs to God, but tell me yet.

⁹And the chief butler told his dream to Joseph and said to him, In my dream I thought there stood a vine before me, ¹⁰and on the vine were three branches. And it was as though it budded, and then its blossoms shot forth and its grapes grew ripe. ¹¹And I had Pharaoh's cup in my hand, and I took some of the grapes, squeezed them into Pharaoh's cup, and delivered Pharaoh's cup into his hand.

¹²Joseph said to him, This is the interpretation of it: the three branches are three days, ¹³for within three days Pharaoh will lift up your head and restore you to your office again, and you will deliver Pharaoh's cup into his hand in the old manner, just as you did when

you were his butler. ¹⁴But think on me when you are in a good case, and show mercy to me, and make mention of me to Pharaoh, and help to bring me out of this house. ¹⁵For I was stolen out of the land of the Hebrews, and here also I have done nothing at all for which they should have put me into this dungeon.

¹⁶When the chief baker saw that he had well interpreted it, he said to Joseph, I thought also in my dream that I had three wicker baskets on my head. ¹⁷And in the uppermost basket were all manner of pastries for Pharaoh, and the birds ate them out of the basket upon my head.

¹⁸Joseph answered and said, This is the interpretation of it: the three baskets are three days, ¹⁹for in three days Pharaoh will take your head from you and will hang you on a tree, and the birds will eat your flesh from off you.

²⁰And it came to pass on the third day, which was Pharaoh's birthday, that he made a feast for all his servants. And he lifted up the head of the chief butler and of the chief baker among his servants. ²¹And he restored the chief butler to his butlership again, and he reached the cup into Pharaoh's hand; ²²but he hanged the chief baker, just as Joseph had said to them. ²³Notwithstanding, the chief butler did not remember Joseph, but forgot him. — M't 14:6

Chapter 41

> Pharaoh's dreams are interpreted by Joseph. He is made ruler over all Egypt. He has two sons, Manasseh and Ephraim. The dearth begins in Egypt.

And it happened at two years' end that Pharaoh dreamed, and thought that he stood by a river's side; ²and there came out of the river seven cows goodly and fat-fleshed, and they fed in a meadow. ³And he thought that seven other cows came up after them out of the river, ugly and lean-fleshed, and they stood by the others on the bank of the river. ⁴And the ugly and lean-fleshed cows ate up the seven healthy and fat cows. And with that, he awoke.

⁵And he slept again and dreamed a second time, that seven ears of plump and goodly grain grew upon one stalk. ⁶And that after them, seven thin ears blasted with the wind sprang up. ⁷And the seven thin ears devoured the seven plump and full ears. And then Pharaoh awoke; and behold, it was a dream.

⁸When the morning came, his spirit was troubled. And he sent and called for all the soothsayers of Egypt and all the wise men thereof, and told them his dream. But there was none of them that could interpret it to Pharaoh.

⁹Then the chief butler spoke to Pharaoh, saying, I do remember my fault this day. ¹⁰Pharaoh was angry with his servants, and put in prison in the chief marshal's house both me and the chief baker. ¹¹And we dreamed, both of us in one night, and each man's dream was of a different meaning. ¹²And there was with us a young man, Hebrew-

born, servant to the chief marshal. And we told him, and he interpreted our dreams for us, according to each of our dreams. ¹³And just as he interpreted them to us, so it came to pass; I was restored to my office again, and the baker was hanged.

Ps 105:17-20

¹⁴Then Pharaoh sent and called Joseph, and they made him hasten out of the prison. And he shaved himself and changed his clothing, and went in to Pharaoh. ¹⁵And Pharaoh said to Joseph, I have dreamed a dream and no one can interpret it; but I have heard of you, that as soon as you hear a dream, you do interpret it.

¹⁶And Joseph answered Pharaoh, saying, God may give Pharaoh an answer of peace without me.

¹⁷Pharaoh said to Joseph, In my dream I thought I stood by a river's side, ¹⁸and there came out of the river seven fat-fleshed and healthy cows, and they fed in the meadow. ¹⁹And then seven other cows came up after them, poor and very ugly and lean-fleshed, so that I never saw their like in all the land of Egypt for ugliness. ²⁰And the seven lean and ugly cows ate up the first seven fat cows. ²¹And when they had eaten them up, a man could not perceive that they had eaten them, because they were still as ugly as they were at the beginning. And I awoke.

²²And I saw again in my dream seven ears of grain spring out of one stalk, full and good, ²³and seven other ears, withered, thin, and blasted with wind, spring up after them. ²⁴And the thin ears devoured the seven good ears. And I have told this to the soothsayers, but no one can tell me what it means.

²⁵Then Joseph said to Pharaoh, Both Pharaoh's dreams are one. And God is showing Pharaoh what he is about to do. ²⁶The seven good cows are years, and the seven good ears are seven years also, and it is but one dream. ²⁷Like-wise, the seven thin and ugly cows that came out after them are seven years; and the seven empty and blasted ears shall be seven years of hunger. ²⁸This is what I said to Pharaoh, that God is showing Pharaoh what he is about to do.

²⁹Behold, there shall come seven years of great plenteousness throughout all the land of Egypt. ³⁰And there shall arise after them seven years of hunger, such that all the plenteousness will be forgotten in the land of Egypt. And the hunger will consume the land, ³¹so that the plenteousness will not once be seen in the land by reason of that hunger that will come after; for it will be exceedingly great. ³²And concerning that the dream was repeated to Pharaoh the second time, it signifies that the thing is certainly prepared by God, and that God will shortly bring it to pass.

³³Now, therefore, let Pharaoh provide for a man of understanding and wisdom, and set him over the land of Egypt. ³⁴And let Pharaoh make officers over the land, and take up the fifth part of the harvest of Egypt in the seven plenteous years. ³⁵And let them gather in all the food of these good years that are coming, and lay up grain under the authority of Pharaoh so that there may be food in the cities. And let

them keep it there, ³⁶so that there may be food in store in the land, in preparation for the seven years of hunger that will come in the land of Egypt, and so that the land will not perish through hunger.

³⁷And the advice pleased Pharaoh and all his servants. ³⁸Then Pharaoh said to his servants, Where shall we find such a man as this, who has the Spirit of God in him? ³⁹And so Pharaoh said to Joseph, Seeing as God has shown you all this, there is no man of understanding or of wisdom like you. ⁴⁰You, therefore, must be over my house; and according to your word must all my people order themselves. Only in the king's seat will I be above you. ⁴¹And he said to Joseph, Behold, I have set you over all the land of Egypt.

Ps 105:21,22
Ac 7:9,10
1Macc 2:53
Dan 2:47,48

⁴²And he took off his ring from his finger and put it upon Joseph's finger, and arrayed him in raiment of fine linen, and put a golden chain about his neck, ⁴³and set him upon the best chariot that he had save one. And they proclaimed before him, Abrech!ᵃ – and that Pharaoh had made him governor over all the land of Egypt.

⁴⁴And Pharaoh said to Joseph, I am Pharaoh; without your will may no one lift up either his hand or foot in all the land of Egypt. ⁴⁵And he called Joseph's name Zaphnath-Paaneah.ᵇ And he gave him Asenath, the daughter of Poti-Pherah priest of On, as a wife.

Then Joseph went abroad in the land of Egypt. ⁴⁶And he was thirty years old when he stood before Pharaoh king of Egypt.ᶜ And then Joseph departed from Pharaoh and went throughout all the land of Egypt. ⁴⁷And in the seven plenteous years they bundled sheaves of grain. ⁴⁸And they gathered up all the food of the seven plenteous years that were in the land of Egypt and stored it in the cities. And he stockpiled within the cities the food from the fields that grew round about every city. ⁴⁹And Joseph laid up grain in store like the sand of the sea in multitude out of measure, until he stopped keeping track. For it was beyond measure.

⁵⁰And two sons were born to Joseph before the years of hunger came, whom Asenath, the daughter of Poti-Pherah priest of On, bore to him. ⁵¹He called the name of the first son Manasseh.* For God (he said) has made me forget all my labour and all my father's household. ⁵²The second he called Ephraim.‡ For God (he said) has caused me to grow in the land of my trouble.

Ge 46:20
*[ie, Forgetting]

‡[ie, Very Fruitful]

⁵³And when the seven years of plenteousness that were in the land of Egypt ended, ⁵⁴then came the seven years of dearth, as Joseph had said. And the dearth was in all lands, but in the land of Egypt there was still food. ⁵⁵When now all the land of Egypt began to hunger, then the people cried out to Pharaoh for bread. And Pharaoh said to all Egypt, Go to Joseph; and what he says to you, that do.

Ac 7:11

⁵⁶And when the dearth was throughout all the land, Joseph made available all that was in the cities and sold it to the Egyptians. And hunger grew severely in the land of Egypt. ⁵⁷And all countries came to Joseph in Egypt to buy grain, because the famine was so severe in all lands.

The Notes

a) 43. Abrech: that is, Tender Father; or as some will, Bow the knee. [As a father of Egypt, Joseph was tender in years. Verse 46 gives his age as thirty.]

b) 45. Zaphnath-Paaneah: these are Egyptian words and mean, As a man to whom secret things are revealed.

c) 46. When he stood before Pharaoh: that is, when he was admitted by Pharaoh into his office, as in 1Samuel 16:21.

Chapter 42

Joseph's brothers come into Egypt to buy grain, and he recognizes them and tries them. Simeon is put in prison. The others return to their father to fetch Benjamin. His father is loathe to let him go, but at the last he granted it.

Ac 7:12

When Jacob saw that there was grain for sale in Egypt, he said to his sons, Why are you negligent? ²Look, I have heard that there is grain sold in Egypt. Go there, and buy us grain from there so that we may live and not die.

³So Joseph's ten brothers went down to buy grain in Egypt. ⁴For Jacob would not send Benjamin, Joseph's brother, with his other brothers. For (he said) some misfortune might happen to him. ⁵And the sons of Israel went to buy grain among others who went, for there was dearth also in the land of Canaan.

⁶And Joseph was governor in the land, and sold grain to all the people of the land. And his brothers came, and they fell flat on the ground before him. ⁷When Joseph saw his brothers, he recognized them, but he made strange with them and spoke roughly to them, saying, Where are you from?

And they said, Out of the land of Canaan, to buy food.

Ge 37:5-11

⁸Joseph recognized his brothers, but they knew him not. ⁹And Joseph remembered the dreams that he had dreamt about them and said to them, You are spies, and have come to see where the land is weak!

¹⁰And they said to him, Nay, my lord, but to buy food your servants are come. ¹¹We are all one man's sons, and mean truly, and your servants are no spies. ¹²And he said to them, Nay indeed, but you have come to see where the land is weak! ¹³And they said, We your servants are twelve brothers, the sons of one man in the land of Canaan. The youngest is yet with our father; and one son, no man knows where he is.

¹⁴Joseph said to them, It is that which I said to you, that you are surely spies. ¹⁵By this you may be proved, for by the life of Pharaoh you will not leave here until your youngest brother comes: ¹⁶send therefore one of you, and let him fetch your brother, and you shall be in prison in the meantime. And by this your words may be proved, whether there is any truth in you – or else, by the life of Pharaoh, you are but spies.

¹⁷And he put them in prison for three days. ¹⁸And Joseph said to them on the third day, Do this and live, for I fear God: ¹⁹If you mean no harm, let one of your brothers be bound in the prison, and you go and bring the necessary food to your households. ²⁰And bring your youngest brother to me so that your words may be believed, and so that you do not die. And they agreed so to do.

²¹Then they said one to another, We truly sinned against our brother, in that we saw the anguish of his soul when he besought us, but would not hear him. Therefore this trouble has come upon us. ²²Reuben answered them, saying, Did I not say to you that you should not sin against the lad? But you would not hear. And now, see, his blood is required of us.ª

Ge 37:21,22

²³They were not aware that Joseph understood them, for he spoke to them by a translator. ²⁴And he turned from them and wept, and then turned to them again and spoke with them. And he took Simeon out from among them and bound him before their eyes. ²⁵And he commanded to fill their sacks with grain, and to put every man's money back in his sack, and to give them food to eat on the way. And it was so done for them.

²⁶And they loaded their donkeys with the grain and departed. ²⁷And, as one of them opened his sack to give his donkey provender in the inn, he saw his money in the mouth of his sack. ²⁸And he said to his brothers, My money is restored to me again, and is even in the mouth of my sack! Then their hearts failed them, and they were astonished and said to one another, How comes it that God deals thus with us?

²⁹And they returned to Jacob their father in the land of Canaan and told him all that had happened them, saying, ³⁰The lord of the land spoke roughly to us, and took us for spies scouting out the country. ³¹And we said to him, We mean truly and are no spies. ³²We are twelve brothers, sons of our father. One is away, and the youngest is now with our father in the land of Canaan. ³³And the lord of the country said to us, This way I may know if you mean truly: leave one of your brothers here with me, and take food necessary for your households, and go; ³⁴and bring your youngest brother back to me. That is how I may know that you are not spies, but mean truly. And thus I will deliver to you your brother again, and you may do your business in the land.

³⁵And as they emptied their sacks, behold, every man's bundle of money was in his sack. And when both they and their father saw the bundles of money, they were afraid.

³⁶And Jacob their father said to them, You have robbed me of my children! Joseph is away, and Simeon is away, and you will take Benjamin away. All these things fall upon me. ³⁷Reuben answered his father, saying, Slay my two sons if I do not bring him back to you! Put him therefore in my hand, and I will bring him to you again. ³⁸But he said, My son shall not go down with you. For his brother is dead, and

he is left alone. Moreover, some misfortune might happen to him along the way when you go, and so would you bring my grey head with sorrow to the grave.^b

The Notes

a) 22. To require his blood of the hand of another is to take vengeance for the evil done to him, as in Genesis 9:5, Psalm 9:12, and Ezekiel 3:18-20.

b) 38. Bring me to my grave: that is, bring me to my death. Isaiah 38:10 and note b.

Chapter 43

When Benjamin was brought, they returned to Egypt with gifts. Simeon is delivered out of prison. Joseph goes aside and weeps. They feast together.

And the dearth waxed sore in the land. ²And when they had eaten up the grain that they had brought out of the land of Egypt, their father said to them, Go again and buy us a little food.

Ge 42:14-16 ³Then said Judah to him, The man firmly warned us, saying, Look that you see not my face unless your brother is with you. ⁴Therefore, if you will send our brother with us, we will go and buy the food. ⁵But if you will not send him, we will not go. For the man said to us, Look that you see not my face unless your brother is with you.

⁶And Israel said, Why did you deal so cruelly with me, as to tell the man that you had yet another brother? ⁷And they said, The man asked us about our kindred, saying, Is your father yet alive? Have you not another brother? And we answered him according to these words. How could we know that he would tell us to bring our brother down with us?

⁸Then said Judah to Israel his father, Send the lad with me, and we will rise and go, so that we may live and not die – both we and you,

Ge 44:32-34 and also our children. ⁹I will be surety for him, and of my hands require him: if I do not bring him to you and set him before your eyes, then let me bear the blame forever. ¹⁰For without this delay, by this time we could have been there twice and returned.

¹¹Then their father Israel said to them, If it must needs be so now, then do this. Take some of the best fruits of the land in your vessels, and bring the man a gift: a little balm, and a little honey, spices and myrrh, dates, and almonds. ¹²And take twice as much money with you. And the money that was brought back in your sacks, take it again with you in your hands. Perhaps it was some oversight. ¹³Take also your brother with you, and arise and go again to the man. ¹⁴And may

v14 e.f. COV. God Almighty give you mercy in the sight of the man, and let you have your other brother and also Benjamin. Meanwhile, I must be as a man robbed of his children.

¹⁵Thus they took the gift and twice as much more money with them, and Benjamin. And they rose up, went down to Egypt, and presented themselves to Joseph. ¹⁶When Joseph saw Benjamin with them,

he said to the steward of his house, Bring these men home, and slaughter an animal and make ready, for they shall dine with me at noon. ¹⁷And the man did as Joseph directed, and brought them to Joseph's house.

¹⁸When they were brought to Joseph's house, they were afraid and said, We have been brought here because of the money that came back in our sacks the first time – to pick a quarrel with us, and to lay something to our charge, to bring us in bondage and our donkeys also. ¹⁹Therefore they went to the man who was the steward of Joseph's house and talked with him at the door, ²⁰and said, Sir, we came here the first time to buy food, ²¹but when we got to an inn and opened our sacks, behold, the full weight of every man's money was in his sack. But we have brought it back with us, ²²and have brought other money also in our hands, to buy food. But we cannot say who put our money in our sacks.

²³And he said, Be of good cheer, fear not. Your God and the God of your fathers has bestowed on you that treasure in your sacks; for I had your money.

And he brought Simeon out to them. ²⁴And he led them into Joseph's house and gave them water to wash their feet, and gave their donkeys provender. ²⁵And they made their gift ready before Joseph came at noon, for they heard that they would dine there.

²⁶When Joseph came home, they brought the gift, which they had in their hands, into the house to him, and fell flat on the ground before him. ²⁷And he welcomed them courteously, saying, Is your father, that old man that you told me of, in good health? And is he yet alive?

²⁸They answered, Your servant our father is in good health and is yet alive. And they bowed themselves and fell to the ground.

²⁹And he lifted up his eyes and saw his brother Benjamin, his mother's son, and said, Is this your youngest brother, of whom you spoke to me? And he said, God be merciful to you, my son.

³⁰And Joseph made haste, for his heart did melt upon his brother, and sought where to weep. And he entered into his chamber to weep there. ³¹And he washed his face and came out, restrained himself, and said to set food on the table. ³²And the servants set a table for him by himself and one for them by themselves. (And for the Egyptians who ate with him, one by themselves, because the Egyptians may not eat food with the Hebrews; for that is an abomination to the Egyptians.ᵃ)

³³And they sat before him, the eldest according to his age and the youngest according to his youth. And the men marvelled among themselves. ³⁴And servants brought them dishes from Joseph's table, but Benjamin's portion was five times as much as any of theirs. And they ate and they drank, and were drunk with him.

The Notes

a) 32. Abomination: that is, it was abhorred by the Egyptians that a Hebrew should eat with them.

Chapter 44

Joseph accuses his brother of theft. Judah becomes surety for Benjamin.

And Joseph directed the steward of his house, saying, Fill the men's sacks with food, as much as they can carry, and put every man's money in his bag mouth; ²and put my silver cup in the mouth of the youngest's sack, and his grain money also. And he did as Joseph had said. ³And in the morning, as soon as it was light, the men were let go with their donkeys.

⁴And when they were out of the city and not yet far away, Joseph said to the steward of his house, Up, and follow after the men and overtake them, and say to them, Why have you rewarded evil for good? ⁵Is that not the cup of which my lord drinks, and does he not prophesy therein? You have done evil, in what you have done.

⁶And he overtook them and said these same words to them. ⁷And they answered him, Why does my lord say such words? God forbid that your servants should so do. ⁸Look, the money that we found in our sacks' mouths, we brought back to you from the land of Canaan. How then could we steal out of my lord's house either silver or gold? ⁹With whomever of your servants it be found, let him die, and let us also be my lord's bondmen.

¹⁰And he said, Now therefore, according to your words, he with whom it is found shall be my servant, but you shall be blameless.

¹¹And at once every man took down his sack to the ground, and every man opened his sack. ¹²And he searched, and began at the eldest and left at the youngest; and the cup was found in Benjamin's sack. ¹³Then they rent their clothes, and loaded every man his donkey and went back to the city.

¹⁴And Judah and his brothers went to Joseph's house, for he was still there, and they fell before him on the ground. ¹⁵And Joseph said to them, What deed is this that you have done? Did you not know that such a man as I can prophesy?

¹⁶Then said Judah, What shall we say to my lord? What shall we say, or what defence can we make? God has found out the wickedness of your servants. Behold, both we and he with whom the cup is found are your servants.

¹⁷And he answered, God forbid that I should so do. The man with whom the cup is found, he shall be my servant. But you, go in peace to your father.

¹⁸Then Judah went to him and said, Oh my lord, let your servant speak a word in my lord's hearing, and be not angry with your servant; for you are even as Pharaoh. ¹⁹My lord asked his servant, saying, Have you a father or a brother? ²⁰And we answered my lord, We have a father who is old, and a young lad that he begat in his age. And the brother of the said lad is dead, and he is all that is left of that mother. And his father loves him. ²¹Then said my lord to his servants, Bring

Ge 42:13

him to me, so that I may set my eyes upon him. ²²And we answered my lord that the lad could not go from his father, for if he should leave his father, he would be but a dead man. ²³Then you said to your servants, Unless your youngest brother comes with you, look that you see my face no more. ²⁴And when we went back to your servant our father, we told him what my lord had said.

Ge 43:3

²⁵And when our father said to us, Go back and buy us a little food, ²⁶we said that we could not go; nevertheless, if our youngest brother goes with us, then will we go. For we may not see the man's face unless our youngest brother is with us. ²⁷Then your servant our father said to us, You know that my wife bore me two sons; ²⁸and the one went out from me, and it is said of a surety that he is torn in pieces by wild beasts, and I have not seen him since. ²⁹If you also take this son away from me and some misfortune happens to him, then shall you bring my grey head with sorrow to the grave.

Ge 43:4,5

Ge 37:33

Ge 42:38

³⁰Now, therefore, when I go to your servant my father, if the lad is not with me, seeing that his life hangs on the lad's life, ³¹then as soon as he sees that the lad has not come, he will die. And so would we your servants bring the grey head of your servant our father with sorrow to the grave. ³²For I your servant became surety for the lad to my father, and said, If I bring him not to you again, I will bear the blame all my life long. ³³Now, therefore, let me your servant stay here in place of the lad and be my lord's bondman, and let the lad go home with his brothers. ³⁴For how can I go to my father, and the lad not with me? Lest I should see the wretchedness that will come on my father.

Ge 43:9

Chapter 45

Joseph makes himself known to his brothers and sends for his father.

And Joseph could no longer contain himself before everyone who stood around him, but directed that they should all go out from him, and that there should be no one with him while he revealed himself to his brothers. ²And he wept aloud, such that the Egyptians and the house of Pharaoh heard it. ³And he said to his brothers, I am Joseph! Does my father yet live?

Ge 42:24

But his brothers could not answer him, for they were abashed at his presence.

⁴And Joseph said to his brothers, Come near to me! And they came near. And he said, I am Joseph your brother, whom you sold into Egypt. ⁵And now, be not grieved about it, neither let it seem a cruel thing in your eyes that you sold me here. For God sent me before you to save life. ⁶For this is the second year of dearth in the land, and five more are coming in which there will be neither plowing nor harvest.

Ac 7:9-13

Ge 37:27,28; 50:20.

⁷Therefore, God sent me before you to make provision, so that you may have posterity in the earth, and to save your lives by a great deliverance. ⁸So now it was not you who sent me here, but God. And he has made me father to Pharaoh, and lord over all his house, and ruler

in all the land of Egypt. ⁹Make haste, and go to my father and tell him, This says your son Joseph: God has made me lord over all Egypt; come down to me, and do not delay. ¹⁰And you shall dwell in the land of Goshen and be by me – you, your children, your children's children, your flocks and beasts, and all that you have. ¹¹There I will make provision for you, because there remain yet five years of dearth – lest you, your household, and all that you have should perish.

¹²Behold, your eyes do see, and the eyes also of my brother Benjamin, that I speak to you by mouth. ¹³Therefore, tell my father of all the honour that I have in Egypt and of everything that you have seen. And make haste, and bring my father here.

¹⁴And he fell on his brother Benjamin's neck and wept, and Benjamin wept on his neck. ¹⁵Moreover, he kissed all his brothers and wept upon them. And after that, his brothers talked with him.

¹⁶And when the news reached Pharaoh's house that Joseph's brothers had come, it pleased Pharaoh well, and all his servants. ¹⁷And Pharaoh said to Joseph, Say to your brothers, Do this: load up your beasts and go. And when you get to the land of Canaan, ¹⁸take your father and your households and come to me, and I will give you the best of the land of Egypt, and you shall eat the fat of the land. ¹⁹And he commanded also, This do: take wagons with you from the land of Egypt for your children and for your wives, and bring your father and come. ²⁰Also, take no thought for your household stuff, for the goods of all the land of Egypt shall be yours.

²¹And the children of Israel did even so. And Joseph gave them wagons at the commandment of Pharaoh, and gave them food also to eat on the way. ²²And he gave to each of them a change of clothing, but to Benjamin he gave three hundred pieces of silver and five changes of clothing. ²³And to his father he sent likewise ten he-donkeys laden with goods out of Egypt, and ten she-donkeys laden with grain, bread, and food, to serve his father on the way. ²⁴Thus he sent his brothers away, and they departed. And he said to them, See that you do not fall out by the way.

²⁵And they departed from Egypt and went into the land of Canaan, to Jacob their father. ²⁶And they told him, saying, Joseph is still alive, and is governor over all the land of Egypt!

And Jacob's heart wavered, for he did not believe them. ²⁷And they told him all the words of Joseph, which he had said to them. But when he saw the wagons that Joseph had sent to carry him, then his spirits revived. ²⁸And Israel said, I have enough if Joseph my son is still alive! I will go and see him before I die.

Chapter 46

> Jacob with all his household goes down to Joseph in Egypt. The genealogy of Jacob. Joseph meets his father.

Israel took his journey with all that he had, and went to Beersheba, and offered offerings to the God of his father Isaac. ²And God spoke to Israel in a vision by night, and called to him, Jacob, Jacob! And he answered, Here am I. ³And he said, I am that mighty God of your father. Fear not to go down into Egypt, for I will make of you there a great people.ᵃ ⁴I will go down with you into Egypt, and I will also bring you up again. And Joseph shall put his hand upon your eyes.ᵇ

⁵And Jacob rose up from Beersheba. And the sons of Israel carried Jacob their father and their children and their wives in the wagons that Pharaoh had sent to carry him. ⁶And they took their flocks, herds, and the goods that they had gotten in the land of Canaan, and went into Egypt, both Jacob and all his seed with him – ⁷his sons and his sons' sons with him, his daughters, and his sons' daughters. And he brought all his seed with him into Egypt.

⁸These are the names of the children of Israel who went into Egypt, both Jacob and his sons:

Reuben, Jacob's first son. ⁹The sons of Reuben: Hanoch, Pallu, Hezron, and Carmi. ¹⁰The sons of Simeon: Jemuel, Jamin, Ohad, Jachin, Zohar, and Shaul the son of a Canaanite woman. ¹¹The sons of Levi: Gershon, Kohath, and Merari. ¹²The sons of Judah: Er, Onan, Shelah, Perez, and Zerah (but Er and Onan had died in the land of Canaan). The sons of Perez: Hezron and Hamul. ¹³The sons of Issachar: Tola, Puah, Jashub, and Shimron. ¹⁴The sons of Zebulon: Sered, Elon, and Jahleel. ¹⁵These were the descendants of Leah, whom she bore to Jacob in Mesopotamia with also his daughter Dinah. All the souls of his sons and daughters make thirty-three.

¹⁶The sons of Gad: Ziphion, Haggi, Shuni, Ezbon, Eri, Arodi, and Areli. ¹⁷The sons of Asher: Jimnah, Ishuah, Isui, Beriah, with also Serah their sister. And the sons of Beriah were Heber and Malchiel. ¹⁸These were the descendants of Zilpah, whom Laban gave to Leah his daughter. And these she bore to Jacob, in number sixteen souls.

¹⁹The sons of Rachel, Jacob's wife: Joseph and Benjamin. ²⁰And to Joseph in the land of Egypt were born Manasseh and Ephraim, whom Asenath, the daughter of Poti-Pherah priest of On, bore to him. ²¹The sons of Benjamin: Belah, Becher, Ashbel, Gera, Naaman, Ehi, Rosh, Muppim, Huppim, and Ard. ²²These were the descendants of Rachel who were born to Jacob, fourteen souls altogether.

²³The son of Dan: Hushim. ²⁴The sons of Naphtali: Jahzeel, Guni, Jezer, and Shillem. ²⁵These were the descendants of Bilhah, whom Laban gave to Rachel his daughter, and she bore these to Jacob, altogether seven souls.

²⁶All the souls that went with Jacob into Egypt, who came out of his loins, besides his son's wives, were altogether sixty-six souls. ²⁷And the sons of Joseph, who were born to him in Egypt, were two souls. So it was that all the souls of the house of Jacob who came into Egypt were seventy.*

²⁸And he sent Judah before him to Joseph, so that he could be shown the way to Goshen. And they went into the land of Goshen.

Jos 24:4
Ac 7:14,15
Isa 52:4

Ex 1:1-5;
6:14-19.

Nu c26
1Ch cc5-7

De 10:22
*[68 + Jacob and Joseph = 70 souls]

²⁹And Joseph made ready his chariot and went to meet Israel his father at Goshen, and presented himself to him and fell on his neck, and wept upon his neck a good while. ³⁰And Israel said to Joseph, Now I am content to die, insomuch as I have seen you, that you are yet alive.

³¹And Joseph said to his brothers and to his father's house, I will go and show Pharaoh, and tell him that my brothers and my father's house, who were in the land of Canaan, have come to me; ³²and how they are shepherds (for they were men who tended pasture animals), and they have brought their flocks and their herds and all that they have with them. ³³If Pharaoh calls you and asks you what your occupation is, ³⁴say, Your servants have worked with pasture animals from our childhood to this time, both we and our fathers. Thus it will be that you may dwell in the land of Goshen, for the Egyptians abhor all shepherds.

The Notes

a) 3. I will make you a great people: that is, I will multiply your seed so that many people shall come thereof.
b) 4. To put his hand upon his eyes is to be present at his death and to bury him, as in Tobit 14:13.

Chapter 47

Jacob comes before Pharaoh, and to him is given the land of Goshen. He binds his son with a vow for his burial.

And Joseph went and told Pharaoh and said, My father and my brothers, and their sheep, their beasts, and all that they have, are come from the land of Canaan and are in the land of Goshen. ²And Joseph took apart five of his brothers and presented them to Pharaoh.

³And Pharaoh said to his brothers, What is your occupation?

Ge 23:4

And they said to Pharaoh, Your servants are shepherds, both we and also our fathers. ⁴They said moreover to Pharaoh, We have come to sojourn in the land, for your servants have no pasture for their flocks, so sore is the famine in the land of Canaan. Now, therefore, let your servants dwell in the land of Goshen.

⁵And Pharaoh said to Joseph, Your father and your brothers have come to you. ⁶The land of Egypt is open before you: in the best place of the land, make both your father and your brothers to dwell. And even in the land of Goshen, let them dwell. Moreover, if you know any men of industry among them, put them in charge of my flocks and herds.

⁷And Joseph brought in Jacob his father and set him before Pharaoh. And Jacob blessed Pharaoh. ⁸And Pharaoh asked Jacob, How old are you?

⁹And Jacob said to Pharaoh, The days of my pilgrimage are 130 years.ᵃ Few and evil have the days of my life been, and have not attained to the years of the life of my fathers in the days of their pilgrimages.

¹⁰And Jacob blessed Pharaoh⁽ᵇ⁾ and went out from him.

¹¹And Joseph prepared dwellings for his father and his brothers, and gave them landholdings in the land of Egypt, in the best of the land – even in the land of Rameses, as Pharaoh commanded. ¹²And Joseph made provision for his father, his brothers, and all his father's household, as young children are fed with food.

¹³There was no food in all the land, for the dearth was exceedingly sore, so that the land of Egypt and the land of Canaan were famished by reason of the dearth. ¹⁴And Joseph brought in all the money that was found in the land of Egypt and of Canaan as payment for the grain that the people bought, and he laid up the money in Pharaoh's house.

¹⁵When money failed in the land of Egypt and of Canaan, all the Egyptians came to Joseph and said, Give us sustenance! Why do you suffer us to die before you? For our money is spent. ¹⁶Then said Joseph, Bring your livestock, and I will give you food for your livestock, if you are without money. ¹⁷And they brought their livestock to Joseph. And he gave them food in exchange for horses, sheep, oxen, and donkeys; thus he fed them with food in exchange for all their livestock that year.

¹⁸When that year was ended, they came to him the next year and said to him, We will not hide it from my lord, that we have neither money nor livestock for my lord. There is no more left for my lord except our bodies and our lands. ¹⁹Why let us die before your eyes, and the land to come to naught? Buy us and our lands for food, and let both us and our lands be bond to Pharaoh. Give us seed so that we may live and not die, and so the land does not go to waste.

²⁰And Joseph bought all the land of Egypt for Pharaoh.⁽ᶜ⁾ For the Egyptians sold every man his land, because the dearth was sore upon them; and so the land became Pharaoh's. ²¹And Joseph appointed the people to the cities, from one side of Egypt to the other. ²²Only the land of the priests he did not buy, because Pharaoh made an ordinance for the priests to eat what was appointed to them, which Pharaoh gave them. Therefore, they did not need to sell their lands.

²³Then Joseph said to the folk, Look, I have bought you this day, and your lands, for Pharaoh. Take here seed, and go and sow the land. ²⁴And of the produce, you shall give the fifth part to Pharaoh. But four parts will be your own, for seed to sow the field, and for you, those of your households, and your children to eat. ²⁵And they answered, You have saved our lives! Let us find grace in the sight of my lord, and let us be Pharaoh's servants.

²⁶And Joseph made it a law over the land of Egypt to this day, that people must give Pharaoh the fifth part, except the land of the priests only, which was not bond to Pharaoh.

²⁷And Israel dwelt in Egypt in the region of Goshen. And they had their landholdings therein, and they grew and multiplied exceedingly. ²⁸Moreover, Jacob lived in the land of Egypt seventeen years, so that the whole age of Jacob was 147 years. ²⁹When the time drew near that

22 e.f. COV.

Israel must die, he sent for his son Joseph and said to him, If I have found grace in your sight, put your hand under my thigh,^d and deal mercifully and truly with me, and do not bury me in Egypt. ³⁰But let me lie by my fathers, and carry me out of Egypt and bury me in their burial place. And he answered, I will do as you have said. ³¹And he said, Swear to me! And he swore to him. And then Israel bowed himself to the head of the bed.

Ge 25:33

The Notes

a) 9. The days of his pilgrimage was all the time that he lived, as in Job 14:14.
b) 10. To bless is here to praise and give thanks, as before in Genesis 14:19.
c) 20. This name Pharaoh was a general name for all the kings of Egypt, just as Abimelech was a name common to all the kings of the Gentiles.
d) 29. To put his hand under his thigh: look in Genesis 24:2, etc., and note a.

Chapter 48

Jacob lies sick. He desires Ephraim and Manasseh for his sons and blesses them.

After these things, tidings were brought to Joseph that his father was sick. And he took with him his two sons, Manasseh and Ephraim. ²Then it was said to Jacob, Behold, your son Joseph comes to you.

And Israel took his strength unto him and sat up on the bed. ³And he said to Joseph, God Almighty appeared to me at Luz in the land of Canaan and blessed me, ⁴and said to me, Behold, I will make you grow and will multiply you, and will make a great number of people of you, and will give this land to you and to your seed after you for an everlasting possession. ⁵Now therefore, your two sons Manasseh and Ephraim, who were born to you before I came to you in Egypt, shall be mine; as Reuben and Simeon they shall be to me. ⁶And the children that you have after them shall be your own, but shall be called with the names of their brothers in their inheritances.

⁷And after I came from Mesopotamia, Rachel died upon my hand in the land of Canaan by the way, when I had but a field's breadth to go to Ephrath. And I buried her there in the way to Ephrath, which is now called Bethlehem.

⁸And Israel saw Joseph's sons and said, Who are these?

⁹And Joseph said to his father, These are my sons, which God has given me here.

And Israel said, Bring them to me, and let me bless them.

¹⁰And the eyes of Israel were dim for age, so that he could not see well. And Joseph brought them to him, and he kissed them and embraced them. ¹¹And Israel said to Joseph, I had not thought to have seen your face, and yet lo, God has shown it to me, and also your sons. ¹²And Joseph took them away from his lap, and they fell on the ground before him.

¹³Then Joseph took them both – Ephraim in his right hand toward Israel's left hand, and Manasseh in his left hand toward Israel's right hand – and brought them to him. ¹⁴But Israel stretched out his right hand and laid it upon the head of Ephraim, who was the younger,ª and his left hand upon Manasseh's head, crossing his hands, though Manasseh was the elder. ¹⁵And he blessed Joseph, saying, May God before whom my fathers Abraham and Isaac did walk, and the God who has fed me all my life long till this day, ¹⁶and the Angel that has delivered me from all evil, bless these lads, so that they may be called after my name and after my fathers Abraham and Isaac, and so that they may grow and multiply upon the earth.

¹⁷When Joseph saw that his father laid his right hand upon the head of Ephraim, it displeased him. And he lifted up his father's hand, to have removed it from Ephraim's head to Manasseh's head, ¹⁸and said to his father, Not so, my father; for this is the eldest. Put your right hand upon his head.

¹⁹And his father would not, but said, I know it well, my son; I know it well. He shall also be a people, and will be great. But of a truth, his younger brother will be greater than he, and his seed shall be full of people. ²⁰And he blessed them, saying, At the example of these sons, the Israelites will bless and say, May God make you as Ephraim and as Manasseh!

Thus he set Ephraim before Manasseh.

²¹And Israel said to Joseph, Behold, I am dying. And God will be with you and bring you again to the land of your fathers. ²²Moreover, I give to you a portion of land above your brothers, which I got out of the hands of the Amorites with my sword and with my bow.

Ge 46:3

Joh 4:5

The Notes

a)   14. The putting on of hands was commonly practised by the Hebrews when they committed or offered anything to God, as in Leviticus 1:4.

Chapter 49

> Jacob blesses all his own sons, and shows them what is to come. He appoints where he wishes to be buried, and dies.

And Jacob called for his sons and said, Come together, so that I may tell you what will befall you in the last days. ²Gather yourselves together and hear, ye sons of Jacob, and hearken unto Israel your father.

³Reuben, you are my eldest son, my might and the beginning of my strength, chief in receiving and chief in power. ⁴As unstable as water were you. You shall therefore not be chief, for you went up upon your father's bed, and then you defiled my couch with going up.

⁵The brothers Simeon and Levi, wicked instruments are their weapons. ⁶Into their secrets come not, my soul; and to their congregation, be not my honour joined! For in their wrath they slew a man, and in their self-will they houghed* an ox. ⁷Cursed is their wrath, for it was

Ge 29:32

Ge 35:22
1Ch 5:1

*That is, lamed it by cutting the sinews on the inside of the knee or ham.

strong, and their fierceness, for it was cruel. I will therefore divide them in Jacob and scatter them in Israel.

⁸Judah, your brethren shall praise you, and your hand shall be in the neck of your enemies, and your father's children shall bow down to you. ⁹Judah is a lion's whelp. From the prey, my son, you are come on high. He laid down and crouched himself as a lion and as a lioness. Who dares stir him up? ¹⁰The sceptre[a] shall not depart from Judah, nor a ruler from between his legs, until Shiloh comes, to whom the people will hearken. ¹¹He will bind his foal to the vine and his donkey's colt to the vine branch, and will wash his garment in wine and his mantle in the blood of grapes. ¹²His eyes are ruddier than wine, and his teeth whiter than milk.

¹³Zebulun shall dwell in the haven of the sea and in the port of ships, and shall reach to Sidon.

¹⁴Issachar is a strong donkey. He hunkered down between two borders, ¹⁵and saw that rest was good and that the land was pleasant, and bowed his shoulder to bear, and became a servant to tribute.

¹⁶Dan shall judge his people,[b] as one of the tribes of Israel. ¹⁷Dan shall be a serpent in the way and an adder in the path, and bite the horse's heels so that its rider shall fall backward. ¹⁸For your salvation I look, Lord!

¹⁹Gad, men of war shall invade him, and he shall turn them to flight.

²⁰From Asher comes fat bread,[c] and he shall give pleasures for a king.

²¹Naphtali is a swift doe, and gives goodly words.

²²That flourishing child Joseph, that flourishing child and fair to the eye; the daughters ran upon the wall. ²³The archers have envied him, and fought with him, and hated him. ²⁴And yet his bow stayed fast, and his arms and his hands were made strong by the hands of the mighty God of Jacob. From him shall come a herdsman, a rock in Israel. ²⁵Your father's God will help you, and the Almighty will bless you with blessings from heaven above, with blessings of the water that lies under, and with blessings of the breasts and of the womb. ²⁶The blessings of your father were great, even as the blessings of my elders, according to the desire of The Highest in the world. And these blessings shall fall on the head of Joseph, and on the top of the head of him that was separated from his brothers.

²⁷Benjamin is a ravishing wolf.[d] In the morning he shall devour his prey, and at night he shall divide his spoil.

²⁸All these are the twelve tribes of Israel. And this is that which their father spoke to them when he blessed them, every man with a separate blessing. ²⁹And he charged them and said to them, I am to be put unto my people. See that you bury me with my fathers, ³⁰in the cave that is in the field of Ephron the Hittite – in the double cave that is in the field before Mamre in the land of Canaan, which Abraham bought from Ephron the Hittite as a possession to bury in. ³¹There they

buried Abraham and his wife Sarah, there they buried Isaac and his wife Rebecca, and there I buried Leah – ³²which field, and the cave that is there, were bought from the children of Heth.

Ge 23:3-20
Ge 25:9,10

³³When Jacob had ended his directions to his sons, he pulled up his feet upon the bed and died, and was put unto his people.

Ac 7:15,16

The Notes

a) 10.*Sceptre* is here taken for royal power and dignity. Here is also prophesied the coming of Christ, as in Isaiah 9:6,7.
b) 16.Judge his people: that is, rule and govern them, as in Exodus 18:21-26.
c) 20.Fat bread: that is, plenteousness of the earth, as crops of grain, etc., with which he shall feed kings and all the people of the earth, as in Nehemiah 9:25.
d) 27.*Wolf* is here taken in a good sense, and signifies a fervent preacher of God's word, as was Paul, in whom this text is fulfilled.

Chapter 50

Jacob is buried. Joseph forgives his brothers the injury that they did to him. And he dies.

And Joseph fell upon his father's face, and wept upon him, and kissed him. ²And Joseph directed his servants who were physicians to embalm his father. And the physicians embalmed Israel ³forty days long; for so long does the embalming last. And the Egyptians bewept him seventy days.

⁴And when the days of weeping were ended, Joseph spoke to the house of Pharaoh, saying, If I have found favour in your eyes, speak to Pharaoh and tell him ⁵that my father made me swear, and said, Lo, I am dying; see that you bury me in the grave that I prepared for myself in the land of Canaan. Now, therefore, let me go and bury my father. And then I will come back.

Ge 47:29-31

⁶And Pharaoh said, Go, and bury your father as he made you swear to do.

⁷And Joseph went up to bury his father. And with him went all the servants of Pharaoh who were the elders of his house, all the elders of Egypt, ⁸all the house of Joseph, his brothers, and his father's house. Only their children and their flocks and herds did they leave behind them in the land of Goshen. ⁹And there went with him also chariots and horsemen, so that they were an exceedingly great company.

¹⁰And when they came to the field of Atad beyond the Jordan, there they made great and exceedingly sore lamentation. And Joseph mourned for his father seven days. ¹¹When the inhabiters of the land, the Canaanites, saw the mourning in the field of Atad, they said, This is a great mourning that the Egyptians make! For this reason, the name of the place is called Abel Mizraim,* which place lies beyond the Jordan.

Ec'us 22:12

*[ie, Mourning of the Egyptians]

¹²And his sons did for Israel as he had bid them. ¹³His sons carried

him into the land of Canaan and buried him in the double cave before Mamre, which Abraham had bought along with the field from Ephron the Hittite, to be a place to bury in. ¹⁴And Joseph returned to Egypt again, with his brothers and everyone who had gone up with him to bury his father, as soon as he had buried him.

¹⁵When Joseph's brothers saw that their father was dead, they said, Joseph might come to hate us, and reward back to us all the evil that we did to him! ¹⁶They sent therefore a word to Joseph, saying, Your father charged us before his death, saying, ¹⁷Thus shall you say to Joseph: Forgive, I pray you, the trespass of your brothers and their sin, for they rewarded you evil. Now, therefore, we pray you: forgive the trespass of the servants of your father's God.

And Joseph wept when they spoke to him.

¹⁸And his brothers came and fell before him and said, Behold, we are your servants.

¹⁹And Joseph said to them, Fear not, for am I not under God? ²⁰You thought to do me evil, but God turned it to good in order to bring to pass as it has happened this day, to save many people alive. ²¹Fear not, therefore. For I will care for you and for your children.

And he spoke kindly to them.

²²Joseph dwelt in Egypt, and his father's house also. And he lived 110 years. ²³And Joseph saw Ephraim's children, even to the third generation. And to Machir the son of Manasseh children were born, and they sat on Joseph's knees.

²⁴Then Joseph said to his brothers, I am dying. But God will surely visit you,ᵃ and bring you out of this land to the land that he swore to Abraham, Isaac, and Jacob. ²⁵And Joseph took an oath of the children of Israel and said,

God will not fail, but will visit you. See therefore
that you carry my bones from here. ²⁶And so
Joseph died when he was 110 years
old. And they embalmed him
and put him in a coffin
in Egypt.

♣

The Notes

a) 24. God will visit you: that is, he will remember you and deliver you out of the bondage that you shall be in under Pharaoh.

The end of the first book of Moses.

A Prologue upon the Book of Exodus

Below are excerpts from William Tyndale's prologue to Exodus, gently updated for today, with his advice on how to read this and all the books of the Pentateuch.

NOTE EVERYTHING EARNESTLY, as things pertaining to your own heart and soul. For as God was to the people of the Old Testament, so will he be till the world's end to us who have received his holy scripture and the testimony of his Son Jesus. As God does all things here for those who believe his promises and hearken to his commandments, and with patience cleave to him and walk with him, so will he do for us if we receive the witness of Christ with a strong faith and endure patiently, following his steps….

• Note how God is found true at the last, and how when all is past remedy and brought into desperation, then he fulfils his promises….

• Note also the mighty hand of the Lord: he plays with his adversaries and provokes them, and stirs them up a little and a little, and does not deliver his people in an hour, so that the patience of his elect and also the worldly wit and wily policy of the wicked, with which they fight against God, may appear….

• Mark the longsuffering and soft patience of Moses, and how he loves the people and is ever between the wrath of God and them…. Yet, do not make Moses a figure of Christ, but an example to all rulers and to all who are in authority, how to rule for God's pleasure and for their neighbour's profit…..

• Note also how God sends his promise to the people and Moses confirms it with miracles, and the people believe. But when trials come, they fall into unbelief and few remain standing. Here you see that not all are Christians who will be so called, and that the cross proves the true from the feigned. For if the cross were not, Christ would have disciples enough. From this you also see what an excellent gift from God true faith is, and impossible to be had without the Spirit of God. For it is above all natural power that a man in times of trial … could then believe steadfastly that God loves and cares for him….

• Of the ceremonies and sacrifices, and the tabernacle with all its glory and pomp, understand that … all was done to keep them from idolatry….

• Finally, God has two testaments: the old and the new. The old is those temporal promises that God made to the children of Israel for a good land … and for wealth, prosperity, and temporal blessings.… The Old Testament was built wholly on keeping the law and ceremonies, and the reward of keeping them was for this life only, as you read (Lev 18:5: A man who does them will live thereby). For neither the law nor ceremonies justified in the heart before God, nor purified for the life to come, insomuch that Moses at his death forty years after the law and ceremonies were given complains, saying, God has not given you a heart to understand, nor eyes to see, nor ears to hear (De 29:4)….

• The New Testament is those everlasting promises that are made to us in Christ the Lord, built on faith, not works. When this testament is preached and believed, the Spirit enters the heart and quickens it, and gives life, and justifies. The Spirit also makes the law a living thing in the heart, so that a person brings forth good works of his own accord without the compulsion of the law. ♣

The Second Book of Moses called
Exodus

Chapter 1

The children of Jacob are numbered. The new Pharaoh oppresses them. The acts of the godly midwives.

THESE ARE THE NAMES of the children of Israel who came to Egypt with Jacob, every man with his household: ²Reuben, Simeon, Levi, Judah, ³Issachar, Zebulun, Benjamin, ⁴Dan, Naphtali, Gad, and Asher. ⁵All the souls that came out of the loins of Jacob were seventy, and Joseph was in Egypt already. ⁶When Joseph was dead, and all his brethren and all that generation, ⁷the children of Israel grew, increased, multiplied, and became a great people, so that the land was full of them.

⁸Then there rose up a new king in Egypt, who did not know Joseph. ⁹And he said to his folk, Look, the people of the children of Israel are more and greater than we. ¹⁰Come, let us play wisely with them, lest they multiply, and then, if any war arises, they join themselves to our enemies and fight against us, and so get out of the land.

¹¹And he set taskmasters over them, to keep them under with burdens. And they built for Pharaoh storage cities: Pithom and Raamses. ¹²But the more the Egyptians afflicted them, the more they multiplied and grew, so that they abhorred the children of Israel. ¹³And the Egyptians held the children of Israel in bondage without mercy, ¹⁴and made their lives bitter to them with cruel labour in clay and brick, and all manner of work in the fields, and in all manner of service which they laid upon them cruelly.

¹⁵And the king of Egypt said to the midwives of the Hebrew women, of which the one's name was Sephora and the other Phua, ¹⁶When you do the office of a midwife for the women of the Hebrews and see in the birth time that it is a boy, kill it. But if it is a girl, let it live.

¹⁷Notwithstanding, the midwives feared God, and did not do as the king of Egypt commanded them, but saved the menchildren. ¹⁸Then the king of Egypt called for the midwives and said to them, Why have you done this, and saved the menchildren? ¹⁹And the midwives answered Pharaoh that the Hebrew women were not like the women of Egypt, but were sturdy women, and were delivered before the midwives got to them. ²⁰And God therefore dealt well with the midwives. And the people multiplied and grew very great. ²¹And because the midwives feared God, he made them houses.ᵃ

²²Then Pharaoh charged all his people, saying, All the menchildren that are born, cast into the river, and save the maidchildren alive.

Margin references: Ge 46:8-20; Ac 7:17; Ac 7:18,19

The Notes

a) 21. He made them houses: that is, he increased, multiplied, and made households of them, giving them both husbands and children.

Chapter 2

Moses is born and cast into the reeds. He is taken up by Pharaoh's daughter. He kills the Egyptian. He flees and marries a wife. The Israelites cry out to the Lord.

And a man from the house of Levi went and took a daughter of Levi, ²and the wife conceived and bore a son. And when she saw that it was a fine child, she hid him three months long. ³And when she could no longer hide him, she took a basket of bulrushes, daubed it with slime and pitch, laid the child in it, and put it in the reeds by the river's edge. ⁴And his sister stood afar off to see what would come of it.

⁵And the daughter of Pharaoh came down to the river to wash herself, while her maids walked along by the river's side. And when she saw the basket among the reeds, she sent one of her maids and caused it to be fetched. ⁶And when she had opened it, she saw the child; and behold, the baby was weeping. And she had compassion on it and said, It is one of the Hebrews' children.

⁷Then his sister said to Pharaoh's daughter, Shall I go and call for you a wet-nurse from the Hebrew women, to nurse the child for you? ⁸And the maiden ran and called the child's mother. ⁹Then Pharaoh's daughter said to her, Take this child away and nurse it for me, and I will reward you for your labour.

And the woman took the child and nursed it up. ¹⁰And when the child was grown, she brought him to Pharaoh's daughter, and he was made her son. And she called him Moses[a] – Because (said she) I took him out of the water.

¹¹And it happened in these days, when Moses had become great, that he went out to his brethren and looked on their burdens, and saw an Egyptian beating one of his brethren, a Hebrew. ¹²And he looked round about, and when he saw that there was no one nearby, he slew the Egyptian[b] and hid him in the sand. ¹³And he went out another day, and behold, two Hebrew men were fighting. And he said to the one who was doing the wrong, Why are you hitting your neighbour? ¹⁴And he answered, Who made you a ruler or a judge over us? Do you intend to kill me like you killed the Egyptian?

Then Moses feared and said, Of a surety, the thing is known! ¹⁵And Pharaoh heard of it, and went about to slay Moses. But he fled from Pharaoh and dwelt in the land of Midian.

And he sat down by a well's side. ¹⁶Now the priest of Midian had seven daughters, who came and drew water and filled the troughs to water their father's sheep. ¹⁷And the shepherds came and drove them away, but Moses stood up and helped them and watered their sheep. ¹⁸And when they returned to Reuel their father,[c] he said, How has it happened that you have come back so soon today? ¹⁹And they answered, There was an Egyptian who delivered us from the shepherds, and also drew water for us and watered the sheep. ²⁰And he said to his daughters, Where is he? Why have you left the man? Go and call him so that he may eat bread with us.

Margin references:
Ex 6:20
1Ch 6:17,18
Heb 11:23

Wis 18:5
Ac 7:20,21

Ac 7:22-28

Ac 7:29
Heb 11:24-27

*[ie, A Stranger There]
‡[ie, God of Help]

²¹And Moses was content to dwell with the man. And he gave to Moses his daughter Zipporah, ²²who bore a son. And Moses called him Gershom;* For he said, I have been a stranger in a strange land. And she bore yet another son, whom he called Eliezer,‡ saying, The God of my father is my helper, and has rid me out of the hands of Pharaoh. ²³And it happened in the process of time that the king of Egypt died. And the children of Israel groaned by reason of their labour, and cried out. And their complaint over their labour came up before God, ²⁴and God remembered his promise to Abraham, Isaac, and Jacob. ²⁵And God looked upon^d the children of Israel and knew them.

The Notes

a) 10. Moses is an Egyptian name, and it signifies drawn out of the water.
b) 12. He slew the Egyptian: that is, he declared himself to have such love for his brethren the Israelites, who were the people of God, that he would rather slay or be slain than that his brother should suffer wrong from the enemy of the Lord. In which act he also showed himself to be predestined by the Lord to be a defence and saver of the Israelites.
c) 18. This Reuel is not Jethro, but is the father of Jethro and the grandfather of Zipporah, and was also the priest of Midian. For it was a like order with them as it was with the Jews, that the son possessed the office of his father.
d) 25. Looked upon them: that is, he had pity and compassion over their sore labours, as in Deuteronomy 26:7.

Chapter 3

> Moses keeps sheep. God appears to him in a bush, and sends him to the children of Israel and to Pharaoh the tyrant.

Moses kept the sheep of Jethro his father-in-law, priest of Midian. And he drove the flock to the back side of the desert,ᵃ and came to the mountain of God, Horeb. ²And the Angel of the Lord appeared to him in a flame of fire out of a bush. And he perceived that the bush burned with fire but was not consumed. ³Then Moses said, I will go over and see this great sight, how it is that the bush is not burning up. ⁴And when the Lord saw that he came to see, he called to him out of the bush and said, Moses, Moses!

And he answered, Here am I.

⁵And he said, Come no closer, but put your shoes off your feet; for the place where you stand is holy ground.ᵇ ⁶And he said, I am the God of your father, the God of Abraham, the God of Isaac, and the God of Jacob.

And Moses hid his face, for he was afraid to look upon God.

⁷Then the Lord said, I have surely seen the trouble of my people who are in Egypt, and have heard their cry, which they have because of their taskmasters. For I know their sorrow, ⁸and have come down to deliver them out of the hands of the Egyptians, and to bring them out

of that land into a good and large land, and into a land that flows with milk and honey;[c] namely, into the place of the Canaanites, Hittites, Amorites, Perizzites, Hivites, and of the Jebusites. [9]Now therefore, behold, the complaint of the children of Israel has come unto me, and I have also seen the oppression by which the Egyptians oppress them. [10]But come, I will send you to Pharaoh so that you may bring my people, the children of Israel, out of Egypt.

[11]And Moses said to God, What? Am I to go to Pharaoh, and to bring the children of Israel out of Egypt?

[12]And he said, I will be with you. And this shall be a certain proof to you that I have sent you: after you have brought the people out of Egypt, you will serve God upon this mountain.

[13]Then said Moses to God, When I come to the children of Israel and say to them, The God of your fathers has sent me to you, and they say to me, What is his name? – what answer should I give them?

[14]Then said God to Moses, I WILL BE WHAT I WILL BE.[d] And he said, This shall you say to the children of Israel: I WILL BE did send me to you. [15]And God said further to Moses, Thus shall you say to the children of Israel: The Lord God of your fathers – the God of Abraham, the God of Isaac, and the God of Jacob – has sent me to you. This is my name forever, and this is my memorial throughout all generations. [16]Go, therefore, and gather the elders of Israel together, and say to them: The Lord God of your fathers, the God of Abraham, the God of Isaac, and the God of Jacob, appeared to me and said, I have been and seen both you and that which is done to you in Egypt. [17]And I have said it, that I will bring you out of the tribulation of Egypt into the land of the Canaanites, Hittites, Amorites, Perizzites, Hivites, and Jebusites, a land that flows with milk and honey.

[18]If it comes to pass that they hear your voice, then go, both you and the elders of Israel, to the king of Egypt, and say to him: The Lord God of the Hebrews has met with us; therefore, let us go three days' journey into the wilderness so that we may sacrifice to the Lord our God. [19]Notwithstanding, I am sure that the king of Egypt will not let you go, unless it be by a mighty hand. [20]Yea, and I will therefore stretch out my hand and smite Egypt with all my wonders, which I will do therein. And after that, he will let you go.[21]And I will get this people favour in the sight of the Egyptians so that, when you go, you will not go empty-handed; [22]but every wife will borrow from her neighbouress, and from the woman sojourning in her house, jewelry of silver and of gold, and clothing. And you shall put them on your sons and daughters, and shall rob the Egyptians.[e]

Ex 11:2,3; 12:35,36.

The Notes

a) 1. Desert: that is, in the wilderness, a place not inhabited.
b) 5. It is a custom of the scripture to call holy that which either the Lord chooses for himself or which is dedicated to the Lord, as in Ex. 22:29-31.
c) 8. By milk and honey is understood an abundance and plenteousness of all things that pertain to the comfort of man.

d) 14. I WILL BE WHAT I WILL BE: that is, I AM, as some do interpret it. Which is, I am the beginning and ending; by me you have all things, and without me you have nothing that is good. John 1:4.

e) 22. Rob the Egyptians: here you may not understand that they steal and therefore you may steal. But note that it was done at God's commandment, and therefore it was a just and righteous thing to be done. For he is not the author of evil.

Chapter 4

Moses receives signs of his calling and is sent into Egypt. His wife Zipporah circumcises her son. Aaron meets with Moses. Moses takes his leave of his father-in-law.

Moses answered and said, See, they will not believe me nor hearken to my voice, but will say, The Lord has not appeared to you. ²Then the Lord said to him, What is that in your hand? And he said, A rod. ³And the Lord said, Cast it on the ground. And it turned into a serpent, and Moses ran away from it. ⁴And the Lord said to Moses, Put forth your hand and take it by the tail. And he put forth his hand and caught it, and it became a rod again in his hand. ⁵The Lord said, By this they may believe that the Lord God of their fathers, the God of Abraham, the God of Isaac, and the God of Jacob, has appeared to you.

⁶And the Lord said furthermore to him, Thrust your hand into your bosom. And he thrust his hand into his bosom and took it out; and behold, his hand was leprous, even as snow. ⁷And he said, Put your hand into your bosom again. And he put his hand into your bosom again and pulled it out of his bosom; and behold, it was turned again like his other flesh. ⁸And the Lord said, If they will not believe you nor hear the voice of the first sign, yet they will believe the voice of the second sign. ⁹But if they will not believe the two signs nor hearken to your voice, then take of the water of the river and pour it on the dry land, and the water that you take from the river will turn to blood upon the dry land.

Jer 1:4-7

¹⁰And Moses said to the Lord, O my Lord! I am not eloquent; no, not in times past, and especially since you have spoken to your servant. But I am slow-mouthed and slow-tongued.

¹¹And the Lord said to him, Who has made man's mouth, or who has made the dumb or the deaf, the seeing or the blind? Have not I, the Lord? ¹²Go, therefore. And I will be with your mouth and teach you what you must say.

M't 10:19,20

¹³But he said, O my Lord, send, I pray you, whom you will.

¹⁴And the Lord was angry with Moses and said, I know Aaron your brother, the Levite; that he can speak. And moreover, behold, he is coming to meet you, and when he sees you, he will be glad in his heart. ¹⁵And you shall speak to him and put the words in his mouth, and I will be with your mouth and with his mouth, and will teach you what you must do. ¹⁶And he will be your spokesman to the people; he will be your mouth,ᵃ and you will be his god. ¹⁷And take this rod in your hand, with which you will do miracles.

¹⁸And Moses went and returned to Jethro his father-in-law again, and said to him, Let me go, I pray you, and return to my brethren who are in Egypt, so that I may see whether they are yet alive. And Jethro said to Moses, Go in peace. ¹⁹And the Lord said to Moses in Midian, return again into Egypt, for they are dead who went about to kill you.   M't 2:20

²⁰And Moses took his wife and his sons and put them on a donkey, and went again to Egypt, and took the rod of God in his hand.

²¹And the Lord said to Moses, When you have come into Egypt again, see that you do all the wonders before Pharaoh that I have put in your hand. But I will harden his heart, so that he will not let the people go. ²²And tell Pharaoh, thus says the Lord: Israel is my eldest son, ²³and therefore says to you, Let my son go, so that he may serve me. If you will not let him go, behold, I will slay your eldest son.

²⁴And it happened along the way, in a lodging place, that the Lord met Moses and would have killed him. ²⁵Then Zipporah took a sharp stone and circumcised her son, and fell at Moses' feet and said, A bloody husband you are to me! ²⁶And the Lord let him go. (She said a bloody husband because of the circumcision.)

²⁷Then the Lord said to Aaron, Go and meet Moses in the wilderness. And he went and met him in the mount of God, and kissed him. ²⁸And Moses told Aaron all the words of the Lord, which he had sent by him, and all the signs that he had charged him to do.

²⁹So Moses and Aaron went and gathered all the elders of the children of Israel. ³⁰And Aaron told all the words that the Lord had spoken to Moses and did the miracles in the sight of the people. ³¹And the people believed. And when they heard that the Lord had visited the children of Israel and had looked upon their tribulation, they bowed themselves and worshipped.[b]

The Notes

a) 16. He will be your mouth: he will speak for you. Compare Job 29:15.
b) 31. They bowed themselves: that is, gave thanks and praised the Lord.

Chapter 5

> Moses and Aaron go to Pharaoh. The people of Israel
> are oppressed more and more, and they cry out against
> Moses and Aaron for it.

Then Moses and Aaron went and told Pharaoh, Thus says the Lord God of Israel: Let my people go, so that they may keep holy day unto me in the wilderness. ²And Pharaoh answered, What fellow is the Lord, that I should hear his voice and let Israel go? I do not know the Lord,[a] neither will let Israel go.

³And they said, The God of the Hebrews has met with us. Let us go, we pray you, three days' journey into the desert, so that we may sacrifice to the Lord our God, lest he smite us either with pestilence or with sword.

⁴Then said the king of Egypt to them, Why do you – Moses and

Aaron – keep the people from their work? Get yourselves to your labour! ⁵And Pharaoh said furthermore, Look, there are many people in the land, and you make them play and let their work stand.

⁶And Pharaoh commanded the same day to the taskmasters over the people and to the officers, saying, ⁷See that you give the people no more straw to make brick with, as you did in time past. Let them go and gather straw for themselves. ⁸And charge them to make the same number of bricks that they used to make in time past, and subtract nothing from it. For they are idle, and therefore clamour, saying, Let us go and make sacrifice to our God! ⁹They must have more work laid upon them so that they may labour, and then they will not turn themselves to false words.

¹⁰Then the taskmasters of the people and the officers went out and told the people, saying, Thus says Pharaoh: I will give you no more straw, ¹¹but go yourselves and gather your straw where you can find it. Yet none of your output may be decreased.

¹²Then the people scattered abroad throughout all the land of Egypt to gather stubble to use instead of straw.

¹³And the taskmasters drove them onward, saying, Complete your work every day, just as when the straw was given to you! ¹⁴And the officers from the children of Israel, whom Pharaoh's taskmasters had set over them, were beaten. And it was said to them, Why have you not fulfilled your task in making brick, both yesterday and today, as well as in times past?

¹⁵Then the officers of the children of Israel went and complained to Pharaoh, saying, Why do you deal thus with your servants? ¹⁶There is no straw given to your servants, and yet they say to us, Make brick. And lo, your servants are beaten, and your people are wickedly treated.

¹⁷And he answered, Idle you are, idle! And therefore you say, Let us go and do sacrifice to the Lord. ¹⁸Go therefore, and work. For no straw will be given you. And see that you deliver still the full quota of brick.

¹⁹When the officers of the children of Israel saw themselves in a grievous dilemma (in that he said, You may subtract nothing from your daily quota of bricks), ²⁰then they met Moses and Aaron standing in their way as they came out from Pharaoh, ²¹and said to them, The Lord look to you and judge! For you have made us stink in the sight of Pharaoh and of his servants,ᵇ and have put a sword into their hands to slay us.

²²Moses returned to the Lord and said, Lord, why do you deal cruelly with this people? And why have you sent me? ²³For since I went to Pharaoh to speak in your name, he has dealt abominably with this folk, and yet you have not delivered your people at all

The Notes

a)   2.I know not the Lord: that is, I do not believe in him, nor have I anything to do with him. And even thus say all hardened hearts that have not the fear of the Lord before their eyes.

b) 21. You have made us stink in the sight of Pharaoh: that is, by your words and means all the wrath and displeasure of Pharaoh has been brought upon us, so that he utterly hates and abhors us.

Chapter 6

God promises deliverance of the Israelites, and to give them the land of Canaan. The genealogy of Reuben, Simeon, and Levi.

Then the Lord said to Moses, Now you shall see what I will do to Pharaoh. For by means of a mighty hand he will let the people go, and by a mighty hand he will drive them out of his land. ²And God spoke to Moses, saying to him, I am the Lord, ³and I appeared to Abraham, Isaac, and Jacob an almighty God; but in my name Jehovah,ᵃ I was not known to them. ⁴Moreover, I appointed to them the land of Canaan, to give them – the land of their pilgrimage, wherein they were strangers. ⁵And I have also heard the groaning of the children of Israel, because the Egyptians keep them in bondage, and have remembered my promise.

⁶Therefore, say to the children of Israel that I am the Lord, and I will bring you out from under the burdens of the Egyptians, and will rid you out of their bondage, and will deliver you with an outstretched arm and with great judgments.ᵇ ⁷And I will take you for my people and will be to you a God, and you will know that I am the Lord your God, who brings you out from under the burdens of the Egyptians. ⁸And I will bring you into the land over which I lifted up my hand,ᶜ to give it to Abraham, Isaac, and Jacob, and will give it to you for a possession; even I, the Lord.

A promise or a testament.

⁹And Moses told this to the children of Israel, but they did not listen to Moses because of their anguish of spirit and cruel bondage.

¹⁰And the Lord spoke to Moses, saying, ¹¹Go and tell Pharaoh king of Egypt to let the children of Israel go out of his land. ¹²And Moses spoke before the Lord, saying, But look, the children of Israel will not hear me; how then will Pharaoh hear me, seeing that I have uncircumcised lips?ᵈ

¹³And the Lord spoke to Moses and Aaron, and gave them a charge concerning the children of Israel and concerning Pharaoh the king of Egypt, to bring the children of Israel out of the land of Egypt.

¹⁴These are the heads of their fathers' houses:

The sons of Reuben, the eldest son of Israel, are these: Hanoch, Pallu, Hezron, Carmi. These are the householders of Reuben.

Ge 46:8-11
Ex 1:2
Nu 26:5-7
1Ch 5:1-6

¹⁵The sons of Simeon are these: Jemuel, Jamin, Ohad, Jachin, Zohar, and Shaul the son of a Canaanite wife. These are the kindreds of Simeon.

¹⁶These are the names of the sons of Levi in their generations: Gershon, Kohath, and Merari. And Levi lived 137 years. ¹⁷The sons of Gershon: Libni and Shimei in their kindreds. ¹⁸The sons of Kohath: Amram, Izhar, Hebron, and Uzziel. And Kohath lived 133 years.

Nu 3:14-39;
26:58-62.
1Ch 6:1-30;
23:3-24.

¹⁹The sons of Merari are these: Mahali and Mushi. These are the kindreds of Levi in their generations.

²⁰And Amram took Jochebed his niece as wife, who bore him Aaron and Moses. And Amram lived 137 years.

²¹The sons of Izhar: Korah, Nepheg, and Zichri.

²²The sons of Uzziel: Mishael, Elzaphan, and Zithri.

²³And Aaron took Elisheba, daughter of Amminadab and sister of Nahshon, as wife, who bore him Nadab, Abihu, Eleazar, and Ithamar.

²⁴The sons of Korah: Assir, Elkanah, and Abiasaph. These are the kindreds of the Korahites.

²⁵And Eleazar, Aaron's son, took as a wife one of the daughters of Putiel, who bore him Phinehas.

These are the principal fathers of the Levites in their kindreds. ²⁶And these are that Aaron and Moses to whom the Lord said, Carry the children of Israel out of the land of Egypt in their companies. ²⁷These are that Moses and Aaron who spoke to Pharaoh, king of Egypt, so that they could bring the children of Israel out of Egypt.

²⁸And in the day when the Lord spoke to Moses in the land of Egypt, ²⁹he spoke to him, saying, I am the Lord; see that you speak to Pharaoh the king of Egypt everything that I say to you.

³⁰And Moses answered before the Lord, I am of uncircumcised lips. How will Pharaoh then listen to me? *Look above in verse 12.*

The Notes

a) 3. Jehovah is the name of God by which no creature is named, and is as much as to say, one that is of himself and depends upon nothing.
b) 6. Judgments are here taken for the wondrous deeds of God, as here for his astonishing plagues, and as Psalm 35:22-26 and Psalm 118:12.
c) 8. To lift up the hand is to promise by an oath, as in Ge 14:22 by Abraham.
d) 12. To be of uncircumcised lips is to have a tongue that lacks skilful speech and lacks eloquence to set forth a matter.

Chapter 7

> The signs by which God will be known. The rod of Moses is turned into a serpent. The sorcerers do even the same. The waters are turned into blood.

And the Lord said to Moses, Behold, I have made you Pharaoh's god,ᵃ and Aaron your brother shall be your prophet. ²You must say everything that I command you, and Aaron your brother is to tell Pharaoh to send the children of Israel out of his land. ³But I will harden Pharaoh's heart, so that I may multiply my miracles and my wonders in the land of Egypt. ⁴And yet Pharaoh will pay no heed to you, so that I may set my hand upon Egypt and bring forth my hosts – even my people, the children of Israel – out of the land of Egypt, with great judgments. ⁵And the Egyptians will know that I am the Lord, when I have stretched forth my hand upon Egypt and have brought out the children of Israel from among them.

⁶Moses and Aaron did as the Lord commanded them. ⁷And Moses was 80 years old and Aaron 83 when they spoke to Pharaoh. ⁸And the Lord spoke to Moses and Aaron, saying, ⁹When Pharaoh speaks to you and says, Show a wonder, then say to Aaron: Take the rod and cast it before Pharaoh. And it will turn into a serpent.

¹⁰Then Moses and Aaron went in to Pharaoh and did just as the Lord had commanded. And Aaron cast forth his rod before Pharaoh and before his servants, and it turned into a serpent. ¹¹Then Pharaoh called for the wise men and enchanters of Egypt, and they did the same through their sorcery; ¹²they cast down every man his rod, and they turned into serpents. But Aaron's rod ate up their rods. ¹³And yet for all that, Pharaoh's heart was hardened, so that he paid them no heed, just as the Lord had said.

2Ti 3:8

¹⁴Then the Lord said to Moses, Pharaoh's heart is hardened, and he refuses to let the people go. ¹⁵Go to Pharaoh in the morning, for he will come to the water; and stand upon the river's edge, ready to meet him. And the rod that turned into a serpent, take in your hand. ¹⁶And say to him: The Lord God of the Hebrews has sent me to you, saying, Let my people go, so that they may serve me in the wilderness. But until now you would not hear. ¹⁷Therefore, thus says the Lord: Hereby you shall know that I am the Lord; behold, I will smite the waters that are in the river with the staff that is in my hand, and they will turn into blood. ¹⁸And the fish that are in the river will die, and the river will stink, so that it will grieve the Egyptians to drink the water of the river.

¹⁹And the Lord spoke to Moses: Say to Aaron, Take your staff and stretch out your hand over the waters of Egypt – over their streams, rivers, ponds, and all the pools of water – so that they may be blood, and so that there may be blood in all the land of Egypt, both in vessels of wood and also of stone.

²⁰And Moses and Aaron did just as the Lord commanded. And he lifted up the staff and smote the waters that were in the river, in the sight of Pharaoh and in the sight of his servants; and all the water that was in the river turned into blood. ²¹And the fish that were in the river died. And the river stank so, that the Egyptians could not drink of the water of the river. And there was blood throughout all the land of Egypt.

The first plague.

Ps 77:11-15; 105:26-29.

²²But the enchanters of Egypt did likewise with their enchantments, so that Pharaoh's heart was hardened and he did not regard them, as the Lord had said. ²³And Pharaoh turned and went home, and set not his heart upon this.ᵇ ²⁴And the Egyptians dug round about the river for water to drink because they could not drink the water of the river. ²⁵And this continued for a week after the Lord smote the river.

The Notes

a) 1. I have made you Pharoah's god: that is, I have made you Pharoah's judge, as in Exodus 22:28 [where *the gods* means *the judges*].

b) 23. He set not his heart thereon: that is, the danger moved him not at all, such as is plainly expressed in Isaiah 47:7.

Chapter 8

The plague of frogs. Moses prays for Pharaoh. The plagues of lice and flies.

Ex 7:16; 9:1; 10:3.

The Lord said to Moses, Go to Pharaoh and tell him, thus says the Lord: Let my people go so that they may serve me. ²If you will not let them go, behold: I will smite all your land with frogs. ³And the river will crawl with frogs, and they will come up and go into your house, and into your chamber where you sleep, and upon your bed, and into the houses of your servants, and upon your people and into your ovens, and upon the victuals that you have in store. ⁴And the frogs will come upon you, your people, and all your servants.

⁵And the Lord said to Moses, Say to Aaron: Stretch forth your hand with your rod over the streams, rivers, and ponds, and bring up frogs upon the land of Egypt. ⁶And Aaron stretched his hand over the water of Egypt, and the frogs came up and covered the land of Egypt.

The second plague.
Ps 105:30

⁷And the sorcerers did likewise with their sorcery, and frogs came up upon the land of Egypt.

⁸Then Pharaoh called for Moses and Aaron and said, Pray to the Lord to take away the frogs from me and from my people, and I will let the people go so that they may do sacrifice unto the Lord. ⁹And Moses said to Pharaoh, Appoint the time for me, when I should pray for you and your servants and your people, to drive away the frogs from you and your house so that they remain in the river only. ¹⁰And he said, Tomorrow. And Moses said, It will be just as you have said, so that you may know that there is none like the Lord our God. ¹¹And the frogs will depart from you and from your houses, and from your servants and your people, and will remain in the river only.

¹²And Moses and Aaron went out from Pharaoh, and Moses cried out to the Lord about the decree of frogs that he had made against Pharaoh. ¹³And the Lord did as Moses asked, and the frogs died out of the houses, courts, and fields. ¹⁴And the people gathered them together into heaps, and the land stank of them.

¹⁵But when Pharaoh saw that he was given respite, he hardened his heart and paid them no heed, as the Lord had said. ¹⁶And the Lord said to Moses, Say to Aaron: Stretch out your rod and smite the dust of the land, so that it may turn to lice in all the land of Egypt. ¹⁷And they did so. And Aaron stretched out his hand with his rod and smote the dust of the earth. And it turned to lice, both in man and beast, so that all the dust of the land turned to lice throughout all the land of Egypt.

The third plague.
Ps 105:31

¹⁸And the enchanters attempted with their enchantments likewise to bring forth lice, but they could not. And the lice were both upon man and beast. ¹⁹Then the enchanters said to Pharaoh, It is the finger of God.[a] Nevertheless, Pharaoh's heart was hardened, and he regarded them not, as the Lord had said.

²⁰And the Lord said to Moses, Rise up early in the morning and stand before Pharaoh, for he will come to the water. And say to him, thus says the Lord: Let my people go so that they may serve me. ²¹If

you will not let my people go, behold: I will send swarms of flies upon you and your servants and your people, and into your houses. And the houses of the Egyptians will be full of flies, and the ground they are on. ²²But that same day I will separate the land of Goshen, where my people are, so that no flies will be there, and so that you may know that I am the Lord upon the earth. ²³And I will put a division between my people and yours. And even tomorrow shall this miracle be done.

²⁴And the Lord did so, and there came noisome flies into the house of Pharaoh and into his servants' houses, and into all the land of Egypt, such that the land was marred with flies. *The fourth plague. Ps 105:31*

²⁵Then Pharaoh sent for Moses and Aaron and said, Go, and do sacrifice unto your God in the land!

²⁶And Moses answered, It is not meet so to do. For we must offer to the Lord our God that which is an abomination to the Egyptians. Look, should we sacrifice that which is an abomination to the Egyptians before their eyes? And would they not stone us? ²⁷We will therefore go three days' journey into the desert and sacrifice to the Lord our God, as he has commanded us.

²⁸And Pharaoh said, I will let you go so that you may sacrifice to the Lord your God in the wilderness. Only go not far away, and see that you pray for me.

²⁹And Moses said, Behold, I will go out from you and pray to the Lord, and the flies will depart from Pharaoh and from his servants and from his people tomorrow. But let Pharaoh deal deceitfully no more, so as not to let the people go to sacrifice to the Lord.

³⁰And Moses went out from Pharaoh and prayed to the Lord. ³¹And the Lord did as Moses had said, and took away the flies from Pharaoh, his servants, and his people, so that there remained not one. ³²But for all that, Pharaoh hardened his heart even then also, and he would not let the people go.

The Notes

a) 19. What the finger of God signifies is expounded in Luke 11, note b.

Chapter 9

The murrain of the beasts. The plague of boils and sores. The horrible hail, thunder, and lightning.

And the Lord said to Moses, Go to Pharaoh and tell him, thus says the Lord God of the Hebrews: Let my people go so that they may serve me. ²If you will not let them go, but will hold them still, ³behold: the hand of the Lord shall be upon your beasts that you have in the field – upon horses, donkeys, camels, oxen, and sheep – with a mighty great murrain. ⁴But the Lord will make a division between the beasts of the Israelites and the beasts of the Egyptians, so that nothing will die of all that belongs to the children of Israel.

⁵And the Lord appointed a time, saying, Tomorrow the Lord will do this thing in the land.

The fifth plague.

⁶And the Lord did the thing on the morrow, and all^a the beasts of Egypt died; but of the beasts of the children of Israel died not one. ⁷And Pharaoh sent to find out, and there was not one of the beasts of the Israelites dead. Notwithstanding, the heart of Pharaoh hardened, and he would not let the people go.

⁸And the Lord said to Moses and Aaron, Take your hands full of ashes out of the furnace, and let Moses sprinkle it up into the air in the sight of Pharaoh. ⁹And it will turn to dust in all the land of Egypt, and will make swelling sores with ulcers both on man and beast in all the land of Egypt.

The sixth plague.

¹⁰And they took ashes out of the furnace and stood before Pharaoh, and Moses sprinkled it up into the air. And there broke out sores with ulcers both in man and beast. ¹¹And the sorcerers could not stand before Moses, for there were boils on the enchanters and upon all the Egyptians. ¹²But the Lord hardened the heart of Pharaoh so that he paid them no heed, as the Lord had said to Moses.

¹³And the Lord said to Moses, Rise up early in the morning and stand before Pharaoh, and tell him, thus says the Lord God of the Hebrews: Let my people go so that they may serve me, ¹⁴or else I will at this time send all my plagues upon your heart, and upon your servants and on your people, so that you may know that there is none like me in all the earth. ¹⁵For now I will stretch out my hand and will smite you and your people with pestilence, so that you will perish from the earth.

Ro 9:17
Ps 47

¹⁶Yet indeed, for this very cause I have stirred you up: to show my power upon you, and to make my name known throughout all the world. ¹⁷If it be so, that you stop my people and will not let them go, ¹⁸behold: tomorrow this time I will send down a mighty great hail – even such a one as has not been in Egypt since it was founded to this time. ¹⁹Send, therefore, and fetch home your beasts and all that you have in the field. For the hail will fall upon all the people and beasts that are found in the field and not brought home, and they will die.

²⁰And as many as feared the word of the Lord among the servants of Pharaoh made their servants and their beasts flee to shelter. ²¹But those who did not regard the word of the Lord left their servants and their beasts in the field.

²²And the Lord said to Moses, Stretch forth your hand toward heaven, so that there may be hail in all the land of Egypt – upon man and beast, and upon all the plants of the field in the land of Egypt.

The seventh plague.

Ps 77:17,18
& 105:32-34.

²³And Moses stretched out his rod toward heaven, and the Lord thundered and hailed, so that the lightning ran along upon the ground. And the Lord so hailed in the land of Egypt ²⁴that there was hail and lightning mingled with the hail, so grievous that there was none such in all the land of Egypt since people had inhabited it. ²⁵And the hail smote in the land of Egypt everything that was in the field, both man and beast. And the hail smote all the plants of the field and broke all the trees of the field. ²⁶Only in the land of Goshen, where the children of Israel were, was there no hail.

²⁷And Pharaoh sent and called for Moses and Aaron, and said to them, I have now sinned. The Lord is righteous, and I and my people are wicked.ᵇ ²⁸Pray to the Lord that the thunder of God and hail may cease, and I will let you go, and you shall remain no longer.

²⁹And Moses said to him, As soon as I am out of the city, I will spread abroad my hands to the Lord. And the thunder will cease and there will be no more hail, so that you may know that the earth is the Lord's. ³⁰But I know that you and your servants do not yet fear the Lord God. ³¹The flax and the barley were smitten, for the barley was in the ear and the flax was in seed, ³²but the wheat and the rye were not smitten because they were late sown.

³³And Moses went out of the city from Pharaoh and spread abroad his hands to the Lord, and the thunder and hail ceased; neither did it rain any more upon the earth.

³⁴When Pharaoh saw that the rain and the hail and thunder had ceased, he sinned again and hardened his heart, both he and his servants. ³⁵Thus was the heart of Pharaoh hardened so that he would not let the children of Israel go, as the Lord had said by Moses.

The Notes

a) 6. This word *all* is not taken here for every single one, but for a great number, or of all sorts of the domestic animals.

b) 27. To be wicked is to be without the knowledge and sense of the goodness of God, and without hope to receive any goodness at his hand, so that we cannot patiently hear any of his truths, nor believe them, nor suffer them to be taught to others. As it appears in all the psalms and in Isaiah 57:20,21.

Chapter 10

The heart of Pharaoh is hardened by God. The grasshoppers. The thick darkness.

The Lord said to Moses, Go in to Pharaoh. Nevertheless, I have hardened his heart and the hearts of his servants so that I may show these my signs amongst them, ²and so that you may tell in the hearing of your children and your children's children of the spectacles that I have displayed in Egypt, and the miracles that I have done among them; so that you may know that I am the Lord.   Ex 4:1

³Then Moses and Aaron went in to Pharaoh and said to him, Thus says the Lord God of the Hebrews: How long will it be, before you will submit yourself to me? Let my people go so that they may serve me. ⁴If you will not let my people go, behold: tomorrow I will bring grasshoppers into your land. ⁵And they will cover the face of the earth so that it cannot be seen, and they will eat the rest of what remains to you, which escaped the hail, and they will eat all your green trees in the field. ⁶And they will fill your houses and all your servants' houses, and the houses of all the Egyptians, in such a manner as neither your fathers nor your fathers' fathers have seen since the time they were upon the earth to this day.   Ex 8:1; 9:1.

And he turned himself about and went out from Pharaoh.

⁷And Pharaoh's servants said to him, How long shall we be thus plagued? Let the people go so that they may serve the Lord their God. Will you not yet acknowledge that Egypt is destroyed?

⁸And then Moses and Aaron were brought again to Pharaoh, and he said to them, Go, and serve the Lord your God. But who are they that will go?

⁹And Moses answered, We must go with young and old; yea, and with our sons, with our daughters, and with our flocks and herds we must go. For we must hold a feast unto the Lord.

¹⁰And he said to them, Shall it be so? The Lord be with you; should I let you go, and your children also? Take heed, for you have some mischief in hand. ¹¹Nay, not so; but you who are men go and serve the Lord. For that was your request.

And they thrust them out of Pharaoh's presence.

¹²And the Lord said to Moses, Stretch out your hand over the land of Egypt for grasshoppers, so that they will come upon the land of Egypt and eat all the plants of the land, and everything that the hail left untouched. ¹³And Moses stretched forth his rod over the land of Egypt, and the Lord brought an east wind upon the land all that day and all night. And in the morning, the east wind brought the grasshoppers; ¹⁴and the grasshoppers went up over all the land of Egypt and lighted in all quarters of Egypt very grievously, such that before them there were no such grasshoppers, nor shall there be after them. ¹⁵And they covered all the face of the earth, so that the land was dark with them. And they ate all the plants of the land and all the fruits of the trees that the hail had left, so that there was no green thing left in the trees or plants of the field throughout all the land of Egypt.

The eighth plague. Ps 105:34, 35.

¹⁶Then Pharaoh called for Moses and Aaron in haste and said, I have sinned against the Lord your God and against you. ¹⁷Forgive me yet my sin only this once, and pray to the Lord your God that he may take away from me this death only.

¹⁸And Moses went out from Pharaoh and prayed to the Lord, ¹⁹and the Lord turned the wind into a mighty strong west wind. And it took away the grasshoppers and cast them into the Red Sea, so that there was not one grasshopper left in all the territory of Egypt. ²⁰But the Lord hardened Pharaoh's heart, so that he would not let the children of Israel go.

Ex 4:21

²¹And the Lord said to Moses, Stretch out your hand toward heaven, and let there be darkness upon the land of Egypt, even such that they may feel the darkness. ²²And Moses stretched forth his hand toward heaven, and there was a thick darkness upon all the land of Egypt three days long, ²³so that no man saw another, neither rose up from the place where he was, for three days. But all the children of Israel had light where they dwelt.

The ninth plague. Ps 105:28

²⁴Then Pharaoh called for Moses and said, Go and serve the Lord! Only let your flocks and your herds remain, but let your children go with you.

²⁵And Moses answered, You must give us also offerings and burnt offerings to sacrifice to the Lord our God. ²⁶Our beasts therefore must go with us, and not one hoof should be left behind, because we must take from them to serve the Lord our God. Moreover, we cannot know with what to serve the Lord until we get there.ᵃ

²⁷But the Lord hardened Pharaoh's heart so that he would not let them go. ²⁸And Pharaoh said to him, Get away from me! And take heed to yourself, that you see my face no more. For whenever you come in my sight, you shall die. ²⁹And Moses said, Let it be as you have said: I will see your face no more.

The Notes

a) 26. This was an outward service, but the true and right service of God is to fear him as a father, to love him, to keep his commandments, and to commit oneself wholly to him, trusting in his mercy only and setting all thought and care upon him. And when we have offended, to repent and to be sorry, and acknowledge our offence, and believe that he will forgive it to us for his truth's sake. 1 Peter 5:6,7 and Psalm 37:3-6.

Chapter 11

The Lord commands to rob the Egyptians. The death of all the first begotten in Egypt.

But the Lord had said to Moses, I will bring yet one more plague upon Pharaoh and upon Egypt, and after that he will let you go from here. And when he lets you go, he will utterly drive you away. ²But tell the people that every man should borrow from his neighbour, and every woman from her neighbouress, articles of silver and articles of gold. (³For the Lord had given the people favour in the sight of the Egyptians. Moreover, Moses was very great in the land of Egypt, both in the sight of Pharaoh and also in the sight of the people.) {vv1-4 e.f. VAR. Ex 3:19-22; 12:31,32. Ps 105:37,38} {Ec'us 45:1-3}

⁴So Moses said, Thus says the Lord: About midnight I will go out among the Egyptians, ⁵and all the firstborn in the land of Egypt shall die, even from the firstborn of Pharaoh, who sits on his seat,ᵃ to the firstborn of the maidservant who is in the mill, and all the firstborn of the domestic animals. ⁶And there will be a great cry throughout all the land of Egypt, such a one as there never was nor shall be. ⁷But among all the children of Israel, not a dog will move his tongue, nor yet man or beast, so that you may know that the Lord puts a difference between the Egyptians and Israel. ⁸And all these your servantsᵇ will come down to me, and fall before me and say, Get out, with all the people that are under you! And then I will depart. {Ex 12:29,30} {Ex 12:23-28}

And he went out from Pharaoh in a great anger. ⁹And the Lord said to Moses, Pharaoh will not regard you, so that many wonders may be wrought in the land of Egypt.

¹⁰And Moses and Aaron had done all these wonders before Pharaoh, but the Lord hardened Pharaoh's heart so that he would not let the children of Israel go out of his land.

The Notes

a)   5. To sit is to bear rule or to minister any kind of office, as in 1Ki 2:4.
b)   8. A sudden change of speaking to divers persons, as in Psalm 16. And this is referred to the end of the chapter that goes before.

Chapter 12

The Passover is eaten. The sweet bread. They must teach their children what the Passover signifies. The destruction of the first begotten in Egypt. The robbery of the Egyptians. The going out of the Israelites.

And the Lord spoke to Moses and Aaron in the land of Egypt, saying, ²This month shall be your chief month; it shall be the first month of the year to you. ³Speak to all the fellowship of Israel and say: Upon the tenth day of this month, let every householder take a lamb (or a kid). ⁴If the household be too few for a whole lamb,ᵃ then let him and the neighbour that is beside his house take it according to the number of souls, and share in the lamb according to what each person can eat. ⁵But it must be a lamb without spot and a male of one year old; and from among the lambs or the goats you must take it.

⁶And you must keep it in until the fourteenth day of the same month. And everyone of the congregation of Israel shall kill it about evening. ⁷And they shall take some of the blood and smear it on the two side posts and on the upper doorpost of the houses in which they eat it. ⁸And they shall eat the flesh that same night, roasted with fire; and with unleavened bread and with bitter herbs shall they eat it. ⁹See that you do not eat it raw or boiled in water, but roasted with fire – the head, feet, and all parts together. ¹⁰And see that you let nothing of it remain until the morning. If anything remains, burn it with fire.

¹¹In this manner shall you eat it: with your loins girded, shoes on your feet, and your staffs in your hands. And you shall eat it in haste, for it is the Lord's Passover.ᵇ ¹²For I will go about in the land of Egypt this same night and will smite all the firstborn in the land of Egypt, both of man and beast. And upon all the gods of Egypt I, the Lord, will execute judgment. ¹³But the blood will be for you a sign upon the houses where you are. For when I see the blood, I will pass over you, and the plague will not be upon you to destroy you when I smite the land of Egypt.

¹⁴And this day shall be for you a remembrance, and you must keep it holy unto the Lord. Throughout your generations after you, you must keep it a holy day, so that it is a custom forever.ᶜ ¹⁵Seven days shall you eat unleavened bread, so that the first day you shall put away leaven out of your houses. For whoever eats leavened bread from the first day until the seventh day, that soul shall be plucked out from Israel. ¹⁶The first day is to be a holy feast for you, and the seventh also. No manner of work is to be done in these days, except only as needed so that everyone may eat; that only may you do. ¹⁷And see that you keep

Margin notes: v3 e.f. COV. | Ex 13:6-10, Lev 23:6, Nu 28:16,17

to unleavened bread. For upon that same day, I will bring your hosts out of the land of Egypt. Therefore you must observe this day, and all your children after you, so that it is a custom forever.^c

¹⁸The fourteenth day of the first month, at evening, you shall eat sweet bread,* continuing till the twenty-first day of the month at evening again. ¹⁹Seven days long, see that there is no leavened bread found in your houses. For whoever eats leavened bread, that soul shall be rooted out from the multitude of Israel, whether he be a stranger or born in the land. ²⁰Therefore, see that you eat no leavened bread, but in all your habitations eat sweet bread.

*[Sweet bread; that is, unleavened bread]

²¹And Moses called for the elders of Israel and said to them, Choose out and take to every household a sheep, and kill the Passover. ²²And take a bunch of hyssop and dip it in the blood that is in the basin, and smear it upon the upper doorpost and on the two side posts. And see that none of you go out at the door of his house until the morning. ²³For the Lord will go about and smite Egypt; but when he sees the blood upon the upper doorpost and on the two side posts, he will pass over the door,^d and will not suffer the destroyer to go into your house to plague you. ²⁴Therefore, see that you observe this thing, so that it is an ordinance for you and your children forever. ²⁵And when you have come into the land that the Lord will give you, as he has promised, see that you keep this service. ²⁶And when your children ask you what manner of service this is that you do, ²⁷you shall say: It is the sacrifice of the Lord's Passover, who passed over the houses of the children of Israel in Egypt as he smote the Egyptians, but saved our houses.

Then the people bowed themselves and worshipped. ²⁸And the children of Israel went and did as the Lord had commanded Moses and Aaron.

²⁹And at midnight the Lord smote all the firstborn in the land of Egypt, from the firstborn of Pharaoh who sat on his seat to the firstborn of the captive that was in prison, and all firstborn of the animals.

The tenth plague.
Ps 105:36
Wis 18:5

³⁰Then Pharaoh arose the same night, and all his servants and all the Egyptians, and there was a great cry throughout Egypt; for there was no house where there was not one dead. ³¹And he called to Moses and Aaron by night, saying, Rise up, and get out from among my people, both you and also the children of Israel! And go, and serve the Lord as you have said. ³²And take your flocks and your herds with you, as you have said, and depart. And bless me also.*

*Look in note a on Ge 27.

³³And the Egyptians were fierce upon the people, and made haste to send them out of the land. For they said, We are all dead men!

³⁴And the people took the dough before it was soured, which they had in store, and bound it in cloths and put it upon their shoulders. ³⁵And the children of Israel had done as Moses had said, and had asked from the Egyptians articles of silver, articles of gold, and garments; ³⁶and the Lord got the people favour in the sight of the Egyptians, and so they borrowed from and robbed the Egyptians.

³⁷Thus the children of Israel took their journey from Rameses to

Succoth, 600,000 men on foot besides children. ³⁸And many common people also went with them; and of sheep, oxen, and livestock, exceedingly many. ³⁹And they baked sweet cakes from the dough that they brought out of Egypt, for it had not soured because they were thrust out of Egypt and could not tarry. Neither had they prepared for themselves any other provision of food.

v40 e.f. LXX and VAR. Gal 3:17.

⁴⁰The time that the children of Israel dwelt in (Canaan and) Egypt was 430 years. ⁴¹And when the 430 years were expired, even the very same day, all the hosts of the Lord departed out of the land of Egypt. ⁴²This is a night to be observed to the Lord, because he brought them out of the land of Egypt. This is a night of the Lord to be kept by all the children of Israel, and by their generations after them.

⁴³And the Lord said to Moses and Aaron, This is the manner of keeping Passover: no stranger may eat of it, ⁴⁴but all the servants that are bought for money you shall circumcise, and then let them eat of it. ⁴⁵A stranger and a hired servant may not eat of it. ⁴⁶In one house it must be eaten; you shall carry none of the flesh out at the doors. More-

Joh 19:36

over, see that you break not a bone of it. ⁴⁷All the congregation of the children of Israel shall observe this.

⁴⁸If a stranger dwells among you and wishes to keep Passover to the Lord, let him circumcise all the males, and then let him come and observe it, and be taken as one that is born in the land. No uncircumcised person shall eat of it. ⁴⁹One manner of law shall be for those who are born in the land and for the strangers that dwell among you. ᵉ

⁵⁰And all the children of Israel did as the Lord commanded Moses and Aaron. ⁵¹And that same day, the Lord brought the children of Israel out of the land of Egypt in their companies.

The Notes

a) 4. That which is here called a sheep is in Hebrew a word indifferently to be taken either for a sheep or a goat.

b) 11. The lamb was called the Passover in order that the very name itself should keep in memory what was signified thereby, which idiom and manner of speaking the scripture often uses, calling the sign by the name of the thing that it signifies, as in Genesis 16:13.

*[See note b on c15 for how the Hebrews indicate a true forever.]

c) 14,17. *Forever* is not here taken for a time without end, but for a long season whose end is not determined, as in Ge 13:15 and Ex 28:43.*

d) 23. *To pass over* is a manner of speech of the scripture, and signifies no more but that as he would plague the wicked, as he did here the Egyptians, so would he show mercy to the faithful, as he did to the Israelites. Exodus 33:19.

e) 49. Those who were born in the land are only those who were born among them, not descending of the stock or lineage of Israel. And the strangers were those who dwelt among the Israelites but were not born among them, as above in this same chapter at verse 19.

Chapter 13

The first begotten must be set apart for the Lord. The memorial of their deliverance. Why they were carried through the wilderness. The bones of Joseph. The pillar of the cloud.

And the Lord spoke to Moses, saying, ²Sanctify unto me^a all the firstborn that open all manner of wombs among the children of Israel, as well of men as of beasts; for they are mine. ³And Moses said to the people, Think on this day, in which you came out of Egypt and out of the house of bondage. For with a mighty hand, the Lord brought you out from there. See, therefore, that you eat no leavened bread. ⁴This day you came out of Egypt, in the month of Abib.* ⁵When the Lord has brought you into the land of the Canaanites, Hittites, Amorites, Hivites, and Jebusites, which he swore to your fathers that he would give you – a land where milk and honey flows – then see that you keep this service in this same month. ⁶Seven days you shall eat sweet bread, and the seventh day shall be a day of feasting unto the Lord. ⁷Therefore, you shall eat sweet bread during seven days. And ensure that there be no leavened bread seen, nor yet any leaven among you, in all your quarters.

⁸And you shall teach your son at that time, saying, This is done because of what the Lord did for me when I came out of Egypt. ⁹Therefore, it shall be a sign for you upon your hand and a reminder between your eyes, so that the Lord's law may be in your mouth. For with a strong hand the Lord brought you out of Egypt.* ¹⁰See, therefore, that you keep this observance in its season from year to year.

¹¹Moreover, when the Lord has brought you into the land of the Canaanites, as he has sworn to you and your fathers, and has given it to you, ¹²then you shall set apart for the Lord all that opens the womb, and all the firstborn among the beasts that you have, if they be males. ¹³And all the firstborn of the donkeys you shall redeem with a sheep; if you do not redeem it, then break its neck. But all the firstborn among your children you shall redeem. ¹⁴And when your son asks you in time to come, saying, What is this? – you shall say to him: With a mighty hand the Lord brought us out of Egypt, out of the house of bondage. ¹⁵And when Pharaoh was loathe to let us go, the Lord slew all the firstborn in the land of Egypt, as well the firstborn of man as of beasts. Therefore, I sacrifice to the Lord all the males that open the womb; but all the firstborn of my children I must redeem. ¹⁶And this shall be as a sign in your hand and as a thing hung up between your eyes, because the Lord brought us out of Egypt with a mighty hand.

¹⁷When Pharaoh had let the people go, God did not carry them through the land of the Philistines, though it was nearby. For God said, The people might have a change of heart when they see war, and turn back to Egypt. ¹⁸Therefore, God led them about through the wilderness that borders on the Red Sea.

The children of Israel went out equipped from the land of Egypt. ¹⁹And Moses took the bones of Joseph with him, for Joseph had made the children of Israel swear, saying, God will surely visit you; therefore, take my bones away from here with you. ²⁰And they took their journey

De 5:6

*That is, the month of April.

De 5:15

*Look in Ps 135:8,9.

Ge 50:24,25
Jos 24:32

from Succoth and pitched their tents in Etham, at the edge of the wilderness. ²¹And the Lord went before them in a pillar of cloud by day to lead them on the way, and by night in a pillar of fire to give them light, so that they could travel both by day and by night. ²²And the pillar of the cloud never departed by day, nor the pillar of fire by night, out of the people's sight.

Nu 14:13,14
1Co 10:1-4
Ne 9:12

The Notes

a) 2. Sanctify: set apart and dedicate. See Genesis 2:3 and note c.

Chapter 14

Pharaoh's heart is hardened. He follows the Israelites with all his host and captains, and is drowned. The Israelites grumble. They go through the Red Sea.

Then the Lord spoke to Moses, saying, ²Tell the children of Israel to turn and pitch their tents before the entrance of Pi Hahiroth, between Migdol and the sea toward Baal Zephon. Pitch just before there, by the sea. ³For Pharaoh will say of the children of Israel, They are entangled in the land; the wilderness has shut them in! ⁴And I will harden his heart so that he will follow after them, so that I may gain honour for myself over Pharaoh and over all his host, and the Egyptians may know that I am the Lord.

And the people did even so.

⁵And when it was told the king of Egypt that the people had fled, then Pharaoh's heart and all his servants turned against the people, and they said, Why have we done this, and let Israel go out of our service? ⁶And Pharaoh made ready his chariots and took his people with him, ⁷and took 600 chosen chariots and all the chariots of Egypt, and captains over all his people. ⁸For the Lord hardened the heart of Pharaoh king of Egypt, so that he pursued the children of Israel – who, for all that, went out openly.

Look in Psalm 136:11-15.

⁹And the Egyptians followed after them with all the horses and chariots of Pharaoh, and with his horsemen and his host, and overtook them where they pitched by the sea, just by the entrance of Pi Hahiroth before Baal Zephon. ¹⁰And Pharaoh drew near. And when the children of Israel lifted up their eyes and saw how the Egyptians followed after them, they were sore afraid and cried out to the Lord. ¹¹Then they said to Moses, Were there no graves for us in Egypt, but you must bring us away to die in the wilderness? Why have you served us thus, to carry us out of Egypt? ¹²Did we not tell you this in Egypt, saying, Let us be in rest and serve the Egyptians? For it would have been better for us to serve the Egyptians than to die in the wilderness.

¹³And Moses said to the people, Fear not, but stand still and behold how the Lord will save you this day. For as you see the Egyptians this day, so shall you see them no more forever till the world's end. ¹⁴The Lord will fight for you, and you will hold your peace.ᵃ

¹⁵The Lord said to Moses, Why do you cry to me?ᵇ Tell the chil-

dren of Israel to go forward. ¹⁶But you, lift up your rod and stretch out your hand over the sea, and divide it apart so that the children of Israel may go on dry ground through the middle of it. ¹⁷And behold, I will harden the hearts of the Egyptians so that they may follow you. And I will gain honour for myself over Pharaoh and over all his host – over his chariots and over his horsemen. ¹⁸And the Egyptians will know that I am the Lord, when I have gained honour for myself over Pharaoh, over his chariots, and over his horsemen.

¹⁹And the angel of God who was going before the host of Israel moved to go behind them. And the pillar of cloud that was before them moved to stand behind them, ²⁰and went between the host of the Egyptians and the host of Israel. It was a dark cloud, but gave light by night, so that all the night long one could not come at the other.

²¹When now Moses stretched forth his hand over the sea, the Lord carried away the sea with a strong east wind that blew all night, and it made the sea to be dry land, and the water divided itself. ²²And the children of Israel went in through the middle of the sea, upon the dry ground. And the water was as a wall to them, both on their right hand and on their left hand. ²³And the Egyptians followed and went in after them, into the middle of the sea, with all Pharaoh's horses and chariots and horsemen.

Job 26:12
J'th 5:10-13
Ps 77:11-20
Ec'us 39:16-18.

²⁴And in the morning watch, the Lord looked upon the host of the Egyptians out of the fiery and cloudy pillar, and he troubled their host, ²⁵and struck off their chariot wheels and cast them down to the ground. Then said the Egyptians, Let us flee from Israel, for the Lord is fighting for them against us! ²⁶Then the Lord said to Moses, Stretch out your hand over the sea, so that the water will come back again upon the Egyptians, upon their chariots and horsemen.

²⁷Then Moses stretched forth his hand over the sea, and it returned to its course early in the morning; and the Egyptians were fleeing toward it. Thus the Lord overthrew the Egyptians in the middle of the sea. ²⁸And the water returned and covered the chariots and the horsemen so that, of all the host of Pharaoh that went into the sea after the Israelites, there remained not one. ²⁹But the children of Israel went on dry land in the middle of the sea, and the water was as a wall to them, both on their right hand and also on the left.

The last plague.

³⁰Thus the Lord delivered Israel that same day out of the hand of the Egyptians, and Israel saw the Egyptians dead upon the sea side. ³¹And when Israel saw the mighty hand that the Lord had shown upon the Egyptians, they feared the Lord, and they believed both the Lord and also his servant Moses.

Isa 11:15,16

Ps 106:7-12

The Notes

a) 14. You will hold your peace: that is, you will be in rest and quietness.
b) 15. To cry to the Lord is to pray to him with full heart and fervent desire, as Moses here did and yet spoke never a word. And both the word *crying* and the making of noise so signify throughout all the psalms, as in Psalms 5:1-3 and 9:9-14.

Chapter 15

Moses and the people sing, with the women. At the prayer of Moses, the bitter waters were made sweet. God must be heard. They come to Elim.

Then Moses and the children of Israel sang this song to the Lord, and said: Let us sing to the Lord, for he is become glorious! The horse and him that rode upon it, he has overthrown in the sea! ²The Lord is my strength and my song, and is become my salvation. He is my God, and I will glorify him; he is my father's God, and I will lift him up on high.

³The Lord is a man of war; Jehovah is his name.ᵃ ⁴Pharaoh's chariots and his host he has cast into the sea; his jolly captains are drowned in the Red Sea. ⁵The deep waters have covered them; they sank to the bottom as a stone.

⁶Your hand, Lord, is glorious in power; your hand, Lord, has altogether dashed the enemy. ⁷And with your great glory you have destroyed your adversaries. You sent forth your wrath, and it consumed them, even as stubble. ⁸With the breath of your anger the water gathered together, and the currents stood still as a rock; the deep water stood solidly in the middle of the sea. ⁹The enemy said, I will follow and overtake them, and will divide the spoil; I will see my desire upon them; I will draw my sword, and my hand will destroy them. ¹⁰But you blew with your breath and the sea covered them, and they sank like lead in the mighty waters.

¹¹Who is like you, O Lord, among the gods? Who is like you, so glorious in holiness, fearful, laudable, and who shows wonders? ¹²You stretched out your right hand and the earth swallowed them. ¹³And you carried with your mercy this people whom you delivered, and brought them with your strength to your holy habitations.

¹⁴The nations heard and were afraid; pangs came upon the Philistines. ¹⁵Then the chiefs of the Edomites were amazed, and trembling came upon the mightiest of the Moabites, and all the inhabiters of Canaan were faint-hearted. ¹⁶Let fear and dread fall on them through the greatness of your arm, and let them be as still as a stone while your people pass through, O Lord – while the people pass through, whom you have gotten. ¹⁷Bring them in and plant them in the mountains of your inheritance – the place, Lord, that you have made to dwell in: the sanctuary, Lord, that your hands have prepared.

¹⁸The Lord reign ever and always!ᵇ ¹⁹For Pharaoh went in on horseback with his chariots and horsemen into the sea, but the Lord brought the waters of the sea upon them, and the children of Israel went on dry land through the middle of the sea.

²⁰And Miriam the prophetess, sister of Aaron, took a timbrel in her hand, and all the women came out after her with timbrels in a dance. ²¹And Miriam sang before them, Sing to the Lord, for he is become glorious indeed; he has overthrown the horse and his rider in the sea!

²²Then Moses brought Israel from the Red Sea, and they went out into the wilderness of Shur. But they traveled three days long in the wil-

Margin notes: Ps 118:6, Isa 12:2; Look in Job 40:6-24; J'th 5:13; J'th 5:14

derness and could find no water. ²³At last they came to Marah, but they could not drink of the waters for bitterness, for they were bitter. Therefore, the name of the place was called Marah.*

*[ie, Bitterness]

²⁴Then the people murmured against Moses, saying, What will we drink? ²⁵And Moses cried out to the Lord, and he showed him a tree branch; and he cast it into the water, and it became sweet.

There the Lord made them an ordinance and a law, and there he put them to the test, ²⁶and said, If you will hearken to the voice of the Lord your God, and will do that which is right in his sight, and will give an ear to his commandments and keep all his ordinances,ᶜ then I will put none of the diseases upon you that I brought upon the Egyptians. For I am the Lord your physician.

Ec'us 38:1-8, esp v5.

²⁷And they came to Elim, where there were twelve wells of water and seventy date trees. And they pitched there by the water.

Nu 33:9

The Notes

a) 3. Jehovah: look in Exodus 6:3 and note a thereon.
b) 18. To reign *ever and always* is a manner of speaking of the Hebrews and means without an end, whereas *[for]ever* by itself means a long time whose end is not appointed, and not for always, as in Ex 12:14 and note c.
c) 26. We must do that which is right in God's sight and as his word teaches us, and not follow our own imaginations.

Chapter 16

The Israelites come into the desert of Sin. They grumble. It rains quails and manna.

And they took their journey from Elim. And all the whole company of the children of Israel came to the wilderness of Sin, which lies between Elim and Sinai, on the fifteenth day of the second month after they had left the land of Egypt.

Nu 33:10,11

²But then the whole multitude of the children of Israel murmured against Moses and Aaron in the wilderness, ³and said to them, Would to God we had died by the hand of the Lord in the land of Egypt, when we sat by the meat pots and had bread to fill our bellies! For you have brought us out into this wilderness to kill this whole assembly with hunger.

⁴Then the Lord said to Moses, Behold, I will rain bread from heaven down to you. And let the people go out and gather it day by day, so that I may prove them, whether they will walk in my law or not. ⁵On the sixth day, let them prepare what they bring in, and let it be twice as much as they gather in daily.

⁶And Moses and Aaron said to all the children of Israel, At evening you will know that it is the Lord who brought you out of the land of Egypt, ⁷and in the morning you will see the glory of the Lord,ᵃ because he has heard your grudging against the Lord. For what are we, that you should murmur against us? ⁸And moreover, Moses said, At evening the Lord will give you flesh to eat, and in the morning bread

enough, because the Lord has heard your murmuring against him. For what are we? Your murmuring is not against us, but against the Lord.

⁹And Moses spoke to Aaron, Say to all the company of the children of Israel: Come forth before the Lord, for he has heard your complaints. ¹⁰And as Aaron was speaking to the whole company of the children of Israel, they looked toward the wilderness, and behold, the glory of the Lord appeared in a cloud. ¹¹And the Lord spoke to Moses, saying, ¹²I have heard the murmuring of the children of Israel. Tell them therefore, and say, that at evening they will eat flesh, and in the morning they will be filled with bread; and you will know that I am the Lord your God.

¹³And at evening quails came, and they covered the ground where the tents lay. And in the morning dew lay round about the host. ¹⁴And when the dew was fallen, behold, it lay upon the ground in the wilderness, small and round and thin, like hoar frost on the ground. ¹⁵When the children of Israel saw it, they said to one another, What is this? For they did not know what it was. And Moses said, This is the bread that the Lord has given you to eat. ¹⁶This is the thing which the Lord has commanded: that you shall gather for each person enough for him to eat – every man to gather a gomer* full for each person in his tent.

¹⁷And the children of Israel did so, and gathered some more, some less, ¹⁸and measured it with a gomer. And to him who had gathered much, nothing remained over, and to him who had gathered little, there was no lack;‡ but each had gathered sufficient for his need.

¹⁹And Moses said to the people, See that no one lets anything remain of it until the morning. ²⁰Notwithstanding, they did not heed Moses, but some of them left part of it until the morning, and it grew full of worms and stank. And Moses was angry with them.

²¹And they gathered it every morning, everyone as much as sufficed for him to eat; for as soon as the heat of the sun* came, it melted. ²²And on the sixth day they gathered twice as much bread: two gomers for one person. And the heads of the people came and told Moses. ²³And he said to them, This is what the Lord has said: Tomorrow is the Sabbath of the holy rest of the Lord. Bake what you will bake and fetch what you will fetch, and that which remains, lay up for yourselves and keep it till the morning.

²⁴And they laid it up till the morning as Moses bade, and it did not stink; neither were there any worms in it. ²⁵And Moses said, Eat that this day, for today it is the Lord's Sabbath. Today you will find none in the field. ²⁶Six days you shall gather it, for the seventh is the Sabbath; there will be none in that day.

²⁷Notwithstanding, some of the people went out in the seventh day to gather; but they found nothing. ²⁸Then the Lord said to Moses, How long will it be before you keep my commandments and laws? ²⁹See, because the Lord has given you a Sabbath, therefore he gives you on the sixth day enough bread for two days. Stay, therefore, everyone at home, and let no one go out of his place on the seventh day.

Margin references:

Ps 78:18-29; 105:40. Wis 16:20

1Co 10:1-3

*[A gomer (or omer): a dry measure of about five pints. Also, a pot holding this measure]

‡2Co 8:15

*Ge 18:1 (the heat of the day) & note a.

Eze 20:10-12

³⁰And the people rested on the seventh day. ³¹And the house of Israel called the bread manna. And it was like coriander seed, and white, and the taste of it was like wafers made with honey.

³²And Moses said, This is what the Lord commands: fill a gomer with it so that it may be kept for your children after you, so they may see the bread with which he fed you in the wilderness, when he had brought you out of the land of Egypt. ³³And Moses spoke to Aaron: Take a pot and put a gomer full of manna in it, and lay it up before the Lord to be kept for your children after you, ³⁴as the Lord commanded Moses. And Aaron laid it up before the testimony, to be kept there.

³⁵And the children of Israel ate manna for forty years, until they came to an inhabited land. And so they ate manna until they came to the borders of the land of Canaan.

³⁶And a gomer is the tenth part of an ephah.

Nu 11:7-9

Ne 9:20,21
J'th 5:13-15

The Notes

a) 7. The glory of the Lord is here taken for the brightness and light that was seen in the cloud, of which glory the apostle makes mention in 2Co 3.

Chapter 17

The Israelites come into Rephidim. They complain. Water is given them out of the rock. Moses holds up his hands and they overcome the Amalekites.

And all the company of the children of Israel went on their journey from the wilderness of Sin at the commandment of the Lord. And they pitched in Rephidim, where there was no water for the people to drink. ²And the people complained loudly against Moses, and said, Give us water to drink! And Moses said to them, Why do you quarrel with me, and why do you tempt the Lord?ᵃ ³But the people thirsted for water there, and murmured against Moses and said, Why have you brought us out of Egypt, to kill us and our children and our animals with thirst?

⁴And Moses cried out to the Lord, saying, What can I do for this people? They are almost ready to stone me!

⁵The Lord said to Moses, Go before the people, and take with you some of the elders of Israel. And take in your hand the rod with which you smote the river, and go. ⁶Behold, I will stand there before you, upon a rock in Horeb; and you shall strike the rock, and water will come out of it so that the people may drink. And Moses did this before the elders of Israel. ⁷And he called the name of the place Massah* and Meribah,‡ because of the contentions of the children of Israel, and because they tempted the Lord, saying, Is the Lord among us or not?

⁸Then Amalek came, and he fought with Israel in Rephidim. ⁹And Moses said to Joshua, Choose out men, and go to fight with Amalek. Tomorrow I will stand on the top of the hill with the rod of God in my hand.

¹⁰And Joshua did as Moses bade him, and fought with the Amalekites. And Moses, Aaron, and Hur went up to the top of the hill.

Nu 20:7-11
Ps 78:15
1Co 10:4
Wis 11:4

*[That is, Temptation]
‡[That is, Contention]

¹¹And when Moses held up his hand, Israel had the better, but when he let his hand down, Amalek had the better.

¹²When Moses' arms were weary, they took a stone and put it under him, and he sat down on it. And Aaron and Hur supported his hands – one on the one side and the other on the other side – and his hands were steady until the sun was down. ¹³And Joshua defeated Amalek and his people with the edge of his sword. ¹⁴And the Lord said to Moses, Write this for a record in a book, and tell it to Joshua. For I will put out the remembrance of Amalek from under heaven.

¹⁵And Moses made an altar and called the name of it Jehovah Nissi.* ¹⁶For he said, The hand is on the seat of the Lord, that the Lord will have war with Amalek throughout all generations.

Wis 11:3

De 25:19

*That is, The Lord Is He That Exalts.

The Notes

a) 2. To tempt the Lord is to provoke him to be angry with them, as in Wisdom 1:2,3,10,11 [ie, in the apocryphal book Wisdom of Solomon].

Chapter 18

Jethro's counsel is accepted by Moses.

Jethro the priest of Midian, Moses' father-in-law, heard of all that God had done for Moses and for Israel his people – how the Lord had brought Israel out of Egypt. ²And he took Zipporah, Moses' wife, after she had been sent back, ³and her two sons – of which one was called Gershom* (for he said, I have been a stranger in a strange land), ⁴and the other was called Eliezer‡ (for he said, The God of my father was my help, and delivered me from the sword of Pharaoh) – ⁵and Moses' father-in-law Jethro went with his two sons and his wife to Moses in the wilderness, where he had pitched his tent by the mount of God. ⁶And he sent word to Moses: I, your father-in-law Jethro, have come to you, and your wife also, and her two sons with her.

*Ex 2:22; 4:20.
‡[ie, God of Help]

⁷And Moses went out to meet his father-in-law, and bowed and kissed him. And they greeted each other and went into the tent. ⁸And Moses told his father-in-law all that the Lord had done to Pharaoh and the Egyptians for Israel's sake, and all the travail that had happened to them along the way, and how the Lord had delivered them. ⁹And Jethro rejoiced over all the good that the Lord had done to Israel, and because he had delivered them out of the hand of the Egyptians. ¹⁰And Jethro said, Blessed be the Lord who has delivered you out of the hand of the Egyptians and out of the hand of Pharaoh – who has delivered his people from under the power of the Egyptians. ¹¹Now I know that the Lord is greater than all gods, since they dealt proudly with them.

¹²And Jethro, Moses' father-in-law, offered burnt offerings and sacrifices to God. And Aaron and all the elders of Israel came to eat bread with Moses' father-in-law before God.

¹³And it chanced, on the morrow, that Moses sat to judge the people; and the people stood around Moses from morning till evening. ¹⁴When his father-in-law saw all that he did for the people, he said,

What is this that you do for the people? Why do you sit by yourself, and let all the people stand around you from morning till evening?

¹⁵And Moses said to his father-in-law, Because the people come to me to seek counsel of God. ¹⁶For when they have a matter, they come to me, and I must judge between each person and his neighbour, and must show them the ordinances of God and his laws.

¹⁷And his father-in-law said to him, It is not good, what you do. ¹⁸You do unwisely, and also this people that is with you, because the thing is too burdensome for you, and you are not able to do it yourself alone. ¹⁹But hear my voice and I will give you counsel, and God will be with you. Be for the people before God, and bring their causes to God, ²⁰and provide for them ordinances and laws, and show them the way in which they must walk and the works they must do. ²¹But also seek out among the people able men who fear God, and men who are true and hate covetousness,ª and make them heads over the people: officers over thousands, over hundreds, over fifty, and over ten. ²²And let them judge the people at all seasons.* If there be any great matter, let them bring that to you, but let them judge all the small causes themselves; and ease yourself, and let them bear the burden with you. ²³If you do this thing, then you will be able to endure what God has charged you with, and all this people may go home quietly.

²⁴And Moses heard the voice of his father-in-law and did all that he had said. ²⁵And he chose able men out of all Israel and made them heads over the people: officers over thousands, over hundreds, over fifty, and over ten. ²⁶And they judged the people at all seasons, and brought the hard causes to Moses, but judged all the small matters themselves.

²⁷And then Moses let his father-in-law depart, and he went into his own land.

De 1:9-18

*To judge: look in Ge 49:16 and note b thereon.

The Notes

a) 21. Able men who fear God, and who are true and hate covetousness: these are the personal qualities that judges should have.

Chapter 19

> The children of Israel come to the mount Sinai. The people of God are holy and a royal priesthood. He who touches the mount dies. God appears to Moses upon the mount in thunder and lightning.

The third month after the children of Israel left Egypt, that same day they came into the wilderness of Sinai. ²For they had departed from Rephidim, and had come to the desert of Sinai and pitched their tents in the wilderness. And there Israel pitched before the mount.

³And Moses went up to God, and the Lord called to him out of the mountain, saying, Thus say to the house of Jacob, and tell the children of Israel: ⁴You have seen what I did to the Egyptians, and how I took you up upon eagles' wings and have brought you unto myself. ⁵Now, therefore, if you will hear my voice and keep that which I appoint, you

Nu 33:15

shall be my own above all nations. For all the earth is mine. ⁶You shall be unto me a kingdom of priests and a holy people. These are the words that you must speak to the children of Israel.

1Pe 2:9

⁷And Moses went and called for the elders of Israel, and laid before them all these words that the Lord had commanded him. ⁸And the people answered all together and said, All that the Lord has said, we will do. And Moses brought the words of the people to the Lord. ⁹And the Lord said to Moses, Lo, I will come to you in a thick cloud, so that the people can hear when I talk with you, and also believe you forever. And so Moses told the words of the people to the Lord. ¹⁰And the Lord said to Moses, Go to the people, and sanctify[a] them today and tomorrow; and let them wash their clothes, ¹¹so that they may be ready by the third day. For on the third day, the Lord will come down in the sight of all the people upon Mount Sinai. ¹²And set marks round about the people and say: Beware that you go not up into the mount, and that you touch not touch the borders of it. For whoever touches the mount will surely die. ¹³Not a hand may touch it, but that he shall either be stoned or else shot through; whether it be beast or man, it shall not live. When the horn blows, then let them come up into the mountain.

Heb 12:18-20.

¹⁴And Moses went down from the mount to the people and sanctified them, and they washed their clothes. ¹⁵And he said to the people, Be ready for the third day, and see that you come not at your wives.[b]

¹⁶And the third day, in the morning, there was thunder and lightning, and a thick cloud upon the mount. And the cry of the horn was exceedingly loud, and all the people that were in the host were afraid. ¹⁷And Moses brought the people out of the tents to meet with God, and they stood at the foot of the mountain.

¹⁸And Mount Sinai was altogether on a smoke, because the Lord descended down upon it in fire. And the smoke of it ascended up like the smoke of a kiln, and all the mount was exceedingly fearful. ¹⁹And the voice of the horn blew, and grew louder and louder.

Moses spoke, and God answered him – and that with a voice. ²⁰And the Lord came down upon Mount Sinai, even to the top of the hill, and called Moses up to the top of the mount. And Moses went up. ²¹And the Lord said to Moses, Go down and warn the people not to press up toward the Lord to see him, and thus many of them perish. ²²And let the priests also who come into the Lord's presence sanctify themselves, lest the Lord smite them.

²³Then Moses said to the Lord, The people cannot come up into Mount Sinai because you directed us, saying, Set marks around the mount and sanctify it.

²⁴And the Lord said to him, Away, and go down! And come up again, both you and Aaron with you. But let not the priests and the people presume to come up to the Lord, lest he smite them.

²⁵And Moses went down to the people and told them.

The Notes

a) 10. To sanctify them is here to purge and cleanse them from the dirt of both their body and garments, as in this same chapter at verses 14 and 22. See also chapter 31:13 and note a.

b) 15. Come not at your wives: that is, when you will serve the Lord, you must put away from you all lusts and fleshly concupiscence, giving yourself wholly to prayer and abstinence, as Paul teaches in 1Corinthians 7:29 that those who have wives should be as though they had none.

Chapter 20

The Ten Commandments are given. The altar of earth.

And God spoke all these words and said, ²I am the Lord your God, who has brought you out of the land of Egypt and out of the house of bondage. ³You shall have no other gods in my sight. ⁴You shall make yourself no graven image, nor any likeness of anything that is in heaven above or in the earth beneath, nor in the water that is beneath the earth. ⁵See that you neither bow yourself down to them nor serve them. For I, the Lord your God, am a jealous God,ᵃ and visit the sin of the fathers upon the children to the third and fourth generation of those who hate me; ⁶and yet show mercy to thousands among those who love me and keep my commandments.

⁷You shall not take the name of the Lord your God in vain, for the Lord will not hold guiltless him who takes his name in vain.

⁸Remember the Sabbath day, to keep it holy. ⁹Six days you may labour and do all that you have to do, ¹⁰but the seventh day is the Sabbath of the Lord your God. In it you shall do no kind of work: neither you nor your son nor your daughter, neither your manservant nor your maidservant, neither your beasts, neither yet the stranger who is within your gates. ¹¹For in six days the Lord made heaven and earth and the sea, and everything that is in them, and rested on the seventh day. On this account the Lord blessed the Sabbath day, and hallowed it.

¹²Honour your father and your mother, so that your days may be long in the land which the Lord your God gives you.ᵇ

¹³You shall not kill.

¹⁴You shall not break wedlock.

¹⁵You shall not steal.

¹⁶You shall bear no false witness against your neighbour.

¹⁷You shall not covet your neighbour's house. Neither shall you covet your neighbour's wife, his manservant, his maid, his ox, his donkey, or anything that is his.

¹⁸And all the people saw the thunder and the lightning, and the noise of the horn, and how the mountain smoked. And when the people saw it, they moved away and stood afar off. ¹⁹And they said to Moses, You talk with us, and we will hear. But let not God talk with us, lest we die.

²⁰And Moses said to the people, Fear not, for God has come to prove you, and so that his fear may be among you, so you do not sin.

²¹And the people stood afar off, and Moses went into the thick cloud where God was. ²²And the Lord said to Moses, Thus must you speak to the children of Israel: You have seen how I have spoken with

Marginal references: De 5:6-10; Ps 81:8-10; Lev 26:1; Ps 97:7-9. De 5:11-15; Lev 26:2. De 5:16-21. De 5:22-26; 18:16. Heb 12:18-21.

you from out of heaven. ²³You shall not make, therefore, alongside me, gods of silver or gods of gold. In no case shall you do it. ²⁴An altar of earth you shall make for me, and offer on it your burnt offerings and your peace offerings, and your sheep and your oxen. And in all the places where I will put the remembrance of my name, there I will come to you and bless you. ²⁵But if you wish to make me an altar of stone, see that you do not make it of hewed stone; for if you lift up your tool upon it, you will pollute it. ²⁶Moreover, you must not go up on steps to my altar, so that your nakedness may not be exposed there.

Margin: De 27:5 / Jos 8:31 / Ge 12:7,8

The Notes

a) 5. I am jealous: that is, I am the Lord who watches and looks narrowly upon your wickedness, and will punish it strictly; and again, who fervently loves your godliness, and will reward it abundantly.

b) 12. To honour father and mother is not only to show obedience to them, but also to help them in their old age if they are poor and needy. Eph 6:1-3, Col 3:20, Mk 7:10-13, Ro 13:9, 1Ti 5:3-8.

Chapter 21

Temporal and civil ordinances.

These are the laws that you shall set before you:

²If you buy a Hebrew servant, he shall serve for six years, and the seventh he shall go out free, paying nothing. ³If he came alone, he shall go out alone. If he came married, his wife shall go out with him. ⁴And if his master has given him a wife and she has borne him sons or daughters, then the wife and her children shall be her master's, and he shall go out alone. ⁵But if the servant says, I love my master and my wife and my children; I do not wish to go out free – ⁶then let his master bring him before the gods,ᵃ and set him at the door or the doorpost and bore his ear through with an awl; and let him be his servant forever.

⁷If a man sells his daughter to be a servant, she shall not go out as the menservants do. ⁸If she does not please her master, so that he gave her to no man as wife, then he shall let her go free. To sell her to a strange nation he shall have no power, because he judged her unworthy. ⁹If he has promised her to his son as wife, he shall deal with her as men do with their daughters. ¹⁰If he takes another wife for his son, still her food, raiment, and lodging he must not diminish.* ¹¹If he does not provide these three things for her, then she shall go out free and pay no money.

¹²He who strikes a person so that he dies shall be slain for it. ¹³ If a man does not lie in wait, but God delivers the deceased into his hand, then I will appoint to you a place where he may flee to. ¹⁴But if a man comes presumptuously upon his neighbour and slays him with guile, you shall take him from my altar, and he shall die. ¹⁵And he who strikes his father or his mother shall die for it.¹⁶He who steals a man and sells him (if it is proved against him) shall be slain for it. ¹⁷And he who curses his father or mother shall be put to death for it.

Margin notes:
Laws.
De 15:12-18 / Jer 34:13,14 / Lev 25:39-42
[Bore with an awl: see De 15:17 and note b]
[ie, because these three things are due to her by reason of the promised marriage to the son]
Nu 35:11, 15-28. De 19:1-13 / Jos 20:1-9
Lev 20:9 / Pr 20:20 / M't 15:4 / Mk 7:10

¹⁸If men fight together, and one strikes another with a stone or with his fist so that he does not die, but is bedridden, ¹⁹if he rises again and walks outdoors upon his staff, then he who hurt him shall be quit, save only that he shall pay for the loss of his time while he lay in bed, and shall pay for his care.

²⁰If a man strikes his servant or his maid with a staff and they die under his hand, it shall be punished. ²¹But if they continue a day or two, it shall not be avenged, for it is his money.

²²When men fight and hurt a woman with child so that her fruit departs from her, and yet no misfortune follows, then the offender shall be fined according to what the woman's husband lays to his charge, and he shall pay as the arbitrators appoint him. ²³But if any misfortune follows, then he shall pay life for life, ²⁴eye for eye, tooth for tooth, hand for hand, foot for foot, ²⁵burn for burn, wound for wound, and stripe for stripe.

²⁶If a man strikes his servant or his maid in the eye and puts it out, he shall let them go free in requital for the eye. ²⁷Also, if he knocks out his servant's or his maid's tooth, he shall let them go out free in requital for the tooth.

²⁸If an ox gores a man or a woman and they die, then the ox shall be stoned and its flesh may not be eaten;ᵇ but its owner shall go quit. ²⁹However, if the ox was wont to run at people in time past, and this was told the owner but he did not restrain it and it has killed a man or a woman, then the ox shall be stoned and the owner shall die also. ³⁰However, if he is required to pay a sum of money, then he shall pay for the deliverance of his life according to the sum imposed. ³¹And whether the ox has gored a son or a daughter, it shall be settled after the same manner. ³²But if it is a servant or a maid that the ox has gored, then the owner shall pay to their master the sum of thirty sickles,ᶜ and the ox shall be stoned.

³³If a man opens up a well or digs a pit but does not cover it, and an ox or a donkey falls into it, ³⁴the owner of the pit shall make it good and give money to their owner, and the dead beast shall be his.

³⁵If one man's ox hurts another's and it dies, then they shall sell the live ox and divide the money, and the dead ox also they shall divide. ³⁶But if it is known that the ox was given to thrust in times past, then, because his master has not restrained him, he shall pay ox for ox, and the dead beast shall be his own.

v19 e.f. COV.

Lev 24:19,20
De 19:21
M't 5:38-42

The Notes

a) 6. Judges and rulers are often called gods in the scripture because they receive their office from God, as in Exodus 22:8. The apostle calls them the ministers of God in Romans 13:1-6.

b) 28. God so abhors murder that the unreasoning beasts must die for it, and their flesh be cast away.

c) 32. A sickle, according to the Hebrews, is an ounce; but according to the Greeks and Latins it is only the fourth part of an ounce. It contains 20 gerahs, as in Ex 30:13, which is about ten pence sterling [1537 value].

Chapter 22

Laws such as are in the chapter above.

Theft.
If a man steals an ox or a sheep and kills it or sells it, he shall restore five oxen for an ox and four sheep for a sheep. ²If a thief is found breaking in and is struck so that he dies, no blood shall be shed for him. ³But if the sun is up when he is found, then there shall be blood shed for him.

A thief shall make restitution. If he does not have means, he shall be sold for his theft. ⁴If the stolen animal is found in his hand alive, whether it be ox, donkey, or sheep, he shall restore double.

⁵If a man harms a field or vineyard by putting his beast to feed in another man's field, he shall make restitution from the best of his own field and from the best of his own vineyard. ⁶If a fire breaks out and catches in the thorns, so that stacks of grain, or standing grain, or the field are consumed, he who kindled the fire shall make restitution.

⁷If a man delivers to his neighbour money or property for safekeeping and it is stolen out of his house, if the thief is found, he shall pay double. ⁸If the thief is not found, then the master of the house shall be brought before the gods* and swear, whether he has put his hand to his neighbour's property.

*[The gods: see note a on Ex c21 just before.]

⁹And in every kind of trespass, whether concerning ox, donkey, sheep, clothing, or any kind of lost thing which another claims to be his, the cause of both parties shall come before the gods. And whom the gods condemn, the same shall pay double to his neighbour.

¹⁰If a man delivers to his neighbour for safekeeping a donkey, ox, sheep, or whatever beast it may be, and it dies, or is hurt, or is driven away, and no one sees it, ¹¹then shall an oath of the Lord[a] go between them, whether he has put his hand to his neighbour's property; and the owner shall accept the oath, and the other need not make it good. ¹²If it is stolen from him, then he shall make restitution to the owner. ¹³If it is torn by wild beasts, then let him bring evidence of the attack, and he need not make it good.

¹⁴When a man borrows an animal from his neighbor, if it is hurt or dies and the owner is not by, he shall make it good. ¹⁵But if the owner is by, he need not make it good; namely, if it is a hired thing and came for hire.

¹⁶If a man beguiles a maiden who is not betrothed and lies with her, he shall endow her and take her as his wife. ¹⁷If her father refuses to give her to him, he shall pay money according to the dowry of virgins.

Witches.
¹⁸You shall not suffer a witch to live.

¹⁹Whoever lies with a beast shall be slain for it.

²⁰He who offers to any gods save to the Lord only, let him die without redemption.

Ex 23:9
Lev 19:33,34
²¹Vex not a stranger, neither oppress him, for you were strangers in the land of Egypt.

²²You shall trouble no widow nor fatherless child. ²³If you trouble

them, they will cry out to me, and I will surely hear their cry. ²⁴And then will my wrath wax hot, and I will kill you by the sword, and your wives shall be widows and your children fatherless.*

²⁵If you lend money to any of my people who is poor among you, you shall not be as a usurer to him, nor oppress him with usury. ²⁶If you take your neighbour's garment as a pledge, see that you return it to him by sundown, ²⁷for that is his only cover for his skin, in which he sleeps; or he will cry out to me and I will hear him, for I am merciful.

²⁸You shall not rail upon the gods,* neither curse the ruler of your people.

²⁹Your harvest fruits[b] (whether they be dry or moist), see that you keep not back. Your firstborn son you shall give me. ³⁰Likewise shall you do with your oxen and your sheep; seven days the firstborn shall be with the dam, and the eighth day you shall give it to me.

³¹You shall be holy people unto me, and therefore you shall eat no flesh that is torn by beasts in the field, but shall cast it to the dogs.

Zec 7:9,10
*Let all oppressors of the poor take heed to this text.

Pledges.

*[The gods: judges and rulers. See note a on Ex 21 above.]

The Notes

a) 11. An oath is the end of strife and division, the which is lawful to be done when it is either to the glory of God or profit of our neighbour, or for the common good; otherwise not, as in Matthew 5:33-37.

b) 29. By tithes and firstfruits are understood the giving of thanks, whereby the heart acknowledges and confesses to have received the harvest from God, as in 1 Timothy 4:4.

Chapter 23

> Here I set no summary, because I would that all people should read the chapter throughout, and the two that are next before also.

You shall not accept a false report, nor put your hand in with the wicked to be an unrighteous witness. ²You shall not follow the crowd to do evil, nor give a testimony so that, to follow many, you turn aside from the truth. ³Neither shall you be partial to a poor man's cause.

⁴When you meet your enemy's ox or donkey going astray, you shall bring them back to him. ⁵If you see your enemy's donkey sinking under his burden, you shall not pass by and leave him alone, but shall help him to lift him up again.

⁶You shall not hinder the right of the poor who are among you in their cause.

⁷Keep yourself far from a false matter, and see that you do not slay the innocent and the righteous. For I will not justify the wicked.

⁸You shall take no gifts,[a] for gifts blind the seeing and pervert the words of the righteous.

⁹You shall not oppress a stranger. For you know the heart of a stranger, because you were strangers in Egypt.

¹⁰Six years you may sow your land and gather in the fruits, ¹¹and the seventh year you shall let it rest and lie still so that the poor of your people may eat; and what they leave, the beasts of the field may eat. In

False witness.

De 22:1-4

De 1:17

Ex 22:21
Lev 19:33, 34.

like manner you shall do with your vineyard and your olive trees. ¹²Six days you shall do your work, and the seventh day you shall keep holy day, so that your ox and your donkey may rest, and the son of your maid and the stranger may be refreshed. ¹³And in all the things that I have said to you, be circumspect. And make no mention of the names of strange gods, nor let any man hear them out of your mouths.

¹⁴Three feasts you shall hold unto me in a year. ¹⁵You shall keep the Feast of Sweet Bread, and eat unleavened bread seven days long as I commanded you, in the time appointed of the month of Abib; for in that month you came out of Egypt. And see that no man appears before me empty-handed. ¹⁶Also, keep the Feast of Harvest when you reap the firstfruits of your labours in the field, and the Feast of Ingathering at the end of the year, when you have gathered in from your labours in the field. ¹⁷Three times in a year shall all your menchildren appear before the Lord Jehovah.

¹⁸You shall not offer the blood of my sacrifice with leavened bread, neither shall the fat of my feast remain until the morning.

¹⁹The first of the firstfruits of your land you shall bring into the house of the Lord your God.

You shall also not stew a kid in its mother's milk.ᵇ

²⁰Behold, I send my angel before you, to keep you in the way and to bring you into the place which I have prepared. ²¹Be on your guard before him, and hear his voice. And anger him not, for he will not spare your misdeeds; yea, and my name is in him. ²²But if you will hearken to his voice and keep all that I tell you, then I will be an enemy to your enemies and an adversary to your adversaries. ²³When my angel goes before you, and has brought you to the Amorites, Hittites, Perezzites, Canaanites, Hivites, and Jebusites, and I have destroyed them, ²⁴see that you worship not their gods, nor serve them, nor do their works; but overthrow them, and break down their places. ²⁵And see that you serve the Lord your God, and he will bless your bread and your water, and I will take all sicknesses away from among you. ²⁶Moreover, there will be no woman childless or unfruitful in your land, and the number of your days I will make full.

²⁷I will send my fear before you, and will kill all the people wherever you go. And I will make all your enemies turn their backs to you in retreat. ²⁸And I will send hornets before you,ᶜ and they will drive out the Hivites, the Canaanites, and the Hittites before you. ²⁹I will not cast them out in one year, lest the land grow into a wilderness and the beasts of the field multiply upon you. ³⁰But little by little I will drive them out before you, until you are increased so that you may inherit the land. ³¹And I will make your boundaries from the Red Sea to the sea of the Philistines, and from the desert to the river.* I will deliver the inhabiters of the land into your hand, and you will drive them out before you. ³²And you must make no league with them nor with their gods. ³³Neither may they dwell in your land, lest they make you sin against me. For if you serve their gods, it will surely be your decay.

The Notes

a) 8. By the receiving of gifts is understood all things by which a person seeks his own profit and honour and not God's, as in Deuteronomy 16:19 and 26:13,14, and Ecclesiasticus 20:29.

b) 19. That is, you shall not cook a kid so long as it is sucking, or, as some think, they should not kill both the dam and the kid.

c) 28. A hornet is like a wasp, but is of a more venomous nature and has a sorer sting, as in Deuteronomy 7:20 and Joshua 24:12.

Chapter 24

Moses ascends up to the mount and writes the words of the Lord. The blood of the covenant. The elders of Israel judge the people.

And he said to Moses, Come up to the Lord, both you and Aaron, and Nadab, Abihu, and the seventy elders of Israel; and worship from afar. ²But let Moses only come near to the Lord, and let not the others come near; and let not the people also come up with him. [v2 e.f. COV.]

³And Moses went and told the people all the words of the Lord and all the laws. And all the people answered with one voice and said, All the words that the Lord has said, we will do. [Ex 19:5-9]

⁴Then Moses wrote down all the words of the Lord, and rose up early and made an altar at the foot of the mountain, and twelve pillars corresponding to the number of the twelve tribes of Israel. ⁵And he sent young men from the children of Israel to sacrifice burnt offerings, and to offer peace offerings^a of oxen to the Lord. ⁶And Moses took half of the blood and put it in basins, and the other half he sprinkled on the altar. ⁷And he took the Book of the Covenant and read it in the audience of the people. And they said, All that the Lord has said, we will do and hear. ⁸And Moses took the blood and sprinkled it on the people and said, Behold, this is the blood of the covenant that the Lord has made with you upon all these words. [The old covenant between Israel and the Lord. Heb 9:18-20, 13-15; 10:4-10.]

⁹Then Moses and Aaron, Nadab and Abihu, and the seventy elders of Israel went up. ¹⁰And they saw the God of Israel,^b and under his feet, as it were, a stone work of sapphire, and as it were the appearance of heaven when it is clear. ¹¹And he did not set his hand against the nobles of the children of Israel, and when they had seen God, they ate and drank.

¹²And the Lord said to Moses, Come up to me, into the hill, and be there. And I will give you tablets of stone, and a law and commandments which I have written to teach them.

¹³Then Moses rose up, and his minister Joshua. And Moses went up into the hill of God. ¹⁴And he said to the elders, Wait here until we come again to you. And see, here are Aaron and Hur with you; if anyone has any matters to deal with, let him go to them.

¹⁵When Moses had gone up into the mount, a cloud covered the hill, ¹⁶and the glory of the Lord abode upon Mount Sinai.^c And the cloud covered it six days, and the seventh day he called to Moses out

of the cloud. ¹⁷And the appearance of the glory of the Lord was like a consuming fire on the top of the hill in the sight of the children of Israel. ¹⁸And Moses went up into the mountain. And Moses was in the mount forty days and forty nights.

Ex c34

The Notes

a)   5. A peace offering is to reconcile God towards people, to be at peace with them and to forgive them their trespasses; or, as some say, for peace obtained after victory in battle. See before at c20:24, and hereafter c32:6.
b)   10. They saw God: that is, they knew certainly that he was there present, and they saw him as in a vision – not in his godly majesty, but as it were by a certain revelation.
c)   16. Of this glory is spoken before at c16:7 and note a thereon.

Chapter 25

The Lord shows Moses the plan for the holy place and the things pertaining to it.

And the Lord spoke with Moses, saying, ²Tell the children of Israel to give me a lift offering.ᵃ From everyone who gives it willingly with his heart, you shall take it. ³And this is the lift offering that you shall take from them: gold, silver, and bronze; ⁴jacinth colour, scarlet, and purple yarns; byss;* goats' hair; ⁵rams' skins that are red and the skins of badgers; sethim wood; ⁶oil for lights; spices for anointing oil and for sweet incense; ⁷onyx stones, and set stones for the ephodᵇ and for the breastlap.ᶜ ⁸And they shall make me a sanctuary,ᵈ so that I may dwell among them. ⁹And as I have shown you the plan of the habitation and of all the furnishings, see that you make it just so in all things.

Ex 35:4-9

*Byss: fine white silk or linen. Look in c35 and note c.

The form of the ark of witness with its poles and cherubims.

¹⁰And they shall make an arkᵉ of sethim wood, two cubits and a half long, a cubit and a half broad, and a cubit and a half high.* ¹¹And you shall overlay it with pure gold both within and without, and make on high upon it a molding of gold round about.
¹²And you shall cast four rings of gold for it, and put them in the four corners – two rings on the one side of it and two on the other. ¹³And you shall make poles of sethim wood and cover them with gold, ¹⁴and put the poles in the rings along by the sides of the ark, to carry it with. ¹⁵And the poles shall remain in the rings of the ark, and must not be taken away. ¹⁶And you shall put in the ark the witness that I will give you.
¹⁷And you shall make a mercy seat of pure gold, two cubits and a half long and a cubit and a half broad. ¹⁸And make two cherubims of thick gold for the two ends of the mercy seat, ¹⁹and set one cherub on one end and the other on the other end of the mercy seat; in that manner, see that you make them on the two ends. ²⁰And the cherubims shall stretch their wings abroad over on high, and shall cover the mercy seat with their wings. And their faces shall look one to another: toward the mercy seat shall the faces of the cherubims be.

*[Cubit: usually meaning the distance from the elbow to the tip of the middle finger. Since this varies among people, a standard building cubit was used. 2Ch 3:3 refers to an "old cubit."]

²¹And you shall put the mercy seat above upon the ark, and in the ark you shall put the witness that I will give you. ²²There I will meet you, and will commune with you from upon the mercy seat, from between the two cherubims that are upon the ark of witness, about all the things that I will give you in commandment for the children of Israel.

The table of showbread with the loaves of bread upon it, and its other utensils.
²³You shall also make a table of sethim wood, of two cubits long, one cubit broad, and a cubit and a half high. ²⁴And cover it with pure gold, and make for it a molding of gold round about. ²⁵And make a rim of four fingers broad round about, and make a golden molding also on the rim round about.

²⁶And make for it four rings of gold, and put them in the corners on the four legs. ²⁷They should be right under the rim, to put in poles to carry the table. ²⁸And you shall make poles of sethim wood and overlay them with gold, to carry the table with. ²⁹And you shall make its dishes, spoons, pots, and bowls for pouring out, of fine gold. ³⁰And you shall set showbread^f upon the table, to be before me always.

The plan of the candlestick with its lamps, snuffers, and other necessaries.
³¹And you shall make a candlestick of pure, thick gold, with its shaft, and with branches, bowls, buds, and flowers extending from it. ³²Six branches shall proceed out of the sides of the candlestick, three out of one side and three out of the other.

³³And there shall be three cups like almonds, with buds and flowers, upon every one of the six branches that proceed out of the candlestick. ³⁴And in the candlestick itself shall be four cups like almonds, with their buds and flowers, ³⁵so that there is a bud under every two branches of the six that proceed out of the candlestick. ³⁶And the buds and the branches shall be altogether one piece of pure, thick gold.

³⁷And you shall make seven lamps, and put them on high upon it so as to give light to the other side that is facing it. ³⁸And its snuffers and firepans shall be of pure gold.

³⁹Out of 100 pounds of fine gold you shall make it, with all the accessories. ⁴⁰And see that you make them according to the plan that was shown you in the mount.

Heb 8:5
Ac 7:44

The Notes

a) 2. *Lift offering* because it was lifted up before the Lord.
b) 7. *Ephod*: a garment somewhat like an amice, except with holes for the arms and it was belted. [An amice is a liturgical vestment consisting of an oblong piece of white linen covering the neck and shoulders, and typically worn over the alb.]
c) 7. A *breastlap*, or *breastflap*, is such a flap as you see in the breast of a cope. [A cope was a long cloak or cape worn as an outer garment, chiefly out of doors. It remains in use as an ecclesiastical garment.]
d) 8. *Sanctuary*: a place hallowed and dedicated to God.
e) 10. *Ark*: a coffer or chest.
f) 30. *Showbread* because it was always in the presence and sight of the Lord.

[Notes a-e are from William Tyndale's own 1530 Pentateuch, with this editor's elucidations. Note f is as it was set forth in the Matthew Bible.]

Chapter 26

This chapter also describes the things pertaining to the holy place.

The form of the ten curtains of the tabernacle with their cherubims and fifty loops

Ex 25:4 And you shall make a habitation with ten curtains of twined byss, jacinth,^a scarlet, and purple yarns; and shall make them with cherubims of embroidered work. ²The length of a curtain shall be twenty-eight cubits and the width four, and they shall be all of the same measure. ³Five curtains shall be joined together one to another, and the other five likewise shall be joined together one to another.

⁴Then shall you make loops of jacinth colour along the edge of the one endmost curtain; that is, in the selvage of the coupling curtain. And likewise shall you do in the edge of the end curtain that is coupled with it on the other side. ⁵Fifty loops shall you make in the one curtain, and fifty in the edge of the other that is coupled with it on the other side, so that the loops are over one against another. ⁶And you shall make fifty rings of gold and couple the curtains together with the rings, so that it may be a habitation.

⁷And you shall make eleven curtains of goats' hair, to be a tent to cover the habitation. ⁸The length of a curtain shall be thirty cubits and the width four, and they shall be all eleven of the same measure. ⁹And you shall couple five by themselves, and the other six by themselves, and shall double over the sixth in the forefront of the tabernacle. ¹⁰And you shall make fifty loops in the edge of the end curtain on the one side – that is, in the coupling curtain – and as many in the edge of the coupling curtain on the other side. ¹¹And you shall make fifty rings of bronze and put them into the loops, and couple the tent together with them so that there may be one covering.

¹²And the extra length that remains of the curtains of the tent, namely the breadth of half a curtain that remains, shall be left on the back sides of the habitation: ¹³a cubit on the one side and a cubit on the other side, of that which remains in the length of the curtains of the tabernacle. It shall be left on either side of the habitation, to cover it.

Ex 25:5 ¹⁴And you shall make another covering for the tent of rams' skins dyed red, and yet another above everything made of badger skins.

The plan of the boards of the tabernacle with their feet, sockets, and bars.

¹⁵And you shall make boards for the habitation of sethim wood, to stand upright. ¹⁶Ten cubits long shall every board be, and a cubit and a half wide. ¹⁷Each board shall have two feet, to couple them together with; and in this way you shall make all the boards of the habitation.

¹⁸And you shall make twenty boards for the habitation on the south side. ¹⁹And you shall make forty sockets of silver and put them under the twenty boards: two sockets under every board, for their two feet. ²⁰In like manner, in the north side of the habitation there shall be twenty boards ²¹and forty sockets of silver: two sockets under every board.

The plan of the corner boards with their feet, sockets, and bars.

²²And for the west end of the habitation you shall make six boards, ²³and two boards more for the two west corners of the habitation, ²⁴so that these two boards are coupled together, beneath and likewise above, with clamps. And so shall it be in both the corners. ²⁵And thus there will be eight boards in all, and sixteen sockets of silver, two sockets under each board.

²⁶And you shall make bars of sethim wood: five for the boards of the one side of the tabernacle, ²⁷five for the other side, and five for the boards of the west end. ²⁸And the middle bar shall go along through the middle of the boards, and bar them together from the one end to the other. ²⁹And you shall cover the boards with gold, and make golden rings for them to put the bars through, and shall cover the bars with gold also. ³⁰And rear up the habitation according to the plan that was shown to you in the mount.

³¹And you shall make a veil of jacinth, scarlet, purple, and twined byss, and shall make it of embroidered work and full of cherubims. ³²And hang it upon four pillars of sethim wood covered with gold, having knobs covered with gold also, and standing upon four sockets of silver. ³³And you shall hang up the veil with rings, and shall bring the ark of witness in within the veil, and the veil shall divide the holy from the most holy.ᵇ ³⁴And you shall put the mercy seat upon the ark of witness in the holiest place. ³⁵And you shall put the table outside the veil, and the candlestick across from the table on the south side of the habitation. And put the table on the north side.

³⁶And you shall make a hanging for the entry to the tabernacle of jacinth, scarlet, purple, and twined byss, and wrought with needlework. ³⁷And you shall make to hang it five pillars of sethim wood, and cover both them and their knobs with gold, and shall cast five sockets of bronze for them.

The Notes

a) 1. Jacinth is a flower which we call a violet, and it is also a precious stone of the colour thereof. But here it is taken only for the colour of jacinth, of which colour the curtains should be, as in verse 4 of c25 above.

b) 33. The most holy place was the secret and inward place of the sanctuary, where stood the ark and the mercy seat, to which none but the priests only could come, and that but once a year. The symbolism of this figure is declared in Hebrews 9:1-10 and 1Kings 6:11-13.*

[*The veil of the holy place in the Jerusalem temple tore in two when Jesus died. M't 27:51; Mk 15:38 & note a.]

Chapter 27

Yet more things pertaining to the holy place.

The form of the altar of the burnt offering with its horns, rings, poles, gridiron, and other accessories.

And you shall make an altar of sethim wood, five cubits long and five cubits broad so that it is foursquare, and three cubits high. ²And make horns for it, proceeding out from the four corners, and cover it with bronze. ³And make its ashpans, shovels, basins, fleshhooks, firepans, and all the utensils of bronze. ⁴And you shall make a gridiron also, like a network of bronze, and put on it four rings in the four corners. ⁵And put it below, so that the gridiron reaches up to the middle of the altar. ⁶And make poles of sethim wood for the altar, cover them with bronze, ⁷and let them be put in rings along by the sides of the altar to carry it with. ⁸And make the altar hollow with boards. Just as it was shown to you in the mount, so let them make it.

The ordering of the furnishings that must stand in the tabernacle.
⁹And you shall make a court[a] for the habitation, which shall have in the south side hangings of twined byss, being 100 cubits long, ¹⁰and twenty pillars upon their twenty sockets of bronze; but the knobs of the pillars and their bands shall be silver. ¹¹Likewise, on the north side there shall be hangings of 100 cubits long and twenty pillars upon their sockets of bronze, and the knobs and bands of silver. ¹²In the breadth of the court westward there shall be hangings of fifty cubits long, and ten pillars with their ten sockets. ¹³And in the breadth of the court eastward, toward the rising of the sun, shall be hangings of fifty cubits: ¹⁴hangings of fifteen cubits on the one side with three pillars on three sockets, ¹⁵and likewise on the other side hangings of fifteen cubits with three pillars on three sockets. ¹⁶And in the gate of the court shall be a veil of twenty cubits, of jacinth, scarlet, purple, and twined byss wrought with needlework, and four pillars on their four sockets.

¹⁷All the pillars round about the court shall be banded with silver, and their knobs shall be of silver and their sockets of bronze. ¹⁸The length of the court shall be 100 cubits, the breadth fifty, and the height five. The hangings shall be of twined byss, and the sockets of bronze. ¹⁹And all the accessories of the habitation used in every manner of service, and its pegs – yea, and the pegs also of the court – shall be bronze.

²⁰And command the children of Israel to give you pure, beaten olive oil to give light, to pour continually into the lamps. ²¹In the tabernacle of witness,[b] outside the veil that is before the witness, Aaron and his sons shall dress the lamps both evening and morning before the Lord. And it shall be a duty forever[c] to your generations after you, that oil be given by the children of Israel.

The Notes

a) 9. The court is that which we call a church yard.
b) 21. It is called the tabernacle of witness because it contained the covenant and witness upon which God desired the children of Israel to trust.
c) 21. Forever: look in Genesis 13:15 and note b.

Chapter 28

Aaron's apparel, and his sons'.

And take unto you Aaron your brother, and his sons with him, from among the children of Israel, so that he may minister to me – Aaron with Nadab, Abihu, Eleazar, and Ithamar, Aaron's sons. ²And you shall make holy garments for Aaron your brother, both honourable and glorious. ³Moreover, tell all who are wise-hearted, whom I have filled with the spirit of wisdom, to make Aaron's garments, to consecrate him with so that he may minister to me. ⁴These are the garments that they shall make: a breastlap,* an ephod, a tunic, a straight coat, a turban, and a sash. And they shall make holy garments for Aaron your brother and his sons, so that he may minister to me.

*Breastlap: see c25 & note c.

⁵And they shall take gold, jacinth, scarlet, purple, and byss. ⁶And they shall make the ephod of gold, jacinth, scarlet, purple, and white twined byss, with embroidered work. ⁷The two sides shall come together, closed up at the edges. ⁸And the sash of the ephod shall be of the same workmanship and of the same stuff: namely, of gold, jacinth, scarlet, purple, and twined byss.

⁹And you shall take two onyx stones and engrave in them the names of the children of Israel, ¹⁰six in one stone and the other six in the other stone, according to the order of their birth. ¹¹As the work of a stone engraver, as signets are graven, so shall you engrave the two stones with the names of the children of Israel, and shall make them to be set in settings of gold. ¹²And you shall put the two stones upon the two shoulders of the ephod, and they shall be stones of remembrance concerning the children of Israel. And Aaron shall bear their names before the Lord upon his two shoulders, for a remembrance.

¹³And you shall make hooks of gold, ¹⁴and two chains of fine gold, linkwork and twisted, and fasten the twisted rope chains to the hooks.

¹⁵And you shall make the breastlap of example^b with embroidered work. Just like the work of the ephod you shall make it: of gold, jacinth, scarlet, purple, and twined byss you shall make it. ¹⁶It shall be foursquare and doubled over, a handbreadth long and a handbreadth wide.* ¹⁷And you shall fill it with four rows of stones. In the first row shall be a sardius, a topaz, and an emerald.‡ ¹⁸The second row: a ruby, sapphire, and a diamond. ¹⁹The third: ligure, agate, and amethyst. ²⁰The fourth: a turquoise, onyx, and jasper. And these shall be set in gold in their enclosures. ²¹And the stones shall be engraved like signets are engraved, with the names of the children of Israel – each stone with its name, corresponding to the twelve tribes.

vv15,29,30 e.f. WT 1530. The MB had breastlap of *judgment* but the note kept breastlap of *example*.
*Wis 18:24
‡Some read, a carbuncle [ie, ruby or other red precious stone].

²²And you shall make for the breastlap two fastening chains of pure gold and twisted work. ²³And you shall make likewise upon the breastlap two rings of gold, and put them on the corners of the breastlap, ²⁴and put the two twisted rope chains of gold in the two rings that are in the corners of the breastlap. ²⁵And the two ends of the two chains you shall fasten in the two hooks, and put them upon the shoulders of the ephod, on the front. ²⁶And you shall make two more rings of gold and put them in the two edges of the breastlap, in the inside borders that face the ephod. ²⁷And yet two other rings of gold you shall make, and put them on the two sides of the ephod beneath, facing the breastlap, where the sides are joined together upon the embroidered sash of the ephod. ²⁸And they shall bind the breastlap by its rings to the rings of the ephod with a cord of jacinth, so that it may lie

close to the embroidered sash of the ephod and the breastlap does not hang loose from the ephod. ²⁹And Aaron shall bear the names of the children of Israel in the breastlap of example upon his heart when he goes into the holy place, for a remembrance before the Lord always. ³⁰And you shall put in the breastlap of example Urim and Thummim,* so that they will be there upon Aaron's heart when he goes in before the Lord.ᵃ And Aaron shall bear the exampleᵇ of the children of Israel upon his heart before the Lord always.

³¹And you shall make the tunic for the ephod altogether of jacinth colour. ³²And there shall be a hole for the head in the middle of it, and let there be a binding of woven work around the collar (as it were the collar of a partlet) so that it does not tear. ³³And beneath, on the hem, you shall make pomegranates of jacinth, of scarlet, and of purple, round about the hem; and put bells of gold between them round about, ³⁴so that there is repeatedly a golden bell and a pomegranate, a golden bell and a pomegranate, round about on the hem of the tunic. ³⁵And Aaron shall have the tunic upon him when he ministers, so that the sound may be heard when he goes into the holy place before the Lord and when he comes out, so that he does not die.

³⁶And you shall make a plate of pure gold and engrave on it, like signets are engraved, THE HOLINESS OF THE LORD.ᶜ ³⁷And put it on a cord of jacinth and tie it to the turban, on the front of it, ³⁸so that it is upon Aaron's forehead; so that Aaron may bear the offerings for sin of the holy things, which the children of Israel have hallowed in all their holy gifts. And it shall be always upon Aaron's forehead so that they may be accepted before the Lord.

³⁹And you shall make the coat of byss. And you shall make the turban of byss, and the sash of needlework.

⁴⁰And you shall make for Aaron's sons also coats, sashes, and headwear honourable and glorious, ⁴¹and you shall put them upon Aaron your brother and on his sons with him, and shall anoint them, fill their hands, and consecrate them so that they may minister to me.

⁴²And you shall make for them linen breeches to cover their privities: from the waist to the thighs they must reach. ⁴³And they shall be upon Aaron and his sons when they go into the tabernacle of witness,* or when they approach the altar to minister in holiness, so that they bear no sin and so die. And this shall be a law forever‡ for Aaron and his seed after him.

*[In 1530 WT had Light and Perfectness instead of Urim and Thummim]

v38 e.f. JR. [In Rogers' 1537 note on v38, he explained that the Hebraism *sin* in the original translation meant *offerings for sin*, as also in Ro 8:3 and 2Co 5:21]

*Witness: look in Ex 27:21 and note b.
‡ Look in Ge 13:15 and note b.

The Notes

a) 30. *Urim* and *Thummim* are Hebrew words. Urim signifies light, and Thummim perfectness. I think one were stones that sparkled and had light in them, and the other were clear stones like crystal. The light signifies the light of God's word, and the perfectness pure, clean living according to the word.

b) 15, etc. It was called the example of the children of Israel because it was a reminder to them to seek God's word and to do according to it.

c)   36. THE HOLINESS OF THE LORD was a name of God made with four letters, which the Hebrews dared not name for the reverence in which they held God. Instead, they said *Adonai*. In Exodus 6:3, we rendered the four letters by the name *Jehovah*.

Chapter 29

The consecration of Aaron and his sons.

This is what you shall do when you hallow them to be my priests. Take one ox and two rams without blemish, ²with unleavened bread, cakes of sweet bread tempered with oil, and wafers of sweet bread anointed with oil (of wheat flour shall you make them). ³And put them in a basket, and bring them in the basket with the ox and the two rams.

⁴And bring Aaron and his sons to the entry to the tabernacle of witness, and wash them with water. ⁵And take the garments, and put upon Aaron the straight coat, the tunic of the ephod, the ephod, and the breastlap. And gird them to him with the embroidered sash of the ephod. ⁶And put the turban on his head, and the holy crown upon the turban. ⁷Then take the anointing oil, and pour it on his head and anoint him. ⁸And bring his sons, put straight coats upon them, ⁹and gird them with sashes – as well Aaron as his sons. And put the headwear on them so that the priest's office may be theirs for a perpetual law.

And fill the hands of Aaron and of his sons, ¹⁰and bring the ox before the tabernacle of witness. And let Aaron and his sons put their hands on its head, ¹¹and kill it before the Lord in the entry of the tabernacle of witness. ¹²And take some of the blood of the ox and put it on the horns of the altar with your finger, and pour out all the blood at the base of the altar. ¹³And take all the fat that covers the inward parts, the membrane that is on the liver, and the two kidneys with the fat that is upon them, and burn them on the altar. ¹⁴But the flesh of the ox with its skin and dung you shall burn with fire outside the host. For it is a sin offering.

Lev 1:3-9

¹⁵Then take one of the rams, and let Aaron and his sons put their hands on the head of the ram. ¹⁶And cause it to be slain, and take some of its blood and sprinkle it round about upon the altar. ¹⁷And cut the ram in pieces, and wash its inwards and its legs and put them together with the pieces and with its head. ¹⁸And burn the whole ram on the altar, for it is a burnt offering to the Lord, and a sweet savourᵃ of the Lord's sacrifice.

¹⁹And take the other ram, and let Aaron and his sons put their hands on his head, ²⁰and let him then be killed. And take some of his blood and put it on the tip of Aaron's right ear and of his sons' ears, and on the thumb of their right hands and the great toe of their right feet. And sprinkle the blood upon the altar round about.

²¹Then take some of the blood that is upon the altar and some of the anointing oil, and sprinkle it upon Aaron and his vestments, and upon his sons and their garments also. Then are he and his clothes holy, and his sons and their clothes holy also.

²²Then take the fat of the ram and his rump, the fat that covers the inwards, the membrane of the liver, the two kidneys and the fat that is upon them, and the right shoulder (for that ram is a full offering), ²³with a loaf of bread, a cake of oiled bread, and a wafer out of the basket of sweet bread that is before the Lord. ²⁴And put it all in the hands of Aaron and in the hands of his sons, and wave them in and out as a wave offering to the Lord. ²⁵Then take it off from their hands and burn it on the altar, there upon the burnt offering, to be a savour of sweetness before the Lord; for it is a sacrifice to the Lord.

²⁶Then take the breast of the ram that is Aaron's full offering and wave it as a wave offering before the Lord; and let that be your part. ²⁷And thus shall you sanctify the breast of the wave offering and the shoulder of the lift offering (which are waved and lifted up of the ram), which is the full offering of Aaron and of his sons. ²⁸And it shall be Aaron's and his sons' due forever from the children of Israel; for it is a lift offering. And the lift offering shall be the Lord's due from the children of Israel, of the sacrifice of their peace offerings which they lift up to the Lord.

²⁹And Aaron's holy garments shall be his sons' after him, in which to anoint them and to fill their hands. ³⁰And that son who is priest in his stead after him shall put them on for seven days, so that he may go into the tabernacle of witness to minister in the holy place.

³¹Then take the ram that is the full offering and boil his flesh in a holy place. ³²And Aaron and his sons shall eat his flesh with the bread that is in the basket in the door of the tabernacle of witness. ³³And they shall eat them because the atonement was made with them, to fill their hands and to sanctify them. But a stranger must not eat of them, because they are holy. ³⁴If any flesh of the full offerings or of the bread remains till morning, you shall burn it with fire; for it must not be eaten, because it is holy. ³⁵And see that you do with Aaron and his sons in all things just as I have commanded you. Fill their hands seven days, ³⁶and offer every day an ox for a sin offering, for reconciliation.

And you shall hallow the altar when you reconcile it, and shall anoint it to sanctify it. ³⁷Seven days you shall reconcile the altar and sanctify it,* so that it may be an altar most holy. No one may touch it but those who are consecrated.

³⁸This is what you shall offer upon the altar: two lambs of one year old, day by day forever. ³⁹One you shall offer in the morning and the other at evening. ⁴⁰And with the one lamb, take a tenth measure of flour mixed with the fourth part of a hin of pressed oil and the fourth part of a hin of wine, for a drink offering. ⁴¹And the other lamb you shall offer at evening, and shall do with it as with the food offering and drink offering in the morning, to be an odour of a sweet savour of the sacrifice of the Lord. ⁴²And it shall be a continual burnt offering among your children after you in the door of the tabernacle of witness before the Lord, where I will meet you, to speak to you there. ⁴³There I will meet with the children of Israel, and will be hallowed in my honour.

---

v27 e.f. COV.

*Look in Ge 2:3 & note c.

⁴⁴And I will sanctify the tabernacle of witness and the altar, and I will sanctify also Aaron and his sons to be my priests. ⁴⁵Moreover, I will dwell among the children of Israel and will be their God. ⁴⁶And they may know that I am the Lord their God, who brought them out of the land of Egypt to dwell among them – even I, the Lord their God.

The Notes

a) 18. What a sweet savour is, look in Lev 1:9 and note a, and Eze 20:41.

Chapter 30

The altar of incense. The bronze laver. The anointing oil.

And you shall make an altar to burn incense in, of sethim wood. ²It shall be a cubit long and a cubit wide foursquare, and two cubits high, with horns proceeding out of it. ³And you shall overlay it with fine gold, both the top and the sides round about, and its horns also. Make a molding of gold round about it, ⁴and two golden rings on either side under the molding, to put poles through to carry it with. ⁵And you shall make the poles of sethim wood and cover them with gold. ⁶And you shall put it before the veil that hangs before the ark of witness, before the mercy seat that is upon the witness where I will meet you.

⁷And Aaron shall burn sweet incense on it every morning when he dresses the lamps, ⁸and likewise at evening when he sets up the lamps. This shall be the daily incense before the Lord throughout your generations. ⁹You shall put no strange incense on it, neither burnt sacrifice nor food offering, neither pour any drink offering on it. ¹⁰And once in a year Aaron shall reconcile upon its horns with the blood of the sin offering of reconciliation. Once in the year shall he reconcile it throughout your generations, and so is it most holy to the Lord.

¹¹And the Lord spoke to Moses, saying, ¹²When you number the children of Israel and count them, every man shall give a reconciliation of his soul to the Lord, so that there will be no plague among them when you count them. ¹³And thus much shall every man who is included in the number give: half a sickle, according to the holy sickle. (A sickle is twenty gerahs.) This half sickle shall be the Lord's lift offering. ¹⁴All who are numbered, from twenty years old and above, shall give this lift offering to the Lord. ¹⁵The rich shall not give more, and the poor shall not go under half a sickle, when they give a lift offering to the Lord for the atonement of their souls.

¹⁶And you shall take the reconciliation money of the children of Israel and put it to the service of the tabernacle of witness; and it shall be a memorial of the children of Israel before the Lord, to make atonement for their souls.

The laver of bronze with its base.

¹⁷And the Lord spoke to Moses, saying, ¹⁸You shall make a laver of bronze, with a base also of bronze, for washing. And set it between the tabernacle of witness and the altar. And put water in it, ¹⁹so that Aaron

vv 8 & 13-14 e.f. COV.

Nu c1

Lev 27:25
Nu 3:47
Eze 45:12

Ex 40:30-32

and his sons may wash their hands and feet there ²⁰when they go into the tabernacle of witness, or when they go to the altar to minister and to burn the Lord's offering, lest they die. ²¹And this shall be an ordinance forever, for him and his seed among your children after you.

²²And the Lord spoke to Moses, saying, ²³Take choice spices: of pure myrrh 500 sickles, of sweet cinnamon half so much, 250 sickles, of sweet calamite 250, ²⁴and of cassia 250, according to the holy sickle; and of olive oil, a hin. ²⁵And make with them a holy anointing oil,ᵃ compounded according to the craft of the apothecary. ²⁶And anoint the tabernacle of witness with it, and the ark of witness, ²⁷the table with all its accessories, the candlestick with all its accessories, the altar of incense, ²⁸the altar of burnt sacrifice and all its accessories, and the laver and its base. ²⁹And sanctify them, that they may be most holy. And no man may touch them but those that are hallowed. ³⁰And anoint Aaron and his sons, and consecrate them to minister to me.

³¹And you shall speak to the children of Israel, saying, This shall be a holy anointing oil for me throughout your generations. ³²No one's flesh shall be anointed with it, neither shall you make any other like it, for it is holy. See, therefore, that you take it for holy. ³³Whoever makes any such like it, or whoever puts any of it upon a stranger, shall perish from among his people.

³⁴And the Lord said to Moses, Take sweet spices – stacte, onycha, sweet galbanum, and pure frankincense – in equal amounts; ³⁵and make incense with them compounded after the craft of the apothecary, mixed together so that it may be made pure and holy. ³⁶And beat it to powder, and put it before the witness in the tabernacle of witness, where I will meet you. But let it be holy to you. ³⁷And see that you make nothing like it, but let it be to you holy for the Lord. ³⁸Whoever makes incense to smell like it shall perish from among his people.

The Notes

a) 25. This holy anointing oil symbolizes the holiness and power of the Holy Spirit, declared or shown by the word of God, and descending down first on the head of Aaron, who is a figure of Christ, and consequently upon the apostles and all the faithful, as in Psalm 133.

Chapter 31

The calling of Bezaleel and Aholiab, the craftsmen. The Sabbath is ordained. The tablets of stone are given to Moses.

Ex 35:30-35

And the Lord spoke to Moses, saying, ²Behold, I have called by name Bezaleel, the son of Uri the son of Hur, of the tribe of Judah. ³And I have filled him with the Spirit of God – with wisdom, understanding, and knowledge in every kind of work, ⁴to develop ingenious arts, to work in gold, silver, and bronze, ⁵and with the skill to engrave stones, to set and carve in wood, and to work in every kind of craft. ⁶And behold, I have given him, to be his companion, Aholiab the son of

Ahisamach, from the tribe of Dan.

And in the hearts of all who are wise-hearted I have put the wisdom to make everything that I have commanded you: ⁷the tabernacle of witness, the ark of witness and the mercy seat that is upon it, all the furnishings of the tabernacle, ⁸the table with its equipment, the pure candlestick with all its accessories, the altar of incense, ⁹the altar of burnt offerings with all its vessels, the laver with its base, ¹⁰the vestments to minister in, the holy garments for Aaron the priest and the garments of his sons to minister in, ¹¹and the anointing oil and sweet incense for the sanctuary. According to everything I have commanded you, so will they do.

¹²And the Lord spoke to Moses, saying, ¹³Speak to the children of Israel and say: You must ensure that you keep my Sabbath, for it will be a sign between me and you in your generations, to know that I the Lord do sanctify you.ᵃ ¹⁴Keep my Sabbath, therefore, as a thing holy to you. He who defiles it shall be slain for it. For whoever works therein, the same soul shall be rooted out from among his people. ¹⁵Six days people may work, but the seventh day is the Sabbath of the holy rest of the Lord, so that whoever does any work in the Sabbath day shall die for it. ¹⁶Therefore, let the children of Israel keep the Sabbath, to observe it throughout their generations as an ordinance forever. ¹⁷For it will be a sign between me and the children of Israel forever. For in six days the Lord made heaven and earth, and the seventh day he rested and was refreshed. [Ge c1; 2:1-3.]

¹⁸And when he had made an end of communing with Moses upon Mount Sinai, he gave him two tablets of witness, which were of stone and written with the finger of God.ᵇ [Ex 24:12; 32:15,16.]

The Notes

a) 13. The Sabbath: besides that it served to come and hear the word of God, to seek his will, and to offer and reconcile themselves to God, it was also a sign to them, and put them in remembrance that it was God who sanctified them with his Holy Spirit [and his word].

b) 18. With the finger of God: that is, with the Spirit of God, or with the power of God, as in Luke 11:20.

Chapter 32

The Israelites worship the golden calf. Moses prays for them, putting God in remembrance of his promise. He breaks the tablets for anger. He chides Aaron. The idolaters are slain. Moses prays God to forgive them or to put him out of the book of life.

And when the people saw that it was a long time before Moses came down from the mountain, they gathered themselves together and went to Aaron and said to him, Up, and make us a god to go before us! For as for this Moses, the fellow that brought us out of the land of Egypt, we do not know what has become of him. [Ac 7:38-41]

²And Aaron said to them, Pluck off the golden earrings that are in the ears of your wives, your sons, and of your daughters, and bring them to me. ³And all the people plucked off the golden earrings that were in their ears and brought them to Aaron. ⁴And he received them from their hands and fashioned the gold with a tool, and made of it a calf of molten metal. And they said, This is your god, O Israel, who brought you out of the land of Egypt!

⁵And when Aaron saw this, he built an altar before it and made a proclamation, saying, Tomorrow shall be a holy day unto the Lord.

⁶And they rose up in the morning and offered burnt offerings, and brought offerings of atonement also. And then they sat down to eat and drink, and rose up again to play.

⁷Then the Lord said to Moses, Go down, for your people whom you brought out of the land of Egypt have ruined everything. ⁸They have at once turned out of the way that I commanded them, and have made themselves a calf of molten metal, and have worshipped it, and have offered to it, and have said, This is your god, O Israel, who brought you out of the land of Egypt! ⁹And the Lord said to Moses, Behold, I see this people, that it is a stiff-necked people. ¹⁰And now therefore, suffer me, that my wrath may wax hot upon them and that I may consume them! And then I will make of you a mighty people.

¹¹Then Moses besought the Lord his God and said, O Lord, why should your wrath wax hot upon your people, whom you have brought out of the land of Egypt with great power and with a mighty hand? ¹²Why should the Egyptians speak and say, He brought them out to their harm – even to slay them in the mountains, and to consume them from off the face of the earth? Turn from your fierce wrath, and have compassion over the wickedness of your people. ¹³Remember Abraham, Isaac, and Israel your servants, to whom you swore by your own self and said to them, I will multiply your seed as the stars of heaven, and all this land that I have promised you, I will give to your seed, and they shall inherit it forever.

¹⁴And the Lord refrained from the harm that he said he would do to his people. ¹⁵And Moses turned his back and went down from the mountain with the two tablets of witness in his hand, which were written on both the leaves. ¹⁶And the tablets were the work of God, and the writing was the writing of God graven upon the tablets.

¹⁷And when Joshua heard the noise of the people as they were shouting, he said to Moses, There is a noise of war in the camp! ¹⁸But he said, It is not the cry of those who have the mastery, nor of those who have the worse, but I hear the noise of singing.

¹⁹And as soon as he came near the camp and saw the calf and the dancing, his wrath waxed hot, and he cast the tablets out of his hand and broke them there at the foot of the mountain. ²⁰And he took the calf that they had made, burned it with fire, pounded it to powder, and strew it in the water and made the children of Israel drink it. ²¹And then Moses said to Aaron, What did this people do to you, that you

have brought so great a sin upon them?

²²And Aaron said, Let not the wrath of my lord wax fierce. You know the people, that they are set on evildoing. ²³They said to me, Make us a god to go before us, because we do not know what has become of Moses, the fellow that brought us out of the land of Egypt. ²⁴And I said to them, Let those who have gold, take and bring it to me. And I cast it into the fire, and this calf came out.

²⁵When Moses saw that the people were naked (for Aaron had made them naked, to their shame, when they rebelled), ²⁶he went and stood in the gate of the camp and said, If any man belongs to the Lord, let him come to me. And all the sons of Levi gathered themselves together and came to him. ²⁷And he said to them, Thus says the Lord of Israel: Let every man put his sword on his side, and go in and out from gate to gate throughout the host, and slay: every man his brother, every man his friend, and every man his neighbour. Nu 25:4,5
1Co 10:6,11

²⁸And the children of Levi did as Moses had said. And there were slain of the people that same day about 3,000 men. ²⁹Then Moses said, Fill your hands* unto the Lord this day, every man upon his son and upon his brother, to bring upon you a blessing this day. *[COV has
consecrate
your hands.
Ex 29:33.]

³⁰And on the morrow, Moses said to the people, You have sinned a great sin. But now I will go up to the Lord to see if I can make an atonement for your sin. ³¹And Moses went again to the Lord and said, O, this people have sinned a great sin, and have made themselves a god of gold. ³²Yet forgive them their sin, I pray you. If not, wipe me out of your book which you have written!ᵃ

³³And the Lord said to Moses, I will put out of my book him who has sinned against me. ³⁴But go, and bring the people into the land, as I said to you. Behold, my angel will go before you. Nevertheless, in the day when I visit, I will visit their sin upon them.ᵇ

³⁵And the Lord plagued the people because they had made the calf, which Aaron made.

The Notes

a) 32. To wipe him out of the book is to put him out of the number of the chosen and to cast him clean out from God, as in Romans 9:3.

b) 34. To visit their sin is to have their sin in remembrance, to punish it. Genesis 50:24 mentions a different kind of visitation of God.

Chapter 33

> The Lord sends an angel before his people. The Lord refuses to go up with the people. The people lament their sin. Moses talks with the Lord and desires to see his face, and is directed to stand upon the rock.

And the Lord said to Moses, Depart, and go from here – both you and the people that you have brought out of the land of Egypt – to the land that I swore to Abraham, Isaac, and Jacob, saying, To your seed I will give it. ²And I will send an angel before you, and will cast out the Canaanites, the Amorites, the Hittites, the Perizzites, the Hivites, and the Ge 15:18-21
Ex 23:28-31

Jebusites, ³so that you may go into a land that flows with milk and honey. But I will not go among you myself, for you are a stiff-necked people, lest I consume you by the way.

⁴And when the people heard this bad tidings, they sorrowed, and no one put on his best raiment.

⁵And the Lord spoke to Moses: Say to the children of Israel: You are a stiff-necked people; I must come once suddenly upon you and make an end of you! But now, put your fine raiment away from you, and I will find out what to do with you.

⁶And the children of Israel laid their fine raiment away from them, there by the foot of Mount Horeb.

⁷And Moses took the tabernacle and pitched it outside the camp, far off from the host, and called it the tabernacle of witness.* And anyone who wanted to ask any question of the Lord went out to the tabernacle of witness, which was outside the host. ⁸And when Moses went out to the tabernacle, all the people rose up and stood, everyone in his tent door, and looked after Moses until he was gone into the tabernacle. ⁹And as soon as Moses entered into the tabernacle, the pillar of cloud descended and stood in the door of the tabernacle, and the Lord spoke with Moses. ¹⁰And when all the people saw the clouden pillar standing in the tabernacle entry, they rose up and worshipped, everyone in his tent door. ¹¹And the Lord spoke to Moses face to face, as a man speaks to his friend. And when Moses turned back into the host, the lad Joshua, his servant the son of Nun, did not leave the tabernacle.

*[Tabernacle of witness: See Ex 27 and note b for why it was so called]

¹²And Moses said to the Lord, See, you said to me, Lead this people forth – but you have not shown me whom you will send with me. And you have said moreover, I know you by name, and, You have also found grace in my sight. ¹³Now, therefore, if I have found favour in your sight, then show me your way, and let me know you, so that I may find grace in your sight. And look on this also: that this nation is your people.

¹⁴And he said, My presence shall go with you, and I will give you rest.

¹⁵And Moses said, If your presence does not go with me, do not carry us away from here. ¹⁶For how can it be known now, that both I and your people have found favour in your sight, unless you go with us? – that both I and your people have pre-eminence before all the people that are upon the face of the earth?

¹⁷And the Lord said to Moses, I will do this also which you have asked, for you have found grace in my sight and I know you by name.

¹⁸And he said, I beseech you, show me your glory!

¹⁹And he said, I will make all my goodness go before you, and I will be called in this name Jehovah before you. And I will show mercy to whom I shew mercy, and will have compassion on whom I have compassion. ²⁰And he said furthermore, You may not see my face, for no man can see me and live.[a]

²¹And the Lord said, Behold, there is a place by me, and there you

shall stand upon a rock. ²²And while my glory goes forth, I will put you in a cleft of the rock, and will put my hand upon you while I pass by. ²³And then I will take away my hand and you shall see my back parts, but my face shall not be seen.

The Notes

a) 20. No man can see my face and live: not that the face of God, which is the face of life, is the cause of death to those that see it. For the saints who are in heaven do indeed see it. But none who live in the body can see nor comprehend the majesty of his face, but must first be purified by death, as Paul declares in 1Corinthians 15:50.

Chapter 34

> The tablets are renewed. The mercy of God. To have fellowship with the Gentiles is forbidden, and their idolatry also. The Feast of Sweet Bread. The first begotten. The Sabbath. The Feast of Three Weeks. The firstfruits. Moses' fast. Moses' face glows.

And the Lord said to Moses, Hew two tablets of stone like the first, so that I may write in them the words that were in the first two tablets, which you broke. ²And be ready for the morning so that you can go early up the mount of Sinai, and stand before me there upon the top of the mount. ³But let no man come up with you, neither let any man be seen throughout all the mount. Neither let the flocks nor herds feed before the hill.

⁴And Moses hewed two tablets of stone like the first ones, rose up early in the morning, and went up into the mount of Sinai as the Lord had directed him. And he took in his hand the two tablets of stone. ⁵And the Lord descended in the cloud and stood with him there, and he called upon the name of the Lord. ⁶And when the Lord walked before him, he cried out, Lord, Lord God, full of compassion and mercy! Who is not lightly angered, but abundant in mercy and truth, ⁷and keeps mercy in store for thousands, and forgives wickedness, trespass, and sin (for there is no man innocent before you), but visits the wickedness of the fathers upon the children, and upon the children's children, even to the third and fourth generation. ⁸And Moses bowed himself to the earth quickly and worshipped, ⁹and said, If I have found grace in your sight, O Lord, then let my Lord go with us (for it is a stubborn people), and have mercy upon our wickedness and our sin, and let us be your inheritance.

Jer 32:18

¹⁰And he replied, Behold, I make a covenant before all this people, that I will do marvels such as have not been done in all the world, neither in any nation. And all the people that are with you will see the work of the Lord; for it is a fearful thing that I will do with you. ¹¹Keep everything that I command you this day, and behold, I will cast out before you the Amorites, Canaanites, Hittites, Perizzites, Hivites, and Jebusites.

Ge 15:18-21
Ex 23:23,28; 33:2.

¹²Take heed to yourself, that you make no compact with the inhabiters of the land where you are going, lest it be a cause of ruin among you. ¹³But overthrow their altars, break their pillars, and cut down their groves; ¹⁴for you must worship no strange god. For the Lord is called jealous because he is a jealous God. ¹⁵Make no agreement with the inhabiters of the land, lest, when they go a-whoring after their gods and sacrifice to their gods, they call you and you eat of their sacrifice; ¹⁶and lest you take their daughters unto your sons, and, when their daughters go a-whoring after their gods, they make your sons go a-whoring after their gods also. ¹⁷You must make no gods of metal for yourselves.

¹⁸The Feast of Sweet Bread you must keep, and seven days you shall eat unleavened bread (as I commanded you) in the time appointed in the month of Abib; for in the month of Abib you came out of Egypt. ¹⁹All that breach the womb[a] shall be mine, and all that breach the womb among your livestock, if it be male, whether ox or sheep. ²⁰But the firstborn of the donkey you shall buy out with a sheep; or, if you do not redeem him, see that you break his neck. All the firstborn of your sons you must redeem. And see that no man appears before me empty-handed.

²¹Six days you shall work, and the seventh you shall rest, both from plowing and reaping. ²²You shall observe the Feast of Weeks with the firstfruits of the wheat harvest, and the Feast of Ingathering at the year's end. ²³Thrice in a year shall all your menchildren appear before the Lord Jehovah, God of Israel. ²⁴For I will cast out the nations before you, and will enlarge your borders so that no man will desire your land while you go up to appear before the face of the Lord your God thrice in the year.

²⁵You shall not offer the blood of my sacrifice with leavened bread, nor shall anything of the sacrifice of the feast of Passover be left till the morning. ²⁶The first of the firstfruits of your land you shall bring to the house of the Lord your God. And see that you do not cook a kid in its mother's milk.

²⁷And the Lord said to Moses, Write down these words, for upon these words I have made a covenant with you and with the children of Israel. ²⁸And Moses was there with the Lord forty days and forty nights, and neither ate bread nor drank water. And he wrote in the tablets the words of the covenant, even ten verses.

²⁹And Moses came down from Mount Sinai with the two tablets of witness in his hand, and he was as yet unaware that the skin of his face shone with beams of light from his communing with the Lord. ³⁰And when Aaron and all the children of Israel looked upon Moses and saw that the skin of his face shone with beams of light,[b] they were afraid to come near him. ³¹But he called them to him, and then Aaron and all the chief men of the company came to him, and Moses talked with them. ³²And at the last, all the children of Israel came to Moses, and he commanded them all that the Lord had said to him in Mount Sinai.

^{33}And as soon as he had made an end of speaking with them, he put a covering upon his face. ^{34}But when he went before the Lord to speak with him, he took the covering off until he came out, and he came out and spoke to the children of Israel that which he was commanded. ^{35}And the children of Israel saw the face of Moses – that the skin of his face shone with beams of light. But Moses put a covering upon his face until he went in to commune with the Lord.

The Notes

a) 19. All that breach the womb: that is, all the firstborn, as in Ge 38:29.
b) 30. The shining of Moses' face is expounded in 2Corinthians 3:13.

Chapter 35

> The Sabbath day. The readiness of the people to offer. Bezaleel and Aholiab are praised by Moses and set to work.

Moses gathered all the company of the children of Israel together and said to them, These are the things that the Lord has commanded to do: ^{2}Six days you shall work, but the seventh day shall be to you the holy Sabbath of the Lord's rest, so that whoever does any work that day shall die. ^{3}Moreover, you must kindle no fire throughout all your habitations on the Sabbath day.   De 5:12-14

^{4}And Moses spoke to all the multitude of the children of Israel, saying, This is the thing that the Lord commanded, saying, ^{5}Give from among you a lift offering to the Lord. All who are willing in their hearts shall bring lift offerings to the Lord: gold, silver, and bronze; ^{6}jacinth,^{a} scarlet, purple, byss, and goats' hair;^{b} ^{7}rams' skins dyed red, badger skins, and sethim wood; ^{8}oil for the lamps; spices for the anointing oil and for the sweet incense; ^{9}and onyx stones and stones to be set in the ephod and in the breastlap.   Ex c25

^{10}And let all who are wise-hearted among you come and make everything that the Lord has commanded: ^{11}the habitation and the tent thereof, with its covering and its rings, boards, bars, pillars, and sockets; ^{12}the ark and its poles, with the mercy seat and the veil that partitions it off; ^{13}the table and its poles, with everything that belongs to it, and the showbread; ^{14}the candlestick for light with its accessories, its lamps, and the oil for the lamps; ^{15}the incense altar and its poles, the anointing oil, and the sweet incense; the hanging for before the tabernacle door; ^{16}the altar of burnt sacrifices and the bronze gridiron that belongs to it, with its poles and all its equipment; the laver and its base; ^{17}the hangings of the court, its pillars, their sockets, and the hanging for the gate of the court; ^{18}the pegs of the habitation and the pegs of the court with their boards: ^{19}and the ministering garments, to minister with in holiness – the holy vestments of Aaron the priest, and the vestments of his sons to minister in.

^{20}And all the company of the children of Israel departed from the presence of Moses. ^{21}And they went (as many as their hearts encouraged them, and as many as their spirits made them willing), and brought lift offerings to the Lord for the making of the tabernacle of witness, and for all its services and for the holy vestments. ²²And the men came with the women (as many as were willing-hearted) and brought bracelets, earrings, rings, belts, and all manner of articles of gold; that is, all who waved* wave offerings of gold to the Lord. ²³And everyone with whom was found jacinth, scarlet, purple, byss,ᶜ goats' hair, red skins of rams, or badger skins, brought it. ²⁴And all who lifted up gold or bronze brought a lift offering to the Lord. And everyone with whom was found sethim wood suitable for any manner of work or service, brought it.

²⁵And all the women who were wise-hearted to work with their hands spun yarn, and brought the spun work of jacinth, scarlet, purple, and byss. ²⁶And all the women who excelled in wisdom of heart spun the goats' hair. ²⁷And the lords brought onyx stones and setting stones for the ephod and the breastlap, ²⁸and spice and oil for the lamps, the anointing oil, and the sweet incense.

²⁹And the children of Israel brought willing offerings to the Lord, both men and women – as many as their hearts made them willing to bring – for all the things that the Lord through Moses had commanded to make.

³⁰And Moses said to the children of Israel, Behold, the Lord has called by name Bezaleel the son of Uri, the son of Hur of the tribe of Judah. ³¹And he has filled him with the Spirit of God – with wisdom, understanding, and knowledge for every kind of work, ³²and to devise artistic works: to work in gold, silver, and bronze, ³³to engrave stones and set them, to carve in wood, and to work in all manner of skilled crafts. ³⁴And he has put in his heart the grace to teach. Both him and Aholiab, the son of Ahisamach of the tribe of Dan, ³⁵he has filled with wisdom of heart to do all kinds of engraving work. They are also embroiderers and needleworkers with jacinth, scarlet, purple, and byss, and are weavers who can make all kinds of things, and can devise ingenious designs.

*[waved: a side to side motion with the items in their hands. The movement was said to indicate that the world belonged to God; hence they were giving back to him what belonged to him.]

Ex 31:1-11

The Notes

a) 6. Jacinth: See above in Exodus 26:1 and note a.
b) 6. Goats' hair is that which we call *camlet*. [Ed: Camlet was a beautiful, light, and costly fabric, which in the 16th and 17th centuries was made of the hair of the Angora goat. It was popular for female apparel.]
c) 23. Byss is fine white, whether it be silk or linen.

Chapter 36

The things Bezaleel and Aholiab made for the holy place of the Lord.

And Bezaleel did the work, and Aholiab, and all the wise-hearted men to whom the Lord had given wisdom and understanding to know how to do all the work for the holy service, in all that the Lord commanded. ²And Moses called for Bezaleel, Aholiab, and all the wise-hearted men in whose hearts the Lord had put wisdom – as many as their hearts encouraged them to come and do the work – ³and they received from Moses all the lift offerings that the children of Israel had brought for making the things of the holy service. And besides that, the people brought willing offerings every morning.

⁴Then all the wise men who were employed in the holy work left the work they were doing ⁵and spoke to Moses, saying, The people are bringing too much, more than enough to serve for the works that the Lord has commanded. ⁶And then Moses gave a charge, and they caused it to be proclaimed throughout the host, saying, See that neither man nor woman prepare anything more for the holy lift offering. And so the people were forbidden to bring more, ⁷because what they had was sufficient for the work to be done – even too much.

⁸And all the wise-hearted men among them who were employed in the work of the habitation made ten curtains of twined byss, jacinth, scarlet, and purple, and made them full of cherubims with embroidered work. ⁹The length of one curtain was twenty-eight cubits and the width four, and they were all the same size. ¹⁰And they joined five curtains by themselves and the other five by themselves. ¹¹And they made fifty loops of jacinth along the edge of the end curtain; that is, in the selvage of the coupling curtain. And they did likewise on the edge of the end coupling curtain on the other side: ¹²fifty loops they made in the one curtain, and fifty in the edge of the coupling curtain on the other side, so that the loops were one over against another. ¹³And they made fifty rings of gold, and coupled the curtains one to another with the rings. And so was it made a dwelling place.   Ex 27:9-18

¹⁴And they made eleven curtains of goats' hair to be a tent over the tabernacle, ¹⁵thirty cubits long apiece and four cubits wide – all eleven of the same size. ¹⁶And they joined five by themselves, and six by themselves, ¹⁷and they made fifty loops along the border of the end coupling curtain on the one side, and fifty in the edge of the coupling curtain on the other side. ¹⁸And they made fifty rings of bronze to couple the tent together, so that it could be one. ¹⁹And they made a covering for the tent of rams' skins dyed red, and yet another of badger skins to go above it all.

²⁰And they made boards of sethim wood for the dwelling place, which stood upright. ²¹Each board was ten cubits long and a cubit and a half wide. ²²And they made two feet for every board of the dwelling place, joining one to another. ²³They made twenty boards for the south side of the habitation, ²⁴and forty sockets of silver for under the twenty boards: two sockets under every board for their two feet. ²⁵And for the other side of the dwelling, toward the north, they made twenty other boards ²⁶with forty sockets of silver: two sockets under every board.   Ex 26:15-30

²⁷Behind, at the rear of the tabernacle toward the west, they made six boards. ²⁸And they made two other boards for the corners of the habitation in the rear, ²⁹and these were joined close, both beneath and also above with clamps; and thus they did for both the corners, ³⁰so

that there were in all eight boards and sixteen sockets, with two sockets under every board. ³¹And they made bars of sethim wood: five for the boards of the one side of the habitation, ³²five for the other, and five for the boards of the west end of the habitation; ³³and they made the middle bar to shoot through the boards, from the one end to the other. ³⁴And they overlaid the boards with gold, and made for them rings of gold to thrust the bars through, and covered the bars with gold.

³⁵And they made a hanging of jacinth, scarlet, purple, and twined byss, with cherubims of embroidered work; ³⁶and for it, they made four pillars of sethim wood and overlaid them with gold. Their knobs were also of gold, and they cast for them four sockets of silver. ³⁷And they made a hanging for the tabernacle entryway of jacinth, scarlet, purple, and twined byss needlework; ³⁸and it had five pillars with their knobs. They overlaid the capitals and the bands with gold, and their five sockets were of bronze.

Chapter 37

The ark of witness. The mercy seat. The table. The candlestick. The lights. The altar and the incense.

Ex 25:10-16

And Bezaleel made the ark of sethim wood, two cubits and a half long, a cubit and a half broad, and a cubit and a half high; ²and he overlaid it with fine gold both within and without. He made a molding of gold to crown it round about, ³and cast for it four rings of gold for the four corners – two rings for one side and two for the other. ⁴And he made poles of sethim wood and covered them with gold, ⁵and put the poles in the rings along by the side of the ark, to carry it with.

Ex 25:17-22

⁶And he made the mercy seat^a of pure gold, two cubits and a half long and one cubit and a half wide. ⁷He made two cherubims of thick gold upon the two ends of the mercy seat: ⁸one cherub on one end and another cherub on the other end of the mercy seat. ⁹And the cherubims spread out their wings above on high and covered the mercy seat. And their faces were one toward the other; even toward the mercy seat were the faces of the cherubims.

Ex 25:23-30

¹⁰And he made the table of sethim wood, two cubits long, a cubit wide, and a cubit and a half high. ¹¹He overlaid it with fine gold, and made a molding of gold round about it. ¹²He also made a rim of a handbreadth wide round about it, and made a molding of gold round about the rim. ¹³And he cast for it four rings of gold and put the rings in the four corners by the legs, ¹⁴under the rim, to put poles in to carry the table. ¹⁵And he made poles of sethim wood to carry the table, and covered them with gold. ¹⁶And he made the vessels that were on the table of pure gold: the dishes, spoons, bowls, and pots to pour with.

Ex 25:31-40

¹⁷And he made the candlestick of pure, thick gold – both the candlestick and its shaft, with branches, bowls, buds, and flowers proceeding out of it. ¹⁸Six branches proceeded out of the sides of it: three out of the one side and three out of the other. ¹⁹And on every branch

were three cups like almonds with buds and flowers, on all six branches that proceeded out of the candlestick. ²⁰And on the candlestick itself were four cups fashioned like almonds with buds and flowers, ²¹with a bud under each pair of branches. ²²And the buds and the branches proceeded out of it, and were all one piece of pure, thick gold. ²³And he made seven lamps for it, and the snuffers and firepans, of pure gold. ²⁴Of 100 pounds of pure gold were it and all its accessories made.

²⁵And he made the incense altar of sethim wood, a cubit long and a cubit wide foursquare, and two cubits high, with horns proceeding out of it. ²⁶And he covered it with pure gold – the top and sides round about and its horns – and made a molding of gold round about it. ²⁷And he attached two rings of gold under the molding on either side of it, to put poles in for carrying it, ²⁸and made poles of sethim wood and overlaid them with gold. ²⁹And he made the holy anointing oil and the sweet, pure incense according to the apothecary's craft.

Ex 30:1-6

The Notes

a) 6. The mercy seat was the place where God spoke to the children of Israel (Ex 25:22; 30:6). It was upon the ark of witness and signified Christ, as it is said in Hebrews, chapter 9.

Chapter 38

> The altar of burnt offerings. The bronze laver. The sum total of that which the people offered for the building of the habitation of the Lord.

And he made the burnt-offering altar of sethim wood, five cubits long and five cubits broad foursquare, and three cubits high. ²And he made horns in the four corners of it, proceeding out of it, and overlaid it with bronze. ³And he made all the accessories of the altar – the pots, shovels, basins, fleshhooks, and coal pans – all of bronze.

Ex 27:1-8

⁴And he made a gridiron, a network of bronze, round about and low beneath on the altar, so that it reached halfway up the altar. ⁵And he cast four rings of bronze for the four corners of the gridiron, to put poles in. ⁶And he made the poles of sethim wood and covered them with bronze, ⁷and put the poles in the rings along by the side of the altar to carry it with. And he made the altar hollow, with boards.

⁸And he made the laver of bronze, and its base also of bronze, in the sight of those who were watching before the door of the tabernacle of witness.

⁹And he made the court with hangings of twined byss of 100 cubits long on the south side, ¹⁰and twenty pillars with twenty sockets of bronze; but the knobs of the pillars and the bands were silver. ¹¹And on the north side the hangings were 100 cubits long with twenty pillars and twenty sockets of bronze, but the knobs and the bands of the pillars were of silver. ¹²And on the west side were hangings of fifty cubits long, and ten pillars with their ten sockets, and the knobs and the bands of the pillars were silver. ¹³And on the east side, toward the sun rising, were hangings of fifty cubits. ¹⁴The hangings of the one side of

Ex 27:9-19

the gate were fifteen cubits long, and their pillars three with their three sockets. ¹⁵And for the other side of the court gate were hangings also of fifteen cubits long, and their pillars three, with three sockets.

¹⁶Now all the hangings round about the court were of twined byss. ¹⁷And the sockets of the pillars were bronze, but the knobs and the bands of the pillars were silver and the capitals were overlaid with silver. All the pillars of the court were banded about with silver. ¹⁸And the hanging of the gate of the court was needlework of jacinth, scarlet, purple, and twined byss, twenty cubits long and five in height, matching the hangings of the court. ¹⁹And the pillars were four, with four sockets of bronze, the knobs of silver, and the capitals overlaid with silver and banded about with silver. ²⁰And all the pegs of the tabernacle and of the court round about were bronze.

²¹Below is the inventory of the habitation of witness, which was taken at Moses' command and carried out by the Levites under the direction of Ithamar, son to Aaron the priest. ²²And Bezaleel the son of Uri, son to Hur of the tribe of Judah, made all that the Lord had commanded Moses; ²³and with him was Aholiab the son of Ahisamach, of the tribe of Dan, a skillful engraver and worker of needlework in jacinth, scarlet, purple, and byss.

²⁴All the gold that was used in the work of the holy place (which was the gold of the wave offering) was 2,900 pounds and 730 sickles according to the holy sickle.

²⁵And the amount of silver that came from the multitude was 10,000 pounds and 1,775 sickles of the holy sickle, ²⁶every man offering half a sickle according to the weight of the holy sickle, of those twenty years old and above who went to be numbered – 603,550 men. ²⁷And the 10,000 pounds of silver went to the casting of the sockets of the sanctuary and the sockets of the veil: 100 sockets made from the 10,000 pounds, being 100 pounds for every socket. ²⁸The 1,775 sickles made knobs for the pillars, and overlaid the capitals and banded them.

²⁹And the bronze of the wave offering was 7,000 pounds and 2,400 sickles. ³⁰With it he made the sockets for the entry of the tabernacle of witness, the bronze altar, the bronze gridiron that belongs to the altar, all the vessels of the altar, the sockets of the court round about, ³¹the sockets of the court gate, all the pegs of the habitation, and all the pegs of the court round about.

Chapter 39

The making of Aaron's and his sons' apparel. Everything that the Lord commanded was offered.

And from the jacinth, scarlet, purple, and twined byss, they made the vestments of ministration to do service in that holy place, and made the holy garments for Aaron's use, as the Lord commanded Moses.

Ex 28:5-8

²They made the ephod of gold, jacinth, scarlet, purple, and twined byss. ³And they hammered gold into thin sheets and cut it into wires,

to work it in with the jacinth, scarlet, purple, and the byss, with embroidered work. ⁴And they made the sides come together, and closed them up by the two edges. ⁵And the embroidery of the sash that was upon it was of the same stuff and with the same work of gold, jacinth, scarlet, purple, and twined byss, as the Lord commanded Moses.

⁶And they fashioned onyx stones enclosed in settings of gold, and engraved as signets are engraved with the names of the children of Israel. ⁷And they put them on the shoulders of the ephod to be a remembrance of the children of Israel, as the Lord commanded Moses.

⁸And they made the breastlap skillfully, as with the ephod, of gold, jacinth, scarlet, purple, and twined byss. ⁹And they made it foursquare doubled over, a handbreadth long and a handbreadth wide. ¹⁰And they filled it with four rows of stones – the first row a sardius, a topaz, and an emerald; ¹¹the second row a ruby, a sapphire, and a diamond; ¹²the third row a ligure, an agate, and an amethyst; ¹³the fourth row a turquoise, an onyx, and a jasper – enclosed round about with gold in all the rows. ¹⁴And the twelve stones were engraved as signets are, with the names of the children of Israel – every stone with its name, corresponding to the twelve tribes.

¹⁵And they made on the breastlap two fastening chains of twisted work and pure gold. ¹⁶And they made two hooks of gold and two gold rings, and put the two rings on the two corners of the breastlap. ¹⁷And they put the two chains of gold in the two rings that were in the corners of the breastlap. ¹⁸And the two ends of the two chains they fastened in the two hooks, and put them on the shoulders of the ephod, on the forefront of it.

¹⁹And they made two other rings of gold and put them on the two other corners of the breastlap, along upon the edge toward the inside of the ephod that faces it. ²⁰And they made yet two other gold rings and put them on the two sides of the ephod, beneath on the foreside of it where the sides go together, above on the embroidery of the ephod. ²¹And they bound the breastlap tightly by its rings to the rings of the ephod with cords of jacinth, so that it would lie tight to the embroidery of the ephod and would not hang loose from the ephod, as the Lord commanded Moses.

²²And he made the tunic for the ephod of woven work and entirely of jacinth. ²³The opening for the head in the tunic was in the middle of it, like the collar of a partlet, with a band round about the collar so that it would not tear. ²⁴And they made on the bottom, on the hem of the tunic, pomegranates of jacinth, scarlet, purple, and twined byss. ²⁵And they made little bells of pure gold and put them between the pomegranates, round about on the hem of the tunic: ²⁶a bell and a pomegranate, a bell and a pomegranate, round about the hem of the tunic, for ministering in as the Lord commanded Moses.

²⁷And they made coats of byss, of woven work, for Aaron and his sons, ²⁸and a turban of byss, fine headwear of byss, linen breeches of twined byss, ²⁹and the sash of twined byss, jacinth, scarlet, and purple

with needlework, as the Lord commanded Moses.

³⁰And they made the plate for the holy crown of fine gold, and wrote upon it with graven work THE HOLINESS OF THE LORD, ³¹and tied it to a cord of jacinth to fasten it up high upon the turban, as the Lord commanded Moses.

Ex 28:36-38

³²Thus was all the work of the habitation of the tabernacle of witness finished. And the children of Israel did according to all that the Lord had commanded Moses. ³³And they brought the habitation to Moses, the tent and all its parts, furnishings, and accessories: the rings, boards, bars, pillars, and sockets; ³⁴the covering of rams' skins dyed red; the covering of badger skins; the hanging veil; ³⁵the ark of witness with its poles and the mercy seat; ³⁶the table, all its equipment, and the showbread; ³⁷the pure candlestick, the lamps prepared for it, all its accessories, and the oil for the lamps; ³⁸the golden altar, the anointing oil, and the sweet incense; the hanging for the tabernacle door; ³⁹the bronze altar and the gridiron of bronze belonging to it, with its bars and all its accessories; the laver with its base; ⁴⁰the hangings of the court with their pillars and sockets; the hanging for the court gate with its boards and pegs; all the equipment that served for the habitation of the tabernacle of witness; ⁴¹and the ministering vestments to serve in the holy place – the holy vestments of Aaron the priest and his sons' garments, to minister in.

⁴²According to everything that the Lord had commanded Moses, just so did the children of Israel do all the work. ⁴³And Moses beheld all the work, and see, they had done it just as the Lord commanded. And then Moses blessed them.*

*Look in Ge 2:3 & note b.

Chapter 40

The tabernacle is reared up. The glory of the Lord appears in a cloud covering the tabernacle.

And the Lord spoke to Moses, saying, ²In the first day of the first month you shall set up the habitation of the tabernacle of witness. ³Put therein the ark of witness, screen off the ark with the veil, ⁴and bring in the table and set it up. Bring in the candlestick and light the lamps, ⁵set the incense altar of gold before the ark of witness, and put the hanging at the door to the habitation. ⁶Set the altar of burnt offering before the door to the tabernacle of witness. ⁷Set the laver between the tabernacle of witness and the altar, and put water in it. ⁸And set up the court around it, and hang the hanging of the court gate.

Ex 30:17-21

⁹And take the anointing oil and anoint the habitation and everything that is in it, and hallow it and everything that belongs there, so that it may be holy. ¹⁰And anoint the altar of the burnt offerings and all its accessories, and sanctify the altar, that it may be most holy. ¹¹And anoint also the laver and its base, and sanctify it.

Nu 7:1

¹²Then bring Aaron and his sons to the door of the tabernacle of witness and wash them with water. ¹³Put upon Aaron the holy vestments, and anoint him and sanctify him so that he may minister to me.

¹⁴Bring his sons also, and put the coats on them, and anoint them as you have anointed their father so that they may be my priests. ¹⁵This anointing they shall have for an everlasting priesthood throughout their generations.

¹⁶And Moses did according to all that the Lord commanded him.

¹⁷Thus was the tabernacle reared up, the first day in the first month in the second year. ¹⁸And Moses reared up the tabernacle and fastened the sockets, set up the boards and put in their bars, reared up the pillars, ¹⁹spread abroad the tent over the habitation, and put the covering of the tent on high above it, as the Lord commanded him.

²⁰And he took and put the testimony in the ark, put in place the poles of the ark, and put the mercy seat on high upon the ark. ²¹And he brought the ark into the habitation, and hung up the veil to screen off the ark of witness, as the Lord commanded him.

²²And he put the table in the tabernacle of witness in the north side of the habitation outside the veil, ²³and set the bread in order before the Lord, just as the Lord had commanded him. ²⁴And he put the candlestick in the tabernacle of witness across from the table, in the south side of the habitation, ²⁵and set up the lamps before the Lord, as the Lord commanded him. ²⁶And he put the golden altar in the tabernacle of witness before the veil, ²⁷and burned sweet incense on it as the Lord commanded him. ²⁸And he set up the hanging in the door of the habitation, ²⁹set the burnt-offering altar before the door of the tabernacle of witness, and offered burnt offerings and food offerings on it, as the Lord commanded him.

³⁰And he set the laver between the tabernacle of witness and the altar, and poured water in it to wash with. ³¹And Moses with Aaron and his sons washed their hands and their feet there, ³²both when they went into the tabernacle of witness and when they went to the altar, as the Lord had commanded Moses. ³³And he reared up the court round about the habitation and the altar, and set up the hanging of the court gate.

And thus Moses finished the work. ³⁴And the cloud covered the tabernacle of witness, and the glory of the Lord filled the habitation, ³⁵so that Moses could not enter into the tabernacle of witness because the cloud abode in it. And the glory of the Lord filled the habitation.

³⁶When the cloud was taken up from the habitation, the children of Israel took their journeys and set out on their travels. ³⁷But if the cloud remained, they journeyed not till it departed. ³⁸For the cloud of the Lord was upon the habitation by day, and fire by night, in the sight of all the house of Israel, in all their journeys.

♣

The end of the second book of Moses.

Side notes:
- vv14-15, e.f. COV. (v14 was missing from the Matthew Bible.)
- Ex 30:17-21
- Nu 9:15
- Nu 9:16-23

The Third Book of Moses
called
Leviticus

Chapter 1

The ordering of burnt offerings, whether they are of small or great animals or birds.

[*]See note b on Ex c27 for why it was called the tabernacle of witness.

AND THE LORD CALLED MOSES and spoke to him out of the tabernacle of witness,* saying, ²Speak to the children of Israel and say to them: Whosoever of you brings a gift to the Lord shall bring it from the domestic animals – from the oxen, sheep, or goats.

³If he brings a burnt offering from the oxen, he shall bring a male without blemish, and shall bring him to the door of the tabernacle of witness so that he may be accepted before the Lord. ⁴And let him put his hand upon the head of the burnt sacrifice,‡ and favour will be given him, to make an atonement for him. ⁵And let him kill the ox before the Lord. And let the priests, Aaron's sons, bring the blood, and let them sprinkle it round about upon the altar that is before the door of the tabernacle of witness. ⁶And let the burnt offering be skinned and cut in pieces. ⁷And then let the sons of Aaron the priest put fire upon the altar, and put wood on the fire. ⁸And let them lay the pieces, with the head and the fat, upon the wood that is on the fire in the altar. ⁹But the inwards and the legs they shall wash in water. And the priest shall burn everything together upon the altar, for a burnt sacrifice and an offering of a sweet odour to the Lord.ᵃ

‡Look in Ge 48:14 and note a.

¹⁰If he offers a burnt sacrifice from the flocks, whether it be from the lambs or from the goats, he shall offer a male without blemish. ¹¹And let him kill it on the north side of the altar before the Lord. And let the priests, Aaron's sons, sprinkle its blood round about upon the altar. ¹²And let it be cut in pieces, with his head and his fat, and let the priest put them upon the wood that lies upon the fire in the altar. ¹³But let him wash the inwards and the legs with water, and then bring it all together and burn it upon the altar. This is a burnt offering and a sacrifice of sweet savour to the Lord.

¹⁴But if he offers a burnt offering from the birds, he shall offer either from the turtle doves or from the young pigeons. ¹⁵And the priest shall bring the bird to the altar and wring its neck apart, and shall burn it on the altar, and let the blood run out on the sides of the altar. ¹⁶And pluck away its crop and its feathers, and cast them beside the altar on the east side, upon the ash heap. ¹⁷And break its wings, but do not pluck them apart. And then let the priest burn it upon the altar, on the wood that lies upon the fire. It is a burnt sacrifice and an offering of a sweet savour to the Lord.

The Notes

a)   9. The sweet odour or savour of a burnt offering is the sacrifice of faith and pure affection, in which God is delighted just as a person delights in the good savour of foods, as it is said of Noah in Genesis 8:20,21.

Chapter 2

> The ordering of food offerings – of sweet cakes, fine flour, frankincense, etc. – without leaven and without honey, but not without salt.

If any soul will offer a food offering to the Lord, his offering shall be fine flour; and he shall pour oil on it and add frankincense, ²and shall bring it to Aaron's sons the priests. And one of them shall take out a handful of the flour and oil with all the frankincense, and burn it for a memorial upon the altar: an offering of a sweet savour to the Lord.ᵃ ³And the rest of the food offering shall be for Aaron and his sons, as a thing most holy of the sacrifices of the Lord. ⁴If anyone brings a food offering that is baked in the oven, let him bring sweet cakes of fine flour mixed with oil, or unleavened wafers spread with oil. ⁵If your food offering is made in a frying pan, then it shall be of sweet flour mixed with oil, ⁶and you shall mince it small and pour oil on it; and so is it a food offering. ⁷If your food offering is a thing broiled on the gridiron, of flour mixed with oil it shall be. ⁸And you shall bring the food offering that is made of these things to the Lord, and shall deliver it to the priest. And he shall bring it to the altar, ⁹and shall lift up part of the food offering for a memorial, and shall burn it upon the altar: an offering of a sweet savour to the Lord. ¹⁰And what is left of the food offering will be for Aaron and his sons, as a thing that is most holy from the offerings of the Lord.

¹¹All the food offerings that you bring to the Lord shall be made without leaven. For you shall burn neither leaven nor honey in any offering to the Lord. ¹²Notwithstanding, you may bring the firstlings of them to the Lord, but they shall not come upon the altar to make a sweet savour.

¹³All your food offerings you must salt with salt. You shall not permit the salt of the covenant of your God to be lacking from your food offering, but in all your offerings you shall offer salt.ᵇ

¹⁴If you offer a food offering of the first ripe grains to the Lord, then take of that which is still green, dry it by the fire, and grind it fine; in this way, offer the food offering from your first ripe fruits. ¹⁵And then pour oil on it and add frankincense, and so is it a food offering. ¹⁶And the priest shall burn part of the ground grain and part of the oil with all the frankincense, for a remembrance. This is an offering to the Lord.

Lev 6:15

The Notes

a) 2. This sweet savour figures the prayers of the meek and faithful, as it is interpreted in Rev 8:3,4, which prayers withstand the fury of the Lord.

b) 13. All offerings must be salted with salt: this signifies that all our good works must be ordered according to the teaching of the apostles and prophets, for then they will be acceptable in the sight of the Lord, if they savour of the salt thereof. Otherwise, they will not.

Chapter 3

The ordering of peace offerings, which were offered for the keeping of peace and made with oxen, sheep, lambs, and goats.

^{Ex 24:5,6} If anyone brings a peace offering from the oxen, whether it be male or female, he shall bring such as is without blemish before the Lord. ²And let him put his hand upon the head of his offering and kill it before the door of the tabernacle of witness. And Aaron's sons, the priests, shall sprinkle the blood upon the altar round about. ³And they shall offer from the peace offering, to be a sacrifice to the Lord, the fat that covers the inwards and all the fat that is upon the inwards, ⁴and the two kidneys with the fat that lies upon the loins. And the membrane that is on the liver, they shall remove with the kidneys.ª ⁵And Aaron's sons shall burn them on the altar with the burnt sacrifice that is upon the wood on the fire. This is a sacrifice of a sweet savour to the Lord.

⁶If anyone brings a peace offering to the Lord from of the flock, whether it be male or female, it shall be without blemish. ⁷If he offers a lamb, he shall bring it before the Lord, ⁸and put his hand upon his offering's head and kill it in the door to the tabernacle of witness. And Aaron's sons shall sprinkle its blood round about the altar. ⁹And from the peace offering they shall bring a sacrifice to the Lord: its fat; the whole rump, which they shall take off hard by the backbone; the fat that covers the inwards and all the fat that is upon the inwards; ¹⁰and the two kidneys, with the fat that lies upon them and upon the loins. And the membrane that is upon the liver, he shall remove with the

vv11 & 16
e.f. COV.
kidneys. ¹¹And the priest shall burn them on the altar, for the food of the offering to the Lord.

¹²If the offering is a goat, he shall bring it before the Lord, ¹³put his hand upon its head, and kill it before the tabernacle of witness. And the sons of Aaron shall sprinkle its blood upon the altar round about. ¹⁴And he shall bring from it his offering for the Lord's sacrifice: the fat that covers the inwards, all the fat that is upon the inwards, ¹⁵and the two kidneys with the fat that lies upon them and upon the loins. And the membrane that is upon the liver, he shall remove with the kidneys. ¹⁶And the priest shall burn them upon the altar, for the food of the Lord's sacrifice and to make a sweet savour.

¹⁷And thus shall all the fat be the Lord's. And it shall be a law forever among your generations after you in your dwelling places, that you shall eat neither fat nor blood.

The Notes

a) 4. By the taking away of the fat, the inwards, the two kidneys, and the membrane, it is signified to us that if we will be a sweet sacrifice unto the Lord, we must cut off all inordinate lusts, immoral desires of the flesh, and the evil use of all our members; and must subdue and mortify our affections, and offer them to God by the mortification of the cross, as says the prophet in Psalm 26:1-6.

Chapter 4

The offering made for sins done out of ignorance.

And the Lord talked with Moses, saying, ²Speak to the children of Israel and say: When a soul sins through ignorance, and has done any of those things which the Lord has forbidden in his commandments to be done:–

³If the anointed priest sins and causes the people to do amiss, he shall bring for his sin that he has done an ox without blemish to the Lord, for a sin offering. ⁴And he shall bring the ox to the door of the tabernacle of witness before the Lord, and shall put his hand upon the ox's head* and kill him before the Lord. ⁵And the anointed priest shall take some of the ox's blood and bring it into the tabernacle of witness, ⁶and shall dip his finger in the blood and sprinkle some of it seven times before the Lord, there before the hanging of the holy place. ⁷And he shall put some of the blood upon the horns of the altar of sweet incense that is in the tabernacle of witness before the Lord, and shall pour all the rest of the blood of the ox upon the bottom of the altar of burnt offerings that is by the door of the tabernacle of witness. ⁸And he shall remove all the fat of the ox that is the sin offering – the fat that covers the inwards, all the fat that is around them, ⁹and the two kidneys with the fat that lies upon them and upon the loins. And the membrane on the liver, let them remove also with the kidneys, ¹⁰as it was removed from the ox of the peace offering. And let the priest burn them on the altar of burnt offerings. ¹¹But the skin of the ox and all his flesh, with his head, his legs, and his inwards with his dung, ¹²he shall carry all together out of the host to a clean place, there where the ashes are poured out, and burn him on wood with fire, there upon the heap of ashes.

¹³If the whole body of the children of Israel sins through ignorance and the thing be hid from their eyes, so that they have committed any of the things which the Lord has forbidden to be done in his commandments and have offended, ¹⁴but the sin that they have sinned becomes afterwards known, then they shall offer an ox for a sin offering. And they shall bring it before the tabernacle of witness, ¹⁵and the elders of the multitude shall put their hands upon its head before the Lord. ¹⁶And the anointed priest shall bring some of its blood into the tabernacle of witness, ¹⁷and dip his finger in the blood and sprinkle it seven times before the Lord, before the veil. ¹⁸And he shall put some of the blood on the horns of the altar that is before the Lord in the tabernacle of witness, and shall pour all the blood upon the bottom of the altar of burnt offerings that is by the door of the tabernacle of witness. ¹⁹And he shall remove all the fat from it and burn it upon the altar, ²⁰and shall do with this ox as he did with the ox of his sin offering. And the priest will make an atonement for them, and so shall it be forgiven them. ²¹And he shall bring the ox outside the host and burn it like he burned the first. This is this the sin offering for the assembly.

²²When a lord sins, and commits through ignorance any of those

*Look in Ge 48 & note a.

Lev 1:5

Lev 3:3-5

things which the Lord his God has forbidden to be done in his commandments, and has thus offended, ²³then when his sin that he has committed is shown to him, he shall bring for his offering a he-goat without blemish, ²⁴and shall lay his hand upon its head and kill it in the place where the burnt offerings are killed before the Lord. This is a sin offering. ²⁵Then let the priest take some of the blood of the sin offering with his finger and put it upon the horns of the burnt-offering altar, pour the blood upon the bottom of the burnt-offering altar, ²⁶and burn all its fat upon the altar, just as he does the fat of the peace offerings. And the priest will make an atonement for him as concerning his sin, and thus it shall be forgiven him.

²⁷If one of the common people of the land sins through ignorance and commits any of the things that the Lord has in his commandments forbidden to be done, and so has trespassed, ²⁸when the sin that he has sinned has come to his knowledge, he shall bring for his offering a she-goat without blemish, for his sin that he has sinned. ²⁹And he shall lay his hand upon the head of the sin offering and slay it in the place of burnt offerings. ³⁰And the priest shall take some of the blood with his finger, put it upon the horns of the burnt-offering altar, and pour all the blood upon the bottom of the altar. ³¹And he shall remove all its fat, as the fat of the peace offerings is removed. And the priest shall burn it upon the altar, for a sweet savour to the Lord. And the priest will make an atonement for him, and it shall be forgiven him.

Lev 3:14-16

³²If he brings a lamb and offers it for a sin offering, he shall bring a female without blemish, ³³and lay his hand upon the head of the sin offering and slay it in the place where the burnt offerings are slain. ³⁴And the priest shall take some of the blood of the sin offering with his finger and put it on the horns of the burnt-offering altar, and shall pour all the blood at the bottom of the altar. ³⁵And he shall remove all its fat, as the fat of the sheep of the peace offerings was removed. And the priest shall burn it on the altar for the Lord's sacrifice, and the priest shall make an atonement for his sin, and it shall be forgiven him.

Chapter 5

Of cursing. The cleansing of one who touches an unclean thing. The purgation of an oath and of sin done by ignorance.

When a soul has sinned and heard the voice of cursing, and is a witness (whether he has seen or known of it), if he has not disclosed it, he shall bear his sin. ²Or, when a person touches any unclean thing (whether it is the carrion of an unclean beast, or of unclean livestock, or unclean vermin) and is not aware of it, he is also unclean and has offended. ³Or, when he touches any uncleanness of man (whatever uncleanness it be that a person may be defiled with) and is not aware of it, and afterwards comes to the knowledge of it, he is a trespasser. ⁴Or, when a soul swears, in that he declares with his lips to do evil or to do good (whatever it be that a person pronounces with an oath), and the thing is out of his mind, but afterwards he comes to the knowledge of it, then he has offended in one of these.

⁵Then, when he has sinned in one of these things, he shall confess that wherein he has sinned. ⁶And he shall bring his trespass offering to the Lord, for his sin that he has sinned, a female from the flock – whether it be a lamb or a she-goat – for a sin offering. And the priest shall make an atonement for him, for his sin.

⁷But if he is not able to bring a sheep, then let him bring for his trespass which he has sinned two turtle doves or two young pigeons to the Lord: one for a sin offering and the other for a burnt offering. ⁸And he shall bring them to the priest, who shall offer the sin offering first, and shall wring its neck but not pluck it clean off. ⁹And let him sprinkle some of the blood of the sin offering on the side of the altar, and let the rest of the blood bleed upon the bottom of the altar; and then it is a sin offering. ¹⁰And let him offer the second for a burnt offering, as the manner is. And so shall the priest make an atonement for him, for the sin that he has sinned, and it shall be forgiven him.

¹¹And yet, if he is not able to bring two turtle doves or two young pigeons, then let him bring as his offering for his sin the tenth part of an ephah of fine flour, for a sin offering. But put no oil upon it, neither put any frankincense on it, for it is a sin offering. ¹²And let him bring it to the priest, and the priest shall take his handful of it and burn it upon the altar for a remembrance,* to be a sacrifice for the Lord. This is a sin offering. ¹³And let the priest make an atonement for him for his sin, whatsoever of these he has sinned, and it shall be forgiven. And the rest shall be the priest's, as it is in the food offering.‡

¹⁴And the Lord communed with Moses, saying, ¹⁵When a soul trespasses and sins through ignorance in any of the holy things of the Lord, for his trespass he shall bring to the Lord a ram without blemish out of the flock, valued at two sickles according to the holy sickle, for a trespass offering. ¹⁶And he shall make restitution for the harm that he has done in the holy thing and add a fifth part more to it, and give it to the priest. And the priest shall make an atonement for him with the ram of the trespass offering, and it shall be forgiven him.

¹⁷When a soul sins and commits any of those things which are forbidden to be done by the commandments of the Lord, though he knew it not, he has yet offended and is in sin. ¹⁸And he shall bring a ram without blemish from the flock – one that is esteemed worthy to be a sin offering – to the priest. And the priest will make an atonement for him, for the unintentional wrong that he did, being unaware, and it shall be forgiven him. ¹⁹This is a trespass offering; for he trespassed against the Lord.

Lev 12:6-8
Lu 2:24

*[A remembrance: a reminder to God and a memorial of his covenant promises]
‡ Lev 2:10

Chapter 6

The offerings for sins that are done willingly. The law of the burnt offerings. The fire must abide evermore upon the altar. The offerings of Aaron and his sons.

And the Lord talked with Moses, saying, ²When a soul sins and trespasses against the Lord, in that he denies to his neighbour that which he gave him for safe-keeping or which was put under his hand, or that which he violently took away or got unrighteously; ³or if he has found that which was lost and denies it with a false oath; or in whatever thing it be that a person does and sins therein; ⁴then, when he has sinned or trespassed, he shall restore that which he took violently away or got wrongfully, or which was delivered to him for safe-keeping, or the lost thing that he found, ⁵or whatever it is about which he has sworn falsely. He shall restore it in the full amount with a fifth part more added to it, and shall give it to him to whom it belongs on the same day that he makes an offering for his trespass.ᵃ ⁶And he shall bring to the Lord - (namely to the priest) for his trespass offering a ram without blemish from the flock, one which is esteemed a worthy trespass offering. ⁷And the priest shall make an atonement for him before the Lord, and all that he has sinned in will be forgiven him.

⁸And the Lord spoke to Moses, saying, ⁹Command Aaron and his sons, saying, This is the law of the burnt offering: The burnt offering shall be upon the hearth of the altar all night until the morning, and the fire of the altar shall burn therein. ¹⁰And the priest shall put on his linen garment, and his linen breeches upon his flesh, and shall take up the ashes left from the fire of the burnt sacrifice in the altar and put them beside the altar. ¹¹Then he shall put off his garments and put on others, and carry the ashes outside the host to a clean place.

¹²The fire that is upon the altar must burn therein and not go out. And the priest shall put wood on the fire every morning, and put the burnt sacrifice upon it; and he shall burn on it the fat of the peace offerings. ¹³The fire must ever burn upon the altar and never go out.*

¹⁴This is the law of the food offering: Aaron's sons shall bring it before the Lord, to the altar; ¹⁵and one of them shall take his handful of the flour of the food offering and of the oil with all the frankincense that is on it, and shall burn it upon the altar for a sweet savour, a reminder to the Lord. ¹⁶And the rest of it, Aaron and his sons may eat. Unleavened it shall be eaten, in the holy place; there in the court of the tabernacle of witness they shall eat it. ¹⁷The part that I have given them of my sacrifice must not be baked with leaven, for it is most holy, as is the sin offering and trespass offering. ¹⁸All the males among the children of Aaron may eat of it, and it shall be a duty forever to your generations in the sacrifices of the Lord. No man may touch it except he that is hallowed.ᵇ

¹⁹And the Lord spoke to Moses, saying, ²⁰This is the offering of Aaron and of his sons, which he shall offer to the Lord in the day when they are anointed: the tenth part of an ephah of flour, which is a daily food offering perpetually, half in the morning and half at night. ²¹It shall be made in the frying pan with oil; and bring it fried. And you shall offer it in small pieces, for a sweet savour to the Lord. ²²And whoever of Aaron's sons is anointed priest in his stead shall offer it, and it will be the Lord's due forever. And it shall be burned complete-

---

vv2-4 e.f. COV.

*Ever: look in Ge 13:15 and note b.

ly, ²³for all the food offerings of the priests must be completely burned, and may not be eaten.

²⁴And the Lord talked with Moses, saying, ²⁵Speak to Aaron and to his sons, and say: This is the law of the sin offering: in the place where the burnt offering is killed, the sin offering shall be killed also before the Lord, for it is most holy. ²⁶The priest who offers it shall eat it in the holy place, there in the court of the tabernacle of witness. ²⁷No man may touch its flesh except he that is hallowed. If any garment be spattered with blood, it shall be washed in the holy place. ²⁸The earthen pot that the meat is boiled in shall be broken, but if it was boiled in a bronze pot, then the pot shall be scoured and rinsed with water. ²⁹All the males among the children of Aaron may eat of the sin offering, for it is most holy. ³⁰Notwithstanding, no sin offering of which the blood was brought into the tabernacle of witness to make reconciliation may be eaten, but must be burned in the fire.

Le 15:12

The Notes

a) 5. To my neighbour satisfaction is due, but to God, repentance. And then the sacrifice of Christ's blood is a full satisfaction, atonement, and appeasement of all wrath.

b) 18. No man may touch it except he that is hallowed: that is, only he who is dedicated, ordained, and appointed to minister before the Lord may touch it, as in Haggai 2:11-14.

Chapter 7

Trespass offerings. Sin offerings and peace offerings.
The fat and the blood may not be eaten.

This is the law of the trespass offering,ᵃ which is most holy: ²In the place where the burnt offering is killed, the trespass offering shall be killed also, and its blood shall be sprinkled round about upon the altar. ³And all its fat shall be offered: the rump and the fat that covers the inwards, ⁴and the two kidneys with the fat that lies on them and upon the loins. And the membrane on the liver shall be removed with the kidneys. ⁵And the priest shall burn them upon the altar, to be an offering to the Lord. This is a trespass offering. ⁶All the males among the priests shall eat thereof in the holy place, for it is most holy.

⁷As the sin offering is, so is the trespass offering: one law serves for both. It shall be for the priest who reconciles with it, ⁸and the priest who offered a person's burnt offering shall have the skin of the burnt offering that he has offered. ⁹And all the food offerings that are baked in the oven, and everything that is prepared upon the gridiron and in the frying pan, shall be for the priest who offers them. ¹⁰But all other food offerings, mixed with oil or dry, shall belong to all the sons of Aaron, and one shall have as much as another.

¹¹This is the law of the peace offerings to be offered to the Lord: ¹²If anyone offers to give thanks, he shall bring for his thank offering sweet cakes mixed with oil, or sweet wafers spread with oil, or fried cakes of fine flour mixed with oil. ¹³And he shall bring his offering

with cakes made of leavened bread for the thank offering of his peace offerings. ¹⁴From them all, he shall offer one to be a lift offering to the Lord, and it shall belong to the priest who sprinkles the blood of the peace offerings. ¹⁵And the flesh of the thank offering from his peace offerings shall be eaten the same day it is offered, and none of it shall be left until the morning.

¹⁶If it is a vowed[b] or a freewill offering that he brings, it shall be eaten the same day that he offers it; but any that remains may be eaten on the morrow. ¹⁷However, as much of the offered flesh as remains until the third day must be burned with fire. ¹⁸For if any of the flesh of the peace offerings be eaten in the third day, then he who offered it will obtain no favour, neither shall it be credited to him, but shall be an abomination. And the soul that eats of it will bear the sin thereof.

¹⁹Flesh that touches any unclean thing shall not be eaten, but burned with fire. As for other flesh, whoever is clean of body may eat of the flesh.

v19 e.f. COV.

²⁰If any soul eats of the flesh of the Lord's peace offerings while his uncleanness is yet upon him, the same soul shall perish from among his people. ²¹Moreover, if a soul touches any unclean thing, whether it be the uncleanness of man or of any unclean beast, or any abomination that is unclean, and then eats of the flesh of the peace offerings that belong to the Lord, that soul shall perish from his people.

²²And the Lord spoke to Moses, saying, ²³Speak to the children of Israel and say: You shall eat no fat of oxen, sheep, or goats. ²⁴And the fat of the beast that dies alone, and the fat of that which is torn by wild beasts, may be used in all manner of ways, but you shall in no case eat of it. ²⁵For whoever eats the fat of a beast of which an offering is brought to the Lord, that soul shall perish from his people. ²⁶Moreover, you shall eat no manner of blood, wherever you dwell, whether it be of bird or of beast. ²⁷Whatever soul it be that eats any manner of blood, the same soul shall perish from his people.

Lev 17:10-12
De 12:23

²⁸And the Lord talked with Moses, saying, ²⁹Speak to the children of Israel and say: Whoever will offer his peace offering to the Lord, shall bring his gift to the Lord from his peace offerings. ³⁰His own hands shall bring the offering to the Lord. The fat upon the breast he shall bring with the breast, to wave it a wave offering before the Lord. ³¹And the priest shall burn the fat upon the altar, and the breast shall be for Aaron and his sons. ³²And the right shoulder he shall give to the priest, to be a lift offering from his peace offerings. ³³And whoever among the sons of Aaron offers the blood of the peace offerings and the fat shall have the right shoulder for his part. ³⁴For I have taken the wave-breast and the lift-shoulder from the children of Israel, from their peace offerings, and have given them to Aaron the priest and to his sons, to be their due forever from the children of Israel.

v35 e.f. COV.

³⁵This was the anointing of Aaron and his sons in the day when they were offered to be priests unto the Lord, and the sacrifices of the Lord ³⁶that the Lord commanded to be given them by the children of

Israel in the day when he anointed them, and to be a duty forever among their generations. ³⁷This is the law of burnt offerings, of food offerings, of sin offerings, of trespass offerings, of full offerings, and of peace offerings, ³⁸which the Lord commanded Moses in the mount of Sinai, in the day when he commanded the children of Israel to offer their offerings to the Lord in the wilderness of Sinai.

The Notes

a) 1. Trespass offering: that is, an offering for trespass. *Trespass,* after the usage of the scripture, sometimes signifies all the past life that we, being ignorant of the truth, lived in infidelity – not only in doing open sins, but also when we have walked in our own righteousness. Psalm 119:12 and 2 Chronicles c28.

b) 16. By vowed offerings are here understood the gifts which are accustomed to be offered and given to God by any outward ceremony, as it was to shave the head or to drink no wine, etc. Numbers 6:1-8. [Ed: Formerly called *vows* in a now-obsolete use, a *vowed offering* is something given to God pursuant to a vow.]

Chapter 8

The anointing and consecration of Aaron and his sons.

And the Lord spoke to Moses, saying, ²Take Aaron and his sons with him, and the garments, the anointing oil, an ox for a sin offering, two rams, and a basket of sweet bread; ³and gather all the community together to the door of the tabernacle of witness.

⁴And Moses did as the Lord commanded him, and the people gathered themselves together to the door of the tabernacle of witness. ⁵And Moses said to the people, This is the thing that the Lord commanded to do. ⁶And Moses brought Aaron and his sons and washed them with water. ⁷He put the straight coat upon Aaron, girded him with a sash, put upon him the tunic, and put the ephod on top. And he girded him with the embroidered sash of the ephod and bound it to him. ⁸And he put the breastlap thereon, and put in the breastlap Urim and Thummim.* ⁹He put the turban on his head; and on the turban, on the forefront of it, he put the golden plate of the holy crown, as the Lord had commanded him.

¹⁰And Moses took the anointing oil and anointed the habitation and everything that was in it, and sanctified them. ¹¹He sprinkled some of the oil upon the altar seven times, and anointed the altar, all its accessories, and the laver with its base, to sanctify them. ¹²And he poured some of the anointing oil on Aaron's head and anointed him, to sanctify him. ¹³And he brought Aaron's sons and put coats upon them, girded them with sashes, and put headwear upon them, as the Lord had commanded him.

¹⁴And the sin offering was brought. And Aaron and his sons put their hands upon the head of the ox of the sin offering. ¹⁵And when it was slain, Moses took some of the blood and put it on the horns of the altar round about with his finger, and purified it. And he poured the

*[Or, Light and Perfection, as WT had in 1530. See Ex 28:30 & note a, and Nu 27:21 & note b.]

blood at the bottom of the altar, and sanctified it and reconciled it. ¹⁶And he took all the fat that was upon the inwards, the membrane that was on the liver, and the two kidneys with their fat, and burned it all upon the altar. ¹⁷But the ox – the hide, his flesh, and his dung – he burned with fire outside the host, as the Lord commanded him.

¹⁸And he brought the ram of the burnt offering. And Aaron and his sons put their hands upon the head of the ram, ¹⁹and it was killed. And Moses sprinkled the blood upon the altar round about, ²⁰cut the ram in pieces, and burned the head, the pieces, and the fat. ²¹He washed the inwards and the legs in water, and burned the ram every whit upon the altar. This was a burnt sacrifice of a sweet savour and an offering to the Lord, as the Lord commanded Moses.

²²And he brought the other ram that was the full offering, and Aaron and his sons put their hands upon the head of the ram. ²³And when it was slain, Moses took some of its blood and put it upon the tip of Aaron's right ear, upon the thumb of his right hand, and upon the great toe of his right foot. ²⁴Then Aaron's sons were brought, and Moses put some of the blood on the tips of their right ears, upon the thumbs of their right hands, and upon the great toes of their right feet; and he sprinkled the blood upon the altar round about.

²⁵And Moses took the fat and the rump, all the fat that was upon the inwards, the membrane of the liver, the two kidneys with their fat, and the right shoulder. ²⁶And from the basket of sweet bread that was before the Lord, he took one sweet cake of oiled bread and one wafer, and he put them on the fat and upon the right shoulder. ²⁷He put all these in Aaron's hands and in his sons' hands, and waved them* as a wave offering before the Lord. ²⁸And then Moses took them from their hands again and burned them on the altar, upon the burnt offering. These are the full offerings of a sweet savour and a sacrifice to the Lord.

*[waved: a side to side motion, with his hands under theirs]

²⁹And Moses took the breast of the ram of the full offerings and waved it as a wave offering before the Lord. And it was Moses' part, as the Lord commanded him.

³⁰And Moses took some of the anointing oil and the blood that was upon the altar, and sprinkled it upon Aaron, upon his vestments, and upon his sons and on their vestments with him, and sanctified Aaron and his garments, and his sons and his sons' garments also. ³¹Then Moses said to Aaron and his sons, Boil the flesh in the door of the tabernacle of witness, and there eat it with the bread that is in the basket of full offerings, as the Lord commanded, saying, Aaron and his sons shall eat it. ³²And that which remains of the flesh and of the bread, burn it with fire.

Ex 29:29-34

Ex 29:35-37

³³And see that you do not depart from the door of the tabernacle of witness seven days long, until the days of your full offerings are at an end. For seven days your hands must be filled, ³⁴as they were this day. This the Lord has commanded to do, to reconcile you. ³⁵See, therefore, that you abide in the door of the tabernacle of witness day and night seven days long, and keep the watch of the Lord so that you do not

die, for so I am commanded.

³⁶And Aaron and his sons did all the things that the Lord had commanded by the hand of Moses.*

*By the hand of: look in 2Ki 19:23 and note a.

Chapter 9

The first offerings of Aaron, for himself and for the people. Aaron blesses the people. The glory of the Lord is shown. The fire coming from above consumes the sacrifice.

And the eighth day, Moses called Aaron and his sons and the elders of Israel, ²and he said to Aaron, Take a calf for a sin offering and a ram for a burnt offering – both without blemish – and bring them before the Lord. ³And to the children of Israel he spoke, saying, Take a he-goat for a sin offering, and a calf and a lamb, both a year old and without blemish, for a burnt sacrifice, ⁴and an ox and a ram for peace offerings, to offer before the Lord, with also a food offering mixed with oil. For today, the Lord will appear to you.

⁵And they brought that which Moses commanded to the tabernacle of witness, and all the people came and stood before the Lord. ⁶And Moses said, This is the thing that the Lord has commanded you to do, and then the glory of the Lord will appear to you. ⁷And Moses said to Aaron, Go to the altar and offer your sin offering, and make an atonement for you and for the people; and then offer the offering of the people and reconcile them also, as the Lord commanded.

⁸And Aaron went to the altar and slew the calf that was his sin offering. ⁹And the sons of Aaron brought the blood to him, and he dipped his finger in the blood, put it upon the horns of the altar, and poured the blood at the bottom of the altar. ¹⁰And the fat and the two kidneys, with the membrane of the liver of the sin offering, he burned upon the altar, as the Lord commanded Moses. ¹¹But the flesh and the hide he burned with fire outside the host.

¹²Afterward, Aaron slew the burnt offering, and his sons brought the blood to him and he sprinkled it round about upon the altar. ¹³And they brought the burnt offering to him in pieces, and the head also, and he burned them upon the altar. ¹⁴And he washed the inwards and the legs and burned them also, upon the burnt offering on the altar.

¹⁵And then he brought the people's offering, and took the goat that was the people's sin offering and slew it, and offered it for a sin offering as he had the first. ¹⁶And then he brought the burnt offering and offered it as the manner was. ¹⁷And he brought the food offering, filled his hand with some of it, and burned it on the altar alongside the burnt sacrifice in the morning.

¹⁸He also slew the ox and the ram that were the people's peace offerings. His sons brought the blood to him, and he sprinkled it upon the altar round about, ¹⁹and took the fat of the ox and of the ram – the rump and the fat that covers the inwards and the kidneys, and the membrane of the liver – ²⁰and placed them on the breasts, and burned

it upon the altar. ²¹But the breasts and the right shoulders Aaron waved before the Lord, as the Lord commanded Moses.

²²And Aaron lifted up his hand over the people and blessed them, and came down from offering the sin offerings, burnt offerings, and peace offerings. ²³Then Moses and Aaron went into the tabernacle of witness, and came out again and blessed the people. And the glory of the Lord appeared to all the people; ²⁴and there came a fire out from before the Lord, and consumed upon the altar the burnt offering and the fat. And all the people saw it, and shouted, and fell on their faces.

Chapter 10

>Nadab and Abihu are slain. Israel mourns for them.
>The priests are forbidden wine. The remainder of the
>sacrifice the priests eat.

And Nadab and Abihu, the sons of Aaron, each took his censer, put fire in it, added incense, and brought strange fire before the Lord, which he had not commanded them to do. ²And there went a fire out from the Lord, and it consumed them. And they died before the Lord.ᵃ

³Then Moses said to Aaron, This is it what the Lord spoke, saying, I must be hallowed in those who come near me,ᵇ and before all the people, I must be glorified. And Aaron held his peace.

⁴And Moses called Mishael and Elzaphan, the sons of Uzziel the uncle of Aaron, and said to them, Go, and carry your brethren* from before the holy place out of the host.

*Brethren: look in Ge 13:8 and note a.

⁵And they went to them and carried them in their coats out of the host, as Moses bade.

⁶And Moses said to Aaron and to Aaron's eldest sons Eleazar and Ithama, Do not uncover your head nor rend your clothes, lest you die and wrath come upon all the people. Let your brethren, the whole house of Israel, weep for the burning which the Lord has burned. ⁷But you, go not out from the door of the tabernacle of witness, lest you die; for the anointing oil of the Lord is upon you.

And they did as Moses bade.

⁸And the Lord spoke to Aaron, saying, ⁹Drink no wine nor strong drink – neither you nor your sons with you – when you go into the tabernacle of witness, lest you die. And let it be a law forever to your children after you, ¹⁰that you may put a difference between holy and unholy, and between unclean and clean, ¹¹and that you may teach the children of Israel all the ordinances that the Lord has commanded them by the hands of Moses.

¹²And Moses said to Aaron, and to Eleazar and Ithamar, his sons who were left, Take the food offering that remains of the sacrifices of the Lord and eat it without leaven beside the altar, for it is most holy. ¹³Eat it, therefore, in the holy place, because it is your due and your sons' due from the sacrifices of the Lord; for so I am commanded. ¹⁴And the wave-breast and lift-shoulder, eat in a clean place – you and your sons and daughters with you. For it is your and your children's

due with you from the peace offerings of the children of Israel. ¹⁵For the lift-shoulder and the wave-breast that they bring with the sacrifices of the fat, to wave before the Lord, shall be yours and your children's with you, and be a law forever,ᶜ as the Lord has commanded.

¹⁶And Moses looked for the goat that was the sin offering, and see, it was burnt. And he was angry with Eleazar and Ithamar, the sons of Aaron who were left alive, and said, ¹⁷Why have you not eaten the sin offering in the holy place, seeing it is most holy, and since it is given you to bear the sin of the people and make atonement for them before the Lord? ¹⁸Look, its blood was not brought in within the holy place. Therefore you should have eaten it in the holy place, as I commanded.

¹⁹And Aaron said to Moses, Behold, this day they offered their sin offering and their burnt offering before the Lord, and it has befallen me after this manner. If I should eat of the sin offering today, would the Lord be pleased with it?ᵈ

²⁰And when Moses heard that, he was content.

[The waving (from side to side) is said to have symbolized the world as belonging to God, while the lifting up symbolized him dwelling on high.]

The Notes

a) 2. From this you see the fruit of a man's good intent without God's word. We may do no other than is commanded.
b) 3. God is hallowed when we obey him and mortify our will to do his.
c) 15. *Forever* is here taken for a time that has an end, and not everlasting, as it is also in Genesis 13:15 and Exodus 12:14 & 17.
d) 19. The offerings were to have been eaten in gladness, but Aaron could not but mourn for his sons.

Chapter 11

Of creatures which are clean, and which unclean.

And the Lord spoke to Moses and Aaron, saying, ²Speak to the children of Israel and say: These are the creatures that you may eat among all the land animals that are on the earth: ³whatsoever among the animals has a hoof that divides into two parts and chews cud, that you may eat. ⁴Nevertheless, these you must not eat of those that chew cud or have hoofs: the camel, for he chews cud but divides not the hoof into two parts; therefore, he shall be unclean to you. ⁵Also the coney, for he chews the cud but divides not a hoof into two parts; therefore, he is unclean to you. ⁶And the hare, for he likewise chews the cud but divides not a hoof into two parts; he is therefore unclean to you. ⁷And the swine, for though he divides the hoof into two parts, yet he chews not the cud, and is therefore unclean to you. ⁸Of their flesh, see that you eat not. And see that you do not touch their carcasses, for they are unclean to you.

Lev 20:24-26.

⁹These you may eat of all that are in the waters: whatever has fins and scales in the waters, seas, and rivers; that you may eat. ¹⁰But all that have not fins and scales in the seas and rivers, of everything that moves and lives in the waters, you shall abhor. ¹¹See that you eat not of their flesh, and also that you abhor their carcasses. ¹²For everything that has no fins or scales in the waters shall be an abomination to you.

¹³These are the birds that you shall abhor and which must not be eaten, for they are an abomination: the eagle, the goshawk, the cormorant, ¹⁴the kite, the vulture and all its kind, ¹⁵all kinds of ravens, ¹⁶the ostrich, the night-crow, the cuckoo, the sparrowhawk and all its kind, ¹⁷the little owl, the stork, the great owl, ¹⁸the water-hen, the pelican, the osprey, ¹⁹the heron, the jay with its kind, the lapwing, and the swallow.

²⁰And all winged creatures that creep and go upon all fours shall be an abomination to you, ²¹except these you may eat of all the winged creatures that move and go upon four legs: those that have no knees above on their legs, to hop with upon the earth. ²²These of them you may eat: the arbe and all its kind, the selaam with all its kind; the hargol and all its kind, and the hagab and all its kind.ᵃ ²³All other winged creatures that move and have four legs shall be an abomination to you; ²⁴by these you shall become unclean. Whoever touches their carcass will be unclean till the evening, ²⁵and whoever carries the carcass of any of them must wash his clothes, and will be unclean until evening.

²⁶Among all manner of animals, they that have hoofs and divide them not into two parts, or that chew not the cud, shall be unclean to you, and everything that touches them shall be unclean. ²⁷And everything that goes upon its hands among all manner of creatures that go on all fours are unclean to you, and as many as touch their carcasses shall be unclean until the evening. ²⁸And he who carries their carcass shall wash his clothes and be unclean until the evening, for such are unclean to you.

²⁹And these are also unclean to you among the things that creep upon the earth: the weasel, the mouse, the toad and all its kind; ³⁰the hedgehog, stellion, the lizard, the snail, and the mole. ³¹These are unclean to you among everything that moves, and all who touch them when they are dead will be unclean until the evening. ³²And whatever any of their dead carcasses falls upon shall be unclean – whatever vessel of wood it be, or clothing, or skin, or bag, or whatever thing it be that any work is done with. And it must be plunged into water, and will be unclean until the evening; and then it will be clean again. ³³Any kind of earthen vessel into which any of them falls is unclean, with all that is in it, and you shall break it. ³⁴Any edible food, if any of the water comes upon it, shall be unclean, and any drink that may be drunk in any such vessels shall be unclean. ³⁵And whether it be oven or kettle, it must be broken, for they are unclean and shall be unclean to you; ³⁶nevertheless yet, the springs and wells and ponds of water shall be clean still. But whoever touches the carcasses shall be unclean. ³⁷If the dead carcass of any such creature falls upon any seed used to sow, it shall yet be clean still, ³⁸but if any water is poured on the seed and afterward the dead carcass falls on it, then it shall be unclean to you.

³⁹If any animal of which you may eat dies, he who touches the dead carcass will be unclean until the evening. ⁴⁰And he who eats of any such dead carcass shall wash his clothes and remain unclean until

margin: Lev 6:28; c15.

the evening. And he also who carries the carcass shall wash his clothes and be unclean until the evening.

⁴¹Everything that crawls upon the earth is an abomination and shall not be eaten. ⁴²And whatever goes upon the breast, and whatever goes upon four or more feet among all that crawls upon the earth, of those see that you eat not, for they are abominable. ⁴³Make not your souls abominable with anything that creeps, neither make your souls unclean with them, so that you are defiled by them. ⁴⁴For I am the Lord your God. Be sanctified, therefore, so that you may be holy, for I am holy; and do not defile your souls with any manner of thing that creeps upon the earth. ⁴⁵For I am the Lord that brought you out of the land of Egypt to be your God. Be holy, therefore; for I am holy.

⁴⁶This is the law concerning beast and bird, and concerning every kind of thing that lives and moves in the water, and all things that creep upon the earth, ⁴⁷so that you may put a difference between unclean and clean, and between the creatures that are eaten and the creatures that are not eaten.

Lev 19:2
1Pe 1:14-16

The Notes

a) 22. The arbe, selaam, hargol, and hagab were kinds of winged creatures that creep or crawl on the ground. The Hebrews themselves do not nowadays know them or the distinctions between the species named.

Chapter 12

A law how women should be purged after delivery.

And the Lord spoke to Moses and said, ²Speak to the children of Israel and say: When a woman has conceived and has borne a manchild, she shall be unclean seven days, in like manner as when she is put apart in the time of her natural infirmity.* ³In the eighth day, the flesh of the child's foreskin shall be cut away,‡ ⁴and she shall continue in the blood of her purifying thirty-three days. She shall touch no hallowed thing, nor come into the sanctuary, until the time of her purifying is up. ⁵If she bears a maidchild, then she shall be unclean for two weeks, as when she has her natural infirmity, and she shall continue in the blood of her purifying sixty-six days.

*[ie, in her monthly period]
‡ Lu 2:21

⁶And when the days of her purifying are up, whether it be a son or a daughter, she shall bring a lamb of one year old for a burnt offering, and a young pigeon or a turtle dove for a sin offering, to the door of the tabernacle of witness, to the priest. ⁷He shall offer them before the Lord and make an atonement for her, and thus will she be purged of her issue of blood.

Lu 2:22-24

This is the law for a woman who has borne a child, whether it be male or female.

⁸But if she is not able to bring a sheep, then let her bring two turtle doves or two young pigeons, one for the burnt offering and the other for the sin offering. And the priest shall make an atonement for her, and she shall be clean.

Chapter 13

The priests are appointed to judge who are the lepers.

And the Lord spoke to Moses and to Aaron, saying, ²When there appears a swelling in any person's flesh, either scabbed or a shiny white, as though the plague of leprosy were in the skin of his flesh,ª then let him be brought to Aaron the priest or to one of his sons the priests, ³and let the priest look on the sore that is in the skin of his flesh. If the hair in the sore has turned white and the sore also seems to go deeper than the skin of his flesh, then it is surely a leprosy; and let the priest look on him and judge him unclean.

⁴If there is but a white spot in the skin of his flesh, and it seems no deeper than the skin and the hair has not turned white, then let the priest confine him seven days, ⁵and let the priest look upon him the seventh day. If the sore seems to him to be stable and to have spread no further in the skin, then let the priest confine him yet seven days more, ⁶and let the priest look on him again the seventh day. Then, if the sore has faded and has not grown abroad in the skin, let the priest judge him clean, for it is but a scurf.* And let him wash his clothes, and then he is clean. ⁷But if the scab grew in the skin after he was seen by the priest again, ⁸if the priest sees that the scab has grown abroad in the skin, let him judge him unclean, for it is surely a leprosy.

*[Scurf: a scaly skin condition with no inflammation]

⁹If the plague of leprosy is in a person, let him be brought to the priest, ¹⁰and let the priest see him. If the swelling appears white in the skin and has also made the hair white, and there is raw flesh in the sore also, ¹¹then it is an old leprosy in the skin of his flesh. And the priest shall judge him unclean; he shall not confine him, for he is unclean. ¹²If a leprosy breaks out in the skin and covers all the skin from the head to the foot, over everywhere the priest looks, ¹³then let the priest look upon him. If the leprosy has covered all his flesh, let him judge the disease clean; for inasmuch as he is altogether white, he is therefore clean.* ¹⁴But if there is raw flesh on him when he is seen, then he shall be unclean. ¹⁵Therefore, when the priest sees the raw flesh, let him judge him unclean; for inasmuch as his flesh is raw, he is unclean, and it is surely a true leprosy. ¹⁶But if the raw flesh changes and turns white, then let him come to the priest, ¹⁷and let the priest see him. If the sore has turned white, let the priest judge the disease clean, and then he is clean.

*[Some: the disease having run its course and not being contagious]

¹⁸When there is a boil in the skin of anyone's flesh and it heals, ¹⁹and afterwards, in the place of the boil, there appears a white swelling or a shiny reddish-white spot, let him be seen by the priest. ²⁰If, when the priest sees him, it appears to go deeper than the skin and the hair has turned white, let the priest judge him unclean, for it is a very leprosy that has broken out in the place of the boil. ²¹But if (when the priest looks on it) there are no white hairs in it, nor is the scab deeper than the skin and it is somewhat faded, then the priest shall confine him separately seven days. ²²If it spreads abroad in the meantime, then let the priest judge him unclean, for it is a leprosy. ²³But if the shiny

white patch has not spread, then it is but the scar from the boil, and the priest shall judge him clean.

24When the skin of a person's flesh is burned with fire so that it is raw, and there appears in the burn a shiny white that is somewhat reddish or altogether white, 25let the priest look upon it. If the hair in that brightness has turned white and it also appears deeper than the other skin, then it is a leprosy that has broken out where the burn was. And the priest shall judge him unclean, for it is a leprosy. 26But if (when the priest looks on it) he sees that there is no white hair in the brightness and that it is no deeper than the other skin, and it is also faded, then let the priest confine him seven days. 27And if (when the priest looks on him the seventh day) it has grown abroad in the skin, let him judge him unclean, for it is a leprosy. 28But if the brightness has not spread in the skin and has become paler, then it is but a swelling in the place of the burn, and the priest shall judge him clean; for it is but the scar from the burn only.

29When either man or woman has an outbreak on the head or in the beard, 30let the priest see it. And if it appears deeper than the skin and there are thin, golden hairs in it, let the priest judge the person unclean, for it is an outbreak of leprosy upon the head or in the beard. 31If (when the priest looks on the outbreak) he sees that it is no deeper than the skin and that there are black hairs in it, let him confine him seven days. 32And let the priest look on the disease the seventh day, and if the outbreak has gone no further and there are no golden hairs therein, and if the scab is not deeper than the skin, 33then let him be shaved. But let him not shave the scab, and let the priest confine him seven days more, 34and let the priest look on the outbreak the seventh day again. If the outbreak has gone no further in the skin nor deeper in it, then let the priest judge him clean. And let him wash his clothes, and then he is clean. 35If the outbreak grows in the skin after he is once judged clean, 36let the priest see him. If it has indeed grown abroad in the skin, let the priest seek no further for any golden hairs, for he is unclean. 37But if he sees that the scab is stable and that there is black hair grown up therein, then the scab is healed and he is clean; and the priest shall judge him clean.

38If there is found in the skin of the flesh of a man or woman a shiny white spot, 39let the priest see it. If there appears in their flesh a shiny white that is somewhat darkish, then it is but freckles grown up in the skin, and the person is clean.

40When the hairs fall out of the head of a man or a woman so that the person is bald, the same is clean. 41If they fall out of his fore-scalp, then he has a receding hairline and is clean. 42But if there is in the bald part a reddish-white scab, then a leprosy has sprung up in their head or fore-scalp. 43And let the priest see it, and if he finds the reddish-white sore swollen in the bald head or fore-scalp, in the manner of a leprosy in the skin of the flesh, 44then the person is a leper and unclean. And the priest shall judge him unclean, for the plague of his head.

vv 40-43 e.f. COV.

*[Warp or woof: here possibly an idiomatic expression referring to raw flax or wool and/or to the yarns spun with it, before being fabricated into a cloth or garment]

⁴⁵Whoever now is leprous, his clothes shall be rent, the head bare, and the mouth muffled; and he shall be called unclean. ⁴⁶And as long as the disease lasts upon him, he shall be unclean, dwell alone, and have his dwelling outside the host.

⁴⁷When the plague of leprosy is in a cloth,[b] whether it be linen or woolen – ⁴⁸yea, and whether it be in the warp or woof* of the linen or of the woolen, or in leather or anything made of skin – ⁴⁹if the plague is pale or somewhat reddish in the cloth or skin, whether it be in the warp or the woof or in anything that is made of skin, then it is a very leprosy and must be shown to the priest. ⁵⁰And when the priest sees the plague, let him shut it up seven days, ⁵¹and let him look on the plague the seventh day. If it has increased in the cloth, whether in the warp or woof, or in a skin, or in anything that is made of skin, then the plague is a consuming leprosy and it is unclean. ⁵²And that cloth shall be burned, or warp or woof, whether it be woolen, linen, or anything that is made of skin in which the plague is. For it is a consuming leprosy and must be burned in the fire.

⁵³If the priest sees that the plague has spread no further in the cloth, or in the warp or woof, or in whatever thing of skin it be, ⁵⁴then let the priest command them to wash the thing containing the plague, and let him shut it up seven days more. ⁵⁵And let the priest look on it again after it is washed. If the plague has not changed in appearance, though it has spread no further, still it is unclean. And see that you burn it in the fire; for it has penetrated inward, whether in part or altogether.

⁵⁶But if the priest sees that the plague is somewhat faded after it is washed, let him tear it out of the cloth, or out of the skin, or out of the warp or woof. ⁵⁷But if it appears any more in the cloth, or in the warp or in the woof, or in anything made of skin, then it is a growing plague. And see that you burn with fire that which contains the plague.

⁵⁸Moreover, if the plague is gone from the cloth, or warp or woof, or whatever thing of skin it be that you have washed, it shall be washed once again, and then it is clean.

⁵⁹This is the law for the plague of leprosy in a cloth, whether it be woolen or linen, or whether it be in the warp or woof, or in anything made of skins, to judge it clean or unclean.

The Notes

a) 2. The leprosy signifies properly man's doctrine, which spreads abroad like a canker, and (to be short) all infections of ungodliness. Therefore, the Levites must give diligent heed to it, for a little leaven sours the whole lump of dough.

b) 47. Of the leprosy of cloths that occurred among the Jews, let them judge. It is evident that we in our time suffer from many leprosies in cloths. [Red leprosy in garments, now believed to be a fungus, had a notable place in history. It was common in the Middle Ages and often occurred before the outbreak of epidemics, which it was believed to herald. Per the OED, other diseases included under the name leprosy in former times probably included unrelated conditions such as psoriasis, scabies, leukoderma or vitiligo, and syphilis. And see chapter 14, note b.]

Chapter 14

The cleansing of a leper and of the house that he is in.

And the Lord spoke to Moses, saying, ²This is the law for a leper when he is to be cleansed. He shall be brought to the priest, ³and the priest shall go out of the host to look upon him. If the plague of leprosy is healed in the leper, ⁴then the priest shall direct that there be brought for him who is to be cleansed two living birds that are clean, cedar wood, a piece of purple cloth, and hyssop. ⁵And the priest shall direct that one of the birds be killed in an earthen vessel with running water. ⁶And the priest shall take the living bird, and also the cedar wood, the purple, and the hyssop, and shall dip them with the living bird in the blood of the slain bird and in the running water, ⁷and sprinkle it upon him who is to be cleansed of his leprosy seven times, and thus cleanse him. And he shall let the living bird go free into the fields.

⁸And he who is cleansed shall wash his clothes, shave off all his hair, and wash himself in water; and then he is clean. And after that he may come into the host, but shall dwell outside his tent seven days. ⁹When the seventh day is come, he shall shave off all the hair upon his head, his beard, and his brows. And fully all the hair that is on him shall be shaven off. And he shall wash his clothes and his flesh in water, and then he will be clean.

¹⁰And when the eighth day is come, let him take two lambs without blemish, a ewe lamb of a year old without blemish, a three-tenths measure of fine flour for a food offering mixed with oil, and a log of oil.ᵃ ¹¹Then let the priest that makes him clean bring the one who is to be made clean with those things before the Lord, to the door of the tabernacle of witness. ¹²And let the priest take one of the lambs and offer it for a trespass offering, and the log of oil, and wave them before the Lord. ¹³And then let him slay the lamb in the place where the sin offering and the burnt offering are slain, there in the holy place. For as the sin offering is, so also is the trespass offering the priest's; for it is most holy.

¹⁴Then let the priest take some of the blood of the trespass offering and put it upon the tip of the right ear of him that is cleansed, and upon the thumb of his right hand and the great toe of his right foot. ¹⁵Then let the priest take some of the log of oil and pour it into the palm of his left hand, ¹⁶and dip his right finger in the oil that is in the palm of his left hand; and let him sprinkle it with his finger seven times before the Lord. ¹⁷And of the rest of the oil that is in his hand, the priest shall put some on the tip of the right ear of him that is cleansed, and upon the thumb of his right hand and the great toe of his right foot, on top of the blood of the trespass offering. ¹⁸And the rest of the oil that is in the priest's hand, he shall pour upon the head of him that is cleansed; and so shall the priest make an atonement for him before the Lord.

¹⁹Then let the priest offer the sin offering and make an atonement for him that is cleansed, for his uncleanness. And then let the burnt offering be slain, ²⁰and let the priest put both the burnt offering and the

M't 8:1-4
Mk 1:40-44
Lu 5:12-14; 7:22.

food offering upon the altar and make an atonement for him; and then he shall be clean.

²¹If he is poor and cannot get so much, then let him bring one lamb for a trespass offering, to wave it and to make an atonement for himself, and a tenth part of fine flour mixed with oil for a food offering, a log of oil, ²²and two turtle doves or two young pigeons that he is able to get; and let the one be a sin offering and the other a burnt offering. ²³And let him bring them on the eighth day to the priest, for his cleansing, to the door of the tabernacle of witness before the Lord.

²⁴And let the priest take the lamb that is the trespass offering and the log of oil, and wave them before the Lord. ²⁵And when the lamb of the trespass offering is killed, the priest shall take some of the blood of the trespass offering and put it upon the tip of the right ear of him who is cleansed, and upon the thumb of his right hand and the great toe of his right foot. ²⁶And the priest shall pour some of the oil into his left hand, ²⁷and shall sprinkle with his finger some of the oil that is in his left hand seven times before the Lord. ²⁸And the priest shall put some of the oil that is in his hand upon the tip of the right ear of him that is cleansed, and upon the thumb of his right hand and the great toe of his right foot, on top of the blood of the trespass offering. ²⁹And he shall pour the rest of the oil that is in his hand upon the head of him that is cleansed, to make an atonement for him before the Lord.

³⁰And he shall offer one of the turtle doves or of the young pigeons, such as he can get – ³¹the one for a sin offering and the other for a burnt offering – upon the altar. And so shall the priest make an atonement for him that is cleansed before the Lord. ³²This is the law for one who has the plague of leprosy, whose hand is not able to get that which pertains to his cleansing.

³³And the Lord spoke to Moses and Aaron, saying, ³⁴When you come to the land of Canaan, which I give you to possess, if I put the plague of leprosy in any house of the land of your possession, ³⁵let him who owns the house go and tell the priest, saying, I think that there is a kind of leprosy in the house. ³⁶And the priest shall command them to rid all things out of the house before the priest goes in to see the plague, so that he does not judge everything that is in the house unclean. And then the priest shall go in and see the house.

³⁷If the priest sees that the plague is in the walls of the house,[b] and that there are sunken pale or red streaks which seem to be lower than the other parts of the wall, ³⁸then let the priest go out at the house doors and shut up the house for seven days. ³⁹And let the priest come again on the seventh day and see it. If the plague has increased in the walls of the house, ⁴⁰let the priest command them to take away the stones in which the plague is, and let them cast them in an unclean place outside the settlement. ⁴¹And scrape the house round about inside, and pour out the dust outside the settlement in an unclean place. ⁴²And let them take other stones and put them in the places of those stones, and other mortar, and plaster the house.

⁴³If now the plague comes back again and breaks out in the house after they have taken away the stones, scraped the house, and plastered the house anew, ⁴⁴let the priest come and see it. And if then he perceives that the plague has eaten further in the house, then it is a consuming leprosy that is in the house, and it is unclean. ⁴⁵Then they shall break down the house – stones, timber, and all the mortar of the house – and carry it out of the settlement to an unclean place. ⁴⁶Moreover, he who goes into the house while it is shut up shall be unclean until night. ⁴⁷And he who sleeps in the house must wash his clothes, and he also who eats in the house must wash his clothes.

⁴⁸But if the priest comes and see that the plague has spread no further in the house after it is newly plastered, then let him judge it clean, for the plague is healed. ⁴⁹And let him take, to cleanse the house, two birds, cedar wood, purple cloth, and hyssop. ⁵⁰And let him kill one of the birds in an earthen vessel with running water, ⁵¹and then take the cedar wood, the hyssop, the purple, and the living bird, and dip them in the blood of the slain bird and in the running water, and sprinkle the house seven times – ⁵²and so cleanse the house with the blood of the bird, the running water, and the living bird, and with the cedar wood, the hyssop, and the purple cloth. ⁵³And he shall let the living bird fly out of the town into the wild fields, and so make an atonement for the house; and it shall be clean.

⁵⁴This is the law for every kind of plague of leprosy and outbreak, ⁵⁵for the leprosy of cloth and house, ⁵⁶and for swellings, scabs, and shiny white patches, ⁵⁷to teach when a thing is unclean or clean. This is the law concerning leprosy.

The Notes

a) 10. A log of oil is a certain measure containing six eggs [about three quarters of a pint or 350 ml], in Greek *Sextarius*.
b) 37. The leprosy of the houses is anything pertaining to houses whereby the dweller might suffer harm in health of body, to his goods, or otherwise, as if it stood in unwholesome air, etc.

Chapter 15

> The manner of purging the uncleanness both of men and women.

And the Lord spoke to Moses and Aaron, saying, ²Speak to the children of Israel and say to them: Everyone who has a running discharge in his flesh is unclean by the reason of his issue. And hereby shall it be known when he is unclean: ³if his flesh runs, or if his flesh congeals by reason of his discharge, then he is unclean. ⁴Every bed on which he lies and everything on which he sits shall be unclean. ⁵Whoever touches his bed must wash his clothes and bathe himself with water, and will be unclean until the evening. ⁶Whoever sits on that whereon he sat shall wash his clothes and bathe himself with water, and be unclean until the evening. ⁷And whoever touches his flesh shall wash his clothes and bathe himself in water, and be unclean until the evening.

⁸If he who has a discharge spits upon a clean person, the person must wash his clothes and bathe himself in water, and will be unclean until the evening. ⁹And whatsoever saddle he rides upon shall be unclean, ¹⁰and whoever touches anything that was under him shall be unclean till the evening. And he that carries any such things shall wash his clothes, bathe himself in water, and be unclean till the evening. ¹¹And whoever he touches (if he has not first washed his hands in water) must wash his clothes and bathe himself in water, and be unclean till the evening. ¹²And if he touches a vessel of earth, it must be broken; and all vessels of wood must be rinsed in water.

Lev 6:28; 11:33.

¹³When he who has a discharge is cleansed of his discharge, let him number seven days after he is clean, and wash his clothes and bathe his flesh in running water, and then he is clean. ¹⁴And the eighth day, let him take two turtle doves or two young pigeons, and come before the Lord at the door of the tabernacle of witness and give them to the priest. ¹⁵And the priest shall offer them, the one for a sin offering and the other for a burnt offering, and make an atonement for him before the Lord as concerning his discharge.

¹⁶If any man's seed departs from him in his sleep, he shall wash his flesh in water and be unclean until the evening. ¹⁷And all the clothes or furs whereon such seed chances shall be washed with water and be unclean till the evening. ¹⁸And if a woman lies with such a man, they shall wash themselves with water and be unclean until the evening.

¹⁹When a woman's natural course of blood runs, she shall be put apart seven days, and whoever touches her shall be unclean till the evening. ²⁰And all that she lies or sits upon, as long as she is put apart, shall be unclean. ²¹Whoever touches her bed shall wash his clothes, bathe himself with water, and be unclean till the evening. ²²And whoever touches anything that she sat upon shall wash his clothes, and wash himself also in water, and be unclean till the evening; ²³so it is that whether he touches her bed or anything whereon she has sat, he shall be unclean till the evening. ²⁴And if a man lies with her in the meantime, he shall be put apart as well as she, and shall be unclean seven days; and all of his bed wherein he sleeps shall be unclean.

²⁵When a woman's blood runs a long time, out of the time of her natural course, as long as her uncleanness runs she shall be unclean, in the same manner as when she is put apart. ²⁶All the beds on which she lies (as long as her issue lasts) shall be to her as her bed when she is put apart, and the things she sits upon shall be unclean, as is her uncleanness when she is put apart. ²⁷And whoever touches them shall be unclean, and shall wash his clothes, bathe himself in water, and be unclean till the evening.

²⁸And when she is cleansed of her issue, let her count seven days after she is clean. ²⁹And the eighth day, let her take two turtle doves or two young pigeons, and bring them to the priest at the door of the tabernacle of witness. ³⁰And the priest shall offer the one for a sin offer-

ing and the other for a burnt offering, and so make an atonement for her before the Lord as concerning her unclean issue.

³¹Make the children of Israel to keep themselves from their uncleanness so that they do not die in their uncleanness, when they have defiled my habitation that is among them.

³²This is the law for him who has a running sore, for him whose seed runs from him in his sleep and is defiled therewith, ³³for her who has an issue of blood as long as she is put apart, for whoever has a running sore, whether it be man or woman, and for him who sleeps with her that is unclean.

Chapter 16

> What Aaron must do before he enters into the holy place. The cleansing of the sanctuary or holy place. Of the Feast of Cleansing. Aaron confesses the sins of the children of Israel over the live goat, and so puts them upon the goat's head.

And the Lord spoke to Moses after the death of the two sons of Aaron, when they had offered before the Lord and died. ²And he said to Moses, Tell Aaron your brother that he is not to go simply at any time into the holy place that is within the veil which hangs before the mercy seat that is upon the ark, so that he does not die. For I will appear in the cloud upon the mercy seat.* ³But in this manner shall Aaron go in, into the holy place: with a bullock for a sin offering and a ram for a burnt offering. ⁴And he shall put the holy linen coat upon him, and shall have the linen breeches upon his flesh, gird himself with a linen sash, and put the linen turban upon his head. For they are holy garments; he shall wash his flesh with water and put them on. ⁵And he shall take from the congregation of the children of Israel two goats for a sin offering and a ram for a burnt offering.

⁶And Aaron shall offer the bullock for his sin offering, and make an atonement for himself and for his house. ⁷And he shall take the two goats and present them before the Lord in the door of the tabernacle of witness. ⁸And Aaron shall cast lots over the two goats: one lot for the Lord and the other for a scapegoat. ⁹And Aaron shall bring the goat upon which the Lord's lot fell and offer it for a sin offering. ¹⁰But the goat on which the lot fell to escape, he shall set alive before the Lord, to reconcile with and to let him go free into the wilderness.

¹¹And Aaron shall bring the bullock of his sin offering and reconcile for himself and for his household, and shall kill him. ¹²And then he shall take a censer full of burning coals out of the altar that is before the Lord, with his handful of sweet incense ground small, and bring them within the veil. ¹³He shall put the incense upon the fire before the Lord so that the cloud of the incense may cover the mercy seat that is upon the witness, so that he does not die. ¹⁴And he shall take some of the blood of the bullock and sprinkle it with his finger before the mercy seat eastward, seven times.

Lev 10:1,2

*By the cloud understand the smoke of the incense. See v 13.

Heb 9:16-22; 10:1-4.

LEVITICUS 16

¹⁵Then he shall kill the goat that is the people's sin offering, bring its blood within the veil, and do with its blood as he did with the blood of the bullock. And let him sprinkle it on the foreside toward the mercy seat, ¹⁶and so reconcile the holy place from the uncleanness of the children of Israel, and from their trespasses and all their sins. And let him so do also for the tabernacle of witness that dwells with them, there among their uncleannesses.

¹⁷And there shall be nobody in the tabernacle of witness when he goes in to make an atonement in the holy place, until he comes out again.* And he shall make an atonement for himself and for his household, and for all the assembly of Israel. ¹⁸Then he shall go out to the altar that stands before the Lord and reconcile it. He shall take some of the blood of the bullock and of the blood of the goat, put it upon the horns of the altar round about, ¹⁹and sprinkle some of the blood upon it with his finger seven times – and so cleanse it and hallow it from the uncleannesses of the children of Israel.

*Lu 1:8-10

²⁰And when he has made an end of reconciling the holy place, the tabernacle of witness, and the altar, let him bring the live goat. ²¹And let Aaron put both his hands on the head of the live goat and confess over him all the misdeeds of the children of Israel, and their trespasses and all their sins, and put them upon the head of the goat. And let him send the goat away by the hands of one who is anointed, into the wilderness. ²²And the goat shall bear all their misdeeds into the wilderness, and he shall let the goat go free in the wilderness.

²³Then let Aaron go into the tabernacle of witness and put off the linen clothes that he put on when he went in into the holy place, and leave them there. ²⁴And let him wash his flesh with water in the holy place, put on his own garments, and then come out and offer his burnt offering and the burnt offering of the people, and so make an atonement for himself and for the people. ²⁵And the fat of the sin offering, let him burn upon the altar.

²⁶And let him who carried out the scapegoat wash his clothes and bathe his flesh in water, and then come into the host again. ²⁷And the bullock of the sin offering and the goat of the sin offering (whose blood was brought in to make an atonement in the holy place), let someone carry out of the host and burn with fire – their skins, their flesh, and their dung. ²⁸And let him who burns them wash his clothes and bathe his flesh in water, and then come into the host again.

*Look in Lev 23:27 and note b.

²⁹And this shall be an ordinance forever to you: on the tenth day of the seventh month you shall humble your souls,* and shall do no work at all – whether it be one of yourselves or a stranger who sojourns among you. ³⁰For on that day an atonement shall be made for you, to cleanse you from all your sins before the Lord, and you shall be clean. ³¹It shall be a sabbath of rest to you, and you shall humble your souls. And it shall be an observance forever. ³²And the priest who is anointed, whose hand was filled to minister in his father's stead, shall make the atonement. He shall put on the holy linen clothes and holy vest-

ments, ³³and reconcile the holy sanctuary, the tabernacle of witness, and the altar; and shall make an atonement also for the priests and for all the people of the congregation. ³⁴And this shall be an everlasting* ordinance to you, to make an atonement for the children of Israel for all their sins once a year.

And it was done just as the Lord commanded Moses.

*Look in Ge 13:15 and note b.

Chapter 17

> All sacrifices must be brought to the door of the tabernacle. To devils they may not offer. Blood and all carrion is forbidden them.

And the Lord talked with Moses, saying, ²Speak to Aaron and to his sons, and to all the children of Israel, and say to them: This is the thing which the Lord charged, saying, ³Whoever he be of the house of Israel that kills an ox, lamb, or goat in the host or out of the host, ⁴and brings them not to the door of the tabernacle of witness to offer an offering to the Lord before the dwelling place of the Lord, blood shall be imputed to that person as though he had shed blood. And that person shall perish from among his people. ⁵Therefore, let the children of Israel bring the offerings they offer in the open field to the Lord, to the door of the tabernacle of witness and to the priest, and offer them for peace offerings to the Lord. ⁶And the priest shall sprinkle the blood upon the altar of the Lord in the door of the tabernacle of witness, and shall burn the fat to be a sweet savour to the Lord. ⁷And let them no more offer their offerings to devils, after whom they go a-whoring. And this shall be an ordinance forever to you throughout your generations.

⁸And you shall say to them: Whoever it may be of the house of Israel or of the strangers who sojourn among you that offers a burnt offering or any other offering, ⁹and who does not bring it to the door of the tabernacle of witness to offer to the Lord, that person shall perish from among his people.

¹⁰And whoever it may be of the house of Israel or of the strangers who sojourn among you that eats any manner of blood, I will set my face against that soul who eats blood, and will destroy him from among his people. ¹¹For the life of the flesh is in the blood, and I have given it to you upon the altar to make an atonement for your souls. For blood shall make an atonement for the soul. ¹²And therefore I said to the children of Israel, See that no soul among you eats blood, nor yet any stranger that sojourns among you.

Lev 3:17; 7:26; 17:14. De 12:16,23; 15:22,23.

¹³Whoever it may be of the children of Israel or of the strangers who sojourn among you who hunts and catches any beast or fowl that may be eaten, he shall pour out the blood and cover it with earth. ¹⁴For the life of all flesh is in the blood. Therefore I said to the children of Israel, You shall eat the blood of no manner of flesh. For the life of all flesh is in its blood, and whoever therefore eats it, shall perish.

¹⁵And whatever soul it may be who eats that which died alone, or that which was torn with wild beasts – whether it be one of yourselves

or a stranger – he shall wash his clothes, bathe himself in water, and shall be unclean till the evening; and then is he clean. ¹⁶But if he does not wash his clothes nor wash his flesh, he shall bear his sin.

Chapter 18

Which degrees of kindred may marry, and which not.

And the Lord talked with Moses, saying, ²Speak to the children of Israel and say to them: I am the Lord your God. ³Therefore, you shall not do the deeds of the land of Egypt where you dwelt, nor the deeds of the land of Canaan where I will bring you. Neither shall you follow their customs. ⁴But do according to my laws, and keep my observances, to walk in them. For I am the Lord your God. ⁵Keep, therefore, my ordinances and my laws – which, if a person does, he will live thereby. For I am the Lord.

⁶See that you go in to none of your nearest kindred to uncover their secrets; for I am the Lord. ⁷The secrets of your father and your mother, see you do not bare; she is your mother, therefore you shall not uncover her secrets. ⁸The secrets of your father's wife you shall not uncover, for they are your father's secrets.*

⁹You shall not uncover the privity† of your sister, the daughter of your father or of your mother, whether she was born at home or without. ¹⁰You shall not uncover the secrets of your son's daughter or your daughter's daughter, for that is your own privity. ¹¹You shall not uncover the secrets of your father's wife's daughter, whom she bore to your father, for she is your sister; you shall therefore not uncover her secrets. ¹²You shall not uncover the secrets of your father's sister, for she is your father's next kin. ¹³You shall not uncover the secrets of your mother's sister, for she is your mother's next kin.

¹⁴You shall not uncover the secrets of your father's brother; that is, you shall not go in to his wife, for she is your aunt. ¹⁵You shall not uncover the secrets of your daughter-in-law; she is your son's wife, therefore uncover not her secrets. ¹⁶You shall not bare the secrets of your brother's wife, for that is your brother's privity. ¹⁷You shall not uncover the privities of the wife and her daughter also. Neither shall you take her son's daughter or her daughter's daughter, to uncover their secrets. They are her next kin; it would therefore be wickedness. ¹⁸You shall not take a wife and her sister then also, to vex her, that you would open up her secrets as long as the wife lives.

¹⁹You shall not go in to a woman to uncover her privity as long as she is put apart for her uncleanness.

²⁰You shall not lie with your neighbour's wife, to defile yourself with her.

²¹You shall not give of your seedᵃ to offer to Moloch,ᵇ so that you do not defile the name of your God. For I am the Lord.

²²You shall not lie with mankind as with womankind, for that is an abomination.

²³You shall lie with no manner of beast, to defile yourself there-

---

Ro 10:5
Gal 3:12
Eze 20:11

Lev 20:11-21.

* † [Secrets or privity: private or secret parts of the body, which would be uncovered in conjugal relations.]

Lev 20:10

Lev 20:1-5

with. Neither shall any woman stand before a beast to lie with it, for that is an abomination.

^{24}Defile not yourselves in any of these things, for with all these things the nations that I cast out before you are defiled. ^{25}And the land is defiled, and I will visit its wickedness upon it, and the land will spew out her inhabiters. ^{26}Keep, therefore, my ordinances and laws. And see that you commit none of these abominations, neither any of you nor any stranger that sojourns among you – ^{27}for all these abominations the people of the land have done who were there before you, and the land is defiled – ^{28}lest the land spew you out, when you have defiled it, as it spewed out the nations that were there before you. ^{29}For whoever commits any of these abominations, the same souls that commit them shall perish from among their people. ^{30}Therefore, see that you keep my ordinances, and follow none of these abominable customs that were practised before you, so that you do not defile yourselves through them. For I am the Lord your God.

Lev 20:22, 23.

The Notes

a) 21. Your seed: that is, your issue (sons, daughters, grandchildren, etc.).
b) 21. Moloch: look in Leviticus 20 and note a.

Chapter 19

> A repetition of certain laws pertaining to the ten commandments. A consideration for the poor. How we ought to judge righteously. How we ought not to be avenged. Witchcraft is forbidden.

And the Lord spoke to Moses, saying, ^{2}Speak to all the multitude of the children of Israel and say to them: Be holy; for I, the Lord your God, am holy. ^{3}See that everyone fears his father and his mother, and that you keep my Sabbaths, for I am the Lord your God. ^{4}You shall not turn to idols nor make yourselves gods of metal. I am the Lord your God.

Lev 11:45
1Pe 1:16

^{5}When you offer your peace offerings to the Lord, you shall offer them so that you may be accepted.* ^{6}And it may be eaten the same day you offer it and on the morrow, but whatever is left on the third day must be burned in the fire. ^{7}If it is eaten the third day, it shall be unclean and not accepted. ^{8}And he that eats it shall bear his sin, because he has defiled the hallowed things of the Lord; and that soul shall perish from among his people.

*[COV: so that he may be merciful to you.]

^{9}When you reap down the ripe grain of your land, you shall not reap down the outermost borders of your fields. Neither shall you gather that which is left behind from harvesting. ^{10}You shall not pluck your vineyard clean, neither gather in the grapes that were overlooked, but you shall leave these things for the poor and the stranger.* I am the Lord your God.

Lev 23:22
*Here should we learn to make provision for the poor.

^{11}You shall not steal, nor lie, nor deal falsely with one another. ^{12}You shall not swear by my name falsely, so that you do not defile

M't 5:33-37
Ex 20:7
De 5:11

the name of your God. I am the Lord.

¹³You shall not defraud your neighbour with cavillations, nor rob him violently. Neither shall the workman's wages remain with you until the morning.

¹⁴You shall not curse the deaf nor put a stumbling block before the blind, but shall fear your God. I am the Lord.

> De 1:17; 16:19. Jas 2:1-9 Ex 23:1-3

¹⁵You shall do no unrighteousness in judgment: you shall not favour the poor nor honour the mighty, but shall judge your neighbour righteously.

¹⁶You shall not go up and down a secret accuser among your people; neither shall you help to shed the blood of your neighbour. I am the Lord.

> v17 e.f. COV. 1Jo 2:9,10; 3:18. M't 18:15 Lu 17:3

¹⁷You shall not hate your brother in your heart, but shall tell your neighbour his fault so that you do not bear sin on his account.

¹⁸You shall not avenge yourself nor bear hate in your mind against the children of your people, but shall love your neighbour as yourself. I am the Lord.

> De 22:9-11 and notes b & c.

¹⁹Keep my ordinances. Let none of your beasts mate with animals of a different kind,ᵃ neither sow your field with mixed seed. Neither shall you put on any garment of mixed linen and wool.ᵇ

²⁰If a man has to do with a woman that is a bondservant and has been promised to another man, and who is neither redeemed nor freedom given her, it shall be punished. But they shall not die, because she was not made free. ²¹And he shall bring for his trespass offering to the Lord, to the door of the tabernacle of witness, a ram for a trespass offering. ²²And the priest shall make an atonement for him with the ram of the trespass offering before the Lord, for the sin that he has done. And it shall be forgiven him, concerning the sin that he has done.

²³And when you come to the land and have planted all manner of trees from which people eat, you shall hold them uncircumcised as concerning their fruit: for three years they shall be uncircumcised to you, not to be eaten from. ²⁴But the fourth year all their fruit shall be holy and acceptable to the Lord, ²⁵and the fifth year you may eat of their fruits and gather them in.* I am the Lord your God.

> *See De 20:6 and note b. Lev 17:14
> ‡[Dismal days: ie, unlucky days, such as some believe Friday the 13th to be.]

²⁶You shall eat nothing with the blood.

You shall use no witchcraft nor observe dismal days.‡

²⁷You shall not round the locks of your heads; neither shall you disfigure the tufts of your beard. ²⁸You shall not cut your flesh for any soul's sake, nor tattoo any marks upon you. I am the Lord.

²⁹You shall not pollute your daughter, that you should maintain her to be a whore, lest the land fall to whoredom and become full of wickedness.

³⁰See that you keep my Sabbaths and fear my sanctuary. I am the Lord.

³¹Turn not to those who work with spirits, neither regard those who observe dismal days, so that you are not defiled by them. For I am the Lord your God.

³²You shall rise up before a grey head and reverence the face of the old man, and dread your God. For I am the Lord. ³³If a stranger sojourns by you in your land, see that you vex him not. ³⁴But let the stranger that dwells with you be as one of yourselves, and love him as yourself; for you were strangers in the land of Egypt. I am the Lord your God.

Ex 22:21; 23:9.

³⁵You shall do no unrighteousness in judgment, neither in meteyard, weight, nor measure. ³⁶But you shall have true balances, true weights, a true ephah, and a true hin. I am the Lord your God, who brought you out of the land of Egypt ³⁷in order that you should observe all my ordinances and laws, and that you should keep them. I am the Lord.

The Notes

a) 19. The beasts may not mate with a contrary kind against the order of nature, much less reasoning creatures made in the image of God, as men and women.

b) 19. The field may not be sown with mixed seed; that is, our deeds and words may not be mixed with hypocrisy. Neither may our garments be made of linen and wool; that is, we may not mix false doctrine with true, nor show a carnal and worldly life under pretence of religion.

Chapter 20

They that give of their seed to Moloch shall die for it.
Other laws and penalties of the nation.

And the Lord talked with Moses, saying, ²Tell the children of Israel: Whosoever he be of the children of Israel or of the strangers that dwell in Israel who gives of his seed to Moloch,ᵃ he shall die for it; the people of the land shall stone him with stones. ³And I will set my face against that fellow and will destroy him from among his people, because he has given of his seed to Moloch, to defile my sanctuary and to pollute my holy name. ⁴And though the people of the land hide their eyes from that fellow when he gives of his seed to Moloch, and do not kill him, ⁵yet I will set my face against that man and against his household; and I will destroy him and all who go a-whoring with him, to commit whoredom with Moloch, from among their people.

Lev 18:21

⁶If any soul turns to enchanters or interpreters of signs, and goes a-whoring after them, I will set my face against that soul and will destroy him from among his people. ⁷Sanctify yourselves therefore, and be holy, for I am the Lord your God. ⁸And see that you keep my observances and do them. For I am the Lord who sanctifies you.

⁹Whoever curses his father or mother shall die for it. His blood is on his head because he has cursed his father or mother.

¹⁰He who breaks wedlock with another man's wife shall die for it, because he has broken wedlock with his neighbour's wife; and so shall she likewise.

Lev 18:20

¹¹If a man lies with his father's wife and uncovers his father's secrets, they shall both die for it. Their blood is upon their heads.

¹²If a man lies with his daughter-in-law, they shall die, both of them. They have wrought abomination; their blood is upon their heads.

¹³If a man lies with mankind after the manner as with womankind, they have both committed an abomination and shall die for it. Their blood is upon their heads.

¹⁴If a man takes a wife and her mother also, it is wickedness. They shall be burned with fire, both him and them, so that there may be no wickedness among you.

¹⁵If a man lies with a beast, he shall die, and you shall slay the beast. ¹⁶If a woman goes to a beast and lies with it, you shall kill the woman and the beast also; they shall die, and their blood is upon their heads.

*[Secrets or secretness: ie, private or secret parts of the body]

¹⁷If a man takes his sister – his father's daughter or his mother's daughter – and see her secrets,* and she see his secrets also, it is a wicked thing. Therefore, let them perish in the sight of their people. He has seen his sister's secretness; he shall therefore bear his sin.

¹⁸If a man lies with a woman in the time of her natural infirmity, and uncovers her secrets and opens up her fountain, and she also opens up the fountain of her blood, they shall both perish from among the people.

Lev 18:10-14.

¹⁹You shall not uncover the secrets of your mother's sister nor of your father's sister. For he who does so uncovers his next kin, and they shall bear their misdoing. ²⁰If a man lies with his uncle's wife, he has uncovered his uncle's secrets; they shall bear their sin and shall die childless.ᵇ ²¹If a man takes his brother's wife, it is an unclean thing. He has uncovered his brother's secrets; they shall be childless for this.

Lev 18:26

²²See, therefore, that you keep all my ordinances and all my laws, and that you do them, so that the land where I bring you to dwell does not spew you out. ²³And see that you walk not in the customs of the nations that I cast out before you, for they did all these things and I abhorred them. ²⁴But I have said to you that you may enjoy their land, and that I will give it to you to possess – even a land that flows with milk and honey.

I am the Lord your God, who has separated you from other nations

Lev c11

²⁵so that you will put a difference between clean beasts and unclean, and between unclean birds and those that are clean. Make not your souls therefore abominable with beasts and birds and all the things that creep on the ground, which I have set apart for you to hold unclean. ²⁶Be holy unto me, for I the Lord am holy, and have severed you from other nations, that you should be mine.

De 18:10-14
1Sam 28:3

²⁷If there is a man or a woman who works with a spirit or who interprets signs, they shall die for it. They shall be stoned with stones, and their blood shall be upon them.

The Notes

a) 2. Under this name *Moloch* is forbidden all manner of idolatry, especially the offering of children to idols, for that is abominable before the Lord. Moloch was an idol of the children of Ammon, whose image was

hollow, having in it seven chambers. One was to offer therein fine flour, another for turtle doves, the third for a sheep, the fourth for a ram, the fifth for a calf, the sixth for an ox. And for him who would offer his son, the seventh chamber was opened. The face of this idol was like the face of a calf, his hands made open, ready to receive from those who stood by.
b) 20. They shall die immediately and shall not await the birth, as Judah would have burned Tamar being great with child. Ge 38:24, Lev 18:29.

Chapter 21

> The priest is forbidden to be at the death of any of his people, a few of his kin excepted. Priests may not be shaven, neither on the head nor yet the beard. The priest's wife must be a maiden. The priest's daughter may not be a harlot.

And the Lord said to Moses, Speak to the priests, the sons of Aaron, and say to them: A priest may not defile himself at the death of any of his people, ²except for his kin that is near to him,ª such as his mother, father, son, daughter, and brother; ³and for his sister, as long as she is a maiden, dwells near him, and was never given to any man – for her, he may defile himself. ⁴But he shall not make himself unclean for a ruler of his people, to pollute himself thereby.

⁵They shall make no baldness on their heads, nor shave off the locks of their beards, nor make any marks in their flesh. ⁶They shall be holy for their God, and not pollute the name of their God. For they offer the sacrifices of the Lord and the bread of their God; therefore, they must be holy.

⁷They shall take no wife who is a whore, or polluted, or put away from her husband; for a priest is holy unto his God. ⁸Set him apart therefore, for he offers up the bread of God. He shall therefore be holy for you; for I, the Lord who sanctifies you, am holy.

⁹If a priest's daughter falls to playing the whore, she pollutes her father; therefore, she shall be burned with fire.

¹⁰He that is the high priest among his brethren, upon whose head the anointing oil was poured and whose hand was filled to put on the vestments, shall not uncover his head nor tear his clothes. ¹¹Neither shall he go to any dead body nor make himself unclean – no, not for his father or mother. ¹²Neither shall he go out of the sanctuary, so that he does not pollute the holy place of his God. For the crown of the anointing oil of God is upon him. I am the Lord.

¹³He shall take a virgin for his wife, ¹⁴but no widow, nor a divorced woman, nor a polluted whore. But he shall take a maiden from his own people as wife, ¹⁵so that he does not defile his seed among his people. For I am the Lord who sets him apart as holy.

¹⁶And the Lord spoke to Moses, saying, ¹⁷Speak to Aaron and say: No man of your seed in their generations who has any deformity upon him may come forward to offer the bread of his God. ¹⁸For none that has any blemish shall come near, whether he be blind, lame, flat-

nosed, or has any misshapen member, ¹⁹or broken-footed, or broken-handed, ²⁰or crook-backed, or has a cataract or bulging eyes, or is mangy or scabbed, or has damaged testicles. ²¹No man who is deformed of the seed of Aaron the priest may come near to offer the sacrifices of the Lord.* If he has a deformity, he shall not come forward to offer the bread of his God. ²²Notwithstanding, he may eat of the bread of his God, even as well of the most holy as of the holy. ²³But he shall not go into the veil nor come near the altar, because he is deformed, and so that he does not pollute my sanctuary. For I am the Lord who sets them apart as holy.

²⁴And Moses told this to Aaron and to his sons, and to all the children of Israel.

*[Deformity in priests: see De 23, note a]

The Notes

a) 2. The priests are warned that they must not partake of the common wailings and lamentations for the dead lest they should thereby be the more unfit to do the sacrifices to which they were properly appointed, and lest they should by their weeping give an occasion to destroy the belief of the resurrection of the dead.

Chapter 22

Who ought to abstain from eating the things that were offered. How, what, and when they should be offered.

And the Lord communed with Moses, saying, ²Bid Aaron and his sons to take heed to the hallowed things of the children of Israel, which they have hallowed unto me, so that they do not pollute my holy name. For I am the Lord. ³Say to them: Whatever man it be of all your seed among your posterity after you who approaches the hallowed things (which the children of Israel shall have hallowed to the Lord), in which man is uncleanness, shall perish before the Lord. I am the Lord.

vv2,3 e.f. WYC.

⁴None of the seed of Aaron who is a leper or has a running sore may eat of the hallowed things until he is clean. And whoever touches any unclean soul, or a man whose seed runs from him by night, ⁵or whoever touches any crawling thing that is unclean to him, or person that is unclean to him, whatever uncleanness he has – ⁶the same soul who has touched any such thing shall be unclean until evening, and shall not eat of the hallowed things until he has washed his flesh with water. ⁷And then, when the sun is down, he will be clean, and may afterward eat of the hallowed things; for they are his food. ⁸Of a beast that dies alone or is rent by wild animals he shall not eat, and so defile himself with it. I am the Lord. ⁹Let them keep therefore my ordinances, lest they heap sin upon themselves and die therein, when they have defiled themselves. For I am the Lord who sets them apart.

Ex 22:31
Eze 44:31

¹⁰No stranger may eat of the hallowed things, neither a guest of the priests nor a hired servant. ¹¹But if the priest buys any soul with money, he may eat of it; and also he who is born in his house may eat of his bread. ¹²If the priest's daughter is married to a stranger, she may not eat of the hallowed lift offerings; ¹³notwithstanding, if the priest's

daughter is a widow or divorced and has no child, but has returned to her father's house again, she may eat of her father's bread as she did in her youth. But no stranger may eat of it.

¹⁴If anyone eats of the hallowed things unwittingly, he shall add a fifth part to it and make good to the priest the hallowed thing. ¹⁵And let the priests see that they do not defile the hallowed things of the children of Israel, which they have offered to the Lord, ¹⁶lest they load themselves with misdoing and trespass in eating their hallowed things. For I am the Lord who hallows them.

¹⁷And the Lord spoke to Moses, saying, ¹⁸Speak to Aaron and his sons, and to all the children of Israel, and say to them: Whoever it be of the house of Israel, or a stranger in Israel, who wishes to offer his offering – whatever vowed or freewill offering it is that they wish to offer to the Lord for a burnt offering, to reconcile themselves – ¹⁹it must be a male without blemish from the oxen, sheep, or goats.

²⁰Let them offer nothing that is deformed, for they shall get no favour with it. ²¹If a person wishes to offer a peace offering to the Lord and separates a vowed or freewill offering from the oxen or the flock, it must be without deformity so that it may be accepted. There may be no blemish in it, ²²whether it be blind, broken, wounded, or have a wart or cyst, an itch, or scabs. See that you offer no such to the Lord, nor put an offering of any such upon the altar for the Lord.

²³An ox or a sheep that has any member out of proportion you may offer for a freewill offering, but for a vowed offering it shall not be accepted. ²⁴You shall not offer to the Lord that which has its testicles bruised, broken, plucked out, or cut away; neither shall you make any such in your land. ²⁵Neither shall you offer from a stranger's hand an offering to your God of any such. For they spoil everything, because they have deformities in them, and therefore cannot be accepted for you.

²⁶And the Lord spoke to Moses, saying, ²⁷When an ox, a sheep, or a goat is born, it shall be seven days under the dam, and from the eighth day forth it may be accepted as a gift in the sacrifice of the Lord. ²⁸And whether it be ox or sheep, you shall not kill the animal and her young both in one day.

²⁹When you wish to offer a thank offering to the Lord,ᵃ you shall so offer it that you may be accepted. ³⁰That same day it must be eaten up, so that you leave none of it until the morrow. For I am the Lord.

³¹Keep now my commandments, and do them, for I am the Lord. ³²And pollute not my holy name, so that I may be hallowed among the children of Israel. For I am the Lord who hallows you, ³³and brought you out of the land of Egypt to be your God. For I am the Lord.

Lev 19:37
Nu 15:40,41
De 4:40

The Notes

a) 29. A thank offering: that is, an offering of thanksgiving. Thanksgiving is when the good deeds, kindnesses, and gifts of God are recited, by which faith toward God is strengthened, the more steadfastly to expect the thing that we ask of God.

Chapter 23

Of the holy days, as the Sabbath, Passover, the Feasts of Weeks and of Firstfruits, the Feast of Trumpets, the Feast of Cleansing, the Feast of the Tabernacles.

And the Lord spoke to Moses, saying, ²Speak to the children of Israel and say to them: These are the feasts of the Lord, which you shall call holy feasts.

The Sabbath.

³Six days you shall work, and the seventh is the Sabbath of rest, a holy feast. You shall do no work therein, for it is the Sabbath of the Lord, wherever you dwell.

Passover or Easter.
Ex 12:14-20; 13:6-10. Nu 28:16-25

⁴These are the feasts of the Lord which you shall proclaim holy in their seasons: ⁵The 14th day of the first month at evening is the Lord's Passover. ⁶And the 15th day of the same month is the Feast of Sweet Bread to the Lord; for seven days you must eat unleavened bread. ⁷The first day shall be a holy feast unto you, so that you may do no laborious work therein. ⁸But you shall offer sacrifices to the Lord seven days, and the seventh day also shall be a holy feast, and you shall do no laborious work therein.

Wave offering of firstfruits.

⁹And the Lord spoke to Moses, saying, ¹⁰Speak to the children of Israel and say to them: When you have come into the land which I give to you and reap down your harvest, you shall bring a sheaf of the firstfruits[a] of your harvest to the priest. ¹¹And he shall wave the sheaf before the Lord, to be accepted for you; the day after the Sabbath the priest shall wave it. ¹²And the same day that he waves the sheaf, you shall offer a lamb without blemish of a year old, for a burnt offering to the Lord, ¹³with the food offering of two tenth-parts of fine flour mixed with oil, to be a sacrifice to the Lord of a sweet savour. And the drink offering that belongs to it shall be the fourth part of a hin of wine. ¹⁴And you shall eat neither bread nor roasted grain nor sweet-boiled new wheat until the same day that you have brought an offering to your God. And this shall be a law forever for your children after you, wherever you dwell.

Feast of Weeks.

¹⁵And you shall count from the morrow after the Sabbath, from the day that you brought the sheaf of the wave offering, seven complete weeks. ¹⁶To the morrow after the seventh week you shall number fifty days, and then you shall bring a new food offering to the Lord. ¹⁷And you shall bring out of your habitations two wave-loaves made of two tenth-parts of fine flour leavened and baked, as firstfruits for the Lord. ¹⁸And you shall bring with the bread seven lambs without deformity of one year of age, one young ox, and two rams. These will serve as burnt offerings to the Lord, with food offerings and drink offerings belonging to the same, to be a sacrifice of a sweet savour to the Lord.

Feast of the Firstfruits.

¹⁹And you shall offer a he-goat for a sin offering, and two lambs of one year old for peace offerings. ²⁰And the priest shall wave them with the bread of the firstfruits before the Lord, and with the two lambs. And they shall be holy to the Lord, and be for the priest. ²¹And you shall make a proclamation the same day that it is a holy feast for you,

and you shall do no laborious work therein. And it shall be a law forever throughout all your habitations for your children after you.

²²When you reap down your harvest, you shall not cut it clean down upon the field. Neither shall you make any after-gathering of the harvest, but shall leave it for the poor and the stranger. I am the Lord your God. Lev 19:9,10

²³And the Lord spoke to Moses, saying, ²⁴Speak to the children of Israel and say: The first day of the seventh month shall be a rest of remembrance for you. To blow horns in a holy feast it shall be, ²⁵and you shall do no laborious work therein, and you shall offer sacrifice to the Lord. Feast of Trumpets.

²⁶And the Lord spoke to Moses, saying, ²⁷Also, the tenth day of the same seventh month is a day of an atonement and shall be a holy feast for you; and you shall humble your souls,ᵇ and offer sacrifice to the Lord. ²⁸Moreover, you shall do no work that day, for it is a day of atonement, to make an atonement for you before the Lord your God. ²⁹For whatever soul it be that does not humble himself that day, he shall be destroyed from among his people. ³⁰And whatever soul does any manner of work that day, the same I will destroy from among his people. ³¹See that you do no manner of work, therefore. And it shall be a law forever for your generations after you in all your dwellings. ³²A sabbath of restᶜ it shall be to you, and you shall humble your souls. The ninth day of the month at evening, and so forth from evening to evening again, you shall keep your sabbath. Feast of Cleansing.

³³And the Lord spoke to Moses, saying, ³⁴Speak to the children of Israel and say: The fifteenth day of the same seventh month shall be the Feast of Tabernacles, for seven days unto the Lord. ³⁵The first day shall be a holy feast, so that you shall do no laborious work therein. ³⁶Seven days you shall offer sacrifice to the Lord, and the eighth day shall be a holy feast for you, and you shall offer sacrifice to the Lord. It is the end of the feast, and you shall do no laborious work therein. Feast of Tabernacles or of Booths.

³⁷These are the feasts of the Lord that you shall proclaim holy feasts, to offer sacrifice to the Lord, burnt offerings, food offerings, and drink offerings every day, ³⁸as well as the Sabbaths of the Lord, and as well as your gifts, all your vowed offerings, and all the freewill offerings that you shall give to the Lord.

³⁹Moreover, in the fifteenth day of the seventh month, after you have gathered in the fruits of the land, you shall keep holy day unto the Lord seven days long. The first day shall be a day of rest, and the eighth day shall be a day of rest. ⁴⁰And the first day you shall take for yourselves the fruits of good trees, the branches of palm trees, the boughs of thick trees, and willows of the brook, and shall rejoice before the Lord seven days. ⁴¹And you shall keep it holy day unto the Lord seven days in the year. And it shall be a law forever for your children after you, to keep that feast in the seventh month. ⁴²And you shall dwell in booths made of boughs and branches for seven days; all who are Israelites by birth shall dwell in shelters of boughs, ⁴³so that vv42,43 e.f. WT 1530. Ne 8:14-17

your children after you may know how I made the children of Israel dwell in booths when I brought them out of the land of Egypt. For I am the Lord your God.

⁴⁴And Moses told all the feasts of the Lord to the children of Israel.

The Notes

a)   10. The firstfruits and tithes were the signs of the faith acknowledging to have received their goods and livestock from the Lord, as it is said, Exodus 22:29 and 23:16.

b)   27. To humble the soul is to chastise the body by abstinence and affliction, as is said, Isaiah 58:3 and note a.

c)   32. Sabbaths, feasts, and new moons signify the joy and gladness of the conscience, the renewing of man, and the rest in which we rest from our own works, not doing our wills but God's, who works in us through his gospel and glad tidings when we earnestly believe it. Ezekiel 20:12.

Chapter 24

> The oil for the lamps, and the illumination of the bread
> of remembrance, or showbread. He who curses must
> be stoned. He who kills shall be killed, etc.

And the Lord spoke to Moses, saying, ²Command the children of Israel to bring you pure oil from beaten olives for light, to pour always into the lamps, ³outside the veil of witness within the tabernacle of witness. And Aaron shall dress them both evening and morning before the Lord always; and it shall be a law forever among your children after you. ⁴And he shall dress the lamps on the pure candlestick before the Lord perpetually.

⁵And you shall take fine flour and bake twelve fine loaves with it.ᵃ Of two tenth-parts shall every loaf be. ⁶Make two rows of them, six per row, on the pure table before the Lord; ⁷and put pure frankincense upon the rows. And it will be bread of remembrance and an offering to the Lord. ⁸Every Sabbath he shall put them in rows before the Lord evermore, given from the children of Israel by an everlasting covenant. ⁹And they shall be for Aaron and his sons. And they shall eat them in the holy place, for they are most holy to him from the offerings of the Lord, for a lasting ordinance.

¹⁰Now the son of an Israelite woman, whose father was an Egyptian, went out among the children of Israel. And this son of the Israelite woman and a man of Israel fought together in the host. ¹¹And the Israelite woman's son blasphemed the Nameᵇ and cursed. And they brought him to Moses. (His mother's name was Shelomith the daughter of Dibri, of the tribe of Dan.) ¹²And they put him in custody until Moses should declare to them what the Lord said to do.

¹³And the Lord spoke to Moses, saying, ¹⁴Bring him who cursed outside the host, and let everyone who heard him put their hands on his head, and let all the people stone him. ¹⁵And speak to the children of Israel, saying, Whoever curses his Godᶜ shall bear his sin, ¹⁶and he who blasphemes the name of the Lord shall die for it; all the people

shall stone him to death. And the stranger as well as the Israelite, if he curses the Name, shall die for it.

¹⁷He who kills any person shall die for it; ¹⁸but he who kills a beast shall pay for it beast for beast. ¹⁹If anyone injures his neighbor, then as he has done, so shall it be done to him: ²⁰break for break, eye for eye, and tooth for tooth. Just as he has maimed another, so shall he be maimed. ²¹So now, he who kills a beast must pay for it, but he who kills a person must die for it. ²²You shall have the same law among you for the stranger as well as for one of yourselves, for I am the Lord your God.

M't 5:38,39

²³And Moses told the children of Israel that they should bring him who had cursed out of the host and stone him with stones. And the children of Israel did as the Lord commanded Moses.

The Notes

a) 5. Twelve fine loaves: the showbreads or the hallowed loaves.
b) 11,16. Name: The Hebrew is *schem*; that is, name that is blessed above all names.
c) 15. Curses: He curses God and blasphemes the name of God who despises and defies God's ordinances, statutes, and commandments, or who magnifies men's precepts and laws above God's, or who sets as much by them as by the precepts of the most merciful God.

Chapter 25

The sabbath of the seven years. And of the year of Jubilee, otherwise called the fiftieth year.

And the Lord spoke to Moses in Mount Sinai, saying, ²Speak to the children of Israel and say to them: When you have come into the land that I give you, let the land rest a sabbath for the Lord. ³Six years you may sow your field, and six years you may cut your vines and gather in your fruits, ⁴but the seventh year shall be a sabbath of rest for the land. The Lord's sabbath it shall be, and you shall neither sow your field nor cut your vines. ⁵You shall not reap the grain that grows by itself, neither gather the grapes that grow without dressing the vines; but it shall be a sabbath of rest for the land. ⁶Nevertheless, you shall keep the sabbath of the land to this intent: that you may eat from it, and your servant, your maid, your hired servant, and the stranger that dwells with you, ⁷and your livestock and the beasts in your land. Everything the land yields may be food.

vv5-7 e.f. cov.

⁸Then count seven weeks of years^a – that is, seven times seven years – and the duration of the seven weeks of years will be forty-nine years to you. ⁹And then you shall make a horn blow in the tenth day of the seventh month, which is the Day of Atonement; ¹⁰then shall you make the horn blow throughout all your land. And you shall hallow the fiftieth year, and proclaim liberty throughout the land to all the inhabitants. It shall be a year of Jubilee*ᵇ to you, and you shall return, every man to his possession and every man to his kindred again. ¹¹A year

*[WT 1530: a year of horns blowing; ie, a trumpet year]

of Jubilee shall that fiftieth year be to you. You shall not sow, neither reap the grain that grows by itself, nor gather the grapes that grow without your labour. ¹²For it is a year of Jubilee, and shall be holy to you; however yet, you may eat whatever the field bears. ¹³And in this year of Jubilee you shall return, every man to his possession again.ᶜ

¹⁴When you sell land to your neighbour, or buy any from your neighbour's hand, you shall not oppress one another. ¹⁵But according to the number of years after the Jubilee year you shall buy from your neighbour, and according to the number of crop years he shall sell to you. ¹⁶For a greater number of years remaining you shall increase the price, and for fewer years you shall reduce the price: for the number of crops, he shall sell to you. ¹⁷And see that no one oppresses his neighbour, but fear your God. For I am the Lord your God. ¹⁸Therefore, follow my ordinances, and keep my laws and do them, so that you may dwell in the land in safety. ¹⁹And the land will give her fruit, and you will eat your fill and dwell therein in safety.

²⁰You may ask, What will we eat in the seventh year, inasmuch as we cannot sow or gather in our crops? ²¹I will send my blessing upon you in the sixth year, and the land will bring forth her fruits for three years. ²²And you will sow in the eighth year, and eat of old fruits until the ninth year; until her crops come, you shall eat of old store.

²³The land shall not be sold forever, because the land is mine, and you are but strangers and sojourners with me; ²⁴and you shall, throughout all the land of your possession, let the land go home free again. ²⁵When your brother becomes poor and has sold away any of his land, if his next kinsman comes to redeem it, he may buy out that which his brother sold. ²⁶If your brother has no man to redeem it for him, yet if his hand can get sufficient to buy the land back, ²⁷then let him count how long it has been sold for and refund the purchaser for the remaining time; and so may he return to his possession again. ²⁸But if his hand cannot get sufficient to buy it back, then that which was sold shall remain in the purchaser's hand until the Jubilee, and in the year of Jubilee it shall come out and he may return to his possession again.

²⁹If a man sells a dwelling house in a walled city, he may buy it back again at any time within a whole year after it is sold; and that shall be the space of time during which he may redeem it. ³⁰But if it is not bought back again within the space of a full year, then the house in the walled city shall be secured forever to the purchaser and to his successors after him, and it shall not go out in the year of Jubilee. ³¹But the houses in villages that have no walls round about them shall be treated like the fields of the country, and may be bought back at any season, and shall go out free in the year of Jubilee.

³²Notwithstanding, the cities of the Levites, and their houses in the cities of their possessions, the Levites may redeem at all seasons. ³³And if a man purchases anything from the Levites, whether it be a house or a city that they possess, the sale shall go out in the trumpet year.* For the houses of the cities of the Levites are their possessions

Ru 4:1-5

*[Trumpet year: that is, the year of Jubilee.]

among the children of Israel. ³⁴But the fields that lie round about their cities shall not be bought, for they are their possessions forever.

³⁵If your brother has become poor and fallen into decay with you, receive him as a stranger or a sojourner, and let him live by you. ³⁶And you shall take no interest from him nor profit, but shall fear your God, so that your brother may live with you. ³⁷You shall not lend him your money at interest, nor lend him of your food to have advantage by it. ³⁸For I am the Lord your God, who brought you out of the land of Egypt to give you the land of Canaan and to be your God.

³⁹If your brother who dwells by you becomes poor and sells himself to you, you shall not let him labour as a bondservant does. ⁴⁰But as a hired servant and as a sojourner he shall be with you, and shall serve you till the year of Jubilee; ⁴¹and then he shall depart from you, both he and his children with him, and return to his own kindred again and to the possessions of his fathers. ⁴²For they are my servants, whom I brought out of the land of Egypt, and shall not be sold as bondmen. ⁴³See therefore that you do not rule over him severely, but fear your God.

⁴⁴If you desire to have bondservants and maids, you shall buy them from the heathen who are round about you, ⁴⁵and from the clans of the strangers who are sojourners among you, and from their descendants with you whom they begat in your land. ⁴⁶And you shall possess them and give them to your children after you, to possess them forever; and they shall be your bondmen. But over your brethren the children of Israel, none shall rule over another severely.

⁴⁷When a stranger and a sojourner nearby you grows rich, and your brother who dwells by him becomes poor and sells himself to the stranger that dwells nearby you or to any of the stranger's kin, ⁴⁸then after he is sold, he may be redeemed. One of his brethren may buy him out – ⁴⁹whether it be his uncle or his uncle's son, or any kinsman among his kindred. Or, if his hand can get enough, he may be released. ⁵⁰He shall reckon with his purchaser from the year that he was sold to the year of Jubilee, and the price of his redemption shall be according to the number of years, as if he were a hired servant. ⁵¹If there be yet many years to the year of Jubilee, then he shall, according to the same, pay the more for his deliverance, of the money that he was sold for; ⁵²if there remain but few years to the trumpet year, then he shall pay accordingly for his redemption: ⁵³and so shall he reckon his wages from year to year. And you shall not let the other rule over your brother severely in your sight. ⁵⁴If he is not bought free in the meantime, then he shall go out in the year of Jubilee, and his children with him. ⁵⁵For the children of Israel are my servants, whom I brought out of the land of Egypt. I am the Lord your God.

Ex 22:21
De 23:19,20
Ez 18:12-18

1Ki 9:22

vv51-53 e.f.
COV, WYC.

The Notes

a)   8. Weeks of years: A week is sometimes taken for the number of seven days, as before in Leviticus 23:15, and sometimes for the number of seven years, as here and in Daniel 9:24.

b) 10. Jubilee (from the Hebrew word *yobel*, which in English signifies a trumpet): a year of singular mirth and joy, and of much rest, in which their grain and all their fruits came forth without sowing, tilling, or any other labours.

c) 13. By this Jubilee is signified the restoring of all things to their perfection, which shall be after the general judgment, in that flourishing world when the chosen will be admitted into liberty from all wretchedness, poverty, anguish, and oppression – when everything which, through the sin of the first man, was taken away, shall be fully restored again in Christ.

Chapter 26

Images are forbidden. Blessed are they that keep those things that God bids, and most cursed are they that keep them not.

You shall make yourselves no idols nor graven image, neither rear up any pillar. Neither shall you set up any image of stone in your land, to bow yourselves to it, for I am the Lord your God. ²Keep my Sabbaths and fear my sanctuary.ᵃ For I am the Lord.

De 28:1-14 ³If you will walk in my observances, and will keep my commandments and do them, ⁴then I will send you rain in the right season, and your land will yield her increase, and the trees of the field will give their fruit. ⁵And the threshing will extend to the wine harvest, and the wine harvest will extend to sowing time, and you will eat your bread in plenteousness and will dwell in your land peaceably. ⁶And I will send peace in your land so that you may sleep, and no one will make you afraid.

And I will rid harmful beasts out of your land, and no sword shall go throughout your land. ⁷And you will chase your enemies, and they will fall before you upon the sword: ⁸five of you will chase a hundred, and a hundred of you will put ten thousand to flight, and your enemies will fall before you upon the sword. ⁹And I will turn to you, and increase you and multiply you, and set up my testament with you. ¹⁰And you will eat old store, and will cast out the old for plenteousness of the new. ¹¹I will make my dwelling place among you, and my soul will

2Co 6:16
Ex 29:45

not loathe you. ¹²And I will walk among you and will be your God, and you will be my people. ¹³For I am the Lord your God, who brought you out of the land of the Egyptians so that you would not be their bondmen; and I broke the bars of your yokes, and made you to walk upright.

De 28:15+ ¹⁴But if you will not hearken unto me nor will do all these my commandments, ¹⁵or if you despise my observances, or if your souls refuse my laws, so that you will not do all my commandments but break my decree, ¹⁶then I will do this to you: I will visit you with vexations, swelling, and fevers that will destroy your eyes, and with sorrows of heart. And you will sow your seed in vain, for your enemies will eat it. ¹⁷And I will set my face against you, and you will fall before your enemies, and they that hate you will rule over you, and you will flee when no man pursues you.

LEVITICUS 26

¹⁸And if for all this you will not yet hearken unto me, then I will punish you seven times more for your sins,ᵇ ¹⁹and will break the pride of your strength. For I will make the heaven* over you as hard as iron, and your land as hard as brass. ²⁰And thus your labour will be spent in vain, because your land will not give her increase. Neither will the trees of the land give their fruits.

²¹And if you walk still contrary to me, and will not hearken unto me, I will bring seven times more plagues upon you, according to your sins. ²²I will send in wild beasts upon you, which will rob you of your children and destroy your livestock, and will make you so few in number that your high roads will grow into a wilderness.

²³And if for all this you will not yet learn, but walk contrary to me, ²⁴then I also will walk contrary to you, and will punish you yet seven times more for your sins. ²⁵I will send a sword upon you, which shall avenge my testament with you. And when you have fled into your cities, I will send the pestilence among you, and will deliver you into the hands of your enemies. ²⁶And I will destroy your provision of bread, so that ten wives will bake your bread in one oven, and your bread will be meted out by weight, and then you will eat and will not be satisfied.

²⁷And if for all this you will not yet hearken unto me, but walk contrary to me, ²⁸then I will walk contrary to you also, wrathfully. And I will also chastise you seven times for your sins, ²⁹so that you will eat the flesh of your sons and the flesh of your daughters. ³⁰And I will destroy your altars built upon high hills and overthrow your images, and will cast your bodies on the bodies of your idols; and my soul will abhor you.

³¹And I will make your cities desolate, and bring your sanctuaries to naught, and will not smell the savours of your sweet odours. ²And I will turn the land into a wilderness, so that your enemies who dwell therein will wonder at it. ³³And I will strew you among the heathen, and will draw out a sword after you, and your land shall be waste and your cities desolate.

³⁴Then will the land enjoy her sabbaths, as long as it lies empty and you are in your enemies' land: even then will the land keep holy day and enjoy her sabbaths. ³⁵And as long as it lies empty, it shall rest, because it could not rest in your sabbaths, when you dwelt therein.

³⁶And upon those who are left alive of you, I will send a faintness into their hearts, in the land of their enemies, so that the sound of a leaf that falls will chase them away. And they will flee as though they fled a sword, and will fall, no man pursuing them. ³⁷And they shall fall one upon another, as it were before a sword, even no man following them. And you will have no power to stand before your enemies. ³⁸And you will perish among the heathen, and the land of your enemies will eat you up. ³⁹And they that are left of you will languish in their unrighteousness, even in their enemies' land; and also in the misdeeds of their fathers will they decay.

*[Heaven: see Genesis 1 and note a]

v26 e.f. COV and JR.

De 28:53

De 28:64

⁴⁰But they may confess their misdeeds and the misdeeds of their fathers, in their trespasses that they have trespassed against me, and because also that they have walked contrary to me. ⁴¹For this, I also will walk contrary to them, and will bring them into the land of their enemies. But then, at the least way, their uncircumcised hearts may be tamed. And then they may make an atonement for their misdeeds; ⁴²and I will remember my bond with Jacob, my testament with Isaac, and my testament with Abraham, and will think on the land.

⁴³For the land will be emptied of them, and will have pleasure in her sabbaths while she lies waste without them. But they may make an atonement for their misdeeds – because they despised my laws and their souls refused my ordinances. ⁴⁴And yet, despite these misdeeds, when they are in the land of their enemies, I will not so cast them away, nor will my soul so abhor them, that I will utterly destroy them and break my covenant with them. For I am the Lord their God. ⁴⁵I will therefore, for their sakes, remember the first covenant made when I brought them out of the land of Egypt in the sight of the heathen, to be their God. For I am the Lord.

⁴⁶These are the ordinances, decrees, and laws that the Lord made between himself and the children of Israel in Mount Sinai, by the hand of Moses.

Margin notes: Mercy is never denied to him that repents. De 4:29-31

The Notes

a) 2. Fear my sanctuary: To fear the sanctuary is to diligently perform the true worshipping and service of God, and to leave off nothing; to observe and keep purity both of mind and body, truly and not hypocritically; to believe that God knows, beholds, does, and rules all things; to beware of offending him; and with all fear and diligence to walk in the paths of his laws.

b) 18. God begins and augments his plagues more and more as the people harden their hearts against him.

Chapter 27

Of divers vowed offerings and the redemption of the same. Of tithes, etc.

And the Lord spoke to Moses, saying, ²Speak to the children of Israel and say to them: If anyone wishes to give a singular vowed offering* to the Lord according to the value of his soul, ³then shall the male from twenty years to forty‡ be set at fifty sickles of silver, after the sickle of the sanctuary, ⁴and the female at thirty sickles. ⁵And from five years to twenty, the male shall be set at twenty sickles and the female at ten sickles. ⁶And from a month to five years, the male shall be set at five sickles of silver and the female at three. ⁷And the man that is forty and above shall be valued at fifteen sickles, and the woman at ten. ⁸If the person is too poor so to be assessed, then let him come before the priest and let the priest set a value for him, according as the hand of him that vowed is able to get.

⁹If an offering be from the beasts of which people bring an offer-

*Margin notes: *[Vowed offerings: see c7 above and note b.] ‡[WT had forty in v3 and below. Others have sixty.]*

ing to the Lord, all that anyone gives of such to the Lord shall be holy. ¹⁰He may not alter it nor exchange it, a good for a bad or a bad for a good. If he exchanges beast for beast, then both the same beast and also the one it was exchanged for shall be holy. ¹¹If it be any manner of unclean beast, of which people may not offer to the Lord, let him bring the beast before the priest, ¹²and let the priest value it. And whether it be good or bad, as the priest sets the value, so shall it be. ¹³And if he wishes to buy it back, let him give a fifth part more in addition to the value it was set at.

¹⁴If any man dedicates his house, it shall be holy to the Lord. And the priest shall set its value: whether it be good or bad, and as the priest has valued it, so shall it be. ¹⁵If he who dedicated it wishes to redeem his house, let him give a fifth part more to the price that it was set at, and it shall be his.

¹⁶If a man hallows^a a piece of his inherited land to the Lord, its value shall be set according to what it bears. If it bears a homer of barley, it shall be set at fifty sickles of silver. ¹⁷If he hallows his field immediately from the year of Jubilee, it shall be worth as it is valued. ¹⁸But if he hallows his field after the year of Jubilee, the priest shall reckon the value with him according to the years that remain till the next trumpet year,* and thereafter it shall be set lower. ¹⁹If he who dedicated the field wishes to redeem it back, let him add a fifth part to the value it was set at, and it shall be his. ²⁰If he does not wish to, it may not be redeemed anymore, ²¹but when the field goes out in the trumpet year it shall be holy to the Lord as a thing devoted; and it shall be the priest's possession.

*[Next trumpet year: that is, the next year of Jubilee]

²²If a man dedicates^a to the Lord a field that he has bought, which is not of his inheritance, ²³then the priest shall reckon with him what it is worth until the year of Jubilee. And he shall give the price that it is set at the same day, and it shall be holy to the Lord. ²⁴But in the year of Jubilee the field shall return to the one from whom he bought it, whose inheritance of land it was.

²⁵And all valuation shall be according to the holy sickle.^b One sickle makes twenty gerahs.

²⁶But the firstborn of the beasts that belong to the Lord, no man may dedicate – whether it be ox or sheep[‡] – for they are the Lord's already. ²⁷If it be an unclean beast, then let him redeem it as it is set and give a fifth part more as well. If it is not redeemed, then let it be sold as it is assessed.

‡[Sheep includes a goat]

²⁸Notwithstanding, no devoted thing that a person devotes to the Lord of all his property, whether it be man or beast or land of his inheritance, may be sold or redeemed. For all devoted things are most holy to the Lord. ²⁹No devoted thing therefore that is devoted from among man may be redeemed, but must needs die.^o

³⁰All tithes from the land, whether it be of the harvest of the field or fruit of the trees, shall be holy to the Lord. ³¹If anyone wishes to redeem anything of his tithes, let him add the fifth part more to it. ³²But

^o[Some: a devoted person must remain in, and therefore die in, the devoted condition]

the tithes of oxen and sheep, and of all that goes under the herdsman's keeping, shall be holy tithes to the Lord. ³³Men shall not look if it be good or bad, nor exchange it. If anyone exchanges it, then both it and the one it was exchanged for shall be holy, and may not be redeemed.

³⁴These are the commandments that the Lord gave Moses, in charge to give to the children of Israel in Mount Sinai.

♣

The Notes

a) 16,22,etc. To *hallow* and to *dedicate* both mean the same. [Ed: the word *sanctify* is sometimes used in the same sense. See Ge 2:3, note c.]
b) 25. Holy sickle and sickle of the sanctuary: these mean the same.

The end of the third book of Moses.

The Fourth Book of Moses
called
Numbers

Chapter 1

All who are able for battle are numbered. The tribe of Levi is appointed to take care of the tabernacle.

AND THE LORD SPOKE TO MOSES in the wilderness of Sinai, in the tabernacle of witness,* on the first day of the second month in the second year after they came out of the land of Egypt, saying, ²Take the count of all the multitude of the children of Israel in their kindreds and households of their fathers, and number them by name, all who are males, head by head, ³from twenty years and above. All who are able to go forth into war in Israel, you and Aaron shall number in their armies.

*[Tabernacle or habitation of witness: see Exodus 27 and note b for why it was so called]

⁴And with you shall be from every tribe a head man in the house of his father. ⁵And these are the names of the men that shall stand with you: of Reuben, Elizur the son of Shedeur; ⁶of Simeon, Shelumiel the son of Zurishaddai; ⁷of the tribe of Judah, Nahshon the son of Amminadab; ⁸of Issachar, Nethaneel the son of Zuar; ⁹of Zebulun, Eliab the son of Helon. ¹⁰Among the children of Joseph: of Ephraim, Elishama the son of Ammihud; of Manasseh, Gamaliel the son of Pedahzur; ¹¹and of Benjamin, Abidan the son of Gideoni. ¹²Of Dan, Ahiezer the son of Ammishaddai; ¹³of Asher, Pagiel* the son of Ocran; ¹⁴of Gad, Eliasaph the son of Deuel; ¹⁵of Naphtali, Ahira the son of Enan. ¹⁶These were counselors of the congregation and lords in the tribes of their fathers, captains over thousands in Israel.

*or, Phegiel

¹⁷And Moses and Aaron took these men above-named, ¹⁸gathered all the congregation together on the first day of the second month, and counted them according to their birth and kindreds and houses of

*[Kindreds: families, related kin]

their fathers by name, from twenty years and above, head by head. ¹⁹As the Lord commanded Moses, so he numbered them, in the wilderness of Sinai.

²⁰And the children of Reuben, Israel's eldest son, in their generations, kindreds, and houses of their fathers, when they were numbered every man by name – all who were males from twenty years and above, as many as were able to go forth in war – ²¹were numbered in the tribe of Reuben 46,500. *Of Reuben.*

²²Among the children of Simeon, their generations in their kindreds and houses of their fathers, when every man's name was counted of all the males from twenty years and above, whoever was fit for the war, ²³were numbered in the tribe of Simeon 59,300. *Of Simeon.*

²⁴Among the children of Gad, their generations in their kindreds and households of their fathers, when they were counted by name from twenty years and above, all who were fit for the war, ²⁵were numbered in the tribe of Gad 45,650. *Of Gad.*

²⁶Among the children of Judah, their generations in their kindreds and houses of their fathers by the number of names, from twenty years and above, all who were able to war, ²⁷were numbered in the tribe of Judah 74,600. *Of Jude.*

²⁸Among the children of Issachar, their generations in their kindreds and houses of their fathers, when their names were counted from twenty years and above, whoever was able for war, ²⁹were numbered in the tribe of Issachar 54,400. *Of Issachar.*

³⁰Among the children of Zebulun, their generations in their kindreds and houses of their fathers by the number of names, from twenty years and above, whoever was fit for the war, ³¹were counted in the tribe of Zebulun 57,400. *Of Zebulon.*

³²Among the children of Joseph, first among the children of Ephraim, their generations in their kindreds and houses of their fathers, when the names of all who were able for the war were counted from twenty years and above, ³³were in number in the tribe of Ephraim 40,500. *Of Joseph; Ephraim*

³⁴Among the children of Manasseh, their generations in their kindreds and houses of their fathers, when the names of all who were able to war were counted from twenty and above, ³⁵were numbered in the tribe of Manasseh 32,200. *Of Manasseh.*

³⁶Among the children of Benjamin, their generations in their kindreds and houses of their fathers by the count of names, from twenty years and above, of all who were able for war, ³⁷were numbered in the tribe of Benjamin 35,400. *Of Benjamin.*

³⁸Among the children of Dan, their generations in their kindreds and houses of their fathers in the sum of names, of all who were able to war from twenty years and above, ³⁹were numbered in the tribe of Dan 62,700. *Of Dan.*

⁴⁰Among the children of Asher, their generations in their kindreds and houses of their fathers, when they were counted by name from *Of Asher.*

twenty years and above, all who were able for war, ⁴¹were numbered in the tribe of Asher 41,500.

Of Naphtali. ⁴²Among the children of Naphtali, their generations in their kindreds and houses of their fathers, when their names were counted from twenty years and above, whoever was fit for war, ⁴³were numbered in the tribe of Naphtali 53,400.

⁴⁴These are the numbers that Moses and Aaron counted with the twelve leaders of Israel, from every house of their fathers a man. ⁴⁵And all the numbers of the children of Israel in the houses of their fathers from twenty years and above, whoever was fit for the war in Israel, ⁴⁶drew to the sum of 603,550.

⁴⁷But the Levites in the tribe of their fathers were not numbered among them. ⁴⁸For the Lord had spoken to Moses, saying, ⁴⁹Only see that you do not number the tribe of Levi, neither take the sum of them among the children of Israel. ⁵⁰But you shall appoint the Levites over the habitation of witness and over all its furnishings, and over everything that pertains to it. For they shall carry the tabernacle and all its apparatus, and they shall attend to it, and shall pitch their tents round about it. ⁵¹And when the tabernacle goes forth, the Levites shall take it down, and when the tabernacle is pitched, they shall set it up; for if any stranger comes near, he shall die. ⁵²The children of Israel shall pitch their tents, every man in his own company and every man by his own standard throughout all their hosts, ⁵³but the Levites shall pitch round about the habitation of witness so that no wrath falls upon the congregation of the children of Israel. And the Levites shall keep watch over the habitation of witness.

⁵⁴And the children of Israel did according to all that the Lord commanded Moses.

Chapter 2

The order of the pitching of the tents round about the tabernacle of witness. The heads and chief lords of the kindreds of Israel are named.

And the Lord spoke to Moses and Aaron, saying, ²The children of Israel shall pitch camp, every man by his own standard with the coats of arms of their fathers' houses, away from the presence of the tabernacle of witness.

On the east side: the company of Judah, Issachar, and Zebulun. ³On the east side, toward the rising of the sun, they of the standard of the host of Judah shall pitch camp with their coat of arms. And Nahshon the son of Amminadab shall be captain over the sons of Judah. ⁴His host and the number of them: 74,600. ⁵And next to him shall the tribe of Issachar pitch, and Nethaneel the son of Zuar shall be captain over the children of Issachar. ⁶His host and the number of them: 54,400. ⁷And then the tribe of Zebulun, with Eliab the son of Helon, captain over the children of Zebulun; ⁸and his host in the number of them: 57,400. ⁹So all who belong to the host of Judah are 186,400 in their companies, and these shall go in the forefront when they journey.

¹⁰And on the south side the standard of the host of Reuben shall lie with their companies, with the captain over the sons of Reuben, Elizur the son of Shedeur. ¹¹His host and the number of them: 46,500. ¹²And fast by him shall the tribe of Simeon pitch, and the captain over the sons of Simeon shall be Shelumiel the son of Zurishaddai. ¹³His host and the number of them: 59,300. ¹⁴And the tribe of Gad also; the captain over the sons of Gad shall be Eliasaph the son of Reuel. ¹⁵And his host and the number of them: 45,650. ¹⁶So all the number that belong to the host of Reuben are 151,450 in their companies, and they shall be the second in the journey.

On the south side: the company of Reuben, Simeon, and Gad.

¹⁷And the tabernacle of witness with the host of the Levites shall go in the midst of the hosts. As they lie in their tents, so shall they proceed in the journey, every man in his position around their standards.

The Levites, with the tabernacle in the midst.

¹⁸On the west side, the standard and the host of Ephraim shall lie with their companies. And the captain over the sons of Ephraim shall be Elishama the son of Ammihud. ¹⁹His host and the number of them: 40,500. ²⁰And fast by him, the tribe of Manasseh, with the captain over the sons of Manasseh, Gamaliel the son of Pedahzur; ²¹and his host and the number of them: 32,200. ²²And the tribe of Benjamin also, with the captain over the sons of Benjamin, Abidan the son of Gideoni; ²³and his host and the number of them: 35,400. ²⁴All the number that belongs to the host of Ephraim are 108,100 in their hosts, and they shall be the third in the journey.

On the west side: the company of Ephraim, Manasseh, and Benjamin.

²⁵And the standard and the host of Dan shall lie on the north side with their companies, with the captain over the children of Dan, Ahiezer the son of Ammishaddai; ²⁶and his host and the number of them: 62,700. ²⁷And fast by him shall the tribe of Asher pitch, with the captain over the sons of Asher, Pagiel the son of Ocran. ²⁸His host and the number of them: 41,500. ²⁹And the tribe of Naphtali also, with the captain over the children of Naphtali, Ahira the son of Enan. ³⁰His host and the number of them: 53,400. ³¹So the whole number of all who belong to the host of Dan is 157,600. And they shall be the last in the journey, with their standards.

On the north side: the company of Dan, Asher, and Naphtali.

³²These were the totals of the children of Israel in the houses of their fathers. All who were numbered of the hosts with their companies were 603,550. ³³And yet the Levites were not numbered among the children of Israel, as the Lord had commanded Moses. ³⁴And the children of Israel did according to all that the Lord commanded Moses: so they pitched with their standards, and so they journeyed, every man in his kindred and in the household of his fathers.

Chapter 3

> The Levites are not numbered to go to battle, but to care for the holy place or sanctuary. They must also pitch their tents next to the habitation.

These are the generations of Aaron and Moses when the Lord spoke to Moses in Mount Sinai. ²These are the names of the sons of Aaron: Nadab, the eldest son, and Abihu, Eleazar, and Ithamar; ³these are the names of the sons of Aaron who were anointed priests, and their hands filled to minister. ⁴But Nadab and Abihu died before the Lord because they brought strange fire before the Lord in the wilderness of Sinai, and they had no children. And Eleazar and Ithamar ministered in the sight of Aaron their father.

⁵And the Lord spoke to Moses, saying, ⁶Bring the tribe of Levi, and set them before Aaron the priest. And let them serve him, ⁷and attend to him and to all the multitude before the tabernacle of witness, to do the service of the habitation. ⁸And they shall keep all the parts and furnishings of the tabernacle of witness and attend to the children of Israel, to minister in the service of the habitation. ⁹And you shall give the Levites to Aaron and his sons, for they are given to him from the children of Israel. ¹⁰And you shall appoint Aaron and his sons to attend to their priest's office; but the stranger who comes near shall die for it.

¹¹And the Lord spoke to Moses, saying, ¹²Behold, I have taken the Levites[a] from among the children of Israel instead of all the firstborn that open the womb among the children of Israel. So the Levites will be mine, ¹³because all the firstborn are mine. For the same day that I smote all the firstborn in the land of Egypt, I hallowed unto myself all the firstborn in Israel, both man and beast. And mine they shall be, for I am the Lord.

¹⁴And the Lord spoke to Moses in the wilderness of Sinai, saying, ¹⁵Number the children of Levi in the houses of their fathers and kindreds, all who are males from a month old and above.

¹⁶And Moses numbered them at the word of the Lord, as he was commanded. ¹⁷And these are the names of the children of Levi: Gershon, Kohath, and Merari. ¹⁸And these are the names of the children of Gershon in their kindreds: Libni and Shimei. ¹⁹And the sons of Kohath in their kindreds were Amram, Izehar, Hebron, and Uzziel. ²⁰And the sons of Merari in their kindreds were Mahli and Mushi. These are the kindreds of Levi in the houses of their fathers.

²¹And of Gershon came the kindreds of the Libnites and the Shimites, who are the kindreds of the Gershonites. ²²The number of them, when all the males were counted from a month old and above, was 7,500. ²³And the kindreds of the Gershonites pitched behind the habitation westward. ²⁴And the head over the most ancient house among the Gershonites was Eliasaph, the son of Lael. ²⁵The office of the children of Gershon in the tabernacle of witness was to keep the habitation and the tent with its covering, and the hanging of the door of the tabernacle of witness, ²⁶the hangings of the court, the curtain of the door of the court (which court went round about the dwelling and the altar), and the cords that pertained to all the service thereof.

²⁷And of Kohath came the kindred of the Amramites, and the kindreds of the Izharites, the Hebronites, and the Uzzielites; and these are the kindreds of the Kohathites. ²⁸And the number of all the males from a month old and above was 8,600, who attended to the holy place. ²⁹And the kindreds of the children of Kohath pitched on the south side

of the dwelling. ³⁰And the head over the most ancient house of the kindreds of the Kohathites was Elizaphan the son of Uzziel. ³¹Their office was to keep the ark, the table, the candlestick, the altar, the holy utensils to minister with, and the veil, with everything that served thereto. ³²And Eleazar, the son of Aaron the priest, was chief over all the heads of the Levites, and had the oversight of those who attended to the holy things.

³³And of Merari came the kindreds of the Mahlites and of the Mushites, and these are the kindreds of the Merarites. ³⁴And the number of them, when all the males from a month old and above were counted, drew to 6,200. ³⁵And the head over the most ancient house among the kindreds of the Merarites was Zuriel the son of Abihail, who pitched on the north side of the dwelling. ³⁶And the office of the sons of Merari was to keep the boards of the dwelling, the bars, the pillars with their sockets, all the tools, and everything that served thereto; ³⁷and also the pillars of the court round about and their sockets, with their pins and cords.

³⁸But at the forefront of the habitation, and before the tabernacle of witness eastward, shall Moses with Aaron and his sons pitch camp, and attend to the sanctuary on behalf of the children of Israel. And the stranger who comes near shall die for it.

³⁹And the whole company of the Levites whom Moses and Aaron numbered at the commandment of the Lord, throughout their kindreds, of all the males a month old and above, was 22,000.

⁴⁰And the Lord said to Moses, Count all the firstborn males among the children of Israel, from a month old and above, and take the number of their names. ⁴¹And you shall appoint the Levites to me, the Lord, instead of all the firstborn among the children of Israel, and the livestock of the Levites for the firstborn livestock of the children of Israel. ⁴²And Moses numbered, as the Lord commanded him, all the firstborn of the children of Israel; ⁴³and all the firstborn males in the sum of names, from a month old and above, were numbered 22,273.

⁴⁴And the Lord spoke to Moses, saying, ⁴⁵Take the Levites for all the firstborn of the children of Israel, and the livestock of the Levites for their livestock, and the Levites shall be mine, who am the Lord. ⁴⁶And for the redemption of the 273 who are more than the Levites in the firstborn of the children of Israel, ⁴⁷take five sickles apiece, after the sickle of the holy place – twenty gerahs per sickle. ⁴⁸And give the money to redeem the excess number of them to Aaron and his sons.

⁴⁹And Moses took the redemption money for the overplus, who were more than the Levites ⁵⁰among the firstborn of the children of Israel; and it came to 1,365 sickles of the holy sickle. ⁵¹And he gave that redemption money to Aaron and his sons at the word of the Lord, even as the Lord commanded Moses.

Sidenotes: The Kohathites are assigned to the south side. The Merarites are assigned to the north side. Moses and Aaron and his sons, on the east side. Ex 30:13; Lev 27:25; Eze 45:12

The Notes

a) 11. *Levite* sometimes signifies only an attendant or servant, as here and Isaiah 66:21.

Chapter 4

The offices of the Levites, everyone according to the flock that he came of.

And the Lord spoke to Moses and Aaron, ²and bade them to take the number of the children of Kohath from among the sons of Levi, in their kindreds and houses of their fathers, ³from thirty years and above to fifty – all who were able to war – to do the work in the tabernacle of witness.

⁴This shall be the office of the children of Kohath in the tabernacle of witness, which is most holy:

⁵When the host is to remove, Aaron and his sons shall first go and take down the veil, and shall cover the ark of witness with it. ⁶And they shall put thereon a covering of badger skins, spread a cloth that is altogether of jacinth above everything, and put in its poles. ⁷And on the show table they shall spread abroad a cloth of jacinth, and put on it the dishes, spoons, bowls, and pots to pour with; and the daily bread shall be thereon. ⁸And they shall spread upon these a covering of purple, cover this with a covering of badger skins, and put in its poles. ⁹And they shall take a cloth of jacinth and cover the candlestick of light, and her lamps, her snuffers, firepans,* and all the oil vessels that pertain to the service, ¹⁰and shall bundle it and all the accessories in a wrapping of badger skins, and put it on carrying poles. ¹¹And upon the golden altar they shall spread a cloth of jacinth and put its poles in place. ¹²And they shall take all the things they use to minister with in the holy place, put a cloth of jacinth on them, wrap them with a covering of badger skins, and put them on carrying poles. ¹³And they shall take away the ashes out of the altar, spread a scarlet cloth on it, ¹⁴and put on it the firepans, the fleshhooks, the shovels, the basins, and everything that pertains to the altar. And they shall spread upon it a covering of badger skins and put the altar's poles in place.

¹⁵And when Aaron and his sons have made an end of covering the sanctuary and all the things of the sanctuary in readiness for the host to remove, then the sons of Kohath shall come in to do the moving. But let them not touch the sanctuary, lest they die. And this shall be the responsibility of the sons of Kohath concerning the tabernacle of witness.

¹⁶And Eleazar, the son of Aaron the priest, shall be responsible to prepare oil for the lights, the sweet incense, the daily food offering, and the anointing oil. And he shall have the oversight of all the dwelling and everything in it, both of the sanctuary and of everything that pertains to it.

¹⁷And the Lord spoke to Moses and Aaron, saying, ¹⁸Destroy not the tribe of the kindreds of the Kohathites from among the Levites. ¹⁹But thus do for them, so that they may live and not die when they approach the most holy place: Aaron and his sons shall go in and direct each man to his service and to his load. ²⁰But let them not go in to see when they are covering the sanctuary, lest they die.

*[Firepans: pans or trays for holding snuffs, ashes, or hot coals as debris. Also sometimes used for heating over a fire, or, when filled with coals, as a heater. Also used to refer to incense burners or censers.]

²¹And the Lord spoke to Moses, saying, ²²Take the number of the children of Gershon in the houses of their fathers and in their kindreds, ²³from thirty years and above to fifty – all who are able to go forth in war – to do service in the tabernacle of witness. ²⁴And this is the service of the kindred of the Gershonites: to serve and to move loads. ²⁵They shall move the curtains of the dwelling, the roof of the tabernacle of witness and its covering, the covering of badger skins that is on high above upon it, the hanging of the door of the tabernacle of witness, ²⁶the hanging of the court, the hanging of the gate of the court that is round about the dwelling and the altar, their cords, all the equipment that serves for them, and everything that is made for them. ²⁷And at the mouth of Aaron and his sons shall all the service of the children of the Gershonites be done, in all that they are to carry and in all their service; and you shall appoint them to all the duties that they are to attend to. ²⁸And that is the service of the kindred of the children of the Gershonites for the tabernacle of witness. And their service shall be under the hand of Ithamar, the son of Aaron the priest.

²⁹And you shall number the sons of Merari in their kindreds and in the houses of their fathers, ³⁰from thirty years and above to fifty – all who are able to go forth in war – to do the service of the tabernacle of witness. ³¹And this is their responsibility in all their service in the tabernacle of witness: the boards of the dwelling, and the bars, pillars, and sockets thereof, ³²the pillars of the court round about and their sockets, pins, and cords, and all that pertains to these. And by name you shall assign the things that they are to carry. ³³That is the service of the kindreds of the sons of Merari in all their service for the tabernacle of witness, under the hand of Ithamar, the son of Aaron the priest.

³⁴And Moses and Aaron and the lords of the multitude numbered the sons of the Kohathites in their kindreds and houses of their fathers, ³⁵from thirty years and above to fifty, and who were able to go forth in the host, to do service in the tabernacle of witness. ³⁶And the number of them in their kindreds was 2,750. ³⁷Those are the numbers of the kindreds of the Kohathites, of all who did service for the tabernacle of witness, whom Moses and Aaron numbered at the commandment of the Lord by the hand of Moses.

³⁸And the sons of Gershon were numbered in their kindreds and in the houses of their fathers, ³⁹from thirty years up to fifty – all who were able to go forth in the host – to do service in the tabernacle of witness. ⁴⁰And the number of them in their kindreds and in the houses of their fathers was 2,630. ⁴¹That is the number of the kindreds of the sons of Gershon, of all who did service for the tabernacle of witness, whom Moses and Aaron did number at the commandment of the Lord.

⁴²And the kindreds of the sons of Merari were numbered in their kindreds and in the houses of their fathers, ⁴³from thirty years up to fifty – all who were able to go forth with the host – to do service in the tabernacle of witness. ⁴⁴And the number of them was in their kindreds 3,200. ⁴⁵That is the number of the kindreds of the sons of Merari,

whom Moses and Aaron numbered at the bidding of the Lord by the hand of Moses.

⁴⁶The whole company that Moses, Aaron, and the lords of Israel numbered among the Levites in their kindreds and households of their fathers, ⁴⁷from thirty years up to fifty – every man to do his office and service, and to carry his load for the tabernacle of witness – ⁴⁸was 8,580. ⁴⁹Whom they numbered at the commandment of the Lord by the hand of Moses, every man for his service and load to carry, as the Lord commanded Moses.

Chapter 5

Who they are that ought to be put out of the host. The confession of sin. The cleansing of sin done out of ignorance. The law of the firstfruits and of jealousy.

And the Lord spoke to Moses, saying, ²Command the children of Israel to put out of the host all the lepers, all who have a discharge, and all who are defiled upon the dead. ³Whether they be males or females, you must put them out of the host so that they do not defile the tents among which you dwell.

⁴And the children of Israel did so, and put them out of the host. Just as the Lord commanded Moses, so did the children of Israel do.

⁵And the Lord spoke to Moses, saying, ⁶Speak to the children of Israel: Whether it be man or woman, when they have sinned any manner of sin that a person does by which they trespass against the Lord, in that the soul has done amiss, ⁷then they shall confess their sins that they have done, and shall make full restitution for the wrong that they have done with a fifth part more added to it, and give it to him whom they trespassed against. ⁸But if he who makes the restitution has no one to give it to, then the restitution that is made shall be the Lord's and the priest's, besides the ram of the atonement offering with which the person makes an atonement for himself.ᵃ

⁹And all the lift offerings, of all the hallowed things that the children of Israel bring to the priest, shall be the priest's. ¹⁰Every person's hallowed things shall be his own, but whatever anyone gives the priest, it shall be the priest's.

¹¹And the Lord spoke to Moses, saying, ¹²Speak to the children of Israel and say to them: If any man's wife goes aside and trespasses against him, ¹³in that another man lies with her carnally, and the thing is hidden from the eyes of her husband and it has not come to light that she is defiled (for there is no witness against her, inasmuch as she was not taken in the act), ¹⁴but the spirit of jealousy comes upon him and he is jealous over his wife, and she is defiled – or perhaps the spirit of jealousy comes upon him and he is jealous over his wife but she is yet undefiledᵇ – ¹⁵then let her husband bring her to the priest. And he shall bring an offering for her, the tenth part of an ephah of barley meal; but he shall pour no oil on it nor put frankincense on it, for it is an offering of jealousy and an offering to remind of sin.

Confession and restitution.

The law for jealousy.

¹⁶And let the priest bring her and set her before the Lord. ¹⁷And let him take holy water in an earthen vessel, and take some of the dust that is in the floor of the habitation and put it into the water. ¹⁸And the priest shall set the wife before the Lord, uncover her head, and put in her hands the offering to remind her, which is the jealousy offering. And the priest shall have the bitter and cursing water in his hand. ¹⁹And he shall adjure her and say to her, If no man has lain with you, and you have not gone aside from your husband and defiled yourself, then this bitter cursing water will not hurt you. ²⁰But if you have gone aside from your husband and are defiled, and some other man has lain with you besides your husband ²¹(and let the priest put her under oath with the invocation of the curse and say to her), may the Lord make you a curse and an oath among your people, so that the Lord makes your thigh rot and your belly to swell; ²²so may go this bitter cursing water into your bowels, so that your belly swells and your thigh rots.

And the wife shall say, Amen, Amen.ᶜ

²³And the priest shall write this curse in a bill and wash it out in the bitter water, ²⁴and shall give the wife some of the bitter cursing water to drink. When the cursing water is in her and is bitter, ²⁵then let the priest take the jealousy offering out of the wife's hand, wave it for a food offering before the Lord, and bring it to the altar. ²⁶And he shall take a handful of the reminder offering and burn it upon the altar, and then make her drink the water. ²⁷And when he has made her drink the water, if she is defiled and has trespassed against her husband, then the cursing water will go into her and be so bitter that her belly will swell and her thigh will rot, and she will be a curse among her people. ²⁸And if she is not defiled but is clean, then she will have no harm, but will be able to conceive.

²⁹This is the law for jealousy, when a wife goes aside from her husband and is defiled, ³⁰or when the spirit of jealousy comes upon a man and he is jealous over his wife. Then he shall bring her before the Lord, and the priest shall administer all this law unto her; ³¹and the man shall be guiltless, and the wife shall bear her sin.

vv19-21 e.f. COV.

The Notes

a) 6-8. This text is to be understood of those trespasses whereby we cause loss to our neighbours in worldly goods (as they call them), and therefore the loss must be restored plus a fifth part more. If the party did not remain to whom the restitution was due, nor any of his lawful heirs, then it must be the wages of the priest, who at that time had no other livelihood.

b) 14, etc. The whole law of jealousy seems to be a fearful warning and admonition to wives to be obedient to their husbands, chaste, mannerly, faithful, and such as give no occasion to be suspected. And to this purpose the law served, while it kept them under control and gave them no license to run at large, whereby they might have come under some suspicion and so have come to this great shame before the congregation.

c) 22. *Amen* is a Hebrew word and signifies so be it, or be it fast and severe, approving and allowing the sentence beforehand. When words are doubled, it augments the confirmation, as in many psalms, John 5:24, etc.

Chapter 6

The law for those who took vows of abstinence upon themselves. The manner of blessing the people.

And the Lord spoke to Moses, saying, ²Speak to the children of Israel and say to them: When either man or woman resolves to vow a vow of abstinence, to fast for the Lord,ᵃ ³he shall abstain from wine and strong drink. And he shall drink no vinegar made from wine or strong drink, nor drink whatever is pressed out of grapes, and shall eat no grapes, fresh or dried, as long as his abstinence endures. ⁴Moreover, he shall eat nothing that comes from the grapevine – no, not so much as the seeds or the skin of the grape.

⁵And as long as the vow of his abstinence endures, no razor nor shears shall come upon his head, until the days are out in which he fasts for the Lord. And he shall be holy, and shall let the locks of his hair grow. ⁶As long as he fasts for the Lord, he shall come at no dead body; ⁷he shall not make himself unclean at the death of his father, mother, brother, or sister, because the abstinence of his God is upon his head.ᵇ ⁸And therefore, as long as his abstinence lasts, he shall be holy unto the Lord.

⁹And if it happens that someone by chance dies suddenly before him and defiles the head of his abstinence, then he must shave his head on the day of his cleansing; that is, on the seventh day he shall shave it. ¹⁰And the eighth day he shall bring two turtle doves or two young pigeons to the priest, to the door of the tabernacle of witness. ¹¹And the priest shall offer one for a sin offering and the other for a burnt offering, to make an atonement for him as concerning that he sinned upon the dead, and shall also hallow his head the same day. ¹²And he shall fast for the Lord in the time of his abstinence, and shall bring a lamb of a year old for a trespass offering. But the days that went before are lost, because his abstinence was defiled.

¹³And this is the law for the abstainer when the time of his fasting is out: he shall be brought to the door of the tabernacle of witness. ¹⁴And he shall bring his offering to the Lord: a he-lamb of a year old without blemish for a burnt offering, a she-lamb of a year old without blemish for a sin offering, and a ram without blemish also for a peace offering; ¹⁵and a basket containing sweet bread made of fine flour mixed with oil, wafers of sweet bread anointed with oil, and the food offerings and drink offerings that pertain thereto. ¹⁶And the priest shall bring him before the Lord and offer his sin offering and his burnt offering, ¹⁷and shall offer the ram for a peace offering to the Lord with the basket of sweet bread. And the priest shall offer also his food offering and his drink offering. ¹⁸And the abstainer shall shave his head in the door of the tabernacle of witness, and shall take the hair of his fasting head* and put it in the fire that is under the peace offering. ¹⁹Then the priest shall take the boiled shoulder of the ram and one sweet cake out of the basket, and one sweet wafer also, and put them in the hand of the abstainer after he has shaven his abstinence off;

*[Fasting head: ie, as kept unshorn during his or her fast]

^{20}and the priest shall wave them to the Lord. This offering shall be holy for the priest, with the wave-breast and lift-shoulder. And then the abstainer may drink wine. ^{21}That is the law concerning the abstainer who has vowed his offering to the Lord of abstinence, besides that which his hand can get. And according to the vow which he vowed, just so must he do, in the law of his abstinence.

^{22}And the Lord talked with Moses, saying, ^{23}Speak to Aaron and his sons, saying, This is how you shall bless the children of Israel, saying to them: ^{24}The Lord bless you and keep you; ^{25}the Lord make his face shine upon you^c and be merciful to you; ^{26}the Lord lift up his countenance upon you, and give you peace. ^{27}For you shall put my name upon the children of Israel, that I may bless them.

The Notes

a) 2. Here it appears what a vow is according to the Old Testament, which was a figure of the vow that a Christian ought to live out, giving and dedicating himself or herself to God, as is spoken in Romans 12:1.

b) 7. To have the abstinence of God upon his head is to show a sign or symbol of refusing the care of bodily things, in that he sets not by the hair of his head or the trimming of his bush or beard, which things the world so greatly esteems.

c) 25. To make his face to shine is to give a sign of his lovingkindness.

Chapter 7

>The offering of the lords and heads of Israel when the tabernacle was set up.

And when Moses had fully set up the habitation, and had anointed it, consecrated it and all its furnishings, and anointed and consecrated the altar also with all its utensils, ^{2}then the rulers of Israel – heads over the houses of their fathers, who were the lords of the tribes that had stood and numbered the people – made offerings. ^{3}They brought their gifts before the Lord: six covered carts and twelve oxen, for every two men a cart, and an ox for each man. And they brought them before the habitation. ^{4}And the Lord spoke to Moses, saying, ^{5}Take it from them, and let them be for the service of the tabernacle of witness. And give them to the Levites, every man according to his office.

^{6}And Moses took the carts and the oxen and gave them to the Levites. ^{7}Two carts and four oxen he gave to the sons of Gershon according to their office, ^{8}and four carts and eight oxen he gave to the sons of Merari according to their office, under the hands of Ithamar the son of Aaron the priest. ^{9}But to the sons of Kohath he gave none, for the office that pertained to them was holy,* and therefore they must transport loads upon their shoulders.

^{10}And the rulers made offerings for the dedication of the altar in the day that it was anointed, and brought their gifts before the altar. ^{11}And the Lord said to Moses, Let the rulers bring their offerings, each day one ruler, for the dedication of the altar.

^{12}He who offered his offering the first day was Nahshon the son of

Nu 1:4

*[The Kohathites carried the ark and items from the most holy place. Nu 4:15.]

Amminadab, of the tribe of Judah. ¹³And his offering was a silver platter of 130 sickles weight and a silver bowl of 70 sickles, of the holy sickle, both of them full of fine wheat flour mixed with oil for a food offering; ¹⁴a spoon of ten sickles of gold, full of incense; ¹⁵ a bullock,* a ram, and a lamb of a year old for burnt offerings; ¹⁶a he-goat for a sin offering; ¹⁷and for peace offerings two oxen, five rams, five he-goats, and five lambs of a year old. And this was the gift of Nahshon the son of Amminadab.

The offering of Nahshon.

*[Bullock: a young bull or bull calf]

¹⁸The second day Nethaneel offered, the son of Zuar and chief over Issachar. ¹⁹And his offering which he brought was a silver platter of 130 sickles weight and a silver bowl of 70 sickles, of the holy sickle, both full of fine flour mixed with oil for a food offering; ²⁰a golden spoon of ten sickles, full of incense; ²¹a bullock, a ram, and a lamb of a year old for burnt offerings; ²²a he-goat for a sin offering; ²³and for peace offerings two oxen, five rams, five he-goats, and five lambs of one year old. And this was the offering of Nethaneel the son of Zuar.

The offering of Nethaneel.

²⁴The third day Eliab the son of Helon, who was chief among the children of Zebulun, brought his offering. ²⁵And his offering was a silver platter of 130 sickles weight and a silver bowl of 70 sickles, of the holy sickle, both full of fine flour mixed with oil for a food offering; ²⁶a golden spoon of ten sickles, full of incense; ²⁷an ox, a ram, and a lamb of a year old for burnt offerings; ²⁸a he-goat for a sin offering; ²⁹and for peace offerings two oxen, five rams, five he-goats, and five lambs of one year old. And this was the offering of Eliab the son of Helon.

The offering of Eliab.

³⁰The fourth day Elizur the son of Shedeur, chief lord among the children of Reuben, brought his offering. ³¹And his gift was a silver platter of 130 sickles weight and a silver bowl of 70 sickles, of the holy sickle, both full of fine flour mixed with oil for a food offering; ³²a golden spoon of ten sickles, full of incense; ³³a bullock, a ram, and a lamb of a year old for burnt offerings; ³⁴a he-goat for a sin offering; ³⁵and for peace offerings two oxen, five rams, five he-goats, and five lambs of a year old. And this was the offering of Elizur the son of Shedeur.

The offering of Elizur.

³⁶The fifth day Shelumiel the son of Zurishaddai, and chief lord among the children of Simeon, offered, ³⁷whose gift was a silver platter of 130 sickles weight and a silver bowl of 70 sickles, of the holy sickle, both full of fine flour mixed with oil for a food offering; ³⁸a golden spoon of ten sickles, full of incense; ³⁹a bullock, a ram, and a lamb of a year old for burnt offerings; ⁴⁰a he-goat for a sin offering; ⁴¹and for peace offerings two oxen, five rams, five he-goats, and five lambs of a year old. And this was the offering of Shelumiel the son of Zurishaddai.

The offering of Shelumiel.

⁴²The sixth day Eliasaph the son of Deuel, the chief lord among the children of Gad, offered, ⁴³whose gift was a silver platter of 130 sickles weight and a silver bowl of 70 sickles, of the holy sickle, both of them full of fine wheat flour mixed with oil for a food offering; ⁴⁴a

The offering of Eliasaph.

golden spoon of ten sickles, full of incense; ⁴⁵a bullock, a ram, and a lamb of a year old for burnt offerings; ⁴⁶a he-goat for a sin offering; ⁴⁷and for peace offerings two oxen, five rams, five he-goats, and five lambs of a year old. And this was the offering of Eliasaph the son of Deuel.

⁴⁸The seventh day Elishama the son of Ammihud, the chief lord of the children of Ephraim, offered. ⁴⁹And his gift was a silver platter of 130 sickles weight and a silver bowl of 70 sickles, of the holy sickle, both full of fine flour mixed with oil for a food offering; ⁵⁰a golden spoon of ten sickles, full of incense; ⁵¹a bullock, a ram, and a lamb of a year old for burnt offerings; ⁵²a he-goat for a sin offering; ⁵³and for peace offerings two oxen, five rams, five he-goats, and five lambs of one year old. And this was the offering of Elishama the son of Ammihud. *The offering of Elishama.*

⁵⁴The eighth day Gamaliel the son of Pedahzur, the chief lord of the children of Manasseh, offered. ⁵⁵And his gift was a silver platter of 130 sickles weight and a silver bowl of 70 sickles, of the holy sickle, both full of fine flour mixed with oil for a food offering; ⁵⁶a golden spoon of ten sickles, full of incense; ⁵⁷an ox, a ram, and a lamb of a year old for burnt offerings; ⁵⁸a he-goat for a sin offering; ⁵⁹and for peace offerings two oxen, five rams, five he-goats, and five lambs of one year old. This was the offering of Gamaliel the son of Pedahzur. *The offering of Gamaliel.*

⁶⁰The ninth day Abidan the son of Gideoni, the chief lord among the children of Benjamin, offered. ⁶¹And his gift was a silver platter of 130 sickles weight and a silver bowl of 70 sickles, of the holy sickle, both full of fine flour mixed with oil for a food offering; ⁶²a golden spoon of ten sickles, full of incense; ⁶³a bullock, a ram, and a lamb of a year old for burnt offerings; ⁶⁴a he-goat for a sin offering; ⁶⁵and for peace offerings two oxen, five rams, five he-goats, and five lambs of a year old. And this was the offering of Abidan the son of Gideoni. *The offering of Abidan.*

⁶⁶The tenth day Ahiezer the son of Ammishaddai, chief lord among the children of Dan, offered. ⁶⁷His gift was a silver platter of 130 sickles weight and a silver bowl of 70 sickles, of the holy sickle, both full of fine flour mixed with oil for a food offering; ⁶⁸a golden spoon of ten sickles, full of incense; ⁶⁹a bullock, a ram, and a lamb of a year old for burnt offerings; ⁷⁰a he-goat for a sin offering; ⁷¹and for peace offerings two oxen, five rams, five he-goats, and five lambs of a year old. And this was the offering of Ahiezer the son of Ammishaddai. *The offering of Ahiezer.*

⁷²The eleventh day Pagiel the son of Ocran, the chief lord among the children of Asher, offered. ⁷³And his gift was a silver platter of 130 sickles weight and a silver bowl of 70 sickles, of the holy sickle, both full of fine flour mixed with oil for a food offering; ⁷⁴a golden spoon of ten sickles, full of incense: ⁷⁵a bullock, a ram, and a lamb of a year old for burnt offerings; ⁷⁶a he-goat for a sin offering; ⁷⁷and for peace offerings two oxen, five rams, five he-goats, and five lambs of one year old. And this was the offering of Pagiel the son of Ocran. *The offering of Pagiel.*

The offering of Ahira. ⁷⁸The twelfth day Ahira the son of Enan, chief lord among the children of Naphtali, offered. ⁷⁹And his gift was a silver platter of 130 sickles weight and a silver bowl of 70 sickles, of the holy sickle, both full of fine flour mixed with oil for a food offering; ⁸⁰a golden spoon of ten sickles, full of incense; ⁸¹a bullock, a ram, and a lamb of a year old for burnt offerings; ⁸²a he-goat for a sin offering; ⁸³and for peace offerings two oxen, five rams, five he-goats, and five lambs of one year old. And this was the offering of Ahira the son of Enan.

⁸⁴Of this manner was the dedication of the altar when it was anointed, to which the rulers of Israel brought twelve platters of silver, twelve silver bowls, and twelve spoons of gold – ⁸⁵every platter containing 130 sickles of silver and every bowl 70, so that all the silver of all the vessels was 2,400 sickles of the holy sickle. ⁸⁶And the twelve golden spoons that were full of incense contained ten sickles apiece of the holy sickle, so that all the gold of the spoons was 120 sickles.

⁸⁷All the oxen that were brought for the burnt offerings were twelve, the rams twelve, and the lambs twelve, of a year old each, with the food offerings and with he-goats for sin offerings. ⁸⁸And all the oxen of the peace offerings were twenty-four, the rams sixty, the he-goats sixty, and lambs of a year old each, sixty. And this was the dedication of the altar after it was anointed.

⁸⁹And when Moses went into the tabernacle of witness to speak with the Lord, he heard the voice of one speaking to him from out of the mercy seat that was upon the ark of witness; from between the two cherubims, he spoke to him.

Chapter 8

The set-up and order of the lamps. The form of the candlestick. The cleansing and offering of the Levites. Their ages of service.

Ex 25:31-40 And the Lord spoke to Moses, saying, ²Speak to Aaron and say to him: When you set up the lamps, see that all seven give light at the forefront of the candlestick. ³And Aaron did just so, and put the lamps upon the forefront of the candlestick, as the Lord commanded Moses. ⁴And the work of the candlestick was of hammered gold, both the shaft and the flowers thereof. And according to the vision that the Lord had shown Moses, just so he made the candlestick.

⁵And the Lord spoke to Moses, saying, ⁶Take the Levites from among the children of Israel and cleanse them. ⁷And this do with them when you cleanse them: sprinkle water of purifying upon them, and make a razor to run along upon all their flesh, and let them wash their clothes; and then they shall be clean. ⁸And let them take a bullock and its food offering of fine flour mixed with oil; and another bullock you shall take to be a sin offering. ⁹Then bring the Levites before the tabernacle of witness, and gather the whole multitude of the children of Israel together. ¹⁰And bring the Levites before the Lord, and let the children of Israel put their hands upon the Levites. ¹¹And let Aaron lift

the Levites before the Lord, for a lift offering given by the children of Israel, and then let them be appointed to attend to the service of the Lord. ¹²And let the Levites put their hands upon the heads of the bullocks, and then offer them – one for a sin offering and the other for a burnt offering to the Lord – to make an atonement for the Levites. ¹³And make the Levites to stand before Aaron and his sons, and have them to be a lift offering to the Lord. ¹⁴Thus you shall separate the Levites from among the children of Israel to be mine. ¹⁵And after that, let them go and work in the service of the tabernacle of witness. Cleanse them and wave them, ¹⁶for they are given to me from among the children of Israel. For I have taken them unto me in the place of all the firstborn that open any womb among the children of Israel.

Nu 3:12

¹⁷For all the firstborn among the children of Israel are mine, both man and beast, because the same time that I smote the firstborn in the land of Egypt, I set them apart for myself. ¹⁸I have taken the Levites in the place of all the firstborn among the children of Israel, ¹⁹and have given them to Aaron and his sons from among the children of Israel, to work in the service of the children of Israel in the tabernacle of witness, and to make an atonement for the children of Israel, so that there will be no plague among the children of Israel if they come near to the sanctuary.

Ex 13:11-15

²⁰And Moses and Aaron and all the congregation of the children of Israel did with the Levites according to all that the Lord commanded Moses. ²¹The Levites purified themselves and washed their clothes, and Aaron waved them before the Lord and made an atonement for them, to cleanse them. ²²And after that, they went in to do their service in the tabernacle of witness before Aaron and his sons. And according as the Lord had commanded Moses concerning the Levites, so they did with them.

²³And the Lord spoke to Moses, saying, ²⁴This shall be the practice of the Levites: from twenty-five years upward they shall go in to attend to the service in the tabernacle of witness. ²⁵And at fifty they shall cease working in the service thereof, and shall labour no more, ²⁶but may minister to their brethren in the tabernacle of witness and there supervise. But they shall do no more service. And see that you do after this manner with the Levites in their serving times.

Chapter 9

The Easter or Passover offering of the clean and unclean. A cloud covering the tabernacle leads the host.

And the Lord spoke to Moses in the wilderness of Sinai, in the first month of the second year after they had come out of the land of Egypt, saying, ²Let the children of Israel offer Passover in its season. ³The fourteenth day of this month, at evening, they shall keep it in its season, according to all the observances and laws thereof.

Ex 12:1-27
Lev 23:5
Nu 28:16
De 16:1,2

⁴And Moses bade the children of Israel to offer Passover, ⁵and they

offered Passover the fourteenth day of the first month at evening in the wilderness of Sinai, and did according to all that the Lord commanded Moses.

⁶And it chanced that certain men who were defiled by a dead body, so that they might not offer Passover the same day, came before Moses and Aaron the same day, ⁷and said, We are defiled upon a dead body. Are we therefore kept back, so that we may not offer an offering to the Lord in the due season among the children of Israel?

⁸And Moses said to them, Wait, so that I may hear what the Lord will command you.

⁹And the Lord spoke to Moses, saying, ¹⁰Speak to the children of Israel and say: If anyone among you or your children after you is unclean by reason of a corpse, or is on the road far off, yet let him still offer Passover to the Lord ¹¹in the fourteenth day of the second month at evening, and eat it with sweet bread and bitter herbs. ¹²And let them leave none of it till the morning, nor break any bone of it. And according to all the ordinance of the Passover, let them offer it. ¹³But if a man was clean and not hindered in a journey, and yet was negligent to offer Passover, the same soul shall perish from his people because he did not bring an offering to the Lord in its due season; and he shall bear his sin.ᵃ ¹⁴And when a stranger dwells among you and wishes to offer Passover to the Lord, according to the ordinance and practice of Passover he shall offer it. And you shall have one law both for the stranger and for him that was born at home in the land.

Ex 40:34

¹⁵And the same day that the habitation was reared up, a cloud covered it on high upon the tabernacle of witness. And in the evening, there was upon the habitation as it were the similitude of fire, until the morning. ¹⁶And so it was always that the cloud covered it by day and the similitude of fire by night. ¹⁷And when the cloud was taken up

Ex 40:36-38

from the tabernacle, then the children of Israel journeyed, and where the cloud abode, there the children of Israel pitched their tents. ¹⁸At the mouth of the Lord the children of Israel journeyed, and at the mouth of the Lord they pitched camp; as long as the cloud abode upon the habitation, they lay still, ¹⁹and when the cloud tarried still upon the habitation a long time, the children of Israel waited upon the Lord and journeyed not. ²⁰So then, if it happened that the cloud abode any space of time upon the habitation, then they kept their tents at the mouth of the Lord, and they journeyed also at the commandment of the Lord. ²¹If it happened that the cloud was upon the habitation from evening till morning and then was taken up in the morning, they rested and then, at the commandment of the Lord, they journeyed. Whether it was by day or by night that the cloud was taken up, they journeyed. ²²But when the cloud tarried two days,ᵇ or a month, or a long season upon the habitation – as long as it tarried there – the children of Israel kept their tents and journeyed not. And as soon as the cloud was taken up, they journeyed: ²³at the mouth of the Lord they rested, and at the commandment of the Lord they journeyed. And thus they kept the watch of the Lord, at the commandment of the Lord by the hand of Moses.

The Notes

a) 13. In like manner it is with us in our spiritual Easter or Passover. Whoever does not reverently believe the redemption of mankind that was thoroughly finished in offering the true lamb, Christ, and will not amend his life, nor turn from vice to virtue in the time of this mortal life, will not belong to the glory of the resurrection, which will be given to the true worshippers of Christ, but will be rooted out from the company of the saints. [Ed: From early Old English to the 16th century, *Easter* and *Passover* were used as synonyms. The true etymology of the word *Easter* disproves any connection with an idol or a pagan feast, as some allege.]

b) 22. Two days, after the Greeks, means certain, a few, or some days.

Chapter 10

> The trumpets of silver and their uses. The Israelites depart from Sinai. The chief rulers of the tribes or hosts are reviewed. Hobab refuses to go with Moses.

And the Lord spoke to Moses, saying, ²Make two trumpets of hammered silver, so that you may use them to call the congregation together and when the host is to journey.

³When they blow with both trumpets, all the multitude shall resort to you at the door of the tabernacle of witness. ⁴But if one trumpet only blows,ᵃ then the rulers who are the heads over the thousands of Israel shall come to you.

⁵And when you blast on a trumpet, at the first blast the hosts that lie on the east parts shall go forward. ⁶And when you blast the second time, then the hosts that lie on the south side shall take their journey. For they shall blast on a trumpet when they set out on their journeys.

⁷But to gather the congregation together, you shall blow and not blast with the trumpet.ᵇ ⁸And the sons of Aaron, the priests, shall blow the trumpets, and shall have them. And this shall be a law for you forever, and among your children after you.

⁹And when you go to war in your land against your enemies who trouble you, you shall blast with the trumpets,ᶜ and you will be remembered before the Lord your God and saved from your enemies. ¹⁰Also, when you are merry in your feast days and in the first days of your months, you shall blow the trumpets over your burnt sacrifices and peace offerings, so that it may bring you in remembrance before your God. I am the Lord your God.

¹¹And it came to pass, the twentieth day of the second month in the second year, that the cloud was taken up from the habitation of witness, ¹²and the children of Israel took their journey out of the desert of Sinai. And the cloud rested in the wilderness of Paran. ¹³And they first took their journey at the mouth of the Lord, by the hand of Moses. ¹⁴The standard of the camp of Judah removed first with their hosts, whose chief lord was Nahshon the son of Amminadab. ¹⁵And over the host of the tribe of the children of Issachar was Nethaneel the son of

Nu 2:3-9

Nu 2:10-16; 3:29.

Zuar. ¹⁶And over the host of the tribe of the children of Zebulun was Eliab the son of Helon. ¹⁷And the habitation was taken down, and the sons of Gershon and Merari went forth bearing the habitation.

¹⁸Then the standard of the camp of Reuben went forth with their hosts, whose chief was Elizur the son of Shedeur. ¹⁹And over the host of the tribe of the children of Simeon was Shelumiel the son of Zurishaddai. ²⁰And over the host of the tribe of the children of Gad was Eliasaph the son of Deuel.

²¹Then the Kohathites went forward and bore the holy things (and the others would set up the habitation before they arrived).

²²Then the standard of the camp of the children of Ephraim went forth with their hosts, whose chief was Elishama the son of Ammihud. ²³And over the host of the tribe of the sons of Manasseh was Gamaliel the son of Pedahzur. ²⁴And over the host of the tribe of the sons of Benjamin was Abidan the son of Gedeoni.

²⁵And hindmost of all the camps came the standard of the camp of the children of Dan with their hosts, whose chief was Ahiezer the son of Ammishaddai. ²⁶And over the host of the tribe of the children of Asher was Pagiel* the son of Ocran. ²⁷And over the host of the tribe of the children of Naphtali was Ahira the son of Enan.

*Or, Phegiel.

²⁸Of this manner were the journeys of the children of Israel with their hosts when they removed.

²⁹And Moses said to Hobab the son of Reuel the Midianite, Moses' father-in-law,ᵈ We are going to the place of which the Lord said, I will give it to you. Come with us, and we will do you good; for the Lord has promised good to Israel.

³⁰But he said to him, I will not, but will go to my own land and to my kindred.

³¹And Moses said, O nay, leave us not! For you know where it is best for us to pitch camp in the wilderness, and you may be our eyes.*

*Eyes: or guide.

³²And if you go with us, look: what goodness the Lord shows upon us, the same we will show upon you.

³³And they departed from the mount of the Lord three days' journey. And the ark of the testament of the Lord went before them in the three days' journey, to search out a resting place for them. ³⁴And the cloud of the Lord was over them by day, when they went out of the tents. ³⁵And when the ark went forth, Moses said, Rise up, Lord, and let your enemies be scattered, and let them that hate you flee before you! ³⁶And when the ark rested, he said, Return, Lord, to the many thousands of Israel.

The Notes

a) 4. To blow with one trumpet signifies to declare the word of salvation simply, in accordance with the unity of the faith.

b) 7. Blow and not blast: they must teach the common people plainly and without sophistry or subtle arguments.

c) 9. Blast with the trumpets: in time of war, they must blast with trumpets. This signifies that when the most need is at hand, then faith, prayer, and the lifting up of the mind to God must chiefly be exercised.

d) 29. Hobab* is the same man who before is called Jethro, just as Solomon is called in some places Jedidiah, following the Hebrew manner. Hobab was the son of Reuel and father to Zipporah, Moses' wife – albeit that, in the second of Exodus, Reuel is called her father, not because he was so indeed, but because he was her father's father, which manner of speaking is not a few times used in the scripture.

*[Hobab: Beloved, or Most Beloved.]

Chapter 11

The people murmur and are punished with fire. They desire meat. They loathe manna. The murmuring and wavering faith of Moses. The Lord divides Moses' burden among seventy of the elders, and they prophesy. Eldad and Medad also prophesy in the host. It rains quail. The meat gluttons are punished.

And the people complained,* and it displeased the ears of the Lord. When the Lord heard it, he was wroth, and the fire of the Lord burned among them and consumed the outermost of the host. ²And the people cried out to Moses, and he made intercession to the Lord and the fire was quenched. ³And they called the name of the place Taberah,‡ because the fire of the Lord had burned among them.

⁴And the common people who were among them fell a-lusting. And the children of Israel also went to and wept, and said, Who can give us meat to eat? ⁵We remember the fish we could eat in Egypt for nothing, and the cucumbers and melons, leeks, onions, and garlic. ⁶But now our souls are wasted away because our eyes look on nothing but manna.

⁷The manna was like coriander seed, and in appearance like bedellion.° ⁸And the people went about and gathered it, ground it in mills or beat it in mortars, baked it in pans, and made cakes of it. And the taste of it was like the taste of an oil cake. ⁹And when the dew fell about the host in the night, the manna fell with it.

¹⁰And when Moses heard the people weeping in their households, everyone in the door of their tent, then the wrath of the Lord waxed hot exceedingly; and it grieved Moses also. ¹¹And Moses said to the Lord, Why do you deal so cruelly with your servant? Why do I not find favour in your sight, seeing as you put the weight of this people upon me? ¹²Have I conceived all this people, or have I begotten them, that you should say to me, Carry them in your bosom (as a nurse bears the sucking child) into the land that you swore to their fathers? ¹³Where could I find meat to give to all this people? For they weep to me, saying, Give us meat, so that we may eat! ¹⁴I am not able to bear all this people alone. It is too heavy for me. ¹⁵And so, if you deal thus with me, kill me, I pray, if I have found favour in your sight, and let me not see my wretchedness!

¹⁶And the Lord said to Moses, Gather to me seventy of the elders of Israel, of whom you know that they are the elders of the people and officers over them, and bring them to the tabernacle of witness, and let them stand there with you. ¹⁷And I will come down and talk with you

*Or, became discontent. Some: did wickedly.

‡That is, Setting on Fire or Consuming by Fire.

°[or bdellium. Probably a precious stone. See Ge 2:12.]

there, and will take of the Spirit that is upon you and put it upon them.ᵃ And they will bear with you the burden of the people, and thus you will not bear it alone. ¹⁸And say to the people, Hallow yourselves for tomorrow, to eat meat. For you have whined in the ears of the Lord, saying, Who can give us meat to eat? For we were happy when we were in Egypt. Therefore, the Lord will give you meat, and you shall eat. ¹⁹You shall eat not only one day, or two or five days, or ten or twenty days, ²⁰but even a month long, and until it comes out at your nostrils[*] and you are ready to spew it out – because you have cast aside the Lord who is among you, and have wept before him, saying, Why did we come out of Egypt?

[*Or, mouths.]

²¹And Moses said, There are 600,000 people on foot among whom I am, and you have said that you will give them meat, and they will eat a month long. ²²Shall the flocks and the herds be slain for them, to provide for them, or could all the fish of the sea be gathered together to serve them?

²³And the Lord said to Moses, Is the Lord's arm too short? You will see whether my word comes to pass for you or not.ᵇ

²⁴And Moses went out and told the people the word of the Lord, and gathered the seventy elders of the people and set them round about the tabernacle. ²⁵And the Lord came down in a cloud and spoke to him, and took of the Spirit that was upon him and put it upon the seventy elders. And as the Spirit rested upon them, they prophesied, and did naught else.ᶜ ²⁶But there remained two of the men in the host: one called Eldad and the other Medad. And the Spirit rested upon them – for they were among those listed also, though they had not gone out to the tabernacle – and they prophesied in the host.

²⁷And a young man ran and told Moses, and said, Eldad and Medad are prophesying in the host. ²⁸And Joshua the son of Nun, the servant of Moses whom he had chosen, answered and said, Master Moses, forbid them! ²⁹And Moses said to him, Are you envious for my sake? Would God that all the Lord's people could prophesy, and that the Lord would put his Spirit upon them.

³⁰And then both Moses and the elders of Israel went into the camp.

³¹And there went forth a wind from the Lord, and it brought quails from the sea and let them fall about the camp, even a day's journey round about on every side of the host, and two cubits deep upon the ground. ³²And the people stood up all that day, all that night, and on the morrow, and gathered quails. And he that gathered the least gathered ten homers full. And they killed them round about the host.

³³But while the flesh was yet between their teeth, before it was chewed up, the wrath of the Lord waxed hot upon the people, and the Lord slew of the people an exceeding mighty slaughter. ³⁴Therefore, they called the name of the place the Graves of Lust,[*] because there they buried the people who lusted.

[*Or, Kibroth-Hattaavah]

³⁵And the people took their journey from the Graves of Lust to Hazeroth, and abode at Hazeroth.

The Notes

a) 17. I will put of the Spirit upon them: that is, I will inspire them with the same Spirit.
b) 23. You will see what comes to pass, etc: This is according to the Greek and the Chaldee. Some say, You will see of what value it shall be.
c) 25. To prophesy is to preach the word to the people, as in 1Corinthians 14:1-5, or to show the wonderful works of God, or to show things to come. But to prophesy and do naught else is here to rule the people of God according to the Spirit, and to govern their subjects with equity, justice, and truth.

Chapter 12

> Aaron and Miriam grudge against Moses. Miriam was stricken with the leprosy, and was healed at the prayer of Moses.

And Miriam and Aaron spoke against Moses because of the wife from India that he had taken; for he had taken to wife a woman of India. ²And they said, Does the Lord speak only through Moses? Does he not speak also by us? And the Lord heard it. ³But Moses was a very meek man, above all the men of the earth.

⁴And the Lord spoke at once to Moses, and to Aaron and Miriam: Come out, you three, to the tabernacle of witness.

And they went out all three.

⁵And the Lord came down in the pillar of the cloud and stood in the door of the tabernacle, and he called Aaron and Miriam. And they went out, both of them. ⁶And he said, Hear my words. If there is a prophet of the Lord among you, I will show myself to him in a vision and will speak to him in a dream. ⁷But my servant Moses is not so, who is faithful in all my house. ⁸To him I speak mouth to mouth, and he sees the sight and the fashion of the Lord, and not through riddles. Why, then, were you not afraid to speak against my servant Moses? (Ex 33:9) (Ex 33:11)

⁹And the Lord was angry with them. And he went his way, ¹⁰and the cloud departed from the tabernacle. And behold, Miriam had become leprous, as it were with snow. And when Aaron looked upon Miriam and saw that she was leprous, ¹¹he said to Moses, O, I beseech you, my lord! Put not the sin upon us that we have foolishly committed and sinned. ¹²O, let her not be as one that came dead out of his mother's womb; for half her flesh is eaten away!

¹³And Moses cried out to the Lord, saying, O God, heal her!

¹⁴And the Lord said to Moses, If her father had spit in her face,ᵃ should she not be ashamed seven days? Let her be shut out of the host seven days, and after that let her be received in again.

¹⁵And Miriam was shut out of the host seven days, and the people did not move on till she was brought in again. ¹⁶And afterward, they removed from Hazeroth and pitched in the wilderness of Paran.

The Notes

a) 14. To spit in her face signifies to punish her and to cause her to see her offence. The Lord is a father, and he punishes his chosen, not to damn them, but to correct them and put them in fear, and to drive them to earnest repentance. After seven days Miriam was received again into the host, and likewise, after full repentance, we must be received again into the congregation.

Chapter 13

Certain men are sent to explore the land of Canaan. They bring back with them a cluster of grapes, for a sign of fertility and fruitfulness.

And the Lord spoke to Moses, saying, ²Send men out to explore the land of Canaan which I am giving to the children of Israel. From every tribe of their fathers send a man, and let them all be such as are leaders among them.

³And at the commandment of the Lord, Moses sent forth out of the wilderness of Paran such men as were all heads among the children of Israel, ⁴whose names are these:

In the tribe of Reuben, Shammua the son of Zaccur.

⁵In the tribe of Simeon, Shaphat the son of Hori.

⁶In the tribe of Judah, Caleb the son of Jephunneh.

⁷In the tribe of Issachar, Igal the son of Joseph.

⁸In the tribe of Ephraim, Hoshea the son of Nun.

⁹In the tribe of Benjamin, Palti the son of Raphu.

¹⁰In the tribe of Zebulun, Gaddiel the son of Sodi.

¹¹In the tribe of Joseph that was of Manasseh, Gaddi the son of Susi.

¹²In the tribe of Dan, Ammiel the son of Gemalli.

¹³In the tribe of Asher, Sethur the son of Michael.

¹⁴In the tribe of Naphtali, Nahbi the son of Vophsi.

¹⁵In the tribe of Gad, Geuel the son of Machi.

¹⁶These were the names of the men whom Moses sent to scout the land. And Moses called the name of Hoshea the son of Nun, Joshua.ª

¹⁷And Moses sent them forth to scout out the land of Canaan, and said to them, Go southward and go up into the high country, ¹⁸to see the land and what it is like: the people who dwell in it, whether they are strong or weak, or few or many; ¹⁹and what the land is that they dwell in, whether it be good or bad; what kind of settlements they dwell in, whether they dwell in tents or walled towns; ²⁰what kind of soil is there, whether it be rich or poor; and whether there are trees there or not. And be of a good courage, and bring back some of the fruits of the land.

And it was about the time that grapes are first ripe. ²¹And they went up and searched out the land, from the wilderness of Zin to Rehob, as men go to Hamath. ²²And they ascended to the south and came to Hebron, where Ahiman was, and Sheshai and Talmai the sons of Anak.* (Hebron was built seven years before Zoan† in Egypt.) ²³And they came to the river of Escol, and they cut down there a branch with one cluster of grapes and carried it on a pole between two men; and

*Look in J'g 1:20 and note d.
†Otherwise Tanis, after the Chaldee.

also some of the pomegranates and some of the figs of the place. ²⁴The river was called Nehel Escol[b] because of the cluster of grapes that the children of Israel cut down there.

²⁵And they turned back again from exploring the land after forty days. ²⁶And they went and came to Moses and Aaron, and to all the multitude of the children of Israel in the wilderness of Paran at Kadesh. And they brought word to them and to all the congregation, and showed them the fruit of the land. ²⁷And they told Moses, saying, We went to the land where you sent us, and surely, it is a land that flows with milk and honey.[c] And here is some of its fruit. ²⁸Nevertheless, the people are strong who dwell in the land, and the cities are walled and exceedingly great. And moreover, we saw the children of Anak there. ²⁹The Amalekites dwell in the south country, and the Hittites, Jebusites, and the Amorites dwell in the mountains, and the Canaanites dwell by the sea and along by the banks of the Jordan.

³⁰Then Caleb stilled the murmur of the people against Moses, saying, Let us go up and conquer the land, for we are able to overcome it! ³¹But the men who had gone up with him said, We are not able to go up against those people, for they are stronger than we. ³²And they brought up to the children of Israel a bad report of the land that they had explored, saying, The land that we have gone through, to search it out, is a land that eats up its inhabitants,[d] and the people that we saw in it are men of stature. ³³And there we saw also giants, the children of Anak who come from the giants.* And we seemed in our sight as it were grasshoppers, and so did we seem in their sight.

*Look in J'g 1:20 and note d concerning the giants.

The Notes

a) 16. *Hoshea* or *Ose* signifies Saving or Saviour. *Joshua* or *Jehoshua* signifies the Salvation of the Lord.
b) 24. *Nehel Escol* signifies by interpretation The River of the Grape, or, as some will, The Valley of the Cluster.
c) 27. Flows with milk and honey: that is, is full of good pastures, herbs, bees, animals, vines, trees, pleasant woods – so that under heaven there was not a more chosen piece of ground for abundance and plenteousness.
d) 32. Eats up its inhabitants: that is, suffers them not to live, but with war and violence from the giants consumes them.

Chapter 14

> The people, despairing of coming to the promised land, murmur against God, and would have stoned Caleb and Joshua. The men who scouted out the land die. Amalek kills the Israelites.

And all the multitude cried out, and the people wept throughout that night. ²And all the children of Israel murmured against Moses and Aaron. And the whole congregation said to them, Would God that we had died in the land of Egypt, or that we had died in this wilderness! ³Why has the Lord brought us to this land to fall upon the sword, so that both our wives and also our children should be taken captive? Is it not better that we return to Egypt again? ⁴And they said one to another, Let us choose a captain and return to Egypt again.

⁵And Moses and Aaron fell on their faces before all the congregation of the multitude of the children of Israel. ⁶And Joshua the son of Nun and Caleb the son of Jephunneh, who were among those who had scouted out the land, tore their clothes,* ⁷and spoke to all the company of the children of Israel, saying, The land that we walked through, to explore it, is a very good land. ⁸If the Lord has pleasure in us, he will bring us into this land and give it to us, which is a land that flows with milk and honey. ⁹But in any event, do not rebel against the Lord. Moreover, do not fear the people of the land, for they are but bread for us. Their shield has departed from them, and the Lord is with us. Fear them not, therefore!

¹⁰And all the whole multitude called for stoning them with stones. But the glory of the Lord appeared in the tabernacle of witness to all the children of Israel. ¹¹And the Lord said to Moses, How long will this people rail upon me?ᵃ And how long will it be before they believe me, for all the signs that I have shown among them? ¹²I will smite them with the pestilence and destroy them, and will make of you a greater nation and a mightier than they.

¹³But Moses said to the Lord, Then the Egyptians will hear it, for you brought this people with your might out from among them. ¹⁴And it will be told to the inhabiters of this land also, for they have heard likewise – that you, the Lord, are among this people, and that you are seen face to face, and that your cloud stands over them, and that you go before them by day in a pillar of cloud, and in a pillar of fire by night. ¹⁵If you should kill all this people, as if they were but one man, then the nations that have heard of your fame will say, ¹⁶Because the Lord was not able to bring this people into the land that he swore to them, therefore he slew them in the wilderness.

¹⁷So now, let the power of my Lord be great in accordance with what you have spoken, saying, ¹⁸The Lord is slow to anger and full of mercy, and suffers sin and trespass; yet leaves no man innocent, and visits the unrighteousness of the fathers upon the children, even upon the third and fourth generations. ¹⁹Be merciful, I beseech you therefore, to the sin of this people, in accordance with your great mercy, and as you have forgiven this people from Egypt even to this place.

²⁰And the Lord said, I have forgiven it, according to your request. ²¹But as truly as I live, all the earth shall be filled with my glory.ᵇ ²²For of all those who have seen my glory and the miracles I did in Egypt and in the wilderness, and yet have tempted me now this ten times and have not hearkened to my voice, ²³not one shall see the land that I swore to their fathers. Neither shall any of them that railed upon me see it. ²⁴But my servant Caleb, because there is another manner of spirit with him, and because he has followed me to the utmost, him I will bring into the land in which he has walked. And his seed shall conquer it, ²⁵and also the Amalekites and Canaanites who dwell in the

*Tore their clothes: look in Ge c37 and note a.

low countries. Tomorrow, turn and go into the wilderness, in the way toward the Red Sea.

²⁶And the Lord spoke to Moses and Aaron, saying, ²⁷How long will this evil multitude murmur against me? I have heard the murmurings of the children of Israel, which they murmur against me. ²⁸Tell them that the Lord says, As truly as I live, I will do with you just as you have spoken in my ears: ²⁹your carcasses shall lie in this wilderness. And all of you who were numbered from twenty years and above who have murmured against me, ³⁰shall not come into the land over which I lifted my hand to make you dwell therein,* except Caleb the son of Jephunneh and Joshua the son of Nun. ³¹And your children, whom you said would be taken captive, I will bring in. And they will know the land which you have refused, ³²but your carcasses will lie in this wilderness. ³³But your children will wander in this wilderness for forty years. They will suffer for your whoredom^c until your bodies are consumed in the wilderness, ³⁴according to the number of the days in which you searched out the land: forty days, for every day a year. So it is that they will bear your unrighteousness forty years, and you shall feel my vengeance. ³⁵I, the Lord, have said that I will do it to all this evil congregation that are gathered together against me. In this wilderness you shall be consumed, and here you shall die.

v29 e.f. COV.

*Look in Ex 6:8 & note c.

³⁶And the men whom Moses had sent to explore the land, and who (when they came back again) made all the people to murmur against it, in that they brought up a slander upon the land, ³⁷died for bringing up that evil slander upon it, and were plagued before the Lord. ³⁸But Joshua the son of Nun and Caleb the son of Jephunneh, who were among the men that went to search out the land, lived still.

³⁹And Moses told the Lord's words to all the children of Israel, and the people took great sorrow. ⁴⁰And they rose up early in the morning and went up to the top of the mountain, saying, Lo, we are here, and will go up to the place of which the Lord spoke,^d for we have sinned.

⁴¹But Moses said, Why would you go in this manner, beyond the word of the Lord? It will not come well to pass. ⁴²Do not go up, for the Lord is not among you to protect you from being slain before your enemies. ⁴³For the Amalekites and the Canaanites are there before you, and you will fall upon the sword because you have turned away from the Lord. And therefore, the Lord will not be with you.

⁴⁴But they were blinded to go up to the hilltop. However, neither the ark of the testament of the Lord nor Moses left the host. ⁴⁵Then the Amalekites and the Canaanites who dwelt upon that mountain came down and smote them and cut them down, even as far as Hormah.

The Notes

a) 11. To rail upon the Lord, or to provoke him, or to resist, withstand, rebel, or strive against him, etc: all such manners of speech, wherever you find them, signify nothing else but than not to believe his words, as in Psalms 5:10 and 9:17.

b) 21. That he will have the earth filled with his glory means that he will be magnified, preached, spoken of, honoured, and praised throughout the earth. Psalm 18:46-49.

c) 33. *Whoredom* for infidelity or idolatry, as 2Ki 9:22 and Wis 14:12.

d) 40. Blind reason, which a while before would not let them believe in God's word, teaches them now to trust in their own works.

Chapter 15

The drink offerings of those who enter into the land. The punishment of the person who sins of arrogance or pride. The man who gathered sticks on the Sabbath is stoned. Decorative trimmings must be made upon the skirts of their garments.

And the Lord spoke to Moses, saying, ²Speak to the children of Israel and say to them: When you have come into the land of your habitation which I am giving to you, ³and you desire to offer an offering upon the fire to the Lord – whether it be a burnt offering or a special vowed or freewill offering, or if it be in your principal feasts, to make a sweet savour* to the Lord from the oxen or from the flock – ⁴then let him who offers his offering to the Lord bring also a food offering of a tenth measure of flour mixed with the fourth part of a hin of oil, ⁵and the fourth part of a hin of wine for a drink offering. And let him offer these with the burnt offering or any other offering, when a lamb is offered. ⁶But with a ram you shall offer a food offering of a two-tenths measure of flour mixed with the third part of a hin of oil, ⁷and for a drink offering you shall offer the third part of a hin of wine, to be a sweet savour to the Lord.

⁸When you offer an ox for a burnt offering or in any special vowed or peace offering to the Lord, ⁹then you shall bring with the ox a food offering of a three-tenths measure of flour mixed with half a hin of oil. ¹⁰And you shall bring for a drink offering half a hin of wine. This is an offering of a sweet savour to the Lord. ¹¹Thus shall you do with one ox or one ram, or a lamb or a kid. ¹²And according to the number of such offerings, you shall increase the food and drink offerings.

¹³All who are from among yourselves shall do these things in this manner when they offer an offering of sweet savour to the Lord. ¹⁴And if a stranger dwells with you or is among your kinfolk and wishes to offer an offering of a sweet savour to the Lord just as you do, so he may do. ¹⁵One ordinance shall serve both for you of the congregation and for the stranger. And it shall be an ordinance forever among your children after you, so that the stranger and you shall be alike before the Lord.ᵃ ¹⁶One law and one practice shall serve both for you and for the stranger who dwells with you.

¹⁷And the Lord spoke to Moses, saying, ¹⁸Speak to the children of Israel and say to them: When you have come into the land where I will bring you, ¹⁹then, when you will eat of the bread of the land, you shall give a lift offering to the Lord. ²⁰You shall give a cake made of the firstlings of your doughs for a lift offering: as the lift offering of the

*[The sweet savour of burnt offerings: Lev c1 and note a]

barn, ²¹so shall you give the firstlings of your dough also to the Lord, as a lift offering throughout your generations.

²²If you forget yourselves and do not observe all these commandments that the Lord has spoken to Moses, ²³ and all that the Lord has commanded you by the hand of Moses from the first day that the Lord began to command among your generations, ²⁴when anything is committed ignorantly before the eyes of the congregation, then all the multitude shall offer a calf for a burnt offering, to be a sweet savour to the Lord, with its food offering and drink offering according to the ordinance, and a he-goat for a sin offering. ²⁵And the priest shall make an atonement for all the multitude of the children of Israel, and it will be forgiven them; for it was ignorance. And they shall bring their gifts with the offering of the Lord and their sin offering before the Lord, for their ignorance. ²⁶And it will be forgiven to all the multitude of the children of Israel – and to the stranger that dwells among you, for the ignorance pertains to all the people.

²⁷If any one soul sins through ignorance, he shall bring a she-goat of a year old for a sin offering. ²⁸And the priest shall make an atonement for the soul that sinned ignorantly with the sin offering before the Lord, and shall reconcile him; and it will be forgiven him. ²⁹And both you who are born one of the children of Israel and the stranger who dwells among you shall have both one law, if you sin through ignorance.

³⁰But the soul that does anything presumptuously, whether he be an Israelite or a stranger, the same has scorned the Lord. And that soul shall be destroyed from among his people, ³¹because he has scorned the word of the Lord and has broken his commandments. That soul therefore shall perish, and his sin shall be upon him.

³²And while the children of Israel were in the wilderness, they found a man gathering sticks on the Sabbath day. ³³And those who had found him gathering sticks brought him to Moses and Aaron, and before the whole congregation. ³⁴And they put him in custody, for it was not declared what should be done with him. ³⁵Then the Lord said to Moses, The man shall die; let all the multitude stone him with stones outside the host.ᵇ

³⁶And all the multitude brought him outside the host and stoned him with stones, and he died as the Lord had commanded Moses.

³⁷And the Lord spoke to Moses, saying, ³⁸Speak to the children of Israel, and bid them to make trimmings upon the skirts of their garments throughout their generations. And let them make the trimmings of ribbons of jacinth. ³⁹And the trimmings shall be for you to look upon so that you remember all the commandments of the Lord and do themᶜ – so that you do not seek a way following your own hearts and following your own eyes, to go a-whoring after them, ⁴⁰but remember and do all my commandments and be holy unto your God. ⁴¹For I am the Lord your God, who brought you out of the land of Egypt to be your God. I am the Lord God.

vv19-21 e.f. COV.

The Notes

a) 15. This commandment was a foreshadowing of gathering the Gentiles and the Hebrews into one church or body in Christ (John 10:16), wherein there is no difference between Hebrew, Jew, or Greek, or the rich or poor, or the citizen and the stranger or foreigner.

b) 35. Necessity did not compel him to gather sticks. Therefore, he deserved this cruel death, inasmuch as he disdained to hear the word of the Lord, to which he was so strictly commanded to give ear on the Sabbath day.

c) 39. Such trimmings should all Christians have deeply fixed in their hearts, considering what they are bound to in the Lord, and by what a God, and what a service they have taken upon them. Thus they may with all diligence and circumspection fulfil that which they have promised, etc. [Promised: In the 16th-century Church of England, the ancient baptismal vows included promises to renounce the devil and all his works, the vain pomp and glory of the world, and the carnal desires of the flesh, so as not to follow or be led by them; and, also, to endeavour to obediently keep God's holy will and commandments, and to walk in the same all the days of our life with God's help. For those who had been baptized as infants, these vows or promises to God were affirmed at their Confirmation.]

Chapter 16

The rebellion and resistance of Korah, Dathan, and Abiram. The earth opened and swallowed them up.

And Korah the son of Izhar, the son of Kohath, the son of Levi, with Dathan and Abiram the sons of Eliab, and On the son of Peleth, the son of Reuben, ²rose up against Moses, with others of the children of Israel – 250 heads of the congregation, counselors and men of renown. ³And they gathered themselves together against Moses and Aaron and said to them, You have done enough! For all the multitude are holy, every one of them, and the Lord is among them. Why therefore lift yourselves up above the congregation of the Lord?

⁴When Moses heard it, he fell upon his face. ⁵And he spoke to Korah and to all his company, saying, Tomorrow the Lord will show who is his and who is holy, and will take them unto him; and whomever he has chosen, he will cause to come to him. ⁶This do: take censers – you, Korah, and all your company – ⁷and put fire in them, and lay incense on them before the Lord tomorrow. And then whomever the Lord choses, the same is holy. You make enough to-do, you children of Levi!

⁸And Moses said to Korah, Hear, you children of Levi: ⁹does it seem but a small thing to you that the God of Israel separated you from the multitude of Israel to bring you to him to do the service of the dwelling place of the Lord, and to stand before the people to minister to them? ¹⁰He has taken you to himself, and all your brethren the sons of Levi with you, and yet you seek the office of the priest also – ¹¹for which cause you and all your company are gathered together against the Lord. For what is Aaron, that you should murmur against him?

¹²And Moses sent for Dathan and Abiram, the sons of Eliab, but they answered, We will not come! ¹³Does it seem a small thing to you

Jude 1:11

that you have brought us out of a land that flows with milk and honey to kill us in the wilderness, but that you should reign over us also? ¹⁴Moreover, you have brought us into no land that flows with milk and honey, neither have you given us any possessions of fields or of vines. Or will you pull out the eyes of these men? We will not come!

¹⁵And Moses was very angry and said to the Lord, Turn not to their offerings! I have not taken so much as a donkey from them, nor have I hurt any of them. ¹⁶Then Moses said to Korah, You and all your company are to be present before the Lord tomorrow – you, them, and Aaron. ¹⁷And take every man his censer, and put incense in them. And come before the Lord, every man with his censer – 250 censers, and Aaron with his censer.

¹⁸And they took every man his censer, put fire in them, and laid incense thereon. And they stood in the door of the tabernacle of witness with Moses and Aaron, ¹⁹and Korah gathered all the congregation in opposition to them at the door of the tabernacle of witness.

And the glory of the Lord appeared to all the congregation. ²⁰And the Lord spoke to Moses and Aaron, saying, ²¹Separate yourselves from this congregation so that I may consume them at once! ²²But they fell upon their faces and said, O most mighty God of the spirits of all flesh, one man has sinned, and will you be angry with all the multitude? <small>Nu 26:11</small>

²³And the Lord spoke to Moses, saying, ²⁴Speak to the congregation and say: Get yourselves away from around the dwellings of Korah, Dathan, and Abiram! ²⁵And Moses rose up and went to Dathan and Abiram, and the elders of Israel followed him. ²⁶And he spoke to the congregation, saying, Get away from the tents of these wicked men, and touch nothing of theirs, lest you perish in all their sins.

²⁷And they got away from the dwelling places of Korah, Dathan, and Abiram on every side. And Dathan and Abiram came out and stood in the door of their tents with their wives, their sons, and their children.

²⁸And Moses said, This is how you may know that the Lord has sent me to do all these works, and that I have not done them of my own mind: ²⁹if these men die the common death of all men, or if they are visited after the visitation* of all men, then the Lord has not sent me. ³⁰But if the Lord does a new thing, and the earth opens her mouth and swallows them and everything that belongs to them so that they go down alive into hell,ᵃ then you may understand that these men have railed upon the Lord.

<small>*That is, punished with the punishment.</small>

³¹And as soon as he had made an end of speaking all these words, the ground that was under them split asunder, ³²and the earth opened her mouth and swallowed them and their households, and all the men who were with Korah, and all their goods. ³³And they and all that belonged to them went down alive into hell, and the earth closed upon them, and they perished from among the congregation. ³⁴And all the Israelites around them fled at their cry, for they said, The earth might swallow us also! <small>Nu 26:9,10</small>

³⁵And then there went out a fire from the Lord, and it consumed the 250 men who were offering incense. ³⁶And the Lord spoke to Moses, saying, ³⁷Speak to Eleazar the son of Aaron the priest, and let him take up the censers out of the burning debris and scatter the fire here and there; ³⁸for the censers of these sinners are hallowed in their deaths.ᵇ And let them be beaten into thin plates and fastened upon the altar. For they offered them before the Lord, and therefore they are holy. And they shall be a sign to the children of Israel.

³⁹And Eleazar the priest took the bronze censers that the men who were burned had offered, and beat them flat and fastened them upon the altar, ⁴⁰to be a reminder to the children of Israel that no stranger who is not of the seed of Aaron should come near to offer incense before the Lord, lest he be made like Korah and his company. So Eleazar did as the Lord had said to him by the hand of Moses.

⁴¹But on the next day, all the multitude of the children of Israel murmured against Moses and Aaron, saying, You have killed the people of the Lord! ⁴²And when the multitude was gathered against Moses and Aaron, they looked toward the tabernacle of witness, and behold: the cloud had covered it, and the glory of the Lord appeared. ⁴³And Moses and Aaron went before the tabernacle of witness. ⁴⁴And the Lord spoke to Moses, saying, ⁴⁵Get away from this congregation, so that I may consume them quickly!

But they fell upon their faces. ⁴⁶And Moses said to Aaron, Take a censer and put fire in it from the altar, and pour on incense, and go quickly to the congregation and make an atonement for them! For there is wrath gone out from the Lord, and a plague has begun.

⁴⁷And Aaron took as Moses commanded him and ran to the congregation; and behold, the plague had begun among the people. And he put on incense and made an atonement for the people. ⁴⁸And he stood between the dead and those who were alive, and the plague ceased.ᶜ ⁴⁹And the number of them that died in the plague was 14,700, besides those that had died in the affair with Korah. ⁵⁰And Aaron went back to Moses at the door of the tabernacle of witness, and the plague ceased.

The Notes

a)   30. To go down alive into hell is to perish by sudden death and to be engulfed by the earth.
b)   38. The censers were hallowed in their deaths because by them was given an example to put others in fear.
c)   48. Aaron is here a figure of Christ, who is the mediator between God and the church, restrains the just vengeance of God for the sins of the world, and helps the chosen when they are in danger.

Chapter 17

Aaron's rod buds and bears blossoms.

vv2-3 e.f.
cov.

And the Lord spoke to Moses, saying, ²Speak to the children of Israel, and take from them twelve rods – from every leader over his father's house, one – and write every man's name upon his rod. ³And write Aaron's name upon the staff of Levi, for each head of their father's house shall have a rod. ⁴And put them in the tabernacle of witness, where I will meet you. ⁵And whom I chose, his rod will blossom, so that I may still the grudgings of the children of Israel against you.

⁶And Moses spoke to the children of Israel. And all the leaders gave him, for each head over their fathers' houses, a rod – even twelve rods. And Aaron's rod was among the rods. ⁷And Moses laid the rods before the Lord in the tabernacle of witness.

⁸And on the morrow, Moses went into the tabernacle; and behold, Aaron's rod, of the house of Levi, had budded. And it bore blossoms and almonds. ⁹And Moses brought out all the rods from before the Lord to all the children of Israel, and they looked upon them. And each man took his rod. [Heb 9:4]

¹⁰And the Lord said to Moses, Bring Aaron's rod back again before the witness, to be kept as a sign for the children of rebellion, so that their murmurings may cease from me and they do not die.

¹¹And Moses did as the Lord commanded him. ¹²And the children of Israel spoke to Moses, saying, Behold, we are destroyed, and all come to naught! ¹³For whoever comes near the dwelling of the Lord, dies. Are we to utterly die away?

Chapter 18

The office of the Levites. The tithes and firstfruits must be given to them. Aaron's heritage.

And the Lord said to Aaron, You and your sons and your father's house with you shall bear the fault of that which is done amiss in the holy place.* And you and your sons with you shall bear the fault of that which is done amiss in your priesthood. ²Your brethren from the tribe of Levi your father may come near; let them be joined to you so that they may assist you. But you and your sons with you shall minister before the tabernacle of witness. ³Let them serve you and serve in all the tabernacle, only do not let them come near the holy vessels or the altar, so that they and also you do not die. ⁴However, let them be by you and attend to the tabernacle of witness, and to all the service of the tabernacle. And let no stranger come near to you.

[*Understand, if you do not take heed that it be not touched.]

⁵Take heed, therefore, to the holy place and to the altar, so that no more wrath falls upon the children of Israel. ⁶Behold, I have taken your brethren the Levites from among the children of Israel to be yours, as gifts given to the Lord to do the service in the tabernacle of witness. ⁷And see that both you and your sons with you take heed to your priest's office, in all things that pertain to the altar and within the veil. And see that you serve, for I have given your priest's office to you for a gift, to serve. But the stranger that comes near shall die.

⁸And the Lord spoke to Aaron: Behold, I have given you my lift offerings. And everything that the children of Israel hallow, I have given to you and to your sons for a lasting ordinance. ⁹These shall be [v8 e.f. COV.]

yours from the most holy sacrifices: all their gifts, with all the food offerings, sin offerings, and trespass offerings that they bring to me. They shall be most holy to you and to your sons. ¹⁰And you shall eat it in the most holy place. All who are males may eat of it, for it shall be holy to you.

¹¹And these shall be yours: the lift offerings of their gifts, in all the wave offerings of the children of Israel. For I have given them to you, and to your sons and your daughters with you, for a lasting ordinance. Whoever is clean in your house may eat of it. ¹²All the best of the oil, the wine, and the wheat – the firstfruits that they give to the Lord – I have given to you. ¹³The firstfruits of all that is in their lands, which they bring to the Lord, shall be yours; and all who are clean in your house may eat of it.

¹⁴All dedicated things in Israel shall be yours. ¹⁵All that opens the womb of all flesh that people bring to the Lord, both of man and beast, shall be yours; however, the firstborn of man shall be redeemed, and the firstborn of unclean beasts shall be redeemed. ¹⁶And their redemptions shall be at a month old, valued at five sickles of silver of the holy sickle. (A sickle makes twenty gerahs.) ¹⁷But the firstborn of oxen, sheep, and goats shall not be redeemed, for they are holy; and you shall sprinkle their blood upon the altar, and shall burn their fat to be a sacrifice of a sweet savour to the Lord. ¹⁸And their flesh shall be yours, as the wave-breast and all the right shoulder is yours. ¹⁹All the holy lift offerings that the children of Israel lift to the Lord, I give to you and to your sons and your daughters with you, for a lasting ordinance. And it shall be a salted covenant* forever before the Lord, to you and to your seed with you.

*A salted covenant: that is, a firm, sure, and stable covenant.

²⁰And the Lord spoke to Aaron: You shall have no inheritance in their land, nor portion among them, for I am your portion and your inheritance among the children of Israel. ²¹And behold, I have given to the children of Levi all the tithes in Israel as an inheritance, for the service that they do in the tabernacle of witness, ²²so that the children of Israel will henceforth not come near the tabernacle of witness, to lade themselves with sin and to die. ²³The Levites shall do the service in the tabernacle of witness, and will bear their own fault, and it shall be a law forever to your children after you. But among the children of Israel they shall have no inheritance. ²⁴For the tithes of the children of Israel, which they lift to the Lord, I have given to the Levites to inherit. Therefore I have said to them, Among the children of Israel, you shall have no inheritance.

²⁵And the Lord spoke to Moses, saying, ²⁶Speak to the Levites and say to them: When you receive from the children of Israel the tithes that I have given you from them as your inheritance, you shall take a lift offering from it for the Lord – a tenth of that tithe. ²⁷And it will be reckoned to you for your lift offering, fully as though you gave grain out of the barn or a full offering from the wine press. ²⁸Thus you shall lift a lift offering to the Lord from all the tithes that you receive from

the children of Israel. And you shall give the Lord's lift offering from it to Aaron the priest. ²⁹From all your gifts you shall take out the Lord's lift offering, the best of all their hallowed things.

³⁰And you shall say to them: When you have taken out the best from it, it will be accounted to the Levites as produce of grain and wine. ³¹And you may eat it anywhere, both you and your households, for it is your reward for your service in the tabernacle of witness. ³²And you bear no sin by reason of this, when you have taken the best of it; neither will you unhallow the hallowed things of the children of Israel. And so you will not die.

Chapter 19

Of the red cow and the sprinkling water. The law for him who dies in a tent or touches any unclean thing.

And the Lord spoke to Moses and Aaron, saying, ²This is the ordinance of the law which the Lord commanded, saying, Speak to the children of Israel, and let them bring to you a red cow without spot, in which is no blemish and which never bore a yoke upon her. ³And you shall give her to Eleazar the priest, and he shall bring her outside the host and cause her to be slain before him. ⁴And Eleazar the priest shall take some of her blood on his finger and sprinkle it straight toward the tabernacle of witness seven times. ⁵And he shall cause the cow to be burned in his sight: the skin, flesh, and blood, with the dung also. ⁶And let the priest take cedar wood, hyssop, and purple cloth, and cast them upon the cow as she burns. ⁷And let the priest wash his clothes and bathe his flesh in water, and then come into the host. And the priest shall be unclean till the evening.

⁸And he who burns her shall wash his clothes in water, and bathe his flesh also in water, and be unclean until evening. ⁹And one who is clean shall go and take up the ashes of the cow and put them outside the host in a clean place, where they shall be kept to make sprinkling water for the multitude of the children of Israel. For it is a sin offering. ¹⁰And let him who gathers the ashes of the cow wash his clothes and remain unclean until evening. And this shall be, for the children of Israel and for the stranger that dwells among them, a lasting ordinance.*

¹¹He who touches any dead person shall be unclean seven days. ¹²And he shall purify himself with the ashes the third day, and then he will be clean the seventh day. But if he does not purify himself the third day, then the seventh day he will not be clean. ¹³Whoever touches a dead person and does not sprinkle himself defiles the dwelling of the Lord, and therefore that soul shall be rooted out of Israel,ᵃ because he has not sprinkled the sprinkling water upon himself. He shall be unclean, and his uncleanness shall remain upon him.

¹⁴This is the law concerning a person who dies in a tent: all who come into the tent and all who are in the tent shall be unclean seven days. ¹⁵And all the open vessels, which have no lid nor covering upon them, are unclean. ¹⁶And whoever touches a person that is slain with a

---

Sprinkling water.

*A lasting ordinance or ordinance forever: see Ge 13:15 & note b.

sword in the fields, or a dead person, or a bone of a dead man, or a grave, shall be unclean seven days.

¹⁷And for an unclean person they shall take some of the burnt ashes of the sin offering and add running water to it in a vessel. ¹⁸And a clean person shall take hyssop, dip it in the water, and sprinkle it upon the tent, all the vessels, and on the souls that were there; or upon the person who touched a bone, or a slain person, or a dead body, or a grave. ¹⁹And the clean person shall sprinkle the unclean person on the third day and the seventh day. And on the seventh day he shall purify himself, wash his clothes, and bathe himself in water; and he shall be clean at evening.

²⁰If anyone is unclean and does not sprinkle himself, the same soul shall be destroyed from among the congregation. For he has defiled the holy place of the Lord and is not sprinkled with sprinkling water; therefore, he is unclean. ²¹And this shall be a perpetual law for them. And he who sprinkles the sprinkling water shall wash his clothes, and he who touches the sprinkling water shall be unclean until evening. ²²And whatever the unclean person touches shall be unclean, and the soul that touches it shall be unclean until the evening.

The Notes

a)   13. As they were defiled by touching the dead, so are the souls of the Christian defiled when they commit deadly sin, which is cleansed with Christ's sacrifice and merits only. And that cleansing is obtained by the passion and death of Christ our Lord. Whosoever disregards his soul shall be rooted out from among the chosen.

Chapter 20

> Miriam dies. The people murmur. They have water out of the rock. Edom denies the Israelites passage through his realm. The death of Aaron, to whose office Eleazar succeeds.

And the whole multitude of the children of Israel came into the desert of Zin in the first month, and the people dwelt at Kadesh. And there Miriam died, and was buried there. ²Moreover, there was no water for the multitude, because of which they gathered themselves together against Moses and Aaron. ³And the people fought with Moses and spoke, saying, Would God that we had perished when our brethren perished before the Lord! ⁴Why have you brought the congregation of the Lord into this wilderness, that both we and our animals should die here? ⁵Why did you bring us out of Egypt, to bring us into this ungracious place, which is no place to sow seed, nor where figs or vines or pomegranates grow, and neither is there any water to drink?

⁶And Moses and Aaron went from the congregation to the door of the tabernacle of witness and fell upon their faces. And the glory of the Lord appeared to them. ⁷And the Lord spoke to Moses, saying, ⁸Take the staff and gather the congregation together, you and your brother Aaron, and tell the rock before their eyes to give forth its water. And

you will bring for them water out of the rock, and will give the company drink, and their beasts also.

⁹And Moses took the staff from before the Lord, as he commanded him. ¹⁰And Moses and Aaron gathered the congregation together before the rock, and he said to them, Hear, ye rebellious! Must we draw you water out of this rock? ¹¹And Moses lifted up his hand with his staff and struck the rock two times. And the water came out abundantly, and the multitude drank, and their beasts also. ¹²But the Lord said to Moses and Aaron, Because you did not believe me, to hallow me as holy in the eyes of the children of Israel, therefore you shall not bring this congregation into the land that I have given them. v12 e.f. JR.

¹³This was the water of strife, because the children of Israel strove with the Lord. But he was shown to be holy among them.

¹⁴And Moses sent messengers from Kadesh to the king of Edom to say, Thus says your brother Israel: You know all the hardship that has happened to us – ¹⁵how our fathers went down into Egypt, and how we dwelt in Egypt a long time, and how the Egyptians dealt ill with both us and our fathers. ¹⁶Then we cried out to the Lord, and he heard our voices and sent an angel, and has brought us out of Egypt. And behold, we are in Kadesh, a town hard by the borders of your country. ¹⁷Let us go in good fellowship through your country. We will not go through the fields or through the vineyards, nor will we drink of the water of the wells. But we will go by the main roadway, and neither turn to the right hand nor to the left until we are past your country. Nu 21:21,22

¹⁸But Edom answered him, See that you come not by me, lest I come out against you with the sword.

¹⁹And the children of Israel said to him, We will go by the beaten way. And if either we or our livestock drink of your water, we will pay for it. We will do no more than pass through by foot only.

²⁰But he said, You shall not go through.

And Edom came out against them with many people and a strong hand. ²¹And thus Edom refused to give Israel passage through his country. And Israel turned away from him.

²²And the children of Israel removed from Kadesh, and went to Mount Hor with all the congregation. ²³And the Lord spoke to Moses and Aaron in Mount Hor, close by the border of the land of Edom, saying, ²⁴Let Aaron be put unto his people. For he shall not come into the land that I have given to the children of Israel, because you disobeyed my mouth at the water of strife. ²⁵Take Aaron and Eleazar his son, and bring them up Mount Hor. ²⁶And strip Aaron out of his vestments and put them upon Eleazar his son, and let Aaron be put unto his people and die there.

²⁷And Moses did as the Lord commanded. And they went up into Mount Hor in the sight of all the multitude. ²⁸And Moses took off Aaron's clothes and put them upon Eleazar his son, and Aaron died there at the top of the mount. And Moses and Eleazar came down out of the mount. ²⁹And all the house of Israel mourned for Aaron thirty days.

Chapter 21

Israel vanquishes King Arad. The fiery serpents bite the people, but when they look at the bronze serpent that the Lord commanded Moses to lift up, they are healed. The kings Sihon and Og are overcome in battle.

And when King Arad, the Canaanite who dwelt in the south parts, heard that Israel was coming by the way that the scouts had found out, he came and fought with Israel, and took some of them prisoners. ²Then Israel vowed a vow to the Lord and said, If you will give this people into our hands, we will destroy their towns. ³And the Lord heard the voice of Israel and delivered the Canaanites over to them. And they destroyed both them and their towns, and called the place Hormah.*

*[ie, Utter Destruction]

⁴Then they departed from Mount Hor toward the Red Sea, to go around the land of Edom. And the souls of the people fainted by the way. ⁵And the people spoke against God and against Moses: Why have you brought us out of Egypt, to die in the wilderness? For here there is neither food nor water, and our souls loathe this light bread.‡

‡ Light bread: or, that is of so little value.

The plague of serpents.

⁶Then the Lord sent fiery serpents among the people, which bit them, so that many people died in Israel. ⁷And the people came to Moses and said, We have sinned, for we have spoken against the Lord and against you. Make intercession to the Lord, to take away the serpents from us!

And Moses made intercession for the people. ⁸And the Lord said to Moses, Make a serpent and hang it up for a sign, and let as many as are bitten look upon it, and they shall live.

⁹And Moses made a serpent of bronze and set it up for a sign. And when the serpents had bitten anyone, they went and looked upon the serpent of bronze and recovered.

¹⁰And the children of Israel removed and pitched in Oboth. ¹¹And they departed from Oboth and lay at Egebarim, in the wilderness that is before Moab on the east side. ¹²Then they removed from there and pitched at the Zered River. ¹³And they departed from there and pitched on the other side of the Arnon, which is a river in the wilderness and comes out of the borderland of the Amorites. For the Arnon River is the border of Moab, between Moab and the Amorites. ¹⁴Therefore it is said in the Book of the War of the Lord,* Go with gusto, both on the river of Arnon ¹⁵and on the river's head, which shoots down to dwell at Ar and leans upon the border of Moab.

*Some think this to be the book of the Judges.

¹⁶And from there they came to Beer, which is the well whereof the Lord said to Moses, Gather the people together so that I may give them water. ¹⁷Then Israel sang this song: Spring up, well! Sing to it – ¹⁸the well that the rulers dug, and the captains of the people, with the help of the lawgiver and with their staffs.

And from this wilderness they went to Mattanah, ¹⁹and from Mattanah to Nahaliel, and from Nahaliel to Bamoth, ²⁰and from Bamoth to the valley that is in the field of Moab in the top of Pisgah,‡ which bows

‡ Per the common translation. Chaldee: a hill.

downward toward Jeshimon.* ²¹And Israel sent messengers to Sihon king of the Amorites, saying, ²²Let us go through your land. We will not turn into your fields nor into your vineyards, neither drink of the water of the wells, but we will go along by the common way until we are past your country.

²³But Sihon would not give Israel leave to pass through his country, but gathered all his people together and went out against Israel in the wilderness. And he came to Jahaz and fought with Israel. ²⁴And Israel smote him with the edge of the sword, and conquered his land from the Arnon River to Jabbok, even as far as the children of Ammon (for the borders of the children of Ammon are strong). ²⁵And Israel took all these places and dwelt in all the settlements of the Amorites – in Heshbon and in all the towns that belong to it. ²⁶For Heshbon was the city of Sihon the king of the Amorites, who earlier had fought with the king of the Moabites and taken all his land out of his hand, even as far as the Arnon. ²⁷And so it is a proverb: Go to Heshbon, and let Sihon's city be built and made ready! ²⁸For there is a fire gone out of Heshbon and a flame from Sihon's city, and it has consumed Ar of the Moabites and the people of the hills of the Arnon. ²⁹Woe be to you, Moab! O people of Chemosh,* you are doomed! His sons are put to flight, and his daughters brought captive to Sihon king of the Amorites. ³⁰Their light is out from Heshbon to Dibon, and we made a wilderness as far as Nophah, which reaches to Medeba.

³¹And thus Israel dwelt in the land of the Amorites. ³²And Moses sent to search out Jazer, and they took the towns belonging to it, and conquered the Amorites that were there. ³³And then they turned and went up toward Bashan. And Og the king of Bashan came out against them, both he and all his people, to make war at Edrei. ³⁴And the Lord said to Moses, Fear him not, for I have delivered him into your hands, with all his people and his land. And you shall do with him as you did with Sihon the king of the Amorites, who dwelt at Heshbon.

³⁵And they smote him and his sons and all his people, until there was nothing left of him. And they conquered his land.

*Greek: desert or wasteland.

The proverb of Heshbon.

*Chemosh is the name of a certain idol.

Chapter 22

> King Balak sends for Balaam to the intent that he should curse Israel, but Balaam can do nothing against the will of the Lord. Balaam's donkey speaks to him in the way.

Afterward, the children of Israel went and pitched camp in the fields of Moab, on the other side of the Jordan River from the city of Jericho. ²And Balak the son of Zippor saw all that Israel had done to the Amorites. ³And the Moabites were sore afraid of the people because they were many, and abhorred the children of Israel. ⁴And Moab said to the elders of Midian, Now this company is going to lick up everyone round about us, like an ox licks up the grass of the field.

And Balak the son of Zippor was king of the Moabites at that time. ⁵And he sent messengers to Balaam the son of Beor, the interpreter*

*[Interpreter: formerly, one who expounded laws and mysteries]

who dwelt at the river of the land of the children of his folk, to call for him, saying, Behold, there is a people come out of Egypt who cover the face of the earth, and lie very close by me. ⁶Come now, and curse this people for me, for they are too mighty for me. Thus perhaps I can smite them, and drive them out of the land. For I know that whom you bless will be blessed and whom you curse will be cursed.

De 23:3-6

⁷And the elders of Moab went with the elders of Midian, and with the reward for the soothsaying in their hands. And they went to Balaam and told him Balak's words. ⁸And he said to them, Tarry here all night and I will bring you word, even as the Lord shall say to me.

And the lords of Moab abode with Balaam.

⁹And God came to Balaam and said, What men are these who are with you?

¹⁰And Balaam said to God, Balak the son of Zippor, king of Moab, has sent to me, saying, ¹¹Behold, there is a people come out of Egypt that covers the face of the earth; come now, therefore, and curse them for me, so that perhaps I may be able to overcome them in battle and drive them out.

¹²And God said to Balaam, You shall not go with them nor curse the people, for they are blessed.

¹³And Balaam rose up in the morning and said to the lords of Balak, Go to your land, for the Lord will not suffer me to go with you.

¹⁴And the lords of Moab rose up and went to Balak and said, Balaam would not come with us.

¹⁵And Balak sent again a greater company of lords, more honourable than they. ¹⁶And they went to Balaam and told him, Thus says Balak the son of Zippor: O, let nothing prevent you from coming to me! ¹⁷For I will greatly promote you, to great honour, and will do whatever you say to me. Come therefore, I pray you; curse this people for me.

Nu 24:12,13

¹⁸And Balaam answered and said to the servants of Balak, If Balak should give me his house full of silver and gold, I can go no further than the word of the Lord my God, to do less or more. ¹⁹Nevertheless, tarry here all night so that I may find out what the Lord will say to me once more.

²⁰And God came to Balaam by night and said to him, If the men come to fetch you, rise up and go with them. But what I say to you, that only you shall do.

²¹And Balaam rose up early, saddled his donkey, and went with the lords of Moab. ²²But God was angry because he went, and the angel of the Lord stood in the way against him. And Balaam was riding upon his donkey, and two servants with him. ²³And when the donkey saw the angel of the Lord standing in the way, his sword drawn in his hand, she turned aside out of the road and went out into the field. And Balaam struck the donkey to turn her into the road.

²⁴And the angel of the Lord went and stood in a path between the vineyards, where was a wall on one side and another on the other side. ²⁵When the donkey saw the angel of the Lord, she wrenched toward

the wall and thrust Balaam's foot against the wall. And he struck her again. ²⁶And the angel of the Lord went further and stood in a narrow place with no way to turn, neither to the right hand nor the left. ²⁷And when the donkey saw the angel of the Lord, she fell down under Balaam. And Balaam was angry and struck the donkey with a staff.

²⁸And the Lord opened the mouth of the donkey, and she said to Balaam, What have I done to you, that you strike me thus three times?

²⁹And Balaam said to the donkey, Because you have defied me. I would that I had a sword in my hand, so that I could now kill you.

³⁰And the donkey said to Balaam, Am I not your donkey, whom you have ridden upon since you were born to this day? Was I ever wont to do so to you?

And he said, Nay.

³¹And the Lord opened the eyes of Balaam so that he saw the angel of the Lord standing in the way, with his sword drawn in his hand. And he bowed himself and fell flat on his face. ³²And the angel of the Lord said to him, Why do you strike your donkey thus three times? Behold, I came out to resist you, for the way is contrary to me. ³³And the donkey saw me and avoided me three times – or else, had she not turned from me, I would surely have slain you and saved her alive.

³⁴And Balaam said to the angel of the Lord, I have sinned. For I did not know that you stood in the way against me. Now therefore, if it displeases your eyes, I will turn back.

³⁵And the angel said to Balaam, Go with the men, but only what I say to you, that say.

And Balaam went with the lords of Balak.

³⁶And when Balak heard that Balaam had come, he went out to meet him at a town of Moab that stood in the borderland of the Arnon River, which was the outermost part of his country. ³⁷And Balak said to Balaam, Did I not send for you, to summon you? Why did you not come to me? Do you think I am not able to promote you to honour?

³⁸And Balaam said to Balak, Lo, I have come to you. But I can say nothing at all save what God puts in my mouth; that must I speak.

³⁹And Balaam went with Balak, and they came to the large city.*
⁴⁰And Balak offered oxen and sheep, and sent for Balaam and for the lords that were with him. ‡

Chapter 23

Balaam blesses the people where he was asked to curse them, and prophesies that they will be a great people.

²²:⁴¹And in the morning, Balak took Balaam and brought him up into the high place of Baal, and from there he saw to the furthest reach of the people of Israel. ¹And Balaam said to Balak, Build me here seven altars, and provide here seven bullocks and seven rams.

²And Balak did as Balaam said, and Balak and Balaam offered on every altar a bullock and a ram. ³And Balaam said to Balak, Stand by the sacrifice while I go to see whether the Lord will come and meet

*Hebrew: city of places or of streets. Some: city full of people in the streets.

‡ v41 begins the next chapter.

me, and whatever he shows me, I will tell you. And he went forthwith.

⁴And God came to Balaam, and Balaam said to him, I have prepared seven altars, and have offered upon every altar a bullock and a ram. ⁵And the Lord put a saying in Balaam's mouth and said, Go back to Balak and say this.

⁶And he went back to Balak, and lo, he was standing by his sacrifice, both he and all the lords of Moab. ⁷And Balaam began his parable and said, Balak the king of Moab has fetched me from Mesopotamia, from the mountains of the east, saying, Come and curse Jacob for me; come and denounce Israel for me! ⁸How can I curse whom God curses not, and how can I denounce whom the Lord does not denounce? ⁹From the top of the rocks I see him, and from the hills I behold him:– Lo, this people will dwell by themselves,ᵃ and will not be reckoned* among other nations. ¹⁰Who can count the dust of Jacob or the number of the fourth part of Israel? I pray God that my soul may die the death of the righteous, and that my last end may be like his.

¹¹And Balak said to Balaam, What have you done to me? I fetched you to curse my enemies, and behold, you bless them!

¹²And he answered and said, Must I not keep and speak that which the Lord has put in my mouth?

¹³And Balak said to him, Come, I pray you, with me to another place from where you may see them – but only the outermost part of them, and will not see them all. And curse them there for me.

¹⁴And he brought him into an open field where people could see far, even to the top of Pisgah, and built seven altars and offered a bullock and a ram on every altar. ¹⁵And Balaam said to Balak, Stand here by your sacrifice while I go yonder. ¹⁶And the Lord met Balaam and put words in his mouth, and said, Go back to Balak and say this.

¹⁷And when he went to Balak, behold, he was standing by his sacrifice, and the lords of Moab with him. And Balak said to him, What says the Lord?

¹⁸And he took up his parable and said, Rise up, Balak, and hear – and hearken to me, son of Zippor! ¹⁹The Lord is not a man, that he can lie, neither the son of a man, that he can repent. Should he say and not do, or should he speak and not make it good? ²⁰Behold, I have begun to bless and have blessed, and cannot go back from it:– ²¹He beheld no wickedness in Jacob nor saw idolatry in Israel.ᵇ The Lord his God is with him, and the triumph* of a king among them. ²²God, who brought them out of Egypt, is as the strength of a wild ox for them, ²³for there is no sorcerer in Jacob nor soothsayer in Israel. When the time comes, it will be said of Jacob and of Israel, What God has wrought! ²⁴Behold, the people will rise up as a lioness and lift itself up as a lion, and will not lie down again until they have eaten of the prey and drunk of the blood of them that are slain.

²⁵And Balak said to Balaam, Neither curse them nor bless them!

²⁶And Balaam answered and said to Balak, Did I not tell you, saying, All that the Lord bids me, that I must do?

Balaam's 1st parable blessing Israel.
*After the Chaldee, destroyed.

Balaam's 2nd parable blessing Israel.
*Chaldee: habitation, dwelling place, or court.

²⁷And Balak said to Balaam, Come, I pray you. I will bring you to yet another place, so perhaps it will please God that you may curse them there. ²⁸And Balak brought Balaam to the top of Peor, which bows toward the wilderness. ²⁹And Balaam said to Balak, Make me here seven altars, and prepare for me here seven bullocks and seven rams. ³⁰And Balak did as Balaam had said, and offered a bullock and a ram on every altar.

The Notes

a) 9. To dwell by oneself is to live in liberty, without trouble and out from under the subjugation of other people, as in Deuteronomy 33:28.

b) 21. There is no people without sin, including Israel, but God looks not on it: he turns not angry in the end; he avenges it not as it deserves, but amends it by his grace.

Chapter 24

Balaam prophesies of the kingdom of Israel and of the coming of Christ. Balak is angry with Balaam. The destruction of the Amalekites and of the Kenites.

When Balaam saw that it pleased the Lord that he should bless Israel, he did not try as he had done twice before to get a soothsaying,* but set his face toward the wilderness, ²and lifted up his eyes and looked upon Israel as they lay in their tribes. And the Spirit of God came upon him, ³and he took up his parable and said, Balaam the son of Beor has said, and the man whose eye is open has said – ⁴he has said who hears the words of God and sees the visions of the Almighty, who falls down and his eyes are opened:–

*[ie, he did not first ask God if he should go]

⁵How goodly are the tents of Jacob, and your habitations, Israel! ⁶Even as the broad valleys, and gardens by the river's side; as the tents that the Lord has pitched, and as cypress trees beside the water.ᵃ ⁷The water shall flow out of his bucket, and his seed shall be many waters. His king shall be higher than Agag, and his kingdom shall be exalted. ⁸God, who brought him out of Egypt, is as the strength of a wild ox for him, and he will devour the nations that are his enemies and break their bones, and will pierce them through with his arrows. ⁹He rested himself and lay down as a lion and as a lioness; who shall stir him up? Blessed is he that blesses you, and cursed is he that curses you.

Balaam's 3rd parable and prophecy of the king Christ.

Nu 23:22
Ho 11:1
M't 2:15

¹⁰And Balak was angry with Balaam, and smacked his hands together and said to him, I sent for you to curse my enemies, and behold, you have blessed them this three times! ¹¹And now, get yourself quickly to your place. I thought that I would promote you to honour, but the Lord has kept you back from honour.

De 23:5
Nu 22:17

¹²And Balaam said to Balak, Did I not tell the messengers whom you sent to me, saying, ¹³If Balak were to give me his house full of silver and gold, I cannot go beyond the mouth of the Lord, to do either good or bad of my own mind? What the Lord says, that I must speak. ¹⁴And now, behold, I go to my people. Come, let me show you what this people will do to your folk in the latter days. ¹⁵And he began his

Nu 22:18

parable and said, Balaam the son of Beor has said, and the man that has his eye open has said – ¹⁶and he has said who hears the words of God and has the knowledge of the Most High, and beholds the vision of the Almighty, and when he falls down has his eyes opened:–

¹⁷I see him, but not now; I behold him, but not near. There shall come a star of Jacob, and arise a sceptre of Israel, who will smite the quarters of Moab and topple all the children of Seth; ¹⁸and Edom shall be his possession. And the land of Seir shall be their enemies, but Israel will do manfully. ¹⁹And out of Jacob shall come he who will destroy the remains of the cities.

²⁰And he looked on the Amalekites and began his parable, and said, Amalek is the first of the nations, but at his latter end shall perish utterly. ²¹And he looked on the Kenites, and took up his parable and said, Strong is your dwelling place, and on a rock you have put your nest. ²²Nevertheless, you shall be a burning to Kain until Ashur takes you prisoner. ²³And he took up his parable and said, Alas, who shall live when God does this? ²⁴The ships will come out of the coast of Chittim* and subdue Ashur and subdue Eber,‡ and he himself will perish at the last.

²⁵And Balaam rose up and went and dwelt in his place, and Balak also went his way.

Balaam's final parables.

*Chittim: the Chaldee & the common translation read, Italy.

‡Eber: ie, the Hebrews, or those who are beyond the Euphrates River.

The Notes

a) 6. By all these similitudes would Balaam declare the felicity of the people of Israel, which came of God, as you have in Ps 111 and Jer 17:7,8.

Chapter 25

The people commit fornication with the daughters of Moab. Phinehas kills Zimri and Cozbi. God commands to kill the Midianites.

And Israel dwelt in Settim. And the people began to commit whoredom with the daughters of Moab, ²who called the people to the sacrifices of their gods. So the people ate and worshipped their gods, ³and Israel coupled himself to Baal Peor.*

Then the Lord was angry with Israel ⁴and said to Moses, Take all the chiefs of the people and hang them up unto the Lord before the sun,ᵃ so that the wrath of the Lord may turn away from Israel. ⁵And Moses said to the judges of Israel, Go, and slay those men that joined themselves to Baal Peor.

⁶And behold, one of the children of Israel came and brought to his brethren a Midianite wife, even in the sight of Moses, and in the sight of all the multitude of the children of Israel as they were weeping in the door of the tabernacle of witness. ⁷And when Phinehas the son of Eleazar, the son of Aaron the priest, saw it, he rose up out of the company, took a weapon in his hand, ⁸and went after the man of Israel into the whorehouse and thrust them through, both the man of Israel and also the woman, even through her belly.‡ And the plague ceased from among the children of Israel; ⁹but 24,000 died in the plague.

*[Baal Peor: the god of the Moabites. The name probably means Lord of the Open Mouth.]

‡After the Chaldean, the Greek, and the common translation: through the shameful or unclean members. Some read, even in the brothel.

¹⁰And the Lord spoke to Moses, saying, ¹¹Phinehas the son of Eleazar, the son of Aaron the priest, has turned my anger away from the children of Israel because he was jealous for my sake among them, so that I did not consume the children of Israel in my jealousy. ¹²Therefore say, Behold, I give to him my covenant of peace; ¹³and he shall have it and his seed after him – even the covenant of the priest's office forever, because he was jealous for his God's sake, and made an atonement for the children of Israel.

¹⁴The name of the Israelite who was smitten with his Midianite wife was Zimri the son of Salu, a lord of an ancient house among the Simeonites. ¹⁵And the name of the Midianite wife was Cozbi the daughter of Zur, a head over the people of an ancient house in Midian.

¹⁶And the Lord spoke to Moses, saying, ¹⁷Vex the Midianites and smite them, ¹⁸because they have troubled you with their wiles, by which they have beguiled you through Peor, and through their sister Cozbi the daughter of a lord in Midian, who was slain in the day of the plague on account of Peor.

The Notes

a) 4. To hang before the sun is to be put to execution openly before all the people.

Chapter 26

> The children of Israel are numbered again when they are about to enter into the land of Canaan.

And after the plague, the Lord spoke to Moses and to Eleazar the son of Aaron the priest, saying, ²Take the number of all the multitude of the children of Israel, from twenty years and above throughout their fathers' houses – all who are able to go to war in Israel.

³And Moses and Eleazar the priest counted them in the fields of Moab by the Jordan River across from Jericho, ⁴those twenty years and above, as the Lord commanded Moses. And the children of Israel who came from Egypt were:

⁵Reuben, the eldest son of Israel. The children of Reuben were: Hanoch, of whom comes the kindred of the Hanochites; and of Pallu comes the kindred of the Palluites; ⁶and of Hezron comes the kindred of the Hezronites; and of Carmi comes the kindred of the Carmites. ⁷These are the kindreds of the Reubenites, who were in number 43,730. *The kindred of Reuben.*

⁸And the son of Pallu was Eliab. ⁹And the sons of Eliab were Nemuel, Dathan, and Abiram. This is that Dathan and Abiram, counselors in the congregation, who strove against Moses and Aaron in the company of Korah, when they strove against the Lord. ¹⁰And the earth opened her mouth and swallowed them, and Korah also; and many died at that time, when the fire consumed 250 men. And they became a sign. ¹¹Notwithstanding, the children of Korah did not die. *Nu c16*

¹²And the children of Simeon in their kindreds were: Nemuel, of whom comes the kindred of the Nemuelites; Jamin, of whom comes the kindred of the Jaminites; Jachin, of whom comes the kindred of *The kindred of Simeon.*

the Jachinites; ¹³Zerah, of whom comes the kindred of the Zarhites; and Shaul, of whom comes the kindred of the Shaulites. ¹⁴These are the kindreds of the Simeonites, in number 22,200.

^{The kindred of Gad.} ¹⁵And the children of Gad in their kindreds were: Zephon, of whom comes the kindred of the Zephonites; and of Haggi comes the kindred of the Haggites; and of Shuni comes the kindred of the Shunites; ¹⁶and of Ozni comes the kindred of the Oznites; and of Eri comes the kindred of the Erites; ¹⁷and of Arod comes the kindred of the Arodites; and of Areli comes the kindred of the Arelites. ¹⁸These are the kindreds of the children of Gad, in number 40,500.

^{The kindred of Judah.} ¹⁹The children of Judah: Er and Onan, who died in the land of Canaan. ²⁰But the children of Judah in their kindred were: Shelah, of whom comes the kindred of the Shelanites; and of Perez comes the kindred of the Parzites; and of Zerah comes the kindred of the Zarhites. ²¹And the children of Perez were: Hezron, of whom comes the kindred of the Hezronites; and Hamul, of whom comes the kindred of the Hamulites. ²²These are the kindreds of Judah, in number 76,500.

^{The kindred of Issachar.} ²³And the children of Issachar in their kindreds were: Tola, of whom comes the kindred of the Tolaites; and Puah, of whom comes the kindred of the Punites; ²⁴and of Jashub comes the kindred of the Jashubites; and of Shimron comes the kindred of the Shimronites. ²⁵These are the kindreds of Issachar, in number 64,300.

^{The kindred of Zebulun.} ²⁶The children of Zebulun in their kindreds were: Sered, of whom comes the kindred of the Sardites; and Elon, of whom comes the kindred of the Elonites; and of Jahleel comes the kindred of the Jahleelites. ²⁷These are the kindreds of Zebulun, in number 60,500.

^{The kindred of Joseph.} ²⁸The children of Joseph in their kindreds were Manasseh and Ephraim. ²⁹The son of Manasseh: Machir, of whom comes the kindred of the Machirites. And Machir begat Gilead, of whom comes the kindred of the Gileadites. ³⁰And these are the children of Gilead: Jeezer, of whom comes the kindred of the Jeezerites; and of Helek comes the kindred of the Helekites; ³¹and of Asriel, the kindred of the Asrielites; and of Shechem comes the kindred of the Shechemites; ³²and of Shemida comes the kindred of the Shemidaites; and of Hepher comes the kindred of the Hepherites. ³³And Zelophehad the son of Hepher had no sons but only daughters. And the names of the daughters of Zelophehad were Mahela, Noa, Hagla, Milcha, and Thirza. ³⁴These are the kindreds of Manasseh, in number 52,700.

^{The kindred of Ephraim.} ³⁵These are the children of Ephraim in their kindreds: Shuthelah, of whom comes the kindred of the Shuthalhites; and Becher, of whom comes the kindred of the Bachrites; and of Tahan comes the kindred of the Tahanites. ³⁶And the son of Shuthelah was Eran, of whom comes the kindred of the Eranites. ³⁷These are the kindreds of the descendants of Ephraim, in number 32,500.

These were the descendants of Joseph in their kindreds.

^{The kindred of Benjamin.} ³⁸And these are the children of Benjamin in their kindreds: Bela, of whom comes the kindred of the Belaites; and of Ashbel comes the

kindred of the Ashbelites; and of Ahiram, the kindred of the Ahiramites; ³⁹and of Shupham, the kindred of the Shuphamites; and of Hupham, the kindred of the Huphamites. ⁴⁰And the children of Bela were Ard and Naaman, from whom come the kindreds of the Ardites and of the Naamites. ⁴¹These are the descendants of Benjamin in their kindreds, and in number 45,600.

⁴²The son of Dan was Shuham, of whom comes the kindred of the Shuhamites. These are the kindreds of Dan in their generations. ⁴³And all the kindreds of the Shuhamites were in number 64,400.

The kindred of Dan.

⁴⁴The children of Asher in their kindreds were: Jimna, of whom comes the kindred of the Jimnites; and Jesui, of whom comes the kindred of the Jesuites; and of Beriah comes the kindred of Beriites. ⁴⁵And the children of Beriah were Heber, of whom comes the kindred of the Heberites; and of Malchiel came the kindred of the Malchielites. ⁴⁶And the daughter of Asher was called Sarah. ⁴⁷These are the kindreds of Asher, in number 53,400.

The kindred of Asher.

⁴⁸The children of Naphtali in their kindreds were: Jahzeel, of whom came the kindred of the Jahzeelites; and Guni, of whom came the kindred of the Gunites; ⁴⁹and of Jezer came the kindred of the Jezerites; and of Shillem the kindred of Shillemites. ⁵⁰These are the kindreds of Naphtali in their generations, in number 45,400.

The kindred of Naphtali.

⁵¹These are the numbers of the children of Israel: 601,730.

⁵²And the Lord spoke to Moses, saying, ⁵³To these the land shall be divided to inherit, according to the number of names. ⁵⁴To many you shall give the greater inheritance, and to few, the lesser; to every tribe the inheritance shall be given according to their number. ⁵⁵Notwithstanding, the land shall be divided by lot, and according to the names of the tribes of their fathers they shall inherit. ⁵⁶And according to their lot you shall divide their land, both to the many and to the few.

⁵⁷These are the Levites in their kindreds: of Gershon came the kindred of the Gershonites; and of Kohath came the kindred of the Kohathites; and of Merari came the kindred of the Merarites. ⁵⁸Also of the kindreds of Levi: the kindred of the Libnites, the kindred of the Hebronites, the kindred of the Mahlites, the kindred of the Mushites, and the kindred of the Korathites.

The numbering of the Levites.

Kohath begat Amram, ⁵⁹and Amram's wife was called Jochebed, a daughter of Levi who was born to him in Egypt. And she bore to Amram, Aaron, Moses, and Miriam their sister. ⁶⁰And to Aaron were born Nadab, Abihu, Eleazar, and Ithamar. (⁶¹But Nadab and Abihu died because they offered strange fire before the Lord.) ⁶²And their number was 23,000, of all the males from a month old and above. But they were not numbered among the other children of Israel because there was no inheritance given to them among the children of Israel.

Lev 10:1,2

⁶³These are the numbers of the children of Israel, whom Moses and Eleazar the priest numbered in the fields of Moab by the Jordan across from Jericho. ⁶⁴And among these there was not a man of the number of the children of Israel whom Moses and Aaron had counted in the

wilderness of Sinai. ⁶⁵For the Lord had said to them that they would die in the wilderness, and that there would not be left a man of them except Caleb the son of Jephunneh and Joshua the son of Nun.

Chapter 27

The law of the inheritance of the daughters of Zelophehad. The land of promise is shown to Moses, in whose stead Joshua is appointed.

Nu 26:33 and c36. Jos 17:3,4

And then the daughters of Zelophehad the son of Hepher, the son of Gilead, the son of Machir, the son of Manasseh, of the kindreds of Manasseh the son of Joseph (whose names were Mahela, Noa, Hagla, Milcha, and Thirza) ²came and stood before Moses and Eleazar the priest, and before the lords and all the multitude, in the door of the tabernacle of witness, saying, ³Our father died in the wilderness, and was not among the company of those who gathered themselves together against the Lord in the congregation of Korah. But he died in his own sin, and he had no sons. ⁴Why should the name of our father be taken away from among his kindred because he had no son? Give to us a possession of land among the brethren of our father.

Nu c16

⁵And Moses brought their cause before the Lord. ⁶And the Lord spoke to Moses, saying, ⁷The daughters of Zelophehad speak that which is right. You shall give them a possession to inherit among their father's brethren, and shall turn the inheritance of their father to them. ⁸And speak to the children of Israel, saying, If a man dies and has no son, you shall turn his inheritance to his daughter. ⁹If he has no daughter, you shall give his inheritance to his brothers. ¹⁰If he has no brothers, you shall give his inheritance to his father's brothers. ¹¹If he has no father's brothers, you shall give his inheritance to him that is next of kin to him, and let him possess it. And this shall be to the children of Israel an ordinance and a law, as the Lord has commanded Moses.

Nu 36:2

¹²And the Lord said to Moses, Go up this Mount Abarim, and see the land that I have given to the children of Israel. ¹³And when you have seen it, you shall be gathered unto your people also, as Aaron your brother was gathered unto his people. ¹⁴For you were disobedient to my mouth in the desert of Zin, in the strife of the congregation, when you did not hallow me at the water before their eyes; that is, the water of strife at Kadesh in the wilderness of Zin.

Nu 20:2-13 De 32:48-52; 33:8.

¹⁵And Moses spoke to the Lord, saying, ¹⁶Let the Lord God of the spirits of all flesh set a man over the congregation, ¹⁷who may go in and out before them,ᵃ and to lead them in and out, so that the congregation of the Lord will not be as a flock of sheep without a shepherd.

¹⁸And the Lord said to Moses, Take Joshua the son of Nun, in whom there is a spirit, and put your hands upon him; ¹⁹and set him before Eleazar the priest and before all the congregation, and give him a charge in their sight. ²⁰And put of your praiseworthiness upon him so that all the company of the children of Israel may hear. ²¹And he shall stand before Eleazar the priest, who shall ask counsel for him

according to the judgment of Urim before the Lord.^b And at the mouth of Eleazar shall he and all the children of Israel with him – all the congregation – go in and out. ^22And Moses did as the Lord commanded him, and he took Joshua and set him before Eleazar the priest and before all the congregation. ^23And he put his hands upon him and give him a charge, as the Lord commanded through the hand of Moses.

Ezr 2:63
Ne 7:65

The Notes

a) 17. To go in and out before them is to govern, teach, comfort, feed, and defend them, etc.

b) 21. According to the judgment of Urim; that is, according to the judgment of the light. See Exodus 28:30. It is very likely that in the ephod there was some bright stone in which the high priest looked and saw the will of God, as it appears in the story of David and Saul, 1Samuel 28:6.

Chapter 28

What must be offered on every feast day.

And the Lord spoke to Moses, saying, ²Give the children of Israel a charge, and tell them to take heed to offer to me the offering of my food in the sacrifice of a sweet savour in its due season. ³And say to them: This is the offering that you shall offer to the Lord: two lambs of a year old without spot, day by day, to be a burnt offering perpetually. ⁴One lamb you shall offer in the morning and the other at evening, ⁵with also the tenth part of an ephah of flour for a food offering mixed with the fourth part of a hin of beaten oil. ⁶This is a daily offering, ordained at Mount Sinai, for a sweet savour in the sacrifice of the Lord. ⁷And the drink offering of the same: the fourth part of a hin with one lamb. And pour the drink offering in the holy place, to be good drink for the Lord. ⁸And the other lamb you shall offer at evening, with the food offering and the drink offering as in the morning – a sacrifice of a sweet savour to the Lord.

⁹And on the Sabbath day: two lambs of a year old apiece and without spot, and two tenth-parts of flour mixed with oil for a food offering, and the drink offering also. ¹⁰This is the burnt offering of every Sabbath, besides the daily burnt offering and its drink offering.

¹¹And in the first day of your months you shall offer a burnt offering to the Lord: two young bullocks, a ram, and seven lambs of a year old without spot; ¹²and also three tenth-parts of flour for a food offering mixed with oil with each bullock, and two tenth-parts of flour for a food offering mixed with oil with the one ram. ¹³And evermore, a tenth-part of flour mixed with oil for a food offering with each lamb. That is a burnt offering of a sweet savour in the sacrifice of the Lord. ¹⁴And their drink offerings shall be half a hin of wine with a bullock, the third part of a hin of wine with a ram, and the fourth part of a hin with a lamb. This is the burnt offering for every month throughout all the months of a year. ¹⁵And one he-goat for a sin offering to the Lord shall be offered with the daily burnt offering and its drink offering.

¹⁶And the fourteenth day of the first month shall be Passover to the Lord. ¹⁷And on the fifteenth day of the same month shall begin a feast, in which, for seven days, people must eat unleavened bread. ¹⁸The first day shall be a holy feast, so that you shall do no manner of laborious work therein. ¹⁹And you shall offer a burnt offering to the Lord: two bullocks, one ram, and seven lambs of a year old without spot, ²⁰with their food offerings of flour mixed with oil – three tenth-parts with a bullock, two tenth-parts with a ram, ²¹and evermore one tenth-part with a lamb, for each of the seven lambs; ²²and a he-goat for a sin offering, to make an atonement for you. ²³And you shall offer these besides the burnt offering in the morning, which is always offered. ²⁴And in this manner you shall offer, throughout the seven days, the food of the sacrifice of a sweet savour to the Lord. And it shall be done as well as the daily burnt offering and its drink offering. ²⁵And the seventh day shall be a holy feast to you, so that you shall do no laborious work therein.

Ex 12:14-20
Lev 23:5-8
De 16:1-8

²⁶And the day of your firstfruits, when you bring a new food offering to the Lord in your weeks, shall be a holy feast to you, so that you shall do no laborious work therein. ²⁷And you shall offer a burnt offering of a sweet savour to the Lord: two young bullocks, a ram, and seven lambs of a year old apiece, ²⁸with their food offerings of flour mixed with oil – three tenth-parts with a bullock, two tenth-parts with a ram, ²⁹and evermore one tenth-part with a lamb, for each of the seven lambs; ³⁰and a he-goat to make an atonement for you. ³¹And this you shall do besides the daily burnt offering and its food offering. And they shall be without spot, with their drink offerings.

Chapter 29

A review of what must be offered in the first day and other days of the seventh month.

The Feast of Trumpets.
Lev 23:23, 24.

And the first day of the seventh month shall be a holy feast to you, and you shall do no laborious work therein. It shall be a day of trumpet blowing to you. ²And you shall offer a burnt offering of a sweet savour to the Lord: one young bullock, one ram, and seven lambs of a year old apiece that are pure. ³And also their food offerings of flour mixed with oil: three tenth-parts with the bullock, two with the ram, ⁴and one tenth-part with one lamb for each of the seven lambs. ⁵And a he-goat for a sin offering, to make an atonement for you, ⁶besides the burnt offering of the month and its food offering, and besides the daily burnt offering and its food offering, with the drink offerings of the same according to their ordinance, for a savour of sweetness in the sacrifice of the Lord.

The Day of Atonement.
Lev 16:29-34; 23:26-32.

⁷And the tenth day of that same seventh month shall be a holy feast to you, and you shall humble your souls and shall do no manner of work therein. ⁸And you shall offer a burnt offering to the Lord of a sweet savour: one bullock, and a ram, and seven lambs of a year old apiece, without fault. ⁹And their food offerings of flour mixed with oil:

three tenth-parts with a bullock, two with a ram, ^{10}and always a tenth-part with a lamb for each of the seven lambs. ^{11}And one he-goat for a sin offering, besides the sin offering of atonement, the daily burnt offering, and the food and drink offerings that belong to the same.

^{12}And the fifteenth day of the seventh month shall be holy day, and you shall do no laborious work therein; and you shall keep a feast to the Lord of seven days long. ^{13}And you shall offer a burnt offering of a sweet savour to the Lord: thirteen bullocks, two rams, and fourteen lambs that are yearlings and pure, ^{14}with oil – three tenth-parts with every one of the thirteen bullocks, two tenth-parts with each of the rams, ^{15}and one tenth-part with each of the fourteen lambs. ^{16}And one he-goat for a sin offering, besides the daily burnt offering with its food and drink offerings.

The Feast of Tabernacles. Lev 23:33-36.

^{17}And the second day: twelve young bullocks, two rams, and fourteen yearling lambs without spot; ^{18}and their food offerings and drink offerings with the bullocks, rams, and lambs, according to their number and following the ordinance. ^{19}And a he-goat for a sin offering, besides the daily burnt offering and its food and drink offerings.

^{20}And the third day: eleven bullocks, two rams, and fourteen yearling lambs without spot; ^{21}and their food and drink offerings with the bullocks, rams, and lambs, according to their number and following the ordinance. ^{22}And a he-goat for a sin offering, besides the daily burnt offering and its food and drink offerings.

^{23}And the fourth day: ten bullocks, two rams, and fourteen lambs, yearlings and pure; ^{24}and their food and drink offerings with the bullocks, rams, and lambs, according to their number and following the ordinance. ^{25}And a he-goat for a sin offering, besides the daily burnt offering and its food and drink offerings.

^{26}And the fifth day: nine bullocks, two rams, and fourteen lambs of one year old apiece without spot; ^{27}and their food and drink offerings with the bullocks, rams, and lambs, according to their number and following the ordinance. ^{28}And a he-goat for a sin offering, besides the daily burnt offering and its food and drink offerings.

^{29}And the sixth day: eight bullocks, two rams, and fourteen yearling lambs without spot, ^{30}and their food and drink offerings with the bullocks, rams, and lambs, following the ordinance. ^{31}And a he-goat for a sin offering, besides the daily burnt offering and its food and drink offerings.

^{32}And the seventh day: seven bullocks, two rams, and fourteen lambs that are yearlings and pure; ^{33}and their food and drink offerings with the bullocks, rams, and lambs, according to their number and following the ordinance. ^{34}And a he-goat for a sin offering, besides the daily burnt offering and its food and drink offerings.

^{35}And the eighth day shall be the conclusion of the feast to you, and you shall do no manner of laborious work therein. ^{36}And you shall offer a burnt offering of a sweet savour to the Lord: one bullock, one ram, and seven yearling lambs without spot; ^{37}and the food and drink offerings with the bullock, ram, and lambs, according to their numbers and following the ordinance. ³⁸And a he-goat for a sin offering, besides the daily burnt offering and its food and drink offerings.

³⁹These things you shall do for the Lord in your feasts – besides your vowed offerings and freewill offerings – in your burnt offerings, food offerings, drink offerings, and peace offerings.

⁴⁰And Moses told the children of Israel everything that the Lord commanded him.

Chapter 30

Of vows: when they are binding and when not.

And Moses spoke to the heads of the tribes of the children of Israel, saying, This is the thing which the Lord commands. ²If any man vows a vow to the Lord, or swears an oath and binds his soul,ᵃ he must not go back on his word, but must fulfil all that proceeds out of his mouth.

³If a damsel vows a vow to the Lord and binds herself, being in her father's house and unmarried, ⁴if her father hears her vow and the bond that she has put upon her soul and holds his peace at it, then all her vows and bonds that she has put upon her soul shall stand in effect. ⁵But if her father forbids her the same day that he hears it, none of her vows or bonds that she put upon her soul will be in effect, and the Lord will forgive her, because her father forbade her.

⁶If she had a husband when she vowed or pronounced anything out of her lips whereby she bound her soul, ⁷and her husband heard it and held his peace at it the same day he heard it, then her vows and her bonds with which she bound her soul shall stand in effect. ⁸But if her husband forbade her the same day that he heard it, then he has made her vow which she had upon her of no effect, and also that which she pronounced with her lips whereby she bound her soul; and the Lord will forgive her.

⁹The vow of a widow or of her who is divorced, and everything that she has bound her soul with, shall stand in effect with her. ¹⁰If she vowed in her husband's house, or bound her soul with an oath, ¹¹and her husband heard it and held his peace and did not forbid her, then all her vows and bonds with which she bound her soul shall stand. ¹²But if her husband annulled them the same day that he heard them, then nothing that proceeded out of her lips in vows or in bonds by which she bound her soul shall stand in effect, because her husband has loosed them; and the Lord will forgive her.

¹³All vows and binding oaths to humble the soul, a woman's husband may establish or break. ¹⁴If her husband holds his peace from one day to another, then he establishes all the vows and bonds that she had upon her, because he held his peace the same day that he heard them. ¹⁵But if he later nullifies them, he shall bear her sin himself.

¹⁶These are the ordinances which the Lord commanded Moses as between a man and his wife, and as between a father and his daughter, being a damsel in her father's house.

The Notes

a) 2. This vow here is that which a person vows to do for a certain space of time, whether it be to fast or to chastise the body or any other thing, as for example concerning vows of abstinence in Numbers c6.

Chapter 31

The Midianites and Balaam are slain. Prisoners of war and livestock carried off as spoils are brought to Moses and equally divided. A gift is given by Israel because none of their men were slain.

And the Lord spoke to Moses, saying, ²Avenge the children of Israel upon the Midianites, and afterward be gathered unto your people. ³And Moses spoke to the folk, saying, Equip some of your men for war, and let them go upon the Midianites and avenge the Lord upon the Midianites. ⁴You shall send to the war a thousand from each of the tribes of Israel. ⁵And there were taken out of the thousands of Israel 12,000 men prepared for war, from every tribe a thousand. ⁶And Moses sent them to war, a thousand from every tribe, with Phineas the son of Eleazar the priest, and the holy vessels, and the trumpets to blow under his hand. ⁷And they warred against the Midianites, as the Lord commanded Moses, and slew all the males. ⁸And they slew the kings of Midian, among others that were slain: Evi, Rekem, Zur, Hur, and Reba – five kings of Midian. And they slew Balaam the son of Beor with the sword. ⁹And the children of Israel took all the women of Midian prisoners with their children, and carried off as spoil all their livestock, their substance, and their goods. ¹⁰And they burned all the towns wherein they dwelt and all their forts with fire. ¹¹And they took all the spoils and all that they could capture, both of man and beast. ¹²And they brought the captives and that which they had taken, all the spoils, to Moses and Eleazar the priest, and to the company of the children of Israel – to the host in the fields of Moab by the Jordan River across from Jericho. ¹³And Moses, Eleazar the priest, and all the lords of the congregation went out of the host to meet them. ¹⁴But Moses was angry with the officers of the army – with the captains over the thousands and over the hundreds who came from the war and battle – ¹⁵and he said to them, Have you saved the women alive? ¹⁶Look, these caused the children of Israel, through Balaam, to commit trespass against the Lord by reason of Peor, and there followed a plague among the congregation of the Lord. ¹⁷Now therefore, slay all the menchildren and the women who have lain carnally with men. ¹⁸But all the women-children who have not lain with men, keep alive for yourselves. ¹⁹And lodge outside the host for seven days everyone who has killed any person, and everyone who has touched any dead body. And purify both yourselves and your prisoners on the third day and the seventh. ²⁰And sprinkle all your garments, and everything

Nu 25:16-18

Jos 13:21,22

Nu 25:18
2Pe 2:15

J'g 21:10-12

Nu 19:11-22

that is made of skins, all work of goats' hair, and everything made of wood.

²¹And Eleazar the priest said to all the men of war who had gone out to battle, This is the ordinance of the law which the Lord commanded Moses: ²²Gold, silver, bronze, iron, tin, and lead, ²³and everything that can withstand fire, you shall make go through the fire; and then it is clean. Nevertheless, it shall be sprinkled with sprinkling water. And everything that cannot withstand fire, you shall make go through the water. ²⁴And wash your clothes the seventh day, and then you are clean. And afterward, come into the host.

²⁵And the Lord spoke to Moses, saying, ²⁶Take the total of both the women and the livestock that were taken – you, Eleazar the priest, and the ancestral heads of the congregation. ²⁷And divide it into two shares, between those who took the war upon themselves and went out to battle, and all the rest of the congregation. ²⁸And take a portion for the Lord from the share of the men of war who went out to battle: one of every 500 of the women, of the oxen, of the donkeys, and of the sheep. ²⁹And you shall take it from their half and give it to Eleazar the priest, a lift offering to the Lord. ³⁰And from the half of the children of Israel take one of every 50 of the women, of the oxen, of the donkeys, and of the sheep, and of all manner of beasts, and give them to the Levites who keep the habitation of the Lord.

³¹And Moses and Eleazar the priest did as the Lord commanded Moses. ³²And the booty and the captives that the men of war had taken was 675,000 sheep, ³³72,000 oxen, ³⁴61,000 donkeys, ³⁵and 32,000 women that had lain by no man.

³⁶The half that was the share of those who went out to war was 337,500 sheep, ³⁷and the Lord's portion of the sheep was 675. ³⁸And the oxen were 36,000, of which the Lord's portion was 72. ³⁹And the donkeys were 30,500, of which the Lord's portion was 61. ⁴⁰And the women were 16,000, of which the Lord's portion was 32 souls. ⁴¹And Moses gave the total that was the Lord's lift offering to Eleazar the priest, as the Lord commanded Moses.

⁴²And the other half, which Moses separated out for the children of Israel apart from the men of war ⁴³(that is to say, the half that fell to the congregation*), it was also 337,500 sheep, ⁴⁴36,000 oxen, ⁴⁵30,500 donkeys, ⁴⁶and 16,000 women. ⁴⁷And Moses took from this half that belonged to the children of Israel one from every fifty, both of the women and of the livestock, and gave them to the Levites who kept the habitation of the Lord, as the Lord commanded Moses.

⁴⁸And the officers over thousands of the army – the captains of the thousands and the captains of the hundreds – came forward. ⁴⁹And they said to Moses, Your servants have counted the men of war that were under our hand, and there is not one man of them missing. ⁵⁰We have therefore brought as a gift to the Lord what every man found of jewelry of gold – chains, bracelets, rings, earrings, and spangles – to make an atonement for our souls before the Lord.

*who were not at the war.

⁵¹And Moses and Eleazar took the gold from them, jewelry of all kinds. ⁵²And all the gold of the lift offering of the Lord from the captains over thousands and hundreds was 16,750 sickles, ⁵³which the men of war had carried off as spoils, every man for himself. ⁵⁴And Moses and Eleazar the priest took the gold from the captains over the thousands and over the hundreds and brought it into the tabernacle of witness, to bring the children of Israel to the remembrance of the Lord.

Chapter 32

> To Reuben and Gad, and to half the tribe of Manasseh, is promised possession of the land beyond the Jordan River eastward if they will bring their brethren into the land of promise.

The children of Reuben and the children of Gad had an exceedingly great multitude of flocks and herds. And when they saw the land of Jazer and the land of Gilead, that it was a suitable place for pasture animals, ²they came and spoke to Moses and Eleazar the priest, and to the lords of the congregation, saying, ³The land of Ataroth, Dibon, Jazer, Nimrah, Heshbon, Elealeh, Shebam, Nebo, and Beon, ⁴which country the Lord smote before the congregation of Israel, is a land for pasture animals, and we your servants have pasture animals. ⁵Therefore (said they), if we have found grace in your sight, let this land be given to your servants to possess, and do not bring us over the Jordan River.

⁶And Moses said to the children of Gad and of Reuben, Shall your brethren go to war and you tarry here? ⁷Why do you discourage the hearts of the children of Israel from going over into the land that the Lord has given them? ⁸This your fathers did, when I sent them from Kadesh Barnea to see the land. ⁹And they went up to the river of Escol and saw the land, but discouraged the hearts of the children of Israel from going into the land that the Lord had given them. ¹⁰And the Lord was wroth at that time and swore, saying, ¹¹None of the men that came out of Egypt, from twenty years old and above, shall see the land that I swore to Abraham, Isaac, and Jacob, because they have not continually followed me – ¹²save Caleb the son of Jephunneh the Kenizzite and Joshua the son of Nun, for they have followed me continually. ¹³And the Lord was angry with Israel, and made them wander in the wilderness for forty years until all the generation that had done evil in the sight of the Lord was consumed. ¹⁴And behold: you are risen up in your father's stead, the progeny of sinful men, to augment the fierce wrath of the Lord toward Israel. ¹⁵For if you turn away from following him, he will yet again leave the people in the wilderness; and so will you destroy all this folk.

¹⁶And they went near him and said, We will build enclosures here for our flocks and for our herds, and settlements for our children. ¹⁷But we ourselves will go ready-armed before the children of Israel until we have brought them to their place. And our children may dwell in the

NUMBERS 32

fortified settlements, because of the inhabiters of the land. ¹⁸And we will not return to our houses until the children of Israel have obtained each one his inheritance. ¹⁹For we would rather not inherit with them on the far side of the Jordan and beyond, because our inheritance is fallen to us on this side of the Jordan eastward.

Jos 1:12-15

²⁰And Moses said to them, If you will do this thing – that you will go all equipped before the Lord to war, ²¹and will go all of you in arms over the Jordan before the Lord until he has cast out his enemies before him, ²²and until the land is subdued before the Lord – then you may return and be without sin against the Lord and against Israel, and this land will be your possession before the Lord. ²³But if you will not do so, behold, you sin against the Lord; and be sure, your sin will find you out. ²⁴Build your settlements for your children and folds for your flocks, and see that you do what you have spoken.

²⁵And the children of Gad and of Reuben spoke to Moses, saying, Your servants will do as my lord commands. ²⁶Our children, our wives, our substance, and all our livestock will remain here in the towns of Gilead, ²⁷but we your servants will go all equipped for the war into battle before the Lord, as my lord has said.

Jos 1:16

Jos 4:12,13

²⁸And Moses commanded Eleazar the priest, Joshua the son of Nun, and the ancestral heads of the tribes of the children of Israel, ²⁹and said to them, If the children of Gad and Reuben will go with you over the Jordan, all prepared to fight before the Lord, then when the land is subdued to you, give them the land of Gilead to possess. ³⁰But if they will not go over with you in arms, then they shall have their possessions among you in the land of Canaan.

³¹And the children of Gad and Reuben answered, saying, That which the Lord has said to your servants, we will do. ³²We will go armed before the Lord into the land of Canaan, and the landholding of our inheritance will be on this side of the Jordan.

Jos 22:1-4
De 3:8-10

³³And Moses gave to the children of Gad and of Reuben, and to half the tribe of Manasseh the son of Joseph, the kingdom of Sihon king of the Amorites and the kingdom of Og king of Bashan – the land that belonged to their towns and cities in the region of the country round about. ³⁴And the children of Gad rebuilt Dibon, Ataroth, Aroer, ³⁵Atroth, Shophan, Jazer, Jogbehah, ³⁶Beth Nimrah, and Beth Haran, strong cities; and they built folds for their flocks. ³⁷And the children of Reuben rebuilt Heshbon, Elealeh, Kirjathaim, ³⁸Nebo, and Baal Meon, and changed their names; and Shibmah also. And they gave names to the settlements they built.

Ge 15:21
De 3:12-17

³⁹And the children of Machir the son of Manasseh went to Gilead and took it, and put out the Amorites that were there. ⁴⁰And Moses gave Gilead to Machir the son of Manasseh, and he dwelt in it. ⁴¹And Jair the son of Manasseh went and took its small towns, and called them the Towns of Jair. ⁴²And Nobah went and took Kenath with the towns belonging to it, and called it Nobah after his own name.

Chapter 33

The stages of Israel's journey and their departures from place to place are enumerated. They are commanded to kill the Canaanites.

These were the stages in the journey of the children of Israel, who went out of the land of Egypt in their companies under Moses and Aaron. ²Moses recorded their departures for each leg of their journey, at the commandment of the Lord. This is the record of their departures, each time they set out on another leg of their journey.

³The children of Israel departed from Rameses the fifteenth day of the first month, on the morrow after Passover. They went out openly in the sight of all Egypt ⁴while the Egyptians buried all their firstborn, whom the Lord had smitten among them. And their gods also the Lord judged and destroyed.* ⁵And so the children of Israel removed from Rameses and pitched camp in Succoth. ⁶And they departed from Succoth and pitched their tents in Etham, which is in the edge of the wilderness. ⁷And they removed from Etham and turned toward the way into Hahiroth, which is before Baal Zephon, and pitched before Migdol. ⁸And they departed from before Hahiroth and went through the middle of the sea into the wilderness, and went a three-day journey in the wilderness of Etham, and pitched in Marah. ⁹And they removed from Marah and went to Elim where there were twelve springs of water and seventy date trees, and they pitched there.

¹⁰And they removed from Elim and lay next to the Red Sea. ¹¹And they removed from the Red Sea and lay in the wilderness of Sin. ¹²And they took their journey out of the wilderness of Sin and set up their tents in Dophkah. ¹³And they departed from Dophkah and lay in Alush. ¹⁴And they removed from Alush and lay at Rephidim, where there was no water for the people to drink. ¹⁵And they departed from Rephidim and pitched in the wilderness of Sinai.

¹⁶And they removed from the desert of Sinai and lodged at the Graves of Lust. ¹⁷And they departed from the Sepulchres of Lust and lay at Hazeroth. ¹⁸And they departed from Hazeroth and pitched in Rithmah. ¹⁹And departed from Rithmah and pitched at Rimmon Perez. ²⁰And they departed from Rimmon Perez and pitched in Libnah.

²¹And they removed from Libnah and pitched at Rissah. ²²And they journeyed from Rissah and pitched at Kehelathah. ²³And they went from Kehelathah and pitched in Mount Shepher. ²⁴And they removed from Mount Shepher and lay in Haradah. ²⁵And they removed from Haradah and pitched in Makheloth.

²⁶And they removed from Makheloth and lay at Tahath, ²⁷and they departed from Tahath and pitched at Terah. ²⁸And they removed from Terah and pitched in Mithkah. ²⁹And they went from Mithkah and lodged in Hashmonah. ³⁰And they departed from Hashmonah and lay at Moseroth. ³¹And they departed from Moseroth and pitched in Bane Jakan. ³²And they went from Bane Jakan and lay at Hor Hagidgad.

Margin notes:
Ex 12:37
*[Their gods: poss. meaning their judges and rulers. Ex 12:12 and c21, note a.]
Ex 13:20
Ex 14:1
Ex 14:21,22
Ex 15:22
Ex 15:27
Ex 16:1
Ex 17:1
Ex 19:1
Nu 11:34
Nu 11:35

³³And they went from Hor Hagidgad and pitched in Jotbathah. ³⁴And they removed from Jotbathah and lay at Abronah. ³⁵And they departed from Abronah and lay at Ezion Geber. ³⁶And they removed from Ezion Geber and pitched in the wilderness of Zin, which is Kadesh.

³⁷And they removed from Kadesh and pitched in Mount Hor, at the edge of the land of Edom. ³⁸And Aaron the priest went up into Mount Hor at the commandment of the Lord and died there, even in the fortieth year after the children of Israel had come out of the land of Egypt, in the first day of the fifth month. ³⁹And Aaron was 133 years old when he died in Mount Hor.

⁴⁰And King Arad the Canaanite, who dwelt in the south of the land of Canaan, heard that the children of Israel were come.

⁴¹And they departed from Mount Hor and pitched in Zalmonah. ⁴²And they departed from Zalmonah and pitched in Punon. ⁴³And they departed from Punon and pitched in Oboth. ⁴⁴And they departed from Oboth and pitched in Egebarim at the border of Moab. ⁴⁵And they departed from Egebarim and pitched in Dibon Gad. ⁴⁶And they removed from Dibon Gad and lay in Almon Diblathaim. ⁴⁷And they removed from Almon Diblathaim and pitched in the mountains of Abarim before Nebo. ⁴⁸And they departed from the mountains of Abarim and pitched in the fields of Moab by the Jordan across from Jericho. ⁴⁹And they pitched along the Jordan, from Beth Jesimoth to the plain of Abel-Satim in the fields of Moab.

⁵⁰And the Lord spoke to Moses in the fields of Moab by the Jordan River across from Jericho, saying, ⁵¹Speak to the children of Israel and say to them: When you have gone over the Jordan into the land of Canaan, ⁵²see that you drive out all the inhabiters of the land before you, and destroy their chapels* and all their images of metal, and pull down all their altars built on hills. ⁵³And possess the land and dwell in it; for I have given you the land to enjoy. ⁵⁴And you shall divide the inheritance of the land by lot among your kindreds, and give to the greater number the greater inheritance and to the fewer the lesser inheritance. And your inheritances shall be in the tribes of your fathers, in the place where every man's lot falls.

⁵⁵But if you will not drive out the inhabiters of the land before you, then those which you let remain of them will be thorns in your eyes and darts in your sides,^a and will trouble you in the land wherein you dwell. ⁵⁶Moreover, it will come to pass that I will do to you as I thought to do to them.

*After the Chaldee, Rabbi Sallo., and Rabbi Abr.: engraved paving stones.

Nu 20:1
Nu 20:22
Nu 20:23-28
De 32:50
Nu 21:4,10-13.
Nu 22:1

The Notes

a) 55. Thorns in your eyes, etc: that is, they will be your rod, scourge, and undoing.

Chapter 34

The coasts and borders of the land of promise. Certain men are assigned to divide up the land.

And the Lord spoke to Moses, saying, ²Command the children of Israel and say to them: When you come into the land of Canaan, this is the land that will fall to your inheritance – the land of Canaan with all her borders:

³Your southern border will be from the wilderness of Zin along by the border of Edom, so that your southern border will be from the side of the Salt Sea* eastward, ⁴and will curve around from the south up to Akrabbim, and then reach to Zin. And it will go forth from the south side of Kadesh Barnea, go on also to Hazar Addar, and go along to Azmon; ⁵and will curve around from Azmon to the river of Egypt, and end at the Great Sea.‡

⁶And your western border will be the Great Sea, which coastline shall be your western border.

⁷And this will be your northern border: you shall take a bearing from the Great Sea to Mount Hor. ⁸And from Mount Hor, you shall take a bearing and go to Hamath; and the border will continue as far as Zedad, ⁹and then reach to Ziphron and end at Hazar Enan. And this will be your northern border.

¹⁰And you shall mark your eastern border from Hazar Enan to Shepham, ¹¹and the border will go down from Shepham to Riblah on the east side of Ain. Then it will descend and reach as far as the side of the sea of Chinnereth eastward, ¹²and then go down along the Jordan River and end at the Salt Sea.

And this will be your land with all its borders round about.

¹³And Moses commanded the children of Israel, saying, This is the land that you will inherit by lot, and which the Lord commanded to give to nine and a half tribes. ¹⁴For the tribe of the children of Reuben have received their lot, according to the households of their fathers, and the tribe of the children of Gad according to their fathers' households, and half the tribe of Manasseh have received their inheritance; ¹⁵that is to say, two and a half tribes have received their inheritance on the other side of the Jordan by Jericho eastward, toward the sun rising.

¹⁶And the Lord spoke to Moses, saying, ¹⁷These are the names of the men who will divide up the land to inherit: Eleazar the priest and Joshua the son of Nun. ¹⁸And you shall take also a lord from every tribe to divide up the land, ¹⁹whose names are these: in the tribe of Judah, Caleb the son of Jephunneh. ²⁰In the tribe of the children of Simeon, Shemuel the son of Ammihud. ²¹In the tribe of Benjamin, Elidad the son of Chislon. ²²In the tribe of the children of Dan, the lord Bukki the son of Jogli. ²³Among the children of Joseph: in the tribe of the children of Manasseh, the lord Hanniel the son of Ephod, ²⁴and in the tribe of the children of Ephraim, the lord Kemuel the son of Shiphtan. ²⁵In the tribe of the sons of Zebulun, the lord Elizaphan the son of Parnach. ²⁶In the tribe of the children of Issachar, the lord Paltiel the son of Azzan. ²⁷In the tribe of the sons of Asher, the lord Ahihud the son of Shelomi. ²⁸In the tribe of the children of Naphtali, the lord Pedahel the son of Ammihud. ²⁹These are they whom the Lord commanded to allocate the inheritance of the children of Israel in the land of Canaan.

Jos 15:1-12

*[ie, the Dead Sea]

‡[ie, the Mediterranean Sea]

Nu 32:28-42
De 3:12-20
Jos 14:3

Jos 14:1,2

Chapter 35

To the Levites must be given towns and pasture lands.
The cities of refuge or sanctuaries. The law of murder.
For one person's witness no one should be condemned.

And the Lord spoke to Moses in the fields of Moab by the Jordan River across from Jericho, saying, ²Command the children of Israel to give the Levites towns and cities to dwell in, from their inheritances of land. And you shall give, in addition to towns for the Levites, pasture lands round about them. ³The towns will be for the Levites to dwell in, and the pasture lands for their herds, flocks, and all manner of beasts of theirs.

⁴And the pasture lands of the towns that you give to the Levites shall reach from the wall of the town outward a thousand cubits round about. ⁵And you shall measure outside the town, and make the outermost border of the eastern side two thousand cubits in length. And the outermost border of the southern side shall be two thousand cubits in length, and the outermost border of the western side two thousand cubits, and the outermost border of the northern side two thousand cubits also. And the town shall be in the middle. And these shall be the pasture lands for their towns.

⁶And among the places that you give to the Levites, there shall be six cities of refuge, which you shall give to the intent that a person who kills another may flee to any of them. And to these cities you shall add forty-two towns more, ⁷so that all the towns and cities that you give the Levites will be forty-eight, with their pasture lands. ⁸And of the places that you shall give out of the landholdings of the children of Israel, you shall give many from the holdings of those who have much, and few out of the holdings of those who have little, so that every tribe shall give to the Levites from their towns in proportion to the inheritance which it received.

⁹And the Lord spoke to Moses, saying, ¹⁰Speak to the children of Israel and say to them: When you have gone over the Jordan into the land of Canaan, ¹¹you shall build cities which will be places of sanctuary for you, so that he who slays a man unintentionally may flee there. ¹²And the cities shall be to flee to from a kinsman avenger, so that he who killed will not die until he has stood before the congregation in judgment. ¹³And of these six sanctuary cities that you shall give, ¹⁴three you shall give on this side of the Jordan River and three in the land of Canaan. ¹⁵And these six sanctuary cities will be for the children of Israel, for the stranger, and for him who dwells among you, so that anyone who kills a person unintentionally may flee there.

¹⁶If anyone strikes another with an iron weapon so that he dies, then he is a murderer and shall die for it. ¹⁷If he strikes another by throwing a stone so that he dies, then he shall die, for he is a murderer and shall therefore be slain. ¹⁸If he hits him with a wooden hand weapon so that he dies, then he shall die, for he is a murderer and shall therefore be slain. ¹⁹The avenger of blood may slay the murderer as

soon as he finds him. ²⁰If anyone shoves another out of hate, or lies in wait and hurls at him so that he dies, ²¹or beats him with his fist out of malevolence so that he dies, he who assaulted the other shall die, for he is a murderer. The avenger of blood may slay him as soon as he finds him.

²²But if he pushed him by chance and not from hate, or flung any manner of thing at him but was not lying in wait, ²³or cast any manner of stone at him so that he died by it but did not see him – and he cast it upon him and he died, but he was not his enemy neither sought him any harm – ²⁴then the congregation shall judge between the slayer and the avenger of blood in such cases. ²⁵And the congregation shall deliver the slayer out of the hand of the avenger of blood, and shall restore him again to the sanctuary city to which he had fled. And he shall dwell there until the death of the high priest who was anointed with holy oil.

Jos 20:4-6

²⁶But if he goes outside the boundaries of the sanctuary city to which he fled, ²⁷and if the blood-avenger finds him outside the boundaries of his place of refuge, he may slay him and be guiltless, ²⁸because he should have remained in his sanctuary city until the death of the high priest. But after the death of the high priest, he may return again to the land of his possession.

²⁹And this shall be an ordinance and a law to you among your children after you in all your habitations.

³⁰Whoever slays shall be slain at the mouth of two or more witnesses; for one witness may not testify against a person to put him to death.ᵃ ³¹Moreover, you shall take no amends-money for the life of a murderer who is worthy to die, but he shall be put to death. ³²Also, you shall take no amends-money for him that has fled to a sanctuary city in order to let him go back and dwell in the land before the death of the high priest.

2Co 13:1

³³And see that you pollute not the land that you are in, for blood defiles the land. And the land cannot be cleansed of the blood that is shed in it otherwise than by the blood of him that shed it. ³⁴Defile not, therefore, the land that you inhabit, and in the midst of which I also dwell. For I am the Lord who dwells among the children of Israel.

The Notes

a)   30. For one man's witness ought no man to be condemned.

Chapter 36

> An order for the marriage of the daughters of Zelophehad. No one from the tribes may intermarry with another, but every man must take for himself a wife from his own tribe.

And the ancestral heads of the children of Gilead the son of Machir, the son of Manasseh, of the kindred of the children of Joseph, came forward and spoke before Moses and the leaders who were the ances-

NUMBERS 36

tral heads among the children of Israel. ²And they said, The Lord commanded my lord to give the land to inherit by lot to the children of Israel. And then my lord commanded in the name of the Lord to give the inheritance of Zelophehad our brother to his daughters. ³Now, when any of the sons of the tribes of Israel take them as wives, then their inheritance will be taken from the inheritance of our fathers and added to the inheritance of the tribe in which they are; and thus it will be taken from the lot of our inheritance. ⁴And when the free year* comes to the children of Israel, then their inheritance will be added to the inheritance of the tribe in which they are, and in this manner their inheritance will be taken away from the inheritance of the tribe of our fathers.

⁵And Moses commanded the children of Israel at the mouth of the Lord, saying, The tribe of the children of Joseph have said well. ⁶This therefore does the Lord command the daughters of Zelophehad, saying, Let them be wives to whom they themselves think best, but only in the kindred of the tribe of their fathers shall they marry, ⁷so that the inheritance of the children of Israel does not roll from tribe to tribe, and so that the children of Israel may abide, everyone in the inheritance of the tribe of his fathers.

⁸And every daughter that possesses any inheritance among the tribes of the children of Israel shall be wife to one of the kindred of the tribe of her father, so that everyone among the children of Israel may enjoy the inheritance of his father, ⁹and so that the inheritance does not go from one tribe to another, but to the intent that in the tribes of the children of Israel everyone may abide in his own inheritance.

¹⁰And as the Lord commanded Moses, so did the daughters of Zelophehad do; ¹¹that is, Mahela, Thirza, Hagla, Milcha, and Noa. And they were married to their father's brothers' sons, ¹²of the kindred of the children of Manasseh the son of Joseph. And thus they had their inheritance in the tribe of the kindred of their father.

¹³These are the commandments and laws which the Lord commanded through Moses for the children of Israel,
in the fields of Moab by the Jordan
River across from
Jericho.

The end of the fourth book of Moses.

Margin notes:
- Nu 33:54; 26:33; 27:1-11.
- *[Free year: the year of Jubilee. Lev c25.]
- Tob 7:12 [In the MB, the content of the apocryphal book Tobit differs from that of later English versions, making it difficult to assign verse numbers. See preface.]

The Fifth Book of Moses
called
Deuteronomy

Chapter 1

A brief review of things that happened before, from pitching camp at Mount Horeb until they got to Kadesh Barnea.

THESE ARE THE WORDS that Moses spoke to all Israel on the other side of the Jordan River* in the wilderness, in the plain by the Red Sea between Paran and Tophel, Laban, Hazeroth, and Dizahab, ²an eleven days' journey from Horeb to Kadesh Barnea by the way that leads to Mount Seir. ³It came to pass, on the first day of the eleventh month in the fortieth year, that Moses spoke to the children of Israel according to all that the Lord had given him in commandment for them, ⁴after he defeated Sihon the king of the Amorites, who dwelt in Heshbon, and Og the king of Bashan, who dwelt at Ashtaroth in Edrei.

⁵On the other side of the Jordan in the land of Moab, Moses began to expound this law, saying, ⁶The Lord our God spoke to us in Horeb,ᵃ saying, You have dwelt long enough in this mount. ⁷Depart, therefore, and take your journey, and go to the hills of the Amorites and to all the places near there: fields, hills, and dales; and to the south; and to the sea's side in the land of Canaan; and to Lebanon, even to the great river Euphrates. ⁸Behold, I have set the land before you. Go in, therefore, and possess the land that the Lord swore to your fathers Abraham, Isaac, and Jacob, to give to them and their seed after them.

⁹And I said to you at that time, I am not able to bear you myself alone. ¹⁰For the Lord your God has multiplied you, so that you are this day as the stars of heaven in number. ¹¹May the Lord God of your fathers make you a thousand times so many more as you are, and bless you as he has promised you! ¹²But how (said I) can I myself alone bear the troubles, burdens, and strife that is among you? ¹³Bring therefore men of wisdom and understanding, proven by experience among your tribes, so that I may set them over you.

¹⁴And you answered me and said, That which you have spoken is good to be done. ¹⁵And then I took the chief men of your tribes, men of wisdom and that were proven, and set them over you as heads over thousands and over hundreds, over fifty and over ten, and officers among your tribes.

¹⁶And I charged your judges at the same time, saying, Hear your brethren, and judge righteously between one person and another, and the stranger that is with him. ¹⁷See that you prefer no man in judgment, but hear the small as well as the great. And be afraid of no one, for the judgment is God's. And the cause that is too hard for you, bring to me and I will hear it. ¹⁸And I commanded you at that time all the things that you should do.

*[The other side of the Jordan River is the east side]

Ex 18:13-26

Judges.

Lev 19:15
Pr 24:23
Ec'us 42:1,2

¹⁹And then we departed from Horeb, and walked through all that great and terrible wilderness that you saw along the way that leads to the hills of the Amorites, as the Lord our God commanded us, and came to Kadesh Barnea. ²⁰And there I said to you, You have come to the hills of the Amorites, which the Lord our God is giving to us. ²¹Behold, the Lord your God has set the land before you. Go up and conquer it. As the Lord God of your fathers says to you, fear not; neither be discouraged.

²²And then you all came to me and said, Let us send men before us to scout out the land, and to bring word back to us about the way we should go up and what cities to go to. ²³And the idea pleased me well, so I took twelve men of you, one from every tribe. ²⁴And they departed and went up into the high country, and came to the river Escol and searched it out. ²⁵And they took some of the fruit of the land in their hands and brought it down to us, and brought word back to us and said, It is a good land that the Lord our God is giving to us.

Nu 13:23-27

²⁶Notwithstanding, you would not consent to go up, but were disobedient to the mouth of the Lord your God.* ²⁷You murmured in your tents and said, Because the Lord hates us,ᵇ therefore he has brought us out of the land of Egypt, to deliver us into the hands of the Amorites and to destroy us. ²⁸How can we go up? Our brethren have discouraged our hearts, saying, The people are greater and taller than we, and the cities are great, and walled even up to heaven; and moreover, we saw the sons of the Anakim there.

*The people, being unfaithful, would not go into the land promised.

Nu 13:28,29

²⁹And I said to you, Dread not, and be not afraid of them. ³⁰The Lord your God who goes before you, he will fight for you, just as he did for you in Egypt before your eyes, ³¹and in the wilderness. You have seen how the Lord your God carried you as a man would carry his child, all through the way that you have gone until you came to this place. ³²And yet for all this, you did not believe the Lord your God, ³³who goes in the way before you to search out a place for you to pitch your tents – in fire by night so that you may see what way to go, and in a cloud by day.

Ex 13:21,22

³⁴And the Lord heard the voice of your words and was wroth, and he swore, saying, ³⁵Not one of these men of this perverse generation will see that good land which I swore to give to your fathers, ³⁶except Caleb the son of Jephunneh. He will see it, and to him I will give the land that he has walked in, and to his children, because he has continually followed the Lord. ³⁷Likewise, the Lord was angry with me because of you, saying, You also will not go into the land. ³⁸But Joshua the son of Nun, who stands before you, he shall go in; encourage him, therefore, for he will divide out the heritage to Israel. ³⁹Moreover, your children, whom you said would be taken captive, and your sons, who know neither good nor bad this day, they will go into the land; to them I will give it and they will enjoy it. ⁴⁰But as for you, turn back and take your journey into the wilderness by the way to the Red Sea.

Nu 14:28-30

Jos 1:6

Nu 14:31

⁴¹Then you answered and said to me, We have sinned against the

Lord. We will go up and fight, according to all that the Lord our God commanded us! And when you had girded on every man his weapons of war, and were ready to go up into the hills, ⁴²the Lord said to me, Say to them: See that you do not go up, and that you fight not, for I am not among you; lest you be plagued before your enemies. ⁴³But when I told you, you would not hear, but disobeyed the mouth of the Lord and went presumptuously up into the hills.ᶜ

⁴⁴Then the Amorites who dwelt in those hills came out against you, and chased you as bees do, and cut you down in Seir, even as far as Hormah. ⁴⁵And you came back again and wept before the Lord. But the Lord would not hear your voice, and inclined not his ears to you. ⁴⁶And so you remained in Kadesh a long season.

Nu 14:39-45

v45 e.f. COV.

The Notes

a) 6. Horeb and Sinai are both one.
b) 27. God is said to hate a person when he puts him out of his heart and gives him not of his grace. Psalms 5:4-6 and 30:7.
c) 43. Here you see the very image of us who live in this most perilous time [c1530-1550]. For even we likewise, where we have God's word, do not believe it, and where we do not have it, there we are bold.

Chapter 2

> A review of that which was done from the time that they departed from Kadesh Barnea to the battle against the kings Sihon and Og.

Then we turned and took our journey into the wilderness by the Way of the Red Sea, as the Lord commanded me. And we made the round of the mountains of Seir a long time. ²Then the Lord spoke to me, saying, ³You have gone around these mountains long enough; turn northward. ⁴And warn the people, saying, You will go through the territory of your brethren, the children of Esau who dwell in Seir, and they will be afraid of you. But take good heed to yourselves, ⁵not to provoke them. For I will not give you any of their land – no, not so much as a foot breadth – because I have given Mount Seir to Esau to possess. ⁶You shall buy food to eat from them with money, and you shall buy water to drink from them with money; ⁷for the Lord your God has blessed you in all the works of your hands, and cared for you as you went through this great wilderness. Moreover, the Lord your God has been with you these forty years so that you have lacked nothing.

⁸And when we departed from our brethren, the children of Esau who dwelt in Seir, by the way of the plain from Elath and Ezion Geber, we turned and went by the way to the wilderness of Moab. ⁹Then the Lord said to me, See that you do not encroach upon the Moabites, neither provoke them to battle. For I will not give you any of their land to possess, because I have given Ar to the children of Lot to possess. ¹⁰The Emimᵃ dwelt there in times past, a people great, many, and tall like the Anakim, ¹¹who also were taken for giants like the Anakim. And the Moabites called them Emim. ¹²In like manner, the

Horites[b] formerly dwelt in Seir, whom the children of Esau cast out and destroyed from before them, and dwelt there in their place, just as Israel did in the land of their possession which the Lord gave them.

[13]Now rise up (said I) and go over the river Zered. And we went over the river Zered. [14]The time in which we traveled from Kadesh Barnea until we crossed over the river Zered was 38 years, until the entire generation of the men of war had died in the host, as the Lord had sworn to them. [15]For indeed, the hand of the Lord was against them, to destroy them out of the host till they were all gone.

[16]And as soon as all the men of war were gone and had died away from among the people, [17]then the Lord spoke to me, saying, [18]You shall go through Ar by the boundary of Moab this day, [19]and will approach near to the children of Ammon. See that you do not encroach upon them nor yet provoke them. For I will not give you any of the land of the children of Ammon to possess, because I have given it to the children of Lot to possess.

([20]That land also was taken for a land of giants, and giants dwelt there in the old time. The Ammonites called them Zamzummim[c] – [21]a people that was great, many, and tall like the Anakim.[d] But the Lord destroyed them before the Ammonites, and they cast them out and dwelt there instead, [22]as he had done for the children of Esau who dwell in Seir; he destroyed the Horites before them and they cast them out, and they dwell in their places to this day. [23]And the Avim who dwelt in Hazzurim, even as far as Gaza, the Caphtorim who came out of Caphtor destroyed; and they dwelt in their places.)

Nu 21:24

[24]Rise up (said the Lord): Take your journey, and go over the river Arnon. Behold, I have given into your hand Sihon, the Amorite king of Heshbon, and his land. Go forth and conquer, and provoke him to battle. [25]This day I will begin to send the fear and dread of you upon all the nations that are under all the gates of heaven, so that when they hear speak of you, they will tremble and quake for fear of you.

Nu 21:21-23

[26]Then I sent messengers from the wilderness of the east to Sihon the king of Heshbon with words of peace, saying, [27]Let me go through your land. I will go always along by the main road, and will neither turn to the right hand nor to the left. [28]I will pay with money for food to eat and for drink to drink. I will go through by foot only – [29]as the children of Esau who dwell in Seir, and the Moabites who dwell in Ar, allowed me to do – until I have crossed over the Jordan into the land that the Lord our God is giving to us.

[30]But Sihon the king of Heshbon would not let us pass by him, because the Lord your God had hardened his spirit and made his heart obstinate in order to deliver him into your hands, as it appears this day. [31]And the Lord said to me, Behold, I have begun to set Sihon and his land before you.* Go forth and conquer, that you may possess his land.

*Or, at your commandment.

[32]Then Sihon and all his people came out against us, to do battle at Jahaz. [33]And the Lord set him before us, and we smote him and his sons and all his people. [34]And we took all his towns at that time, and

destroyed all the towns with men, women, and children, and let nothing remain, ³⁵except the livestock that we seized for ourselves and the spoils from the towns that we took. ³⁶From Aroer, which lies upon the side of the river Arnon, and from the town on the river to Gilead, there was not one town too strong for us. The Lord our God delivered all to us. ³⁷Only upon the land of the children of Ammon you did not encroach, nor along the river Jabbok, nor the towns in the mountains, nor wherever the Lord our God forbade us.

Nu 21:24,25

The Notes

a) 10. Emim: a kind of giants, so called because they were terrible and cruel. For *Emim* signifies terribleness.
b) 12. Horites: a kind of giants whose name signifies noble, because out of pride they called themselves nobles or gentry.
c) 20. Zamzummim: a kind of giants whose name signifies vicious. They were ruffians, cruel, thieves, and robbers.
d) 21. Anakim (or Enakims): also giants. See Judges 1:20 and note d.

Chapter 3

A review of events from the victory over the two kings of Sihon and Og to the installation of Joshua in Moses' stead.

Then we turned and went up by the way to Bashan. And Og the king of Bashan came out against us, he and all his people, to do battle at Edrei. ²And the Lord said to me, Fear him not, for I have delivered him, all his people, and his land into your hand, and you will deal with him as you dealt with Sihon king of the Amorites, who dwelt at Heshbon. ³And so the Lord our God also delivered into our hands Og the king of Bashan and all his folk. And we smote him until nothing was left to him.

Nu 21:33-35
De 29:7,8

⁴And we took all his cities and towns at that time, for there was not a place that we did not take from them – even sixty of them, all the region of Argob, the kingdom of Og in Bashan. ⁵All these places were fortified with high walls, gates, and bars, besides a great many unwalled towns.* ⁶And we utterly destroyed them, like we dealt with with Sihon king of Heshbon, destroying all the towns with men, women, and children. ⁷But all the livestock and the spoils of these places we seized for ourselves.

*Such as villages and thoroughfare towns.

⁸And thus at that time we took the land out of the hand of two kings of the Amorites on the other side of the Jordan, from the river of Arnon to Mount Hermon ⁹(which Hermon the Sidonians call Sirion, but the Amorites call it Senir). ¹⁰We took all the towns in the plain, all Gilead, and all Bashan to Salcah and Edrei, towns of the kingdom of Og in Bashan. ¹¹For only Og king of Bashan remained of the remnant of the giants. Behold, his iron bed is yet at Rabbah with the children of Ammon, nine cubits long and four cubits wide, by the cubits of a man.‡

‡[Cubit: see marginal note on Ex 25:10]

¹²And when we had conquered this land, I gave the area from Aroer, which is by the river of Arnon, and half of Mount Gilead and

its towns, to the Reubenites and Gadites. ¹³The rest of Gilead and all Bashan, the kingdom of Og, I gave to half the tribe of Manasseh. (The whole region of Argob with all Bashan used to be called the land of giants. ¹⁴Jair the son of Manasseh took all the region of Argob to the borders of Geshur and Maachah, and called the settlements of Bashan after his own name, Bashan Havoth Jair,* as it is to this day.) ¹⁵And I gave half Gilead to Machir. ¹⁶And to Reuben and Gad I gave from Gilead to the river of Arnon (at the middle of the river is the border), and to the Jabbok River, which is the border of the children of Ammon; ¹⁷the plains also; and the Jordan River (which is the border) from Chinnereth to the sea in the plain, namely the Salt Sea at the foot of Mount Pisgah eastward.

*That is, pasturelands or villages belonging to Jair.

vv16-17 e.f. COV & JR

¹⁸And I charged you at the same time (you Reuben and Gad), saying, The Lord your God has given you this land to enjoy. But see that you go armed before your brethren the children of Israel, all who are men of war among you. ¹⁹Your wives only, your children, and your livestock – for I know that you have much livestock – will stay in the towns that I have given you, ²⁰until the Lord has given rest to your brethren as well as to you, and until they also have conquered the land that the Lord your God has given them beyond the Jordan. And then return again, every man to the possession that I have given you.

²¹And I warned Joshua at the same time, saying, Your eyes have seen all that the Lord your God has done to these two kings. Just so will the Lord do to all the kingdoms where you go. ²²Fear them not, for the Lord your God, he it is that fights for you.

²³And I besought the Lord at the same time, saying, ²⁴O Lord God, you have begun to show your servant your greatness and your mighty hand, for there is no God in heaven or in earth that can do your works or match your power. ²⁵Let me go over and see the good land that is beyond the Jordan, that goodly high country, and Lebanon!

²⁶But the Lord was angry with me on your account and would not hear me, but said to me, Be content, and speak henceforth no more to me about this matter. ²⁷Go up into the top of Pisgah, and there lift up your eyes west, north, south, and east, and behold it with your eyes. For you shall not cross over this Jordan. ²⁸Moreover, instruct Joshua, and encourage and strengthen him. For he shall go over before his people, and he will divide out to them the land that you will see.

Nu 27:12,13
De 34:1-5

²⁹And so we remained in the valley beside Beth Peor.

Chapter 4

An exhortation to give diligent heed to the law, and that they should not take away from it or add anything to it. Images may not be worshipped nor yet made. The three cities of refuge.

And now hearken, Israel, to the ordinances and laws that I teach you, to do them, so that you may live and go and conquer the land which the Lord God of your fathers gives you. ²You must add nothing to the word that I give you nor take anything away from it,ᵃ so that you may keep the commandments of the Lord your God which I command you. ³Your eyes have seen what the Lord did in the case of Baal Peor; all the people who followed Baal Peor, the Lord your God has destroyed from among you. ⁴But you who cleave unto the Lord your God are alive, every one of you this day.

⁵Behold, I have taught you ordinances and laws such as the Lord my God commanded me, so that you may do according to them in the land you go to possess. ⁶Keep them, therefore, and do them. For therein lie your wisdom and understanding in the sight of the nations – which, when they have heard all these ordinances, may say, O, what a wise and understanding people is this great nation! ⁷For what nation is so great that it has gods as nigh to it as the Lord our God is nigh to us, in all things, when we call upon him? ⁸Yea, and what nation is so great that it has ordinances and laws as righteous as all this law that I set before you this day? ⁹Only take heed to yourself, and keep your soul diligently, so that you do not forget the things that your eyes have seen, and so that they do not depart out of your heart all the days of your life. But teach them to your children and your children's children.

¹⁰The day that I stood before the Lord your God in Horeb – when he said to me, Gather the people together for me so that I may make them hear my words, that they may learn to fear me as long as they live upon the earth, and may teach their children – ¹¹you came and stood also at the base of the mountain. And the mountain burned with fire, even up to the midst of heaven, and there was darkness, clouds, and mist. ¹²And the Lord spoke to you out of the fire. And you heard the voice of the words but saw no image; there was only a voice.ᵇ ¹³And he declared to you his covenant which he commanded you to keep, namely ten verses, and wrote them in two tablets of stone. ¹⁴And the Lord instructed me at that time to teach you ordinances and laws for you to observe in the land to which you go to possess.

¹⁵Take heed to yourselves diligently, as pertaining to your souls. For you saw no manner of image that day, when the Lord spoke to you in Horeb out of the fire. ¹⁶Take care not to corrupt yourselves by making for yourselves graven images, of whatever likeness it be – whether the likeness of man or woman, ¹⁷or of any manner of beast that is on the earth, or of any manner of feathered fowl that flies in the air, ¹⁸or of anything that crawls on the earth, or of any manner of fish that is in the water beneath the earth – ¹⁹yea, and so that you do not lift up your eyes to heaven and, when you see the sun and the moon and the stars and whatever is contained in heaven, should be deceived, and should bow yourself to them, and serve the things that the Lord your God has given to all nations that are under all quarters of heaven.

²⁰For the Lord took you and brought you out of the iron furnace of Egyptᶜ so that you, as a people, should be his heritage, as it has come to pass this day. ²¹Furthermore, the Lord was angry with me on your account, and swore that I would not go over the Jordan, and that I would not go to that good land that the Lord your God is giving you to

Ps 19:7-11

Teach your children.

inherit. ²²For I must die in this land, and will not go over the Jordan. But you will go over and conquer that good land.

²³Take heed to yourselves therefore, that you forget not the covenant of the Lord your God which he made with you, and that you make no graven image of anything that the Lord your God has forbidden you. ²⁴For the Lord your God is a consuming fire and a jealous God.ᵈ ²⁵If, after you have gotten children and children's children and have dwelt long in the land, you corrupt yourselves and make graven images after the likeness of whatsoever it be, and work wickedness in the sight of the Lord your God, to provoke him, ²⁶I call heaven and earth as witnesses to you this day that you will shortly perish from off the land that you go over the Jordan to possess. You will not prolong your days therein, but will shortly be destroyed. ²⁷And the Lord will scatter you among the nations, and you will be left few in number among the people where the Lord will bring you. ²⁸And there you will serve gods that are the works of man's hand – wood and stone, which do not see nor hear nor eat nor smell.

²⁹Nevertheless, you may seek the Lord your God even there, and will find him if you seek him with all your heart and with all your soul. ³⁰In your tribulation, and when all these things are come upon you in the latter days, you may turn to the Lord your God and may hearken to his voice. ³¹For the Lord your God is a merciful God. He will not forsake you nor destroy you, neither forget the covenant made with your fathers, which he swore to them.

³²For ask, I pray you, of the days that are past, which were before you. Since the day that God created man upon the earth, or from one side of heaven to the other, has there been anything like this great thing, or has any such thing been heard of, as it is now: ³³that a nation has heard the voice of God speaking out of fire, as you have heard, and yet lived? ³⁴Or has God ever undertaken to go and take for himself a people from among the nations, through trials and signs and wonders, and through war, with a mighty hand and an outstretched arm, and with mighty, terrible sights, as the Lord your God did for you in Egypt before your eyes?

³⁵To you these things were shown so that you may know that the Lord, he is God, and that there is none but he. ³⁶Out of heaven he made you hear his voice, to instruct you. And upon earth he showed you his great fire, and you heard his words out of the fire. ³⁷And because he loved your fathers, therefore he chose their seed after them, and brought you out of Egypt with his presence and with his mighty power, ³⁸to thrust out nations greater and mightier than you before you, and to bring you in and give you their land as an inheritance, as it has come to pass this day.

³⁹Understand therefore this day, and turn it to your hearts, that the Lord, he is God in heaven above and upon the earth beneath; there is no other. ⁴⁰Keep, therefore, his ordinances and his commandments, which I give you this day, so that it may go well with you and with

your children after you, and so that you may prolong your days upon the land which the Lord your God is giving you your life long.

⁴¹Then Moses set apart three cities on the other side of the Jordan toward the sun rising, ⁴²so that anyone could flee there who had killed his neighbour unintentionally, not having hated him in time past. He therefore could flee to one of these cities and live: ⁴³Bezer in the wilderness, in the plain country among the Reubenites; Ramoth in Gilead, among the Gadites; and Golan in Bashan, among the Manassites.

⁴⁴This is the law that Moses set before the children of Israel, ⁴⁵and these are the testimonies, ordinances, and statutes that Moses declared to the children of Israel after they came out of Egypt, ⁴⁶when they were on the other side of the Jordan in the valley beside Beth Peor, in the land of Sihon king of the Amorites who dwelt at Heshbon, whom Moses and the children of Israel smote after they came out of Egypt. ⁴⁷They conquered his land and the land of Og king of Bashan – two kings of the Amorites on the other side of the Jordan toward the sun rising – ⁴⁸from Aroer on the bank of the river Arnon to Mount Sion which is called Hermon, ⁴⁹and all the plains on the other side of the Jordan eastward, to the sea in the plain at the foot of Mount Pisgah.

Ex 21:12,13
Nu 35:9-15
De 19:1-7

Nu 21:21-25; 33-35.

The Notes

a) 2. To add to the word and to take away from it is to judge and to think otherwise of the will of God than is shown to us in the scripture, as in Deuteronomy 12:29-32 and Proverbs 30:5,6.

b) 12. The voice is everything. To that image ought men to bow their hearts.

c) 20. By the iron furnace is understood anguish, great sorrow, and anxiety of heart. See 1 Kings 8:51 and Jeremiah 11:4.

d) 24. Because God proves those who are his people by affliction, therefore he is called a consuming fire (Hebrews 12:29); and also because he consumes the unfaithful without any remedy. For there is nothing that can resist his anger toward them. And he is called jealous because he cannot suffer that any should fall away from him.

Chapter 5

The ten commandments of the law. No image may be made.

And Moses called to all Israel and said to them, Hear, Israel, the ordinances and laws that I speak in your ears this day; and learn them, and take heed that you do them.

²The Lord our God made a covenant with us in Horeb. ³The Lord did not make this bond with our fathers, but with us, who are all here alive this day. ⁴The Lord spoke with you face to face[a] in the mount, out of the fire. ⁵And I stood between the Lord and you at the same time, to make known to you the word of the Lord. For you were afraid of the fire, and therefore went not up into the mount. And he said:

⁶I am the Lord your God who brought you out of the land of Egypt, the house of bondage. ⁷You shall therefore have no other gods in my presence.

Ex 19:3-9

Ex 20:2,3

⁸You shall make no graven image for yourselves in the likeness of anything that is in heaven above, in the earth beneath, or in the water beneath the earth. ⁹You shall neither bow yourself to them nor serve them. For I, the Lord your God, am a jealous God, visiting the wickedness of the fathers upon the children, even in the third and the fourth generation, among those who hate me; ¹⁰but show mercy upon thousands among those who love me and keep my commandments.

¹¹You shall not take the name of the Lord your God in vain, for the Lord will not hold guiltless him who takes his name in vain.

¹²Keep the Sabbath day, to hallow it, as the Lord your God has commanded you. ¹³Six days you shall labour and do all that you have to do, ¹⁴but the seventh day is the Sabbath of the Lord your God. On that day you shall do no manner of work: neither you nor your son nor your daughter, nor your servant nor your maid, nor your ox nor your donkey, nor any of your beasts, nor the stranger that is within your gates, so that your servant and your maid may rest as well as you. ¹⁵And remember that you were a servant in the land of Egypt, and how the Lord God brought you out from there with a mighty hand and an outstretched arm; for which cause the Lord your God commanded you to keep the Sabbath day.

¹⁶Honour your father and your mother, as the Lord your God has commanded you, so that you may prolong your days, and so that it may go well with you in the land that the Lord your God is giving you.

¹⁷You shall not kill.

¹⁸You shall not break wedlock.

¹⁹You shall not steal.

²⁰You shall not bear false witness against your neighbour.

²¹You shall not lust after your neighbour's wife. You shall not covet your neighbour's house, field, servant, maid, ox, or donkey, nor anything that is your neighbour's.

²²These words the Lord spoke to the whole multitude of you in the mount, out of the fire, cloud, and darkness with a loud voice, and added no more to it. And he wrote them in two tablets of stone and delivered them to me.

²³But as soon as you heard the voice out of the darkness and saw the hill burn with fire, you came to me – all the heads of your tribes and your elders – ²⁴and you said, Behold, the Lord our God has shown us his glory and his greatness, and we have heard his voice out of the fire, and we have seen this day that God may talk with a man and he yet live. ²⁵And now, why should we die, consumed by this great fire? If we hear the voice of the Lord our God any more, we might die; ²⁶for what is any flesh, that he should hear the voice of the living God speaking out of the fire as we have done, and should yet live? ²⁷You go and hear everything that the Lord our God says, and you tell us all that the Lord our God says to you, and we will hear it and do it.

²⁸And the Lord heard the voice of your words when you spoke to me. And he said to me, I have heard the voice of the words of this

people, which they have spoken to you. They have well spoken all that they have said. ²⁹O that they had such a heart in them as to fear me and keep all my commandments always, so that it might go well with them and with their children forever! ³⁰Go, and say to them to go into their tents again. ³¹But you stand here before me, and I will tell you all the commandments, ordinances, and laws that you must teach them, so that they may do them in the land that I am giving them to possess.

Jer 24:5-7; 31:31-33.

³²Take heed, therefore, that you do as the Lord your God has commanded you, and turn not aside either to the right hand or to the left. ³³But walk in all the ways that the Lord your God has commanded you, so that you may live, and so that it may go well with you, and so that you may prolong your days in the land that you shall possess.

Walk straight.
De 17:11
Jos 1:7

The Notes

a) 4. Face to face (Chaldee, word to word): that is to say, with such manifest words and signs that it cannot be denied but that it was God.

Chapter 6

The law must be earnestly printed in their hearts. To keep it in memory, they must write it on the doors and posts of their houses and teach it to their children.

These are the commandments, ordinances, and laws that the Lord your God has appointed, that you should learn them and do them in the land that you are going to possess; ²that you may fear the Lord your God,ᵃ to keep all his ordinances and his commandments that I am commanding you – you and your children and your children's children all the days of your life – so that your days may be prolonged. ³Hear, therefore, Israel, and take heed that you observe them so that it may go well with you, and so you may multiply greatly, seeing as the Lord God of your fathers has promised you a land that flows with milk and honey.*

v1 e.f. COV.

*[Milk and honey: see Ex 3, note c, and Nu 13, note c]

⁴Hear, Israel: the Lord your God is Lord alone, ⁵and you shall love the Lord your God with all your heart, with all your soul, and with all your might. ⁶And these words that I command you this day must be in your heart, ⁷and you must impress them upon your children,ᵇ and must speak of them when you are at home in your house and as you walk by the way, and when you lie down and when you rise up. ⁸And you shall bind them for a sign upon your hand, and they shall be notes of remembrance between your eyes, ⁹and you shall write them upon the posts of your house and upon your gates.

¹⁰And when the Lord your God has brought you into the land that he swore to your fathers Abraham, Isaac, and Jacob to give you – with great and goodly cities that you did not build, ¹¹houses full of all manner of goods that you did not provide, wells that you did not dig, and vines and olive trees that you did not plant – and when you have eaten and are full, ¹²then beware lest you forget the Lord who brought you out of the land of Egypt, the house of bondage. ¹³But fear the Lord your God, and serve him, and swear by his name.ᶜ ¹⁴See that you do not

follow strange gods from the gods of the nations that are around you, ¹⁵for the Lord your God is a jealous God among you,ᵈ lest the wrath of the Lord your God wax hot upon you and destroy you from the earth.

¹⁶You must not tempt the Lord your God like you did at Massah. ¹⁷But see that you keep the commandments of the Lord your God, his testimonies, and his observances that he has commanded you. ¹⁸See that you do that which is right and good in the sight of the Lord, so that you may prosper, and so that you may go and conquer that good land which the Lord swore to your fathers – ¹⁹so that the Lord may cast out all your enemies before you, as he has said.

<small>Right in God's sight is that which he commands.</small>

²⁰When your son asks you in time to come, saying, What is the meaning of the precepts, observances, and laws that the Lord our God has commanded you? – ²¹then you shall say to your son: We were bondmen to Pharaoh in Egypt, but the Lord brought us out of Egypt with a mighty hand. ²² The Lord showed signs and wonders both great and severe upon Egypt, Pharaoh, and all his household before our eyes, ²³and brought us out of there to bring us into and give us the land that he swore to our fathers. ²⁴And therefore he commanded us to do all these ordinances, and to fear the Lord our God, for our wellbeing always, and so that he may preserve us, as it has come to pass this day. ²⁵Moreover, it will be our righteousness before the Lord our Godᵉ if we take heed to keep all these commandments, as he has charged us.

<small>Teach your children.</small>

The Notes

a) 2. To fear God is to honour him by putting your confidence in him, and by leading a good and righteous manner of life in his sight.
b) 7. Impress these words and commandments upon your children: that is, exercise your children in them and put them in practise with them.
c) 13. Swear by the Lord's name: see beneath in De 10:20 and note a.
d) 15. God is jealous: see Ex 20:5, note a, and De 4:24, note d.
e) 25. The outward deed is righteousness for the avoidance of punishment, threats, and curses, and to obtain temporal blessings. But for the life to come, you must have the righteousness of faith and thereby receive the forgiveness of sins, promise of inheritance, and power to work out of love.

Chapter 7

> The Israelites may make no covenant or pact with the Gentiles. They must destroy their idols. God loves and blesses those who keep the commandments, but those who are contrary he hates and punishes. Idolaters must be slain.

When the Lord your God has brought you into the land where you are going, to possess it, and has cast out many nations before you – the Hittites, the Girgashites, the Amorites, the Canaanites, the Perrizites, the Hivites, and the Jebusites, seven nations greater in number and mightier than you – ²and when the Lord your God has set them before you so that you can smite them, see that you utterly destroy them. And make no covenant with them, nor have compassion on them. ³Also, you must make no marriages with them. Neither give your daughters to their sons nor take their daughters for your sons, ⁴for they will make your children depart from me and serve strange gods, and then the wrath of the Lord will wax hot upon you and quickly destroy you.

⁵But this is how you must deal with them: overthrow their altars, break down their pillars, cut down their groves, and burn their images with fire. ⁶For you are a holy nation for the Lord your God. The Lord your God has chosen you out of all the nations that are upon the earth to be a distinct people for himself. ⁷It was not because of the multitude of you above all nations that the Lord had a longing to you and chose you, for you were fewest of all nations. ⁸But because the Lord loved you, and to keep the oath he had sworn to your fathers, therefore he brought you out of Egypt with a mighty hand and delivered you out of the house of bondage, even from the hand of Pharaoh king of Egypt.ᵃ

⁹Understand, therefore, that the Lord your God, he is God – and a true God, who keeps his covenant and mercy with those who love him and keep his commandments, even throughout a thousand generations, ¹⁰but rewards those who hate him before his face,* so that he reduces them to nothing. And he will not defer the time for him who hates him, but will reward him before his face. ¹¹Keep, therefore, the commandments, ordinances, and laws that I command you this day, to do them.

¹²If you hearken to these laws, and observe and do them, then the Lord your God will keep his covenant with you and the mercy that he swore to your fathers, ¹³and will love you, bless you, and multiply you. He will bless the fruit of your womb and the fruit of your field – your wheat, your wine and your oil, the fruit of your oxen, and the flocks of your sheep – in the land that he swore to your fathers to give you. ¹⁴You will be blessed above all nations. There will be neither man nor woman unfruitful among you, nor any unfruitful among your livestock. ¹⁵Moreover, the Lord will turn away from you all manner of infirmities, and will put none of the evil diseases of Egypt (which you know) upon you, but will send them on those who hate you.

¹⁶You must destroy all the nations that the Lord your God delivers over to you. Your eye must have no pity on them. Neither may you serve their gods, for that will be your decay. ¹⁷If you should say in your heart, These nations are greater than I; how can I cast them out? – ¹⁸fear them not. Remember what the Lord your God did to Pharaoh and to all Egypt, ¹⁹and the great proofs that your eyes saw, and the signs and wonders, and mighty hand and outstretched arm by which the Lord your God brought you out. Just so will the Lord your God do with all the nations of which you are afraid. ²⁰Also, the Lord your God will send hornets* among them, until those who remain and hide themselves from you are destroyed. ²¹See that you fear them not, for the Lord your God is among you, a mighty God and a terrible.

²²The Lord your God will put out these nations before you little by little. You may not consume them at once, lest the beasts of the field

*Before his face: in his presence while he looks on.

Ex 23:25,26; 9:1-11.

Ex 23:27,28
*Hornets: see note c on Ex 23.

Ex 23:29

increase upon you. ²³And the Lord your God will deliver them over to you, and will stir up a mighty tempest among them until they are destroyed. ²⁴And he will deliver their kings into your hand, and you will destroy their names from under heaven. No one shall stand before you until you have destroyed them.

²⁵The images of their gods you must burn with fire. And see that you do not covet the silver or gold that is on them, nor take it for yourself, lest you be ensnared by it.ᵇ For it is an abomination to the Lord your God. ²⁶Bring not, therefore, the abomination into your house, lest you be a damned thing as it is; but utterly reject it and abhor it. For it is a thing that must be destroyed.

The Notes

a) 7-8. God's own goodness and his own faithfulness cause him to work.
b) 25. Whatever gold or silver, honour or profit, calls from the word of God, belongs to the images of their gods and must therefore be abhorred.

Chapter 8

Moses puts the Israelites in remembrance of the afflictions and blessings of their forty years in the wilderness.

All the commandments that I give you this day you must mind and do, so that you may live, multiply, and go and possess the land that the Lord swore to your fathers. ²And think on all the way through which the Lord your God led you this forty years, in the wilderness, to humble you and to prove you, to make known what was in your heart – whether you would keep his commandments or not. ³He humbledᵃ you and made you hunger, and fed you with manna that neither you nor your fathers knew of, to make you know that a man must not live by bread only, but by all that proceeds out of the mouth of the Lord must a man live. ⁴Your clothing did not become worn upon you, neither did your feet swell this forty years.ᵇ

The word is life.

⁵Understand therefore in your heart, that as a man disciplines his son, even so does the Lord your God discipline you. ⁶Keep, therefore, the commandments of the Lord your God, so that you walk in his ways and so that you fear him. ⁷For the Lord your God is bringing you into a good land – a land of rivers of water, and of springs that spring out both in valleys and hills; ⁸a land of wheat and of barley, of vines, fig trees, and pomegranates; a land of olive trees with oil, and of honey – ⁹a land where you will not eat bread in scarceness, and where you will lack nothing; a land whose stones are iron and out of whose hills you shall dig bronze. ¹⁰When you have eaten, therefore, and filled yourself, then bless the Lord for the good land which he has given you.

¹¹But beware not to forget the Lord your God, so that you would not keep his commandments, laws, and observances that I give you this day. ¹²Yea, and when you have eaten and filled yourself, and have built goodly houses and dwell in them, ¹³and when your herds and

your flocks are numerous, your silver and your gold is multiplied, and everything that you have is increased, ¹⁴then beware, lest your heart rise up and you forget the Lord your God who brought you out of the land of Egypt, the house of bondage, ¹⁵and who led you through a wilderness both great and terrible, with fiery serpents and scorpions, and with thirst where there was no water – who brought the water out of the rock of flint, ¹⁶and who fed you in the wilderness with manna that your fathers knew not of, to humble you and to prove you so that he might do you good at your latter end.

¹⁷And beware that you say not in your heart, My power and the strength of my own hand has done for me all these things. ¹⁸But remember the Lord your God, and that it is he who gave you the power to do manfully, in order to make good the promise that he swore to your fathers, as it has come to pass this day. ¹⁹For if you forget the Lord your God and follow strange gods, and serve them and worship them, I testify to you this day that you will surely perish. ²⁰Like the nations that the Lord destroys before you, so will you perish, because you would not hearken unto the voice of the Lord your God.

The Notes

a) 3. Humbled: that is, grieved and afflicted.
b) 4. Here you may see that those who believe God's word and live according to it will want nothing, but God will care for them in all things if they commit themselves wholly to his provision. 1Peter 5:10.

Chapter 9

> They are forbidden to trust in their own strength. A review of certain things that were done after the law was given till the murmuring at the Graves of Lust.

Hear, Israel! You are going over the Jordan this day, to go and conquer nations greater and mightier than yourself, and cities great and walled up to heaven,ᵃ ²and people great and tall – even the children of the Anakim, whom you know and of whom you have heard it said, Who is able to stand before the children of Anak? ³But understand this day that the Lord your God, who goes over before you as a consuming fire, he will destroy them, and he will conquer them before you. And you will cast them out and will reduce them to nothing quickly, as the Lord has said to you.

⁴Speak not in your heart, after the Lord your God has cast them out before you, saying, For my righteousness the Lord has brought me in to possess this land. Nay, but for the wickedness of these nations the Lord casts them out before you. ⁵It is not for your righteousness' sake and right heart that you go to possess their land; but partly for the wickedness of these nations does the Lord your God cast them out before you, and partly to perform that which the Lord your God swore to your fathers Abraham, Isaac, and Jacob.

⁶Understand, therefore, that it is not for your righteousness' sake

Where man's righteousness is.

that the Lord your God is giving you this good land to possess, for you are a stiff-necked people. ⁷Remember, and do not forget, how you provoked the Lord your God in the wilderness. For since the day that you came out of the land of Egypt until you came to this place, you have rebelled against the Lord. ⁸Also in Horeb you angered the Lord, so that the Lord was angry with you, even to have destroyed you, ⁹after I went up into the mount to receive the tablets of stone (the tablets of the covenant that the Lord made with you), and abode in the hill forty days and forty nights, neither eating bread nor drinking water. ¹⁰And the Lord delivered to me two tablets of stone written with the finger of God, and in them it was written according to all the words that the Lord had spoken to you in the mount out of the fire, in the day when the people were gathered together.

¹¹And when the forty days and forty nights were ended, the Lord gave me the two tablets of stone, the tablets of the testament, ¹²and said to me, Up, and get down quickly from here! For your people whom you have brought out of Egypt have corrupted themselves: they have turned at once out of the way that I commanded them, and have made themselves a god of metal.

¹³Furthermore, the Lord spoke to me, saying, I see this people, how they are a stiff-necked people. ¹⁴Let me alone so that I may destroy them and put out their name from under heaven. And I will make of you a nation both greater and bigger than they.

¹⁵And I turned away and came down from the mount, and the mountain was burning with fire. And I had the two tablets of the covenant in my hands. ¹⁶And when I looked, I saw that you had sinned against the Lord your God and made for yourselves a metal calf, and had turned at once out of the way that the Lord had commanded you. ¹⁷Then I took the two tablets and cast them out of my two hands, and broke them before your eyes.

¹⁸And I fell before the Lord just as at the first time, forty days and nights, and neither ate bread nor drank water, over all the sins that you had done wickedly in the sight of the Lord, provoking him. ¹⁹For I was afraid of the wrath and fierceness with which the Lord was angry with you, even to have destroyed you. But the Lord heard my petition at that time also. ²⁰The Lord was very angry with Aaron also, even to have destroyed him, but I made intercession for Aaron also at the same time. ²¹And I took your sin, the calf that you had made, and burned it with fire, and pounded it and ground it to fine powder. And I cast the dust into the brook that descended down from the mount.

²²Also, at Taberah, at Massah, and at the Sepulchres of Lust,* you angered the Lord. ²³Yea, and when the Lord sent you from Kadesh Barnea, saying, Go up and conquer the land that I have given you, – you disobeyed the mouth of the Lord your God, and neither believed him nor hearkened to his voice. ²⁴Thus you have been disobedient to the Lord since the day that I knew you.

²⁵And I fell before the Lord. Forty days and forty nights I lay there,

because the Lord was minded to have destroyed you. ²⁶But I made intercession to the Lord and said, O Lord God, destroy not your people and your inheritance, whom you have delivered through your greatness, and whom you have brought out of Egypt with a mighty hand. ²⁷Remember your servants Abraham, Isaac, and Jacob, and look not to the stubbornness of this people, nor to their wickedness and sin, ²⁸lest the people of the land from which you brought them say, Because the Lord was not able to bring them into the land that he promised them, and because he hated them, therefore he carried them out to destroy them in the wilderness. ²⁹Moreover, they are your people and inheritance, whom you brought out with your mighty power and with your outstretched arm.

Learn to pray.
Ex 34:9

The Notes

a) 1. *Walled up to heaven* is a figurative expression, signifying that the walls were high and not easy to be won.

Chapter 10

A repetition of some of the journeys of the Israelites. The renewing of the tablets. An exhortation to give heed to the law.

At the same time the Lord said to me, Hew two tablets of stone like the first, and come up to me in the mount. And make an ark of wood, ²and I will write in the tablets the words that were in the first tablets, which you broke, and you shall put them in the ark. ³So I made an ark of sethim wood, hewed two tablets of stone like the first, and went up into the mountain with the two tablets in my hand. ⁴And he wrote in the tablets as in the first writing – the ten verses that the Lord spoke to you in the mount out of the fire, in the day when the people were gathered together – and he gave them to me. ⁵And I departed and came down from the hill, and put the tablets in the ark that I had made. And there they remained, as the Lord commanded me.

Ex 34:1

⁶And the children of Israel took their journey from Beroth of the children of Jaakan to Moserah (where Aaron later died and was buried, and Eleazar his son became priest in his stead). ⁷And from there they went to Gudgodah, and from Gudgodah to Jotbathah,* a land of rivers of water. ⁸And at that time the Lord set apart the tribe of Levi to bear the ark of the covenant of the Lord, and to stand before the Lord and minister to him, and to bless in his name, to this day. ⁹Therefore, the Levites have no part nor inheritance with their brethren. The Lord is their inheritance, as the Lord your God has promised them.

*Or, Gabgadah or Jotbath

¹⁰And I tarried in the mount just as in the first time, forty days and forty nights. And the Lord hearkened to me at that time also, so that the Lord would not destroy you. ¹¹And the Lord said to me, Up, and go forth in the journey before the people, and let them go in and conquer the land that I swore to their fathers to give to them.

¹²And now, Israel, what is it that the Lord your God requires of

^{De 6:5}
^{M't 22:37-40}
^{Jos 22:5}

you but to fear the Lord your God, to walk in all his ways, to love him, and to serve the Lord your God with all your heart and with all your soul, ¹³so that you will keep the commandments of the Lord and his ordinances that I give you this day, for your wellbeing? ¹⁴Behold, heaven and the heaven of heavens is the Lord your God's, and the earth with all that is in it. ¹⁵Only, the Lord had a longing to your fathers, to love them, and therefore chose you, their seed after them, out from all the nations, as it has come to pass this day.

¹⁶Circumcise therefore the foreskin of your hearts, and be no longer stiff-necked. ¹⁷For the Lord your God, he is God of gods and Lord of lords, a great God, a mighty and a terrible, who regards no man's person nor takes gifts, ¹⁸but does right to the fatherless and widow, and loves the stranger, to give him food and raiment. ¹⁹Love, therefore, the stranger. For you were strangers yourselves in the land of Egypt.

²⁰You shall fear the Lord your God and serve him, and cleave unto him, and swear by his name.[a] ²¹For he is worthy of your praise, and he is your God who has done these great and terrible things for you, which your eyes have seen. ²²Your fathers went down into Egypt with seventy souls, and now the Lord your God has made you as the stars of heaven in multitude.

The Notes

a) 20. To swear that which is true in a cause of faith, or for the honour of God or profit of your neighbour, is lawful. And then Moses wills that the oath be made by the name of God, by which he means that, if we must swear, we refer the oath to God alone, though we swear by a book or other thing, as Paul swore by his conscience in Romans 9:1.

Chapter 11

> An exhortation to regard the law; and how they ought
> to have it in their hearts always, and before their eyes,
> and to speak of it when they rise up, when they sit
> down, and when they walk by the way, etc.

Love the Lord your God, and keep his observances, his ordinances, his laws, and his commandments always. ²And call to mind this day the things that your children have neither known nor seen: the instruction of the Lord your God; his greatness, his mighty hand, and his outstretched arm; ³his miracles and the acts that he did among the Egyptians, even to Pharaoh the king of Egypt and to all his land; ⁴what he did to the army of the Egyptians, to their horses and chariots – how he brought the water of the Red Sea upon them as they pursued you, and how the Lord has reduced them to nothing to this day; ⁵what he did with you in the wilderness until you came to this place; ⁶and what he did to Dathan and Abiram, the sons of Eliab the son of Reuben – how the earth opened her mouth and swallowed them with their households, their tents, and all their property that was in their possession, in the midst of Israel.

^{Nu 16:28-33;}
^{26:9,10.}

⁷For your eyes have seen all the great deeds of the Lord, what he

has done. ⁸Keep, therefore, all the commandments that I give you this day, so that you may be strong and go and conquer the land that you are going to possess, ⁹and so that you may prolong your days in the land that the Lord swore to your fathers, to give to them and to their seed – a land that flows with milk and honey.

¹⁰For the land that you go to possess is not like the land of Egypt where you are from, where you sowed your seed and watered it with your labour,ᵃ like a vegetable garden. ¹¹But the land that you are going over to possess is a land of hills and valleys, and it drinks the water of the rain of heaven, ¹²and is a land which the Lord your God cares for. The eyes of the Lord your God are always upon it, from the beginning of the year to the latter end of the year.

¹³If you hearken, therefore, to the commandments that I give you this day – loving the Lord your God and serving him with all your hearts and with all your souls – ¹⁴then he will give rain to your land in due season, both the first rain and the latter,ᵇ and you will gather in your wheat, your wine, and your oil. ¹⁵And he will send grass in your fields for your animals, and you will eat and fill yourselves.

¹⁶But beware that your hearts do not deceive you, so that you turn aside and serve strange gods and worship them. ¹⁷For then the wrath of the Lord will wax hot upon you, and he will shut up the heaven so that there is no rain and your land will not yield her fruit, and so that you will perish quickly from off the good land that the Lord gives you.

¹⁸Lay up, therefore, these my words in your hearts and in your souls, and bind them for a sign on your hands, and let them be as notes of remembrance between your eyes. ¹⁹And teach them to your children, so it will be that you talk about them when you sit in your house and when you walk by the way, and when you lie down and when you rise up. ²⁰Yea, and write them upon the doorposts of your house and upon your gates, ²¹so that your days and the days of your children may be multiplied upon the land that the Lord swore to give to your fathers, as long as the days of heaven last upon the earth.

De 6:6-9
Pr 3:1-4

²²For if you keep all these commandments that I give you, so that you do them, and love the Lord your God, walk in all his ways, and cleave unto him, ²³then the Lord will cast out all these nations that are both greater and mightier than yourselves, and you will conquer them. ²⁴All the places that the soles of your feet tread shall be yours, from the wilderness and from Lebanon and from the river Euphrates – even to the most distant sea* shall your territory be. ²⁵No one will be able to stand before you; the Lord your God will cast the fear and dread of you upon all the lands you go to, as he has said to you.

Jos 1:1-5

*[ie, the Mediterranean Sea]

²⁶Behold, I set before you this day a blessing and a curse: ²⁷a blessing if you hearken to the commandments of the Lord your God that I give you this day, ²⁸and a curse if you will not hearken to the commandments of the Lord your God, but turn out of the way that I command you this day, to go after strange gods that you have not known. ²⁹When the Lord your God has brought you into the land that you are

De 30:19,20

going to possess, then put the blessing upon Mount Gerizim and the curse upon Mount Ebal, ³⁰which are on the other side of the Jordan on the back side of the road toward the going down of the sun, in the land of the Canaanites who dwell in the plains opposite Gilgal beside the grove of Moreh. ³¹For you shall cross over to go and possess the land that the Lord your God is giving you, and shall conquer it and dwell in it. ³²Take heed, therefore, to do all the commandments and laws that I set before you this day.

The Notes

a) 10. Watered it with your labour: for lack of rain, water was usually brought over all Egypt from the river Nile by manual labour.

b) 14. The first and the latter rains: that is, according to the Hebrew, the rain in October, which is after harvest, and the rain in springtime.

Chapter 12

The Israelites must destroy and flee from idolatry. They must eat no blood. They must only do that thing which God commands.

These are the ordinances and laws that you shall observe to do in the land that the Lord God of your fathers is giving you to possess, as long as you live upon the earth. ²See that you destroy all the places where the nations you conquer serve their gods – upon high mountains, on high hills, and under every green tree. ³Overthrow their altars, break their pillars, and burn their groves with fire. And hew down the images of their gods, and destroy their names out of that place.

⁴See that you do not worship the Lord your God in their way. ⁵But you shall seek out the place that the Lord your God will have chosen out of all your tribes, to put his name there and there to dwell, and there you must go. ⁶And there you shall bring your burnt sacrifices and your offerings, your tithes, the lift offerings of your hands, your vowed and freewill offerings, and the firstborn of your herds and your flocks. ⁷And there you shall eat before the Lord your God, and you shall rejoice in all that you lay your hands on – both you and your households – because the Lord your God has blessed you.

⁸You must do nothing as we do here this day, every man what seems good in his own eyes. ⁹For you have not yet come to rest, nor to the inheritance that the Lord your God is giving you. ¹⁰But you shall go over the Jordan and dwell in the land that the Lord your God is giving you to inherit, and he will give you rest from all your enemies round about, and you will dwell in safety. ¹¹Therefore, when the Lord your God has chosen a place to make his name dwell, there you shall bring all that I command you – your burnt sacrifices and your offerings, your tithes, the lift offerings of your hands, and all the observant offerings that you have vowed to the Lord. ¹²And you shall rejoice before the Lord your God – you, your sons and your daughters, your servants and your maids, and the Levite who is within your gates, since he has neither part nor inheritance with you. ¹³Take heed that you do not offer your burnt offerings in just any place you see, ¹⁴but in

Marginal references: De 7:5; De 14:22-27; 16:5-7; De 29:14-19; De 10:9; 14:27,29; 18:1-8.

the place that the Lord shall have chosen among one of your tribes; there you shall offer your burnt offerings, and there you shall do all that I command you. ¹⁵Nothwithstanding, you may kill and eat meat in all your towns and cities, whatever your soul desires, according to the blessing that the Lord your God has given you. Both the clean and the uncleanᵃ you may eat, such as the roe and the hart.* ¹⁶Only eat not the blood, but pour it upon the earth as water.

¹⁷You may not eat within your gates the tithe of your grain, your wine, or your oil, nor the firstborn of your herds or your flocks, nor any of the vowed offerings that you vow, nor your freewill offerings, nor the lift offerings of your hands. ¹⁸These you must eat before the Lord your God in the place that the Lord your God has chosen – you, your son and your daughter, your servant and your maid, and the Levite that is within your gates – and you shall rejoice before the Lord your God in all that you put your hand to. ¹⁹And beware that you do not forsake the Levite as long as you live upon the earth.

²⁰If, when the Lord your God has enlarged your territory as he has promised you, you say, I would like to eat meat (because your soul longs to eat meat) – then you may eat meat, whatever your soul desires. ²¹If the place that the Lord your God has chosen to put his name is too far from you, then you may kill animals of the herds and the flocks that the Lord has given you, as I have commanded you, and you may eat in your own town whatever your soul desires. ²²As the roe and the hart are eaten, so you may eat it; the uncleanᵃ and the clean indifferently you may eat. ²³But be uncompromising not to eat the blood. For the blood, that is the life, and you may not eat the life with the flesh; ²⁴you may not eat it, but must pour it upon the earth like water. ²⁵See you eat it not, therefore, so that it may go well with you and with your children after you, when you will have done that which is right in the sight of the Lord.

²⁶But the holy things that you have and your vowed offerings, you must take with you and go to the place that the Lord has chosen, ²⁷and you shall offer your burnt offerings, both flesh and blood, upon the altar of the Lord your God. And the blood of your offerings you shall pour out upon the altar of the Lord your God, and shall eat the flesh.

²⁸Take heed and hear all these words that I command you, so that it may go well with you and with your children after you forever, when you do that which is good and right in the sight of the Lord your God. ²⁹When the Lord your God has destroyed before you the nations you go to conquer, and when you have conquered them and dwelt in their lands, ³⁰beware that you are not taken in a snare after they are destroyed before you, and that you do not ask about their gods, saying, How did these nations serve their gods, so I may do likewise? ³¹Nay, you shall not do so for the Lord your God. For every abomination that the Lord hated, they did for their gods. For they burned both their sons and their daughters with fire for their gods. ³²But whatever I command you, take heed to do: add nothing to it, and take nothing away.

De 15:19-22

* Roe and hart are types of deer.

Ec'us 7:31

De 14:23; 16:11.

De 18:9-14
Jos 1:7

Add nought nor take ought away.

The Notes

a) 15,22. The clean and the unclean you may eat: unclean only as pertaining to sacrifice, such as beasts that had deformities, but they may not eat of the unclean that was forbidden. [See De 15:19-22 and note c.]

Chapter 13

The false prophet must be put to death. God proves our faith by false miracles.

<small>v1 e.f. WYC.</small>

If there arises among you a prophet or a dreamer of dreams who foretells a sign or a wonder, ²and the sign or wonder that he has spoken of comes to pass, and then he says, Let us go after strange gods (which you have not known) and let us serve them – ³hearken not to the words of that prophet or dreamer of dreams. For the Lord your God proves you,ᵃ to make known whether you love the Lord your God with all your hearts and with all your souls. ⁴For you must walk after the Lord your God and fear him, and keep his commandments and hearken to his voice, and serve him and cleave unto him. ⁵And that prophet or dreamer of dreams must die for it, because he has spoken to turn you away from the Lord your God who brought you out of the land of Egypt and delivered you from the house of bondage, to thrust you out of the way that the Lord your God commanded you to walk in. And so you must put the evil away from you.

<small>Zec 10:2</small>

⁶If your brother, the son of your mother, or your own son, or your daughter, or the wife that lies in your bosom, or your friend who is as your own soul to you, entices you secretly, saying, Let us go and serve strange gods (which you and your fathers have not known, ⁷from among the gods of the people who are round about you, whether they are near to you or far off from you, from the one end of the land to the other) – ⁸see that you do not consent to him nor hearken to him. No, let not your eye pity him nor have compassion on him, and do not shield him, ⁹but cause him to be slain. Your hand shall be first upon him to kill him, and then the hands of all the people. ¹⁰And you shall stone him with stones so that he dies, because he has gone about to thrust you away from the Lord your God who brought you out of Egypt, the house of bondage. ¹¹And all Israel will hear and fear, and will do no more any such wickedness as this among them.

<small>De 17:2-5</small>

¹²If you hear concerning one of the towns that the Lord your God has given you to dwell in, ¹³that certain people, being the children of Belial,ᵇ have gone out from among you and have moved the inhabiters of their town, saying, Let us go and serve strange gods (which you have not known), ¹⁴then seek and make search and enquire diligently. If it is true, and the thing of a surety that such abomination is wrought among you, ¹⁵then you shall smite the dwellers of that place with the edge of the sword, and shall destroy it without mercy, and everything that is in it – even the very livestock – with the edge of the sword. ¹⁶And gather all the spoils from it into the middle of the streets, and

burn with fire the town and all the spoils, every whit, for the Lord your God. And it shall be a heap forever, and shall not be rebuilt. ¹⁷And see that nothing of the damned thing remains in your hand, so that the Lord may turn from his fierce wrath and show you mercy, and may have compassion on you, and multiply you as he has sworn to your fathers – ¹⁸when you have hearkened to the voice of the Lord your God, to keep all his commandments which I give you this day, so that you do what is right in the eyes of the Lord your God.

The Notes

a) 3.God gives us his word and confirms it with his miracles to prove who has a true heart. We must take heed to the scripture lest false prophets or false miracles deceive us.

b) 13.*Belial* by interpretation signifies worthlessness, or, as some will, wickedness. Therefore, immoral, wicked, and cursed people, who cast the yoke of God off their necks and will not obey God, are called the sons, daughters, children, or men of Belial, as in J'g 19:22, 1Sam 1:16 & 2:12, etc.

Chapter 14

The ways and customs of the Gentiles must not be followed. Which animals are clean to eat and which not.

You are the children of the Lord your God.ᵃ Do not cut yourselves or shave any baldness above your eyes for anyone's death. ²For you are a holy people to the Lord your God, and the Lord has chosen you to be a distinct people for himself from all the nations that are upon the earth.

³You shall eat no manner of abomination. ⁴These are the beasts that you may eat of: oxen, sheep, and goats; ⁵hart, roe, and fallow deer; wild goat, wild ox, antelope, and giraffe. ⁶And all beasts that divide the hoof in two and chew the cud you may eat. ⁷Nevertheless, these you shall not eat of those that chew cud or divide the hoof: the camel, the hare, and the coney. For they chew cud but divide not the hoof, and therefore are unclean to you. ⁸And also the swine, for though he divides the hoof, yet he chews not cud, and therefore is unclean to you. You shall not eat the flesh of these nor touch their dead carcasses. *(Lev 11:1-8, 26.)*

⁹These you may eat of all that are in the waters: everything that has fins and scales. ¹⁰And whatever does not have fins and scales, of that you may not eat, for that is unclean to you. *(Lev 11:9-12)*

¹¹Of all clean birds you may eat, ¹²but these are they of which you may not eat: the eagle, the goshawk, the cormorant, ¹³the buzzard, the vulture, the kite and her kind, ¹⁴all kind of ravens, ¹⁵the ostrich, the night-crow, the cuckoo, the sparrowhawk and all her kind, ¹⁶the little owl, the great owl, the water-hen, ¹⁷the pelican, the osprey, the stork, ¹⁸the heron, the jay in his kind, the lapwing, and the swallow. *(Lev 11:13-19.)*

¹⁹And all winged creeping insects are unclean to you and may not be eaten of, ²⁰but of all clean winged insects you may well eat. *(Lev 11:20-23.)*

²¹You shall eat of nothing that dies alone, but may give it to the stranger that is within your gates to eat, or may sell it to a foreigner.

For you are a holy people to the Lord your God.

Ex 23:19 — You shall not stew a kid in its mother's milk.

De 12:11 — ²²You shall tithe of all the crops that come from the field year by year. ²³And you shall eat before the Lord your God, in the place that he has chosen to make his name dwell, the tithe of your grain, your wine, and your oil, as well as the firstborn of your herds and flocks, so that you may learn to fear the Lord your God always. ²⁴But if the way is too long for you, and the place where the Lord your God has chosen to set his name is so far from you that you cannot carry what the Lord your God has blessed you with, ²⁵then sell it for money, and take the money in your hand and go to the place that the Lord your God has chosen. ²⁶And spend that money for whatever your soul desires – whether oxen, sheep, wine and good drink, or whatever your soul desires – and eat there before the Lord your God and be merry: you, your household, ²⁷and the Levite that is in the town. See that you forsake not the Levite, for he has neither part nor inheritance with you.*

vv24-26 e.f. COV.

*De 10:9; 12:12; 18:1, 2; 26:11-13.

²⁸At the end of three years, you shall bring forth all the tithes of your harvest the same year and lay it up within your own gates. ²⁹And the Levite may come, because he has neither part nor inheritance with you, and the stranger, the fatherless, and the widow in your town may eat and fill themselves, so that the Lord your God may bless you in all the works of your hand which you do.

The Notes

a) 1. They are here called the children of the Lord because above all other people of the world they were endowed with the gifts and blessings of the Lord. Romans 3:1,2.

Chapter 15

The forgiveness of debts in the seventh year. If the Israelites obey God, they are promised that they will not suffer poverty. How and after what manner to lend.

At the end of every seven years you shall make a free year. ²And this is the manner of the free year: whosoever lends with his hand to his neighbour may not ask to receive back from his neighbour or from his brother that which he has lent, because it is called the Lord's free year. ³From a stranger you may require it, but to him who is your brother you shall remit it – ⁴and that in every case, so that there will be no beggar among you. For the Lord will bless the land that the Lord your God gives you as an inheritance to possess, ⁵provided that you hearken unto the voice of the Lord your God, to observe and do all these commandments that I give you this day. ⁶Yea, and then the Lord your God will bless you as he has promised you, and you will lend to many nations and will borrow from none, and will reign over many nations, but none will reign over you.

v3 e.f. COV. Ec'us 4:1-6

De 29:9

⁷When one of your brethren among you is poor, in any of the towns within your land that the Lord your God gives you, see that you harden not your heart nor withdraw your hand from your poor brother,

⁸but open your hand to him and lend him sufficient for his need. ⁹And beware that there be not a mark of Belialᵃ in your heart, such that you would say, The seventh year, the year of freedom, is at hand! – and therefore it grieves you to look upon your poor brother, and you give him nothing, and he then cries to the Lord against you, and it should be sin to you. ¹⁰But give to him. And let it not grieve your heart to give, because for that thing the Lord your God will bless you in all your works and in all that you put your hand to. ¹¹The land will never be without the poor, and so I command you, saying, Open your hand to your brother who is needy and poor in your land.

¹²If your brother a Hebrew sells himself to you, or a Hebrewess, that person shall serve you six years, and the seventh year you shall let him go free from you. ¹³And when you send him out free from you, you shall not let him go away empty-handed, ¹⁴but shall give him some of your sheep, and some of your wheat and of your wine, and shall share with him that which the Lord your God has blessed you with. ¹⁵And remember that you were a servant in the land of Egypt, and the Lord your God delivered you from there. Therefore, I command you this thing today. *[Ex 21:2]*

¹⁶But if your servant says to you, I do not want to go away from you – because he loves you and your house and is well at ease with you – ¹⁷then take an awl and nail his ear to the door with it, and let him be your servant forever. And with your maidservant you shall do likewise.ᵇ ¹⁸But let it not grieve your eyes to let them go out from you, for they have been worth double a hired servant to you in their six years of service. And the Lord your God will bless you in all that you do. *[Ex 21:5,6]*

¹⁹All the firstborn males that come of your herds and of your flocks you shall hallow to the Lord your God. You shall not plow with the firstborn of your oxen nor clip the firstborn of your sheep, ²⁰but shall eat them before the Lord your God year by year in the place that the Lord has chosen, both you and your household. ²¹But if there be any deformity in an animal, whether it be lame or blind, or whatever bad blemish it has, you shall not offer it to the Lord your God. ²²Rather, you shall eat it in your own town, the unclean and the clean alike,ᶜ just as the roe and the hart are eaten. ²³Only, eat not its blood, but pour it upon the ground like water. *[v19 e.f. COV.]*

The Notes

a) 9. *A mark of Belial:* here, for the wicked and adverse counsel of Belial. [Re Belial, see also note b on chapter 13 above.]

b) 17. The intent of this law is to cause them to abhor bondage, to which abhorrence this open shame should drive them. For God wills not that the love of any man should be dearer to him than liberty. [Some: The manifest dishonour of this symbolic act agrees with the whole spirit of the law, which seeks to protect personal freedom and always to re-establish it.]

c) 22. The unclean and clean (and likewise in chapter 12 at verses 15 and 22): In the Hebrew it is possible in all these places to apply the cleanness or uncleanness to the person who eats or to the beast that is eaten. [Concerning beasts, here *unclean* means unfit for sacrifice. See c12, note a.]

Chapter 16

Of Passover, the Feast of Weeks, the Feast of Tabernacles. What officials ought to be appointed.

Observe the month of Abib,^a and offer Passover to the Lord your God. For in the month of Abib the Lord your God brought you out of Egypt by night. ²You shall therefore offer Passover to the Lord your God, and sheep and oxen, in the place where the Lord will choose to make his name dwell. ³You shall eat no leavened bread with it, but shall eat the bread of tribulation seven days long; for you came out of the land of Egypt in haste. And thus you may remember the day you came out of the land of Egypt all days of your life. ⁴And ensure that no leavened bread is seen in all your territories seven days long, and that nothing remains until the morning of the flesh that you offered on the first day at evening.

⁵You may not offer Passover in just any of the towns that the Lord your God gives you, ⁶but in the place where the Lord your God will choose to make his name dwell. There you shall offer Passover at evening, at the time of the going down of the sun, in the same season that you came out of Egypt. ⁷And you shall boil and eat it in the place that the Lord your God has chosen, and depart the next day and go to your tent. ⁸Six days you shall eat sweet bread,* and the seventh day is for the people to come together to the Lord your God, when you may do no work.

⁹Then you shall reckon seven weeks; and begin to count down the seven weeks when you begin to put the sickle to the crops. ¹⁰And keep the Feast of Weeks to the Lord your God, giving a freewill offering from your hand to the Lord your God according as the Lord your God has blessed you. ¹¹And rejoice before the Lord your God – you, your son, your daughter, your servant and your maid, the Levite that is within your gates,^b the stranger, the fatherless, and the widows who are among you – in the place which the Lord your God has chosen to make his name dwell. ¹²And remember that you were a servant in Egypt, and observe and do these ordinances.

¹³You shall observe the Feast of Tabernacles seven days long, after you have gathered in your crops and your wine. ¹⁴And you shall rejoice in your feast – you and your son, your daughter, your servant, your maid, the Levite, the stranger, the fatherless, and the widows who are in your towns and cities. ¹⁵Seven days you shall keep holy day to the Lord your God in the place which the Lord will choose; for the Lord your God will bless you in all your fruits and in all the works of your hands, and therefore you will be glad.

¹⁶Three times in the year shall all your males appear before the Lord your God, in the place that he will choose, for the Feast of Sweet Bread, the Feast of Weeks, and the Feast of Tabernacles.* And they shall not appear before the Lord empty-handed, ¹⁷but every man with the gift of his hand according to the blessing of the Lord your God, which he has given you.

De 14:23; 16:16.

*[Sweet bread is unleavened bread]

*Or, Feast of Booths.

¹⁸You shall appoint judges and officials within all the gates that the Lord your God will give you, throughout your tribes. And let them judge the people righteously. ¹⁹Do not make false interpretations of the law, nor be partial to any person. Neither take any reward, because gifts blind the wise and pervert the words of the righteous. ²⁰But in all things follow righteousness, so that you may live and enjoy the land that the Lord your God gives you.

²¹You shall plant no grove, of whatever trees it may be, near to the altar of the Lord your God that you will make. ²²You shall set up no pillar, which the Lord your God hates.

Judges.

Ex 23:6-8.

The Notes

a) 1. Abib: that is, April, when all things do spring afresh. Exodus 23:15.
b) 11. By *gates* is oft-times understood cities or towns, and jurisdiction, rule, and governance, as also in this same chapter in verse 18.

Chapter 17

> The pain and punishment for idolatry. Doubtful matters must be referred to the high judges. The punishment of a rebel or presumptuous adversary of the law. The making of a king.

You shall offer to the Lord your God no ox nor sheep in which is any deformity, whatever ill-favouredness it may be; for that is an abomination to the Lord your God.

²If there be found among you, in any of the towns which the Lord your God gives you, a man or woman who has wrought wickedness in the sight of the Lord your God, in that they have gone beyond what he has appointed, ³and they have gone and served strange gods and worshipped them – whether it be the sun or moon or anything contained in heaven which I forbade – ⁴and it was told you and you have heard of it, then you shall enquire diligently. And if it is true, and the thing of a surety that such abomination is wrought in Israel, ⁵then you shall bring out to your gates^a the man or the woman who has committed that wicked thing and stone them with stones, and they shall die.

⁶At the mouth of two or three witnesses shall he that is worthy of death die; but at the mouth of only one witness he shall not die. ⁷And the hands of the witnesses shall be first upon him to kill him, and afterward the hands of all the people. So shall you put wickedness away from you.

2Co 13:1

⁸If a matter is too hard for you in judgment, between blood and blood, plea and plea, or blow and blow, in matters of dispute within your towns, then arise and go up to the place that the Lord your God has chosen. ⁹And go to the priests, the Levites, and to the judge that will be in those days, and ask; and they will show you how to judge. ¹⁰And see that you do according to what they of that place (which the Lord has chosen) show you; and see that you observe and do according to all that they instruct you. ¹¹According to the law that they teach

you and manner of judgment that they tell you, see that you do. And do not swerve from what they show you, neither to the right hand nor to the left.

¹²And that person who will do presumptuously, such that he will not hearken to the priest who stands there to minister before the Lord your God, nor to the judge, shall die. And thus shall you put away evil from Israel. ¹³And all the people will hear, and will fear, and will no more do presumptuously.

¹⁴When you have come into the land that the Lord your God gives you, and are enjoying it and dwelling therein, if you say, I would like to set a king over me, like all the nations that are about me – ¹⁵then you may make a king over you, one whom the Lord your God will choose. It must be one of your brethren whom you make king over you; you may not set a stranger over you, who is not of your brethren. ¹⁶But let him not hold too many horses, so that he does not bring the people again to Egypt through the multitude of horses, seeing that the Lord has said to you, You shall henceforth go no more again that way. ¹⁷Also, he must not have too many wives, lest his heart turn away. Neither shall he gather for himself too much silver and gold.

¹⁸And when he is set upon the seat of his kingdom, he shall write out for himself this second law in a book, taking a copy from the priests, the Levites; ¹⁹and he shall keep it with him. And he shall read in it all days of his life so that he may learn to fear the Lord his God, and to keep all the words of this law and these ordinances, to do them; ²⁰and so that his heart does not rise up above his brethren; and so that he does not turn from the commandment, either to the right hand or to the left. Thus may both he and his children prolong their days in his kingdom in Israel.

Margin references: De 5:32; Jos 1:7; Kings; 1Ki 10:26, 28,29; 11:1-6; 10:21,27 (of Solomon).

The Notes

a) 5. Openly in the gates, and not secretly in prison. And with lawful testimony, not torturing them or making them swear against themselves or perjure themselves.

Chapter 18

The Levites could have no possessions. They must flee idolatry. The prophet Christ is promised. A false prophet must be slain, and how he may be known.

The priests, the Levites – all the tribe of Levi – shall have no part nor inheritance with Israel. The offerings of the Lord and his inheritance they shall eat, ²but shall have no inheritance among their brethren; the Lord, he is their inheritance, as he has said to them. ³And this shall be the priest's due from the people and from those who offer, whether it be ox or sheep: they must give to the priest the shoulder, the two cheeks, and the maw. ⁴And the firstfruits of your grain, wine, and oil, and the first shearings from your sheep you must give him. ⁵For the Lord your God has chosen him out of all your tribes to stand and minister in the name of the Lord, both him and his sons forever.

Margin references: Nu 18:20; De 10:8,9; 12:12; 14:27.

⁶If a Levite comes out of any of your towns, or from any place of Israel where he is a sojourner, and comes with all the desire of his heart to the place that the Lord has chosen, ⁷he may minister there in the name of the Lord his God, as all his brethren the Levites do who stand there before the Lord. ⁸And they shall have like portions to eat, besides that which comes to them from the patrimony of their elders.

⁹When you have come into the land that the Lord your God is giving you, see that you do not learn to do after the abominations of those nations. ¹⁰Let there not be found among you anyone who makes his son or his daughter go through fire, or who uses witchcraft,* or a maker of dismal days,† or one who observes the flight of birds, or a sorcerer, ¹¹or a charmer, or one who counsels with spirits, or a prophesier, or one who asks advice of the dead.° ¹²For all who do such things are an abomination to the Lord, and because of these abominations, the Lord your God is casting them out before you. ¹³Be pure, therefore, with the Lord your God. ¹⁴For these nations that you will conquer hearken to choosers out of days and prophesiers, but the Lord your God does not permit that to you.

¹⁵The Lord your God will stir up a prophet like me among you,ᵃ from among your brethren. And to him you must hearken, ¹⁶according to all that you desired of the Lord your God in Horeb, in that day when the people were gathered, saying, Let me hear the voice of my Lord God no more, nor see this great fire any more, that I die not! ¹⁷And the Lord said to me, They have well spoken. ¹⁸I will raise up for them a prophet like you from among their brethren, and will put my words into his mouth, and he will speak to them all that I shall command him. ¹⁹And whosoever will not hearken to the words that he will speak in my name, I will require it of him.

²⁰But the prophet who presumes to speak anything in my name that I did not command to speak, and he who speaks in the name of strange gods, that prophet shall die. ²¹And if you ask in your heart, How can I know that which the Lord has not spoken? – ²²When a prophet speaks in the name of the Lord, if the thing does not follow or come to pass, that is the thing which the Lord has not spoken, but the prophet has spoken it presumptuously. Be not afraid therefore of him.

*Or, magic arts.
†Some: who have regard to times.
°They ask advice of the dead who conjure spirits in the night, thinking that they are departed souls.

Ex 20:18,19

Heb 10:9,16

The Notes

a) 15. Christ is here promised, a preacher of better tidings than Moses.

Chapter 19

The sanctuary towns. The punishment of those who bear false witness.

When the Lord your God has destroyed the nations whose land the Lord your God gives you, and you have conquered them and dwell in their cities and in their houses, ²you shall appoint three cities in the land that the Lord your God gives you to possess. ³You shall prepare the roads, and divide the territory of the land that the Lord your God

Nu c 35
Jos 20:1-9

gives you to inherit into three parts, so that whoever commits manslaughter may flee there.

⁴And this is the cause of the slayer⁽ᵃ⁾ who may flee there and be saved: If he kills his neighbour unintentionally, and did not hate him in time past – ⁵as when a man goes into the woods with his neighbour to hew wood and, as his hand makes a stroke with the axe, the head slips from the helve, hits his neighbour, and he dies – that man may flee to one of the same cities and be saved, ⁶lest the avenger of blood follow after the slayer while his heart is hot and overtake him, because the way is long, and slay him. And yet, there was no cause deserving of death in him, inasmuch as he did not hate his neighbour in time past. ⁷Therefore I command you, saying, See that you set apart three cities.

⁸And if the Lord your God enlarges your territory, as he swore to your fathers, and gives you all the land that he said he would give to your fathers ⁹(provided you keep all these commandments that I give you this day, to do them, and that you love the Lord your God and walk in his ways always), then you shall add three more cities to those three, ¹⁰so that innocent blood is not shed in the land that the Lord your God gives you to inherit, and thus blood should come upon you.

¹¹But if there is any man who hates his neighbour, and lies in wait for him, rises up against him, and strikes him so that he dies, and he flees to any of these cities, ¹²then let the elders of his town send and fetch him from there and deliver him into the hands of the avenger of blood; and he shall die. ¹³Let your eye have no pity on him. And so shall you put away innocent blood from Israel; and happy are you.

¹⁴You shall not remove your neighbour's mark, which they of old time set in the inheritance that you receive in the land that the Lord your God gives you to enjoy.

De 17:6
M't 18:16
Joh 8:17,18
2Co 13:1
1Ti 5:19

¹⁵One witness shall not rise up against a person concerning any manner of trespass or sin, whatever sin anyone sins; but at the mouth of two witnesses or of three witnesses shall all matters be tried.

¹⁶If an unrighteous witness rises up against someone to accuse him of wrongdoing, ¹⁷then let both parties to the dispute stand before the Lord, before the priests and the judges who shall be in those days. ¹⁸And let the judges make diligent enquiry. And if the witness be found false, and to have given false witness against the other, ¹⁹then you shall do to him as he had thought to do to his fellow. And thus shall you put evil away from you, ²⁰and others will hear and fear, and will henceforth commit no more any such wickedness among you. ²¹And let your eye have no compassion; but life for life, eye for eye, tooth for tooth, hand for hand, and foot for foot.

Ex 21:23-25
Lev 24:19, 20.
M't 5:38-42

The Notes

a) 4. Here are shown two kinds of manslaughter, one done willingly and of set purpose, the other unwillingly. For even he that kills with the hand may before God be no manslayer, and again he who is angry and grudges, although he does not kill with the hand, cannot but be a manslayer before God, because he wishes his neighbour ill. As it is said in 1John 3:15.

Chapter 20

Who ought to go to battle. The law of arms among the Israelites. They must kill the Canaanites.

When you go out to battle against your enemies, and see horses and chariots and people more than you, be not afraid of them; for the Lord your God, who brought you out of the land of Egypt, is with you. ²And when you are come near to a battle, let the priest come out and speak to the people, ³and say to them: Hear, Israel! You have come to do battle against your enemies. Let not your hearts faint; neither fear, nor be panicked nor a-dread of them. ⁴For the Lord your God goes with you, to fight for you against your enemies and to save you.

⁵And let the officers speak to the people, saying, If any man has built a new house and has not dedicated it, let him go and return to his house, lest he die in the battle and another dedicate it.ᵃ ⁶And if any man has planted a vineyard and has not made it common,ᵇ let him go and return again to his house, lest he die in the battle and another make it common. ⁷And if any man is betrothed to a wife and has not taken her, let him go and return again to his house, lest he die in the battle and another take her. ⁸And let the officers speak further to the people and say: If any man fears and is fainthearted, let him go and return to his house, lest his brother's heart be made faint as well as his. ⁹And when the officers have made an end of speaking to the people, let them make captains of war over them.

¹⁰When you come near to a city or town to fight against it, offer the people peace. ¹¹And if they answer you peaceably and open their gates to you, then let all the people there be tributaries to you and serve you. ¹²But if they will make no peace with you, then make war against that place and besiege it. ¹³And when the Lord your God has delivered it into your hands, smite all its males with the edge of the sword. ¹⁴But the women, children, animals, and all that is there – all its spoils – take for yourself. And eat the spoils of your enemies which the Lord your God gives you. ¹⁵Thus you shall do with all the places that are a great way off from you, but not the places of these nations. ¹⁶In the cities and towns of these nations which the Lord your God is giving you to inherit, you shall save alive nothing that breathes, ¹⁷but you shall destroy them without redemption – the Hittites, the Amorites, the Canaanites, the Perrizites, the Hivites, and the Jebusites – as the Lord your God has commanded you, ¹⁸so that they do not teach you to do all the abominations that they do for their gods, and you should thus sin against the Lord your God.

¹⁹When you have besieged a place for a long time, in making war against it to take it, do not destroy the trees by taking an axe to them. For you may eat from them, so do not destroy them. For the trees of the fields are no men, that they might come against you to besiege you. ²⁰Nevertheless, those trees which you know people cannot eat from you may destroy and cut down; and make bulwarks against the city or town that makes war with you, until it is overthrown.

De 7:1,2
Jos 6:17,18;
8:8; 10:8-11.

The Notes

a) 5. Dedicate his house: the Levites, I suppose, hallowed their houses like we do our ships.

b) 6. To make a vineyard common: during the three first years, the fruit could not be eaten [Lev 19:23]. In the fourth year, it could be offered [Lev 19:24; and as an offering, the priests could eat of it]. Then, in the fifth year, the fruit could be eaten by everyone [Lev 19:25], and this is to make it common; namely, to bring it to the use of the lay people.

Chapter 21

The method of compurgation for a person found dead, when it is not known how he was slain. How we ought to take as a wife a woman captured in war. The right of the first begotten. The punishment of the son who is disobedient to his father and mother.

If anyone is found slain in the land that the Lord your God gives you to possess, lying in the fields, and it is not known who has slain him, ²then let your elders and your judges come out and measure the distances to the towns that are round about the slain person. ³And let the elders of the town that is nearest to the slain person take a heifer that has never been worked nor has pulled in the yoke, ⁴and let them bring her to a valley where there is neither plowing nor seeding, and strike off her head there in the valley.

⁵Then let the priests the sons of Levi come forth. For the Lord your God has chosen them to minister and to bless in the name of the Lord, and therefore at their mouth shall all pleas and blows be tried. ⁶And all the elders of the town that is nearest to the slain person shall wash their hands over the heifer that is beheaded in the plain, ⁷and shall answer and say: Our hands have not shed this blood, neither have our eyes seen it. ⁸Be merciful, Lord, to your people Israel, whom you have delivered, and put not innocent blood upon your people Israel. And the blood shall be forgiven them; ⁹and so shall you put innocent blood* from you, when you shall have done that which is right in the sight of the Lord.

¹⁰When you go to war against your enemies, and the Lord your God has delivered them into your hands and you have taken them captive, ¹¹and you see among the captives a beautiful woman and have a desire for her, so that you would have her as your wife,ᵃ ¹²then bring her home to your house. And let her shave her head, trim her nails, ¹³and put away the clothing that she was taken in. And let her remain in your house and mourn for her father and her mother a month long. And after that, go in to her and marry her, and let her be your wife. ¹⁴Or, if you have no liking for her, then let her go where she wishes; for you may not sell her for money nor make merchandise of her, because you have afflicted her.ᵇ

¹⁵If a man has two wives, one loved and the other hated, and they have borne him children (both the loved and also the hated), if the firstborn is the son of the hated wife, ¹⁶then, when he distributes his

---

Nu 35:33

De 17:8,9
Ec'us 45:15-17.

*The Chald. transl: he who sheds innocent blood.

v14 e.f. JR.

goods among his children, the man may not put the firstborn son of the beloved before the son of the hated, who is indeed the firstborn. ¹⁷But he shall acknowledge the son of the hated wife for his firstborn and give him double of all that he has. For he is the first of his strength, and to him belongs the right of the firstborn.

¹⁸If any man has a son who is stubborn and disobedient, so that he will not hearken to the voice of his father and voice of his mother – and they have instructed him, but he would not hearken to them – ¹⁹then let his father and his mother take him and bring him out to the elders of that town and to the gate of that same place. ²⁰And they shall say to the elders of the town, This our son is stubborn and disobedient, and will not hearken to our voice; he is a rioter and a drunkard. ²¹Then let all the men of that place stone him with stones unto death. Thus shall you put evil away from you, and all Israel will hear and fear.

²²If someone has committed a trespass deserving of death, and is put to death for it and hanged on tree, ²³let not his body remain all night upon the tree, but bury him the same day. For the curse of God is on him that is hanged. Defile not your land, therefore, which the Lord your God gives you to inherit.

Jos 8:29
Ga 3:13

The Notes

a) 11. Here they were permitted to take a wife from the Gentiles, but were first to shave her head and cut her nails etc. This ceremony signified that she should be instructed to cut away the wantonness, superfluous attire, and sensual manners of the Gentiles, lest the clean people of the Jews should shortly abhor her, if she continued in her old manners.

b) 14. Have afflicted her: that is, have afflicted, vexed, and grieved her by taking away her father, country, and goods, etc., as in Ps 38:6-8.

Chapter 22

> What you ought to do when you find your neighbour's beast going astray. A man shall not wear women's clothing nor a woman men's clothing. To wear a coat of wool and flax is also forbidden. The punishment of a person who accuses another unrighteously, of an adulterer also, and of him who forces a maiden.

If you see your brother's ox or sheep going astray, you shall not withdraw yourself from them, but shall bring them back home to your brother. ²If your brother is not near to you, or if you do not know who the owner is, then bring them to your own house and let them be with you until your brother asks after them, and then deliver them back to him. ³In like manner shall you do with his donkey, with his mantle, and with all your brother's things that he has lost and you have found. And you may not withdraw yourself.

⁴If you see that your brother's donkey or ox has fallen down along the road, you shall not withdraw yourself from them but shall help him to lift them up again.

⁵A woman shall not wear that which belongs to a man, neither shall

a man put on woman's clothing. For all who do so are abominations to the Lord your God.

⁶If you chance upon a bird's nest with fledglings or eggs by the road, in whatsoever tree it may be or on the ground, and the dam sitting upon the young or upon the eggs, you shall not take the mother with the young. ⁷But you shall in any case let the dam go and take the young, so that you may prosper and prolong your days.ᵃ

⁸When you build a new house, you shall make a parapet for the roof,* so that you do not lay a burden of blood upon your house if anyone falls off.

⁹You shall not sow your vineyard with diverse seed,ᵇ lest you hallow the seed which you have sown with the fruit of your vineyard.

¹⁰You shall not plow with an ox and a donkey together.ᶜ

¹¹You shall not wear a garment made of mixed wool and flax.ᶜ

¹²You shall put ribbons as trim upon the four sections of the vesture that you cover yourself with.

¹³If a man takes a wife and, when he has lain with her, hates her, ¹⁴and lays shameful things to her charge, and brings up an evil name upon her and says, I took this wife and, when I came to her, I found her not a maiden – ¹⁵then let the father of the damsel and the mother bring forth the evidences of the damsel's virginity to the elders of the town at the gate. ¹⁶And let the damsel's father say to the elders, I gave my daughter to this man as wife, but he hates her. ¹⁷And lo, he lays shameful things to her charge, saying, I did not find your daughter a maiden. And yet, these are the evidences of my daughter's virginity. – And let them spread the cloth before the elders of the town. ¹⁸Then let the elders of that town take that man and chastise him; ¹⁹and fine him one hundred sickles of silver and give them to the father of the damsel, because he has brought up an evil name upon a maiden in Israel. And she shall be his wife, and he may not put her away all his days.

²⁰But if the thing be of a surety that the damsel was not found a virgin, ²¹let them bring her to the door of her father's house, and let the men of that town stone her to death because she has wrought immorality in Israel, to play the whore in her father's house. And so shall you put evil away from you.

²²If a man be found lying with a woman who has a wedded husband, then let them both die – the man who lay with the wife and also the wife. So shall you put away evil from Israel.

²³If a maiden is promised to a husband and then a man finds her in town and lies with her, ²⁴then you shall bring them both out to the gates of that same town and stone them to death – the damsel because she did not cry out, being in the town, and the man because he has violated his neighbour's wife. And you shall put evil away from you.

²⁵But if a man finds a betrothed damsel in the field and forces her and lies with her, then the man that lay with her shall die alone. ²⁶And to the damsel you shall do no harm, because there is in the damsel no cause of death. For as when a man rises up against his neighbour and

*The roofs are flat in those countries.
Lev 19:19

slays him, so is this matter; ²⁷for he found her in the fields, and the betrothed damsel cried out, but there was no man to help her.

²⁸If a man finds a maiden that is not betrothed, and takes her and lies with her and is found out, ²⁹then the man who lay with her shall give to the damsel's father fifty sickles of silver. And she shall be his wife, because he has taken her; and he may not put her away all his days.

³⁰No man shall take his father's wife nor uncover his father's covering.

De 19:11

v29 e.f. JR.

The Notes

a) 7. You shall not kill the mother, etc. This law wills no more but that, in dealing mercifully with beasts, we should learn mercifulness toward our neighbours.

b) 9. Not with diverse seed, for then one could harm the other. Likewise, people's manners and dealing may not be double, but single, simple, agreeing in opinions, and not of contrary sects and diverse doctrines.

c) 10,11. To not plow with an ox and a donkey, and to not wear a garment of mixed woollen and linen, mean both one thing and are expounded in Leviticus 19, note b.

Chapter 23

What manner of men may not be admitted to minister.
Pollutions that happen in the night. Usury.

No man who is castrated or has his privy members cut off may come into the congregation of the Lord.ᵃ ²And he that is born of a common woman shall not come in the congregation of the Lord; no, in the tenth generation he may not enter into the congregation of the Lord. ³The Ammonites and the Moabites shall not come into the congregation of the Lord; no, not in the tenth generation; no, they may never come into the congregation of the Lord, ⁴because they did not meet you with bread and water in the way when you came out of Egypt, and because they hired against you Balaam the son of Beor, the interpreter of Mesopotamia, to curse you. (⁵Nevertheless, the Lord your God would not hearken to Balaam, but turned the curse into a blessing upon you because the Lord your God loved you.) ⁶You shall never, therefore, seek that which is prosperous or good for them all of your days forever.

⁷You shall not abhor an Edomite, for he is your brother. Neither shall you abhor an Egyptian, because you were a stranger in his land. ⁸The children that are begotten of them may come into the congregation of the Lord in the third generation.

⁹When you go out with the army against your enemies, keep yourselves from all wickedness, for the Lord is among you. ¹⁰If there be any man that is unclean by the reason of uncleanness that chances him by night, let him go out of the camp, ¹¹and not come in again until he has washed himself with water, before the evening. And then, when the sun is down, let him come into the camp again.

¹²You shall have a place outside the camp to which you shall resort, ¹³and you shall have a sharp point at the end of your weapon. And

when you ease yourself, dig with it, and turn and cover that which is departed from you.ᵇ ¹⁴For the Lord your God walks in your host, to protect you and to set your enemies before you. Let your camp be pure, so that he will see no unclean thing among you and turn from you.

¹⁵You shall not deliver back to his master the servant who has escaped from his master to you. ¹⁶Let him dwell with you – there among you, in whatever place he himself likes best – in one of your towns where it is good for him. And do not oppress him.

¹⁷There shall be no whore among the daughters of Israel, nor whore-keeper among the sons of Israel. ¹⁸Neither shall you bring the earnings of a whore or the price of a dog into the house of the Lord your God, for any manner of vowed offering. For both of them are abominations to the Lord your God.

¹⁹You shall be no usurer to your brother, neither in money nor in food, nor in any manner of thing that is lent upon interest. ²⁰To a stranger you may lend upon interest, but not to your brother, so that the Lord your God may bless you in all that you set your hand to in the land where you are going, to conquer it.

Nu c30
Ec 5:2-5

²¹When you have vowed an offering to the Lord your God, see you be not slack to pay it, or he will surely require it of you, and it will be sin to you. ²²If you leave vowing, it will be no sin to you, ²³but that which is once gone out of your lips you must keep. Do what you have vowed to the Lord your God of a free will, which you have spoken with your mouth.

M't 12:1

²⁴When you come into your neighbour's vineyard, you may eat of grapes your bellyful at your own pleasure, but you shall put none in your bag. ²⁵When you go into your neighbour's grainfield, you may pluck the ears with your hand, but you may not move a sickle upon your neighbour's standing grain.

The Notes

a) 1. To come into the congregation is to have an office or ministry among the congregation, which no deformed person may have for fear that his deformity should be an occasion to disdain the office or ministry to which he was ordained.

b) 13. If such policies must be had in soldiers' tents to keep them clean, how much more in cities and towns. If such a thing, which of itself is not evil, must be so earnestly seen to, what singular provision ought there be to prevent open whoredom, adultery, theft, robbery, extortion, etc.

Chapter 24

Divorce is permitted. He that is newly married shall not be compelled to go to war. Grain remaining in the field after harvest must be left for the poor.

M't 5:31,32;
19:3-10.

When a man has taken a wife and married her, if she finds no favour in his eyes because he has discovered some uncleanness in her, then let him write her a bill of divorce, put it in her hand, and send her out of his house. ²If, after she has departed from his house, she goes and becomes another man's wife, ³and the second husband hates her and writes her a bill of divorce, puts it in her hand, and sends her out of his house, or if the second husband dies, ⁴the first husband who sent her away may not take her back to be his wife, inasmuch as she is defiled. For that is an abomination in the sight of the Lord. Do not defile with sin the land that the Lord your God gives you to inherit. — Jer 3:1

⁵When a man takes a new wife, he shall not go to war nor be charged with any business, but shall be free at home one year and rejoice with the wife that he has taken. — De 20:7

⁶No man shall take the bottom or the upper millstone in pledge,ᵃ because then he takes a man's life in pledge.

⁷If any man be found kidnapping any of his brethren the children of Israel, and trades him or sells him, the kidnapper shall die; and you shall put the evil away from you.

⁸Take heed to yourself concerning the plague of leprosy, that you observe diligently to do according to everything that the priests the Levites teach you. As I commanded them, so you shall observe to do. ⁹Remember what the Lord your God did to Miriam along the way, after you had come out of Egypt. — De 17:12; Nu 12:10

¹⁰If you lend your brother any manner of assistance, you shall not go into his house to get a pledge, ¹¹but shall stand outside, and the man you lend to shall bring the pledge out to you at the door. ¹²Furthermore, if it be a poor person, do not lie down to sleep with his pledge in your possession, ¹³but return the pledge to him by sundown, and let him sleep in his own mantle and bless you. And it will be righteousness to you before the Lord your God.

¹⁴You shall not withhold the wages of the needy and poor among your brethren, nor of a stranger that is in your land within your gates. ¹⁵Give him his wages the same day. Let not the sun go down on them, for he is needy and sustains his life thereby. Otherwise, he may cry out against you to the Lord, and it will be sin to you. — v14 e.f. cov. Lev 19:13; Tob 4:14; Ec'us 7:20

¹⁶The fathers shall not die for the children, nor the children for the fathers, but every man shall die for his own sin.

¹⁷Hinder not the right of the stranger nor of the fatherless, nor take a widow's cloak in pledge, ¹⁸but remember that you were a servant in Egypt and how the Lord your God delivered you out of there. Therefore, I command you to do this thing.

¹⁹When you cut down your harvest in the field and have overlooked a sheaf in the field, you shall not go back and fetch it. It shall be for the stranger, the fatherless, and the widow, so that the Lord your God may bless you in all the works of your hand. ²⁰When you beat down your olive trees, you shall not strip the branches clean after you, but it shall be for the stranger, the fatherless, and the widow. ²¹And when you gather in from your vineyard, you shall not gather it clean up after you, but it shall be for the stranger, the fatherless, and the widow. ²²And remember that you were a servant in the land of Egypt. Therefore, I command you to do these things. — Lev 19:9,10

The Notes

a) 6. By the bottom or upper millstone is signified anything that is a necessity to a borrower or debtor, whereby he feeds and sustains himself. This no creditor may take from him. Especially, he may not keep a debtor from the craft and occupation by which he chiefly lives by imprisoning him (which some most cruelly do), lest he be compelled to pay his debt with double disadvantage: one, that his millstone is idle in the meantime, and second, that he is constrained to go further into debt in other ways, or to sell goods without which he cannot live, to make payment.

Chapter 25

The punishment of offenders. The law of raising up seed for the brother who is dead.

When there is strife between people, let them go to the law; and let the judges justify the righteous and condemn the trespasser. ²And if the trespasser is deserving of stripes, then let the judge cause to take him down and to beat him before his face, commensurate with his trespass, to a certain number. ³Forty stripes he may give him, but no more,* lest if he should exceed and beat him above that with many stripes, your brother should appear despicable before your eyes.

⁴You shall not muzzle the ox that treads out the grain.‡

⁵When brothers reside together and one of them dies childless, the wife of the dead man shall not be given out to a stranger, but her brother-in-law shall go in to her and take her as wife and marry her. ⁶And the eldest son whom she bears shall stand in the name of his dead brother,ᵃ so that his name is not put out in Israel.

⁷But if the man will not take his sister-in-law, then let her go to the elders at the gate and say: My brother-in-law refuses to stir up a name in Israel for his brother; he will not marry me. ⁸Then let the elders of his town call him and commune with him. If he stands and says, I will not take her, – ⁹then let his sister-in-law go to him in the presence of the elders, loose his shoe off his foot, spit in his face, and answer and say: So shall it be done to that man who will not build his brother's house. ¹⁰And his name shall be called in Israel, the unshod house.

¹¹If, when men are fighting together one with another, the wife of the one runs up to deliver her husband out of the hands of his assailant, and puts forth her hand and takes him by the secrets, ¹²then cut off her hand. And let not your eye pity her.ᵇ

¹³You shall not have in your bag two manner of weights, a great and a small. ¹⁴Neither shall you have in your house diverse measures, a great and a small. ¹⁵But you shall have a perfect and a just measure, so that your days may be lengthened in the land that the Lord your God gives you. ¹⁶For all who do such things, and all who do unrighteously, are abominations to the Lord your God.

¹⁷Remember what Amalek did to you by the way after you came out of Egypt. ¹⁸He met you by the way and smote the hindmost of you, all who were over-laboured and dragging behind, when you were faint

---

Marginal notes:
*This is why St. Paul had no more at any time; 2Co 11:24.
‡1Co 9:9, 1Ti 5:18.
Ex 17:8,16
Nu 24:20
1Sam 15:2

and weary; and he feared not God. ¹⁹Therefore, when the Lord your God has given you rest from all your enemies round about in the land which the Lord your God gives you to inherit and possess, see that you put out the name of Amalek from under heaven. And do not forget.

The Notes

a) 6. Shall stand in the name of the dead brother: that is, so that he would be as the child of the dead brother and not of the one who begat him.
b) 12. God wills that a woman be more modest than either to exercise the feat of a man in fighting or to touch that member.

Chapter 26

The firstfruits and tithes to the Levites, fatherless, widows, and strangers.

When you have come into the land that the Lord your God is giving you to inherit, and have enjoyed it and are dwelling in it, ²take some of the first of all the fruit of the earth that you will have brought in from the land that the Lord your God gives you, put it in a basket, and go to the place where the Lord your God will choose to make his name dwell. ³And you shall go to the priest that will be in those days and say to him: I acknowledge this day to the Lord your God that I have come into the country that the Lord swore to our fathers to give us.

⁴And the priest shall take the basket out of your hand and set it down before the altar of the Lord your God. ⁵And you shall speak and say before the Lord your God, The Syrians would have destroyed my father,ᵃ but he went down into Egypt. And he sojourned there with a few folk, and grew there to a nation great, mighty, and full of people. ⁶And the Egyptians afflicted us, troubled us, and oppressed us with cruel bondage. ⁷But we cried out to the Lord God of our fathers, and the Lord heard our voice and looked on our adversity, labour, and oppression. ⁸And the Lord brought us out of Egypt with a mighty hand and an outstretched arm, and with great terribleness, and with signs and wonders. ⁹And he has brought us into this place and has given us this land that flows with milk and honey.* ¹⁰And now, lo, I have brought the firstfruits of the land which the Lord has given me.

Then set it before the Lord your God, and worship before the Lord your God, ¹¹and rejoice over all the good things that the Lord your God has given to you and to your house – to you, the Levite, and the stranger that is among you.

¹²When you have made an end of tithing all the tithes of your increase in the third year, the year of tithing, and have given it to the Levite, the stranger, the fatherless, and the widow, and they have eaten in your gates and filled themselves, ¹³then say before the Lord your God: I have brought you hallowed things out of my house and given them to the Levite, the stranger, the fatherless, and the widow, according to all the commandments that you gave me. I have not skipped over your commandments nor forgotten them. ¹⁴I have not eaten of the tithes in

Margin notes:
Ex 23:16; 34:26.

*[Milk and honey: see note c on Ex c3 and note c on Nu c13]

my mourning, nor taken away from them in uncleanness, nor given any of them for the dead; but I have hearkened to the voice of the Lord my God, and done according to all that he commanded me. ¹⁵Look down from your holy habitation, from heaven, and bless your people Israel and the land that you have given us, as you swore to our fathers – a land that flows with milk and honey.

¹⁶This day the Lord your God has commanded you to do these ordinances and laws. Keep them, therefore, and do them with all your heart and all your soul. ¹⁷You have set up the Lord this day to be your God,ᵇ and to walk in his ways and to keep his observances, his commandments, and his laws, and to hearken to his voice. ¹⁸And the Lord has set you up this day to be a distinct people unto him, as he promised you, and to keep his commandments, ¹⁹and to make you high above all the nations that he has made – in praise, in name, and in honour – so that you may be a holy people for the Lord your God, as he has said.

Margin notes: v14 e.f. COV.; M't 22:37-40, Mk 12:30,31, Lu 10:27

The Notes

a) 5. The Chaldee version reads, The Syrian went about to destroy my father; meaning (as some suppose) Laban the Syrian, of whom it is written in Genesis 31. The LXX reads, My father left, or forsook, Syria. The common translation [Latin Vulgate] reads, The Syrian persecuted my father, signifying, as some interpret, that Syria, the country of their fathers, had expelled them and thrust them out.

b) 17. Or, you have caused to be said that the Lord should be to you for your God; or, as many will, he made you to say (that is, he was the cause that you should say) that the Lord should be to you for your God.

Chapter 27

An altar must be built after they go over the Jordan River. The blessings in Mount Gerizim. The curses in Mount Ebal.

And Moses with the elders of Israel commanded the people, saying, Keep all the commandments that I give you this day. ²And when you have gone over the Jordan River into the land that the Lord your God is giving you, set up great stones and plaster them with plaster. ³And write upon them all the words of this law, when you have gone over, so that you may come into the land which the Lord your God gives you – a land that flows with milk and honey, as the Lord God of your fathers has promised you. ⁴When you have gone over the Jordan, see that you set up these stones, as I command you this day, on Mount Ebal. And plaster them with plaster, ⁵and build there unto the Lord your God an altar of stones. And see that you lift up no iron upon the stones, ⁶but you shall make the altar of the Lord your God of rough stones, and offer burnt offerings thereon to the Lord your God. ⁷And you shall offer peace offerings, and shall eat there and rejoice before the Lord your God. ⁸And you shall write upon the stones all the words of this law, plainly and well.

Margin notes: Jos 8:30-35; Ex 20:25

⁹And Moses with the priests the Levites spoke to all Israel, saying, Take heed and hear, Israel! This day you have become the people of the Lord your God. ¹⁰Hearken therefore to the voice of the Lord your God, and do his commandments and his ordinances which I command you this day. ¹¹And Moses charged the people the same day, saying, ¹²These shall stand upon Mount Gerizim to bless the people when you have gone over the Jordan: Simeon, Levi, Judah, Issachar, Joseph, and Benjamin. ¹³And these shall stand upon Mount Ebal to curse: Reuben, Gad, Asher, Zebulun, Dan, and Naphtali. ¹⁴And the Levites shall begin and say to all the people of Israel with a loud voice:

¹⁵Cursed be he that makes any carved image or image of metal (an abomination to the Lord, the work of the hands of the craftsman), and puts it in a secret place. And all the people shall answer and say: Amen. Ex 20:4

¹⁶Cursed be he that curses his father or his mother. And all the people shall say, Amen. Ex 21:15

¹⁷Cursed be he that removes his neighbour's landmark. And all the people shall say, Amen.

¹⁸Cursed be he that makes the blind to go out of his way. And all the people shall say, Amen,

¹⁹Cursed be he that hinders the right of the stranger, fatherless, and widow. And all the people shall say, Amen. De 24:14-18

²⁰Cursed be he that lies with his father's wife, because he has uncovered his father's covering. And all the people shall say, Amen.

²¹Cursed be he that lies with any manner of beast. And all the people shall say, Amen.

²²Cursed be he that lies with his sister, whether she be the daughter of his father or of his mother. And all the people shall say, Amen.

²³Cursed be he that lies with his mother-in-law. And all the people shall say, Amen.

²⁴Cursed be he that smites his neighbour secretly. And all the people shall say, Amen.

²⁵Cursed be he that takes a reward to slay innocent blood. And all the people shall say, Amen.

²⁶Cursed be he that maintains not all the words of this law, to do them. And all the people shall say, Amen.

Chapter 28

The promises of the blessings to those who regard the commandments, and the curses to those who are contrary.

If you will hearken diligently to the voice of the Lord your God, to observe and do all his commandments which I give you this day, the Lord will set you on high above all the nations of the earth. ²And all these blessings will come on you and reach you, if you will hearken to the voice of the Lord your God: Lev 26:3-12

³Blessed shall you be in the town, and blessed in the fields. ⁴Blessed shall be the fruit of your body, the fruit of your ground, and

the fruit of your beasts – the fruit of your oxen and your flocks of sheep. ⁵Blessed shall your alms basket be, and your store of supplies. ⁶Blessed shall you be both when you go out and blessed when you come in.

⁷The Lord will smite the enemies that rise against you before your face. They will come out against you one way and flee before you seven ways. ⁸The Lord will command the blessing to be with you in your storehouses and in all that you set your hand to, and will bless you in the land which the Lord your God gives you.

De 2:7

⁹The Lord will make you a holy people for himself, as he has sworn to you, if you will keep the commandments of the Lord your God and walk in his ways. ¹⁰And all the nations of the earth will see that you are called after the name of the Lord, and they will be afraid of you. ¹¹And the Lord will make you rich – in goods, in the fruit of your body, in the fruit of your beasts, and in the fruit of your ground – in the land that the Lord swore to your fathers to give you.

De 11:13-15

¹²The Lord will open for you his good treasure, even the heaven, to give rain to your land in due season, and to bless all the labours of your hand. And you will lend to many nations but will not need to borrow yourself. ¹³And the Lord will set you before and not behind, and you will be above only and not beneath, if you hearken to the commandments of the Lord your God that I give you this day to keep and to do. ¹⁴And see that you do not turn aside from any of these words that I command you this day, either to the right hand or to the left,ᵃ to go after strange gods to serve them.

Bar 1:19-22
Dan 9:10-14

¹⁵But if you will not hearken to the voice of the Lord your God, to keep and to do all his commandments and ordinances which I command you this day, then all these curses will come upon you and overtake you:

¹⁶Cursed shall you be in the town, and cursed in the field. ¹⁷Cursed shall your alms basket be, and your stores. ¹⁸Cursed shall be the fruit of your body and the fruit of your land, and the fruit of your oxen and the flocks of your sheep. ¹⁹And cursed shall you be when you go in and when you go out.

²⁰And the Lord will send upon you cursing, vanity, and complaint, in all that you set your hand to – whatever you do – until you are destroyed and reduced to nothing quickly, because of the wickedness of your inventions, in that you have forsaken the Lord. ²¹And the Lord will make the pestilence cleave to you until he has consumed you from off the land that you are entering to enjoy. ²²And the Lord will smite you with swelling, with fevers, heat, burning, drought, harsh winds, and blight. And they will follow you until you perish.

Lev 26:25, 14-16.

Lev 26:20

²³And the heaven that is over your head will be as brass, and the earth that is under you as iron. ²⁴And the Lord will turn the rain of the land into powder and dust; even from heaven they will come down upon you until you are brought to nothing. ²⁵And the Lord will plague you before your enemies; you will come out one way against them and

flee seven ways before them, and will be scattered among all the kingdoms of the earth. ²⁶And your dead body will be meat for all manner of birds of the air and for the beasts of the earth, and no man will scare them away.

²⁷And the Lord will smite you with the sores of Egypt, and with hemorrhoids, scabs, and manginess, and you will not be healed from them. ²⁸And the Lord will smite you with madness, blindness, and bewilderment of heart. ²⁹And you will grope at noonday like the blind grope in darkness, and will not come to the right way.

And you will suffer wrong only, and be robbed forevermore, and no one will assist you. ³⁰You will be betrothed to a wife and another will lie with her. You will build a house and another will dwell in it. You will plant a vineyard and will not make it common.* ³¹Your ox will be slain before your eyes and you will not eat of it. Your donkey will be forcibly taken away, even before your face, and will not be restored to you again. Your sheep will be given to your enemies, and no one will help you. De 20:6,7
*[Common: see note b on c20 above]

³²Your sons and your daughters will be given to another nation, and your eyes will see and look numbly upon them all day long, but your hand will not be able to deliver them. ³³A nation that you do not know will eat the fruit of your land and all your labours, and you will but suffer violence only and be oppressed always, ³⁴so that you will be clean beside yourself for the sight that your eyes shall see. v32 e.f. COV.

³⁵The Lord will smite you with malignant ulceration in the knees and legs, so it will be that you cannot be healed – even from the sole of the foot to the top of the head.

³⁶The Lord will bring both you and your king which you have set over you into a nation that neither you nor your fathers have known, and there you will serve strange gods, even wood and stone. ³⁷And you will go to waste, and be made an example and a laughingstock to all the nations where the Lord will carry you. De 17:14,15
2Ch 33:7
2Ki 24:12-16
Jer 24:1

³⁸You will carry much seed out into the field, but will gather only a little in, because the grasshoppers will destroy it. ³⁹You will plant a vineyard and dress it, but will neither drink of the wine nor gather of the grapes, for the worms will eat them. ⁴⁰You will have olive trees in all your territories, but will not be anointed with the oil, for your olive trees will be rooted out. ⁴¹You will have sons and daughters but will not keep them, for they will be carried away captive. ⁴²All your trees and the fruit of your land will be ruined by severe weather.* *Or, grasshoppers. Some read, by vermin.

⁴³The strangers that are among you will climb up on high above you, and you will come down a-low beneath. ⁴⁴He will lend to you and you will not lend to him; he will be before, but you behind.

⁴⁵Moreover, all these curses will come upon you and follow you and overtake you until you are destroyed, because you hearkened not to the voice of the Lord your God, to keep the commandments and ordinances that he commanded you. ⁴⁶And they will be upon you as miracles and wonders,ᵇ and upon your seed forever. ⁴⁷And because

you did not serve the Lord your God with joyfulness and with a good heart, for the abundance of all things, ⁴⁸therefore you will serve your enemy, whom the Lord will send upon you, in hunger and thirst, in nakedness, and in need of all things. And he will put a yoke of iron upon your neck until he has destroyed you.

⁴⁹And the Lord will bring a nation upon you from afar, even from the end of the world, as swiftly as an eagle flies – a nation whose tongue you will not understand, ⁵⁰and a hard-faced nation that will not regard the person of the old nor have compassion on the young. ⁵¹And he will eat the fruit of your land and the fruit of your animals until he has destroyed you – so that he will leave you no grain, wine, nor oil, neither the young of your oxen nor the flocks of your sheep, until he has reduced you to nothing. ⁵²And he will pen you in, in all your cities, until the high and strong walls in which you trusted have come down through all your land. He will besiege you at all your gates throughout all your land which the Lord your God has given you.

⁵³And you will eat the fruit of your own body* – the flesh of your sons and of your daughters which the Lord your God has given you – in the straitness and siege wherewith your enemy will besiege you. ⁵⁴And it will grieve the man who before has lived tenderly and luxuriously among you to look upon his brother, or upon the wife that lies in his bosom, or on his remaining children which he has yet left, ⁵⁵for fear of giving to any of them some of the flesh of his children that he is eating, because there is nothing left for him in that straitness and siege wherewith your enemy will besiege you at all your gates. ⁵⁶Yea, and the woman who before has lived so tenderly and luxuriously among you that she dared not venture to set the sole of her foot on the ground, for softness and tenderness, will be grieved to look upon the husband that lies in her bosom, or on her son or her daughter, ⁵⁷even because of the afterbirth that has come out from between her legs and the children that she has borne, because she will eat them secretly, for need of all things, in the straitness and siege wherewith your enemy will besiege you in your gates.

⁵⁸If you will not be diligent to do all the words of this law that are written in this book, to fear this glorious and fearful name of the Lord your God, ⁵⁹the Lord will smite both you and your seed with astonishing plagues, and with great plagues of long continuance, and with evil sicknesses of long duration. ⁶⁰Moreover, he will bring upon you all the diseases of Egypt that you were afraid of, and they will cleave to you. ⁶¹As well, the Lord will bring all manner of sicknesses and all manner of plagues which are not written in the book of this law upon you, until you have come to naught. ⁶²And you will be left few in number, though before you were as the stars of heaven in multitude, because you would not hearken unto the voice of the Lord your God.

⁶³And as the Lord was pleased to do you good and to multiply you, even so he will be pleased to destroy you and to reduce you to nothing. And you will be wasted from off the land to which you are

*2Ki 6:24-29
Jer 19:9
La 2:20; 4:8-10. Bar 2:2,3.
Eze 5:10

De 10:22
Jer 31:37

going to enjoy. ⁶⁴And the Lord will scatter you among all nations, from the one end of the world to the other, and there you will serve strange gods which neither you nor your fathers have known – even wood and stone.

⁶⁵And you will be among these nations for no short season, and yet will have no rest for the sole of your foot. For the Lord will give you there a trembling heart and dazed eyes and sorrow of mind. ⁶⁶And your life will hang before you, and you will fear both day and night, and will have no trust in your life. ⁶⁷In the morning you will say, Would God it were night! and at night you will say, Would God it were morning! – for the fear of your heart that you will feel, and for the sights that your eyes will see.

⁶⁸And the Lord will bring you into Egypt again by ships, by the way which I said to you that you should see it no more. And there you shall be offered for sale to your enemies as bondmen and bondwomen, and yet no one will buy you.

Ex 14:13

The Notes

a) 14. To turn aside to the right hand is to add to the word of God, and to turn aside to the left is to take away, as in Proverbs 4:25-27.
b) 46. Miracles do sometimes strengthen the weakness of the faithful, but they blind the unfaithful and are to them a witness of damnation.

Chapter 29

> The people are exhorted to observe the commandments in consideration of benefits received, but if they break them, are threatened to be plagued.

These are the words of the covenant that the Lord commanded Moses to make with the children of Israel in the land of Moab, besides the covenant that he made with them in Horeb.

²And Moses called to all Israel and said to them, You saw all that the Lord did before your eyes in the land of Egypt, to Pharaoh and to all his servants and to all his land – ³the great proofs that your eyes have seen, and those great miracles and wonders. ⁴And yet the Lord has not given you a heart to perceive, nor eyes to see, nor ears to hear, to this day.

Ex 19:4

Jos 24:19,20

⁵And I have led you forty years in the wilderness, and your clothes have not worn out upon you, nor have your shoes worn out upon your feet. ⁶You have eaten no bread, nor drunk wine or strong drink, so that you may know how he is the Lord your God. ⁷And at the last you came to this place, and Sihon the king of Heshbon and Og king of Bashan came out against you to battle; but we smote them, ⁸and took their land and gave it as an inheritance to the Reubenites, the Gadites, and the half-tribe of Manasseh. ⁹Keep, therefore, the words of this covenant, and do them, so that you may understand all that you ought to do.

De 8:3,4

Nu 21:23,24; 33-35.
De 31:3,4

¹⁰You stand here this day, every one of you, before the Lord your

De 4:1-6

God – the heads of your tribes, your elders, your officials, all the men of Israel, ¹¹your children, your wives, and the strangers that are in your host, from the hewer of your wood to the drawer of your water – ¹²in order that you should come under the covenant of the Lord your God, and under the oath that the Lord your God makes with you this day, ¹³to make you a people for himself; and so that he may be to you a God, as he has said to you and as he swore to your fathers Abraham, Isaac, and Jacob. ¹⁴Also, I do not make this bond and this oath with you only, ¹⁵but both with him that stands here with us this day before the Lord our God and, also, with him that is not here with us this day.

Jos 9:21-27

¹⁶For you know how we dwelt in the land of Egypt, and how we came through the midst of the nations that we passed through. ¹⁷And you have seen their abominations, and their idols of wood, stone, silver, and gold that they had. ¹⁸Yet there may be among you a man or woman, or kindred or tribe, who in their heart turn away this day from the Lord our God, to go and serve the gods of these nations. And there may be among you some root that bears gall and wormwood – ¹⁹one who, when he hears the words of this curse, blesses himself in his heart, saying, I shall have peace; I will therefore follow the inclination of my own heart (so that the drunken may perish with the thirsty[a]). ²⁰And so the Lord will not be merciful to him, but then the wrath of the Lord and his jealousy will smoke against that person. And all the curses that are written in this book will light upon him, and the Lord will blot his name out from under heaven, ²¹and will separate him for evil out from all the tribes of Israel, according to all the curses of the covenant that is written in the book of this law.

²²So it will be that the generations to come of your children who will rise up after you, and the stranger who will come from a far land, will observe (when they see the plagues of that land and the diseases with which the Lord has smitten it) ²³how all the land is burned up with brimstone and salt, so that it is not sown, nor is fruitful, nor does any grass grow in it, as with the overthrowing of Sodom, Gomorrah, Admah, and Zeboim, which the Lord overthrew in his wrath and anger. ²⁴And then shall all nations also ask, Why has the Lord done such things to this land? O, how fierce is this great wrath?

Jer 22:6-9
1Ki 9:6-9

²⁵And people will say, Because they left the testament of the Lord God of their fathers, which he made with them when he brought them out of the land of Egypt. ²⁶And they went and served strange gods and worshipped them – gods that they knew not, and which had given them nothing. ²⁷And, therefore, the wrath of the Lord waxed hot upon that land, to bring upon it all the curses that are written in this book. ²⁸And the Lord cast them out of their land in anger, wrath, and great furiousness, and cast them into a strange land, as it has come to pass this day.

²⁹These are the secrets of the Lord our God, which are revealed to us and our children forever in order that we should do all the words of this law.[b]

The Notes

a) 19. That the drunken may perish with the thirsty: by this is signified that both the wicked teacher and the disciple who receives evil doctrine shall perish together. Some read, so that the drunken may be put to the thirsty; some, so that drunkenness may be put to thirst.

b) 29. Secrets revealed: that is, the Lord has revealed his will to us before all other people.

Chapter 30

The word of God is not far from them that seek for it,
but in their mouths and hearts.

When all these words are come upon you, whether it be the blessing or the curse which I have set before you, yet if you turn into your heart (being among all the nations where the Lord your God has thrust you), ²and come back to the Lord your God, and hearken unto his voice according to all that I command you this day – both you and your children, with all your heart and all your soul – ³then the Lord your God will turn your captivity and have compassion upon you, and will go and bring you back from all the nations among which the Lord your God will have scattered you.

⁴Though you were cast into the extreme parts of heaven, even from there will the Lord your God gather you, and from there fetch you, ⁵and bring you into the land that your fathers possessed; and you may enjoy it. And he will show you kindness, and multiply you above your fathers. ⁶And the Lord your God will circumcise your heart and the heart of your seed to love the Lord your God with all your heart and all your soul, so that you may live. ⁷And the Lord your God will put all these curses upon your enemies, and on those who hate you and persecute you. — De 10:16 — Ps 54:4-7

⁸But you must turn and hearken to the voice of the Lord, and do all his commandments which I command you this day; ⁹and the Lord your God will make you to abound in all the works of your hand and in the fruit of your body, in the fruit of your beasts and fruit of your land, and in riches. For the Lord will turn again and rejoice over you, to do you good, as he rejoiced over your fathers, ¹⁰if you hearken to the voice of the Lord your God to keep his commandments and ordinances which are written in the book of this law – if you turn to the Lord your God with all your heart and all your soul. — Jer 32:37,38

¹¹For the commandment that I give you this day is not separated from you nor far off. ¹²It is not in heaven, that you need to say, Who will go up for us into heaven and get it for us, so that we may hear it and do it? ¹³Neither is it beyond the sea, that you should say, Who will go over the sea for us and get it for us, so that we may hear it and do it? ¹⁴But the word is very near to you, even in your mouth and in your heart, for you to do it. — Ro 10:6-8

¹⁵Behold, I have set before you this day life and good, death and evil, ¹⁶in that I command you this day to love the Lord your God and

to walk in his ways, and to keep his commandments, his ordinances, and his laws, so that you may live and multiply, and so that the Lord your God may bless you in the land to which you go to possess.

¹⁷But if your heart turns away, so that you will not hear, but go astray and worship strange gods and serve them, ¹⁸I pronounce to you this day that you will surely perish, and that you will not prolong your days upon the land that you pass over the Jordan to go and possess. ¹⁹I call heaven and earth as witnesses to you this day, that I have set before you life and death, blessing and cursing. But choose life, so that you and your seed may live, ²⁰in loving the Lord your God, hearkening to his voice, and cleaving unto him. For he is your life and the length of your days, so that you may dwell upon the land that the Lord swore to your fathers Abraham, Isaac, and Jacob, to give them.

De 4:26

Ec'us 15:17

Chapter 31

Moses, being ready to die, directs Joshua to govern the people in his stead. This book Deuteronomy is written and laid in the tabernacle beside the ark. The Levites are charged to read it to the people.

And Moses went and spoke these words to all Israel, ²and said to them, I am 120 years old this day, and can no more go out and in.^a Also, the Lord has said to me, You shall not go over this Jordan River. ³The Lord your God, he will go over before you. And he will destroy these nations before you, and you shall conquer them. And Joshua will go over before you, as the Lord has said. ⁴And the Lord will do to them as he did to Sihon and Og, the kings of the Amorites, and to their lands, when he destroyed them.

⁵And when the Lord has delivered them to you, see that you do to them according to all the commandments that I have given you. ⁶Pluck up your hearts and be strong. Dread not, nor be afraid of them; for the Lord your God himself will go with you, and will neither let you go nor forsake you.

⁷And Moses called to Joshua and said to him in the sight of all Israel, Be strong and bold! For you must go with this people to the land that the Lord has sworn to their fathers to give them, and you shall give it to them to inherit. ⁸And the Lord, he will go before you, and he will be with you, and will not let you go nor forsake you. Fear not therefore, nor be faint-hearted.

Jos 1:6-9
1Ki 2:2,3

⁹And Moses wrote this law and delivered it to the priests, the sons of Levi who bore the ark of the testament of the Lord, and to all the elders of Israel. ¹⁰And he commanded them, saying, At the end of seven years, in the time of the free year in the Feast of the Tabernacles, ¹¹when all Israel has come to appear before the Lord your God in the place which he has chosen, see that you read this law before all Israel in their ears. ¹²Gather the people together – men, women, children, and the strangers that are within your gates – so that they may hear, learn, and fear the Lord your God, and may be diligent to keep all the words

Nu 3:31

of this law; ¹³and so that their children who know nothing may hear, and may learn to fear the Lord your God for as long as you live in the land that you are going over the Jordan to possess.

¹⁴And the Lord said to Moses, Behold, your days are come, that you must die. Call Joshua, and come and stand in the tabernacle of witness so that I may give him a charge.

And Moses and Joshua went and stood in the tabernacle of witness. ¹⁵And the Lord appeared in the tabernacle, even in the pillar of the cloud. And the pillar of the cloud stood over the door of the tabernacle. ¹⁶And the Lord said to Moses, Behold, you must sleep with your fathers. But this people will go a-whoring after strange gods, the gods of the land into which they are going, and will forsake me and break the covenant that I have made with them. ¹⁷And then my wrath will wax hot against them, and I will forsake them and will hide my face from them,[b] and they shall be consumed. And when much adversity and tribulation is come upon them, then they will say, Because our God is not among us, these tribulations have come upon us. ¹⁸But I will hide my face at that same time because of all the evil that they shall have wrought, in that they have turned to strange gods.

De 29:4

¹⁹Now, therefore, write this song; and teach it to the children of Israel and put it in their mouths, so that this song may be my witness to the children of Israel. ²⁰For when I have brought them into the land that I swore to their fathers, which runs with milk and honey, then they will eat and fill themselves and wax fat, and will turn to strange gods and serve them, and rail on me and break my testament. ²¹And then, when much evil and tribulation has come upon them, this song will answer before them and be a witness; it will not be forgotten out of the mouths of their seed. For I know their imaginations, which they are going about even now before I have brought them into the land that I swore to them.

²²And Moses wrote the song at that same time and taught it to the children of Israel.

²³And the Lord gave Joshua the son of Nun a charge and said, Be bold and strong, for you shall bring the children of Israel into the land that I swore to them, and I will be with you.

²⁴When Moses had made an end of writing out the words of the law in a book, to the end of them, ²⁵he commanded the Levites who bore the ark of the testament of the Lord, saying, ²⁶Take the book of this law and put it by the side of the ark of the testament of the Lord your God, and let it be there for a witness to you. ²⁷For I know your stubbornness and your stiff neck. Behold, while I am yet alive with you this day, you have been disobedient to the Lord; and how much more after my death? ²⁸Gather to me all the elders of your tribes and your officials so that I may speak these words in their ears and call heaven and earth to witness against them. ²⁹For I am sure that after my death they will utterly corrupt themselves, and turn from the way that I have commanded you. And tribulation will come upon you in the latter

days, when you have wrought wickedness in the sight of the Lord, to provoke him with the works of your hands.

³⁰And Moses spoke in the ears of all the congregation of Israel the words of this song, even to the end:

The Notes

a) 2. To go in and out is to exercise the office of a minister and leader among them, as Christ says of the ministers and pastors. John 10:1-5.
b) 17. To hide his face is as much as not to hear, and to take away the evidences of his kindness, as when he gives no ear to us or our prayers, nor shows us any evidence of love, but sets before our eyes grievous afflictions and even very death. As in Job 13:24 and Micah 3:4.

Chapter 32

The song of Moses. He goes up to the top of Mount Abarim to see the land of promise.

Hear, O heaven,ᵃ what I shall speak; and hear, O earth, the words of my mouth. ²My doctrine drops as does the rain, and my speech flows as does the dew – as the drizzle upon the tender plants and as the drops upon the grass. ³For I will call on the name of the Lord: magnify the might of our God!

⁴He is a rock,ᵇ and perfect are his deeds. For all his ways are with equity. God is faithful and without wickedness; both righteous and just is he.

v5 e.f. cov. ⁵The perverse and crooked generation has ruined themselves for him, and are not his children because of their deformities.

⁶Do you so reward the Lord? O foolish nation, and unwise! Is not he your father and your owner? Has he not made you and established you? ⁷Remember the days that are past; consider the years from time to time. Ask your father, and he will show you; your elders, and they will tell you.

⁸When the Most High gave the nations an inheritance and divided the sons of Adam, he put the borders of the nations fast by the multitude of the children of Israel. ⁹For the Lord's part is his folk, and Jacob is the portion of his inheritance.ᶜ ¹⁰He found him in a desert land, in a dry ground and a roaring wilderness. He led him about, and gave him understanding, and kept him as the apple of his eye. ¹¹As an eagle that stirs up her nest and flutters over her young, he stretched out his wings and took him up, and he bore him on his shoulders.ᵈ ¹²The Lord alone was his guide, and there was no strange god with him.

¹³He set him up upon a high land, and he ate the crops of the fields. And he gave him honey to suck out of the rock and oil out of the hard stone, ¹⁴with butter from the cows and milk from the flocks, with the fat of lambs, fat rams, he-goats with fat kidneys, and with wheat. And from the blood of grapes they drank wine.ᵉ

¹⁵But Israel waxed fat and kicked: you were fat, thickset, and

smooth. And he let go of God who made him, and disregarded the rock that saved him.

¹⁶They angered him with strange gods, and with abominations provoked him. ¹⁷They offered to field devils and not to God, and to gods that they knew not, and to new gods that came newly up, which their fathers feared not.

¹⁸Of the rock that begat you, you are unmindful, and have forgotten God who made you.

¹⁹And when the Lord saw it, he was angry, because of the provocations of his sons and daughters. ²⁰And he said, I will hide my face from them* and will see what their end shall be. For they are a contrary generation, and children in whom is no faith.

²¹They have angered me with that which is no god, and provoked me with their vanities. And I, in return, will anger them with those who are no people, and will provoke them with a foolish nation.

²²For fire is kindled in my wrath, and will burn to the bottom of hell, and will consume the land with her fruits, and set afire the bottoms of the mountains.

²³I will heap calamities upon them, and will spend all my arrows at them. ²⁴They shall pine away through hunger, and be consumed by fevers and bitter sicknesses. I will also send the teeth of beasts upon them, and poison serpents.

²⁵Without, the sword shall rob them of their children, and within, in the chamber, will be fear – for both young men and young women, and the suckling babes with the men of grey heads.

²⁶I have determined to scatter them throughout the world, and to make away the remembrance of them from among men. ²⁷Were it not that I feared the railing of their enemies,* lest their adversaries would be proud and say, Our high hand has done all these works, and not the Lord!

²⁸For it is a nation that has an unhappy prospect, and has no understanding in them. ²⁹I would they were wise and understood this, and would consider their latter end. ³⁰How comes it that one should chase a thousand, and two put ten thousand of them to flight? – unless their rock had sold them, and because the Lord had delivered them over.

³¹For our rock is not as their rock. Of this our enemies are judges themselves. ³²Their vines are of the vines of Sodom and of the fields of Gomorrah. Their grapes are grapes of gall and their clusters are bitter. ³³Their wine is the poison of dragons and the cruel gall of asps.

³⁴Are not such things laid in store with me, and sealed up among my treasures?

³⁵Vengence is mine, and I will reward. Their feet will slide when the time comes; for the time of their destruction is at hand, and the time that shall come upon them makes haste. ³⁶For the Lord will do justice for his people and have compassion on his servants. For it shall be seen that their power will fall, and at the last they will be imprisoned and forsaken.

*See before in 31:17 and note b.

Ro 10:19

Jer 15:14

v24 e.f. COV.
Jer 5:6
Joe 1:6

*[WYC: But I delayed for the ire of enemies, etc.]

v31 e.f. COV.

Ro 12:19
Heb 10:30

³⁷And it shall be said, Where are their gods, and their rock in which they trusted? – ³⁸the fat of whose sacrifices they ate, and they drank the wine of their drink offerings? Let them rise up and help you and be your protection!

³⁹See now how it is, that I, I am he; and there is no God but I. I can kill and make alive, and what I have smitten, that I can heal. Neither is there any that can deliver any man out of my hand.

⁴⁰For I will lift up my hand to heaven and will say, I live ever!

⁴¹If I whet the lightning of my sword and take in hand to do justice, I will show vengeance on my enemies, and will reward them that hate me. ⁴²I will make my arrows drunken with blood, and my sword shall eat flesh over the blood of the slain, over the captive, and over the bare head of the enemy.ᶠ

⁴³Rejoice, heathen, with his people! For he will avenge the blood of his servants, and will avenge himself upon his adversaries, but will be merciful to the land of his people.

⁴⁴And Moses went and spoke all the words of this song in the ears of the people, both he and Joshua the son of Nun. ⁴⁵And when Moses had spoken all these words to the end before all Israel, ⁴⁶then he said to them, Set your hearts upon all the words that I testify to you this day.ᵍ Command them to your children, to observe and do all the words of this law. ⁴⁷For it is not a vain word to you, but it is your life, and through this word you may prolong your days in the land that you are going over the Jordan to conquer.

⁴⁸And the Lord spoke to Moses that same day, saying, ⁴⁹Go up this mountain Abarim to Mount Nebo, which is in the land of Moab across from Jericho, and look upon the land of Canaan that I am giving to the children of Israel to possess. ⁵⁰And die in the mount that you go up to, and be gathered unto your people, as Aaron your brother died in Mount Hor and was gathered unto his people. ⁵¹For you trespassed against me among the children of Israel at the waters of strife, at Kadesh in the wilderness of Zin, because you did not hallow me* among the children of Israel. ⁵²You will see the land before you, but will not go into the land that I am giving to the children of Israel.

*To hallow is to show and honour as holy. Nu 20:2-13; 27:12-14. De 33:8

The Notes

a)   1. The prophets customarily, when they speak with a fervent affection, speak to things that have no life as if they were speaking to people. Isaiah 1:2. And here Moses, thinking that the children of Israel would not earnestly hear him and that he would lose his labour, wills yet heaven and earth to hear him, and to be his witnesses that he recited this song to them.

b)   4. Rock: God is called a rock because he and his word last forever, he is ever to be trusted, he is a perfect comfort to believers, and he is their singular defence at all times. 2Samuel 22:2-4, Psalm 62:6,7.

c)   9. Only the faithful, who are signified by Jacob, are God's portion. The unbelievers do not belong to him.

d)   11. To bear them on his shoulders is to save and keep them from evil, and to let them have the pleasure of his goodness.

e) 14. By these things named is signified an abundance of all good things, as it is said in Psalm 63:3-5.

f) 42. Here he recites three plagues of the sword: that many will be slain; that they will be led captive and brought into bondage; and that their head would become bare, that is, their kingdom and priesthood would be taken away from them.

g) 46. To testify the word is to preach the word, and therefore the word is called a testimony or witness. Psalm 119:14.

Chapter 33

As Moses is dying, he blesses all the tribes of Israel.

This is the blessing wherewith Moses, God's man, blessed the children of Israel before his death, ²saying, The Lord came from Sinai and showed his beams of light from Seir unto them, and appeared gloriously from Mount Paran. And he came with thousands of saints, and in his right hand a law of fire for them. ³How did he love the people? All his saints are in his hand.* They set themselves down at your feet and received your words. ⁴Moses gave us a law, which is the inheritance of the congregation of Jacob; ⁵and he was king in Israel, when he gathered the heads of the people and the tribes of Israel together.

⁶Reuben will live, and shall not die, but his people will be few in number.

⁷This is the blessing upon Judah. He said, Hear, Lord, the voice of Judah, and bring him to his people! Let his hands fight for him, but you be his help against his enemies.

⁸And of Levi he said, Let your perfectness and your light* be as the man of your mercy,ᵃ whom you tempted at Massah, and with whom you strove at the waters of strife. ⁹He who says to his father and mother, I saw him not, and to his brethren, I knew not, and to his son, I knew not – for they have observed your words and kept your testament – ¹⁰they shall teach Jacob your precepts, and Israel your laws. They shall put incense before your nose and whole sacrifices upon your altar. ¹¹Bless, Lord, their strength, and accept the works of their hands. Smite the backs of those who rise against them and of those who hate them, so that they do not rise again.

¹²Concerning Benjamin, he said, The beloved of the Lord will dwell in safety through him, and keep himself in the haven through him continually, and will dwell between his shoulders.

¹³And of Joseph he said, Blessed by the Lord is his land, with the goodly fruits of heaven; with dew, and with springs that lie beneath; ¹⁴with fruits brought forth by the sun, and with the ripe fruit of the months; ¹⁵with the tops of mountains that were from the beginning, and with pleasant hills that last forever; ¹⁶and with goodly fruit of the earth and of the fulness thereof. And the goodwill of him who dwells in the bush* shall come upon the head of Joseph, and upon the top of the head of him who was separated from among his brethren. ¹⁷His beauty is as a firstborn ox, and his horns as the horns of a wild ox. And

*Wis 3:1-4

*[Others: your Thummim and Urim. See note a.]

*Ex 3:2

with them he will push the nations together, even to the ends of the world. These are the many thousands of Ephraim and the thousands of Manasseh.

¹⁸And of Zebulun he said, Rejoice, Zebulun, in your going out; and you, Issachar, in your tents. ¹⁹They will call the people to the hill, and there they will offer the offerings of righteousness. For they will suck of the abundance of the sea and of treasure hid in the sand.ᵇ

²⁰And of Gad he said, Blessed is the room-maker Gad.ᶜ He dwells as a lion, and caught the arm, and also the top of the head. ²¹He saw his beginning, and that a part of the teacher* was hid there;† and came with the heads of the people and executed the righteousness of the Lord and his decrees with Israel.

²²And of Dan he said, Dan is a lion's whelp; he shall spring from Bashan.

²³And of Naphtali he said, Naphtali, he shall have an abundance of pleasure and be filled with the blessing of the Lord, and will have his possessions in the southwest.

²⁴And of Asher he said, Asher will be blessed with children. He will be accepted with his brethren, and will dip his foot in oil. ²⁵Your shoes will be iron and bronze, and your age will be as your youth.ᵈ

²⁶There is none like the God of Israel. He that sits upon heaven shall be your help. His glory is in the clouds, ²⁷which is the dwelling place of God from the beginning, and from under the arms of the world. He will cast out your enemies before you and say, Destroy! ²⁸And Israel shall dwell in safety alone,* and the eyes of Jacob shall look upon a land of grain and wine; moreover, his heaven will drop with dew. ²⁹Happy are you, Israel! Who is like you, a people saved by the Lord, your shield and helper and the sword of your glory? And your enemies will hide themselves from you, and you will walk upon their high hills.

*Or (as some will) the lawgiver.
†The Chald. transl., was buried there.

*Look in Nu 23:9 and note a about this word, to dwell by himself.

The Notes

a) 8. That is, let your priest's office be happy and fortunate before God and man through prayer, teaching, and good example, as it was with Moses. This is the light and perfectness which Moses put in the breastlap of judgment (Ex 28:30, Nu 27:21). The Chaldee version reads, With perfectness and light you clothed the man that was found holy.
b) 19. That is, they will have an abundance of riches from merchandise coming by sea and from metals of the earth.
c) 20. Room-maker: because by war he obtained territory, for he was a valiant warrior.
d) 25. As to why Simeon is left out, there appears no cause that is evident and worthy to be believed.

Chapter 34

Moses dies. Israel weeps. Joshua succeeds in Moses' place.

And Moses went from the fields of Moab up into Mount Nebo, which is the top of Pisgah across from Jericho. And the Lord showed him all the land of Gilead, even to Dan; ²and all Naphtali, the land of Ephraim and Manasseh, and all the land of Judah to the most distant sea;* ³the south; and the region of the plain of Jericho, the city of palm trees, to Zoar. ⁴And the Lord said to him, This is the land that I swore to Abraham, Isaac, and Jacob, saying, I will give it to your seed. I have shown it to you before your eyes, but you will not go over there.

*[ie, the Mediterranean Sea]

Ge 12:7; 15:18.

⁵So Moses the servant of the Lord died there in the land of Moab, at the commandment of the Lord. ⁶And he buried him in a valley in the land of Moab beside Beth Peor, but no man knows of his grave to this day.

⁷And Moses was 120 years old when he died, and yet his eyes were not dim nor his cheeks sunken. ⁸And the children of Israel wept for Moses in the fields of Moab thirty days, and the days of weeping and mourning for Moses were ended.

⁹And Joshua the son of Nun was full of the spirit of wisdom, for Moses had put his hand upon him. And all the children of Israel hearkened to him, and did as the Lord commanded Moses. ¹⁰But there arose never since a prophet in Israel like Moses, whom the Lord knew face to face, ¹¹in all the miracles and wonders that the Lord sent him to do in the land of Egypt against Pharaoh and all his servants and all his land, ¹²and in all the mighty deeds and great terrible things that Moses did in in the sight of all Israel.

Nu 27:18-23

The end of the fifth book of Moses.

www.ingramcontent.com/pod-product-compliance
Lightning Source LLC
Chambersburg PA
CBHW082150070526
44585CB00020B/2159